The Modern Short Story
and Magazine Culture, 1880–1950

The Modern Short Story and Magazine Culture, 1880–1950

Edited by Elke D'hoker and Chris Mourant

University Press

Edinburgh University Press is one of the leading university presses in the UK. We publish academic books and journals in our selected subject areas across the humanities and social sciences, combining cutting-edge scholarship with high editorial and production values to produce academic works of lasting importance. For more information visit our website: edinburghuniversitypress.com

© editorial matter and organisation Elke D'hoker and Chris Mourant, 2021, 2022
© the chapters their several authors, 2021, 2022

Edinburgh University Press Ltd
The Tun – Holyrood Road
12(2f) Jackson's Entry
Edinburgh EH8 8PJ

First published in hardback by Edinburgh University Press 2021

Typeset in 10.5/13 pt Sabon by
Servis Filmsetting Ltd, Stockport, Cheshire

A CIP record for this book is available from the British Library

ISBN 978 1 4744 6108 5 (hardback)
ISBN 978 1 4744 6109 2 (paperback)
ISBN 978 1 4744 6110 8 (webready PDF)
ISBN 978 1 4744 6111 5 (epub)

The right of Elke D'hoker and Chris Mourant to be identified as the editors of this work has been asserted in accordance with the Copyright, Designs and Patents Act 1988, and the Copyright and Related Rights Regulations 2003 (SI No. 2498).

Contents

List of Figures		vii
	Introduction Elke D'hoker and Chris Mourant	1
1	The 'wire-puller': L. T. Meade, *Atalanta* and the Development of the Short Story Whitney Standlee	25
2	The Short Story Series of Annie S. Swan for *The Woman at Home* Elke D'hoker	44
3	Hubert Crackanthorpe and *The Albemarle*: A Study of Contexts David Malcolm	65
4	'It is astonishing how little literature has to show of the life of the poor': Ford Madox Ford's *The English Review* and D. H. Lawrence's Early Short Fiction Annalise Grice	86
5	*Rhythm* and the Short Story Louise Edensor	108
6	For Love or Money: Popular 1920s Artist Stories in *The Royal* and *The Strand* Emma West	130
7	Fiction for the Woman of To-day: The Modern Short Story in *Eve* Alice Wood	150

8   Calling Parrots in Walter de la Mare and Elizabeth
    Bowen: A Communion in *The London Mercury*   169
    Yui Kajita

9   Virginia Woolf and Aldous Huxley in *Good
    Housekeeping* Magazine   187
    Saskia McCracken

10 Virginia Woolf and the Magazines   208
    Dean Baldwin

11 *Horizon* Magazine and the Wartime Short Story,
    1940–1945   229
    Ann-Marie Einhaus

12 John Lehmann's War Effort: *The Penguin New Writing*
    (1940–1950)   250
    Tessa Thorniley

13 Voicing 'the native tang of idiom': *Lagan* Magazine,
    1943–1946   273
    Tara McEvoy

14 The Short Story in *Wales* (1937–1949): 'Though we write
    in English, we are rooted in Wales'   293
    Daniel Hughes

Bibliography   311
Notes on Contributors   328
Index   333

List of Figures

Figure 6.1 Frank Gillett's illustration accompanying Morley Roberts's story 'Brown of Boomoonoomana'. © British Library Board, *The Strand*, March 1921.   134

Figure 6.2 Helen McKie's illustration accompanying Robert Magill's story 'Gossamer for Goddesses'. © British Library Board, *The Royal*, January 1921.   143

Figure 9.1 Illustration accompanying Ambrose O'Neill's story 'The Astounding History of Albert Orange'. © British Library Board, *Good Housekeeping* Magazine, February 1932.   203

Figure 10.1 Cover of *Harper's Bazaar*, March 1938.   214

Figure 10.2 Illustration accompanying Virginia Woolf's story 'The Shooting Party', *Harper's Bazaar*, March 1938.   217

Figure 10.3 Leslie Gill's illustration accompanying Virginia Woolf's story 'The Duchess and the Jeweler', *Harper's Bazaar*, May 1938.   221

Figure 10.4 Illustrations accompanying Virginia Woolf's story 'Lappin and Lapinova', *Harper's Bazaar*, April 1939.   226

Introduction

Elke D'hoker and Chris Mourant

This essay collection aims to spotlight the intertwined fates of the modern short story and periodical culture in the period 1880–1950, the heyday of magazine short fiction in Britain. Through case studies that focus on particular magazines, short stories and authors, the different chapters investigate the presence, status and functioning of short stories within a variety of periodical publications – highbrow and popular, mainstream and specialised, middlebrow and avant-garde. The perspective of this investigation is twofold: the collection considers the impact of the contexts and co-texts of a given magazine on the production, publication and reception of short stories, while it also assesses the specific positioning and role of the short stories within the textual and ideological whole of the periodical text. In this way, this collection reflects and crystallises several recent developments within the fields of periodical studies and short fiction studies, at the same time as it opens up new areas for future scholarship.

The material turn in short fiction studies

With regard to the study of the short story, first, this book participates in the movement towards more contextual and material approaches in short fiction studies since the turn of the twentieth century. After the formalist focus of the 1980s and 1990s – with the critics of the 'new short story theories' – short fiction studies became more attuned to context, ideology and history.[1] Several critical studies have sought to situate the short story within a national tradition or to align it with specific historical contexts or new movements in criticism and theory.[2] At the same time, the near exclusive focus on the short stories of a handful of celebrated authors gave way to a consideration of broader trends within the development of the short story form. With regard to the British short story, this opening up has led to a welcome adjustment of the disproportionate attention to the modernist short story in favour of a renewed consideration of, for instance, late-Victorian, post-colonial or contemporary work.[3] The increased critical attention to the emergence of the short story at the nineteenth-century *fin de siècle*, in particular, has coincided with a more detailed exploration of the importance of the periodical press for the short story of the period. Here too, the initial focus on the proto-modernist short fiction of such little magazines as *The Yellow Book* and *The Savoy* has given way to a fuller exploration of the large spectrum of magazines that were publishing short stories at the time. In 2006, Mike Ashley's *The Age of the Storytellers* impressively showed just how much short fiction was being published in the serial press between 1880 and 1950. And in 2007, Winnie Chan's *The Economy of the Short Story in British Periodicals of the 1890s* convincingly posited the need for a material turn in short fiction studies by highlighting the prominent role periodicals such as *The Strand*, *The Yellow Book* and *Black and White* played in the development of the modern short story.[4] Other critical studies followed suit: Bashir Abu-Manneh, for instance, investigated the consolidation of the middlebrow short story in *The New Statesman*; Ann-Marie Einhaus analysed the war stories published in *The Strand* and *The English Review* in her book *The Short Story and the First World War*; and Dean Baldwin, in *Art and Commerce in the British Short Story*, provided an authoritative overview of the market and economics of short story publication in the period 1880–1950.[5]

As Baldwin's study shows, the material turn in short fiction studies is not limited to a consideration of the magazine context. As critics have increasingly recognised, the various publication contexts of the short story – collections, cycles, anthologies, digital platforms and newspapers – influence the way a short story is read, understood and produced. Arguably that influence is greater for the short story than for the novel. For, as Bruno Monfort claimed in a prescient article from the early 1990s, unlike the novel, the short story's unit of publication usually exceeds its textual unit. Hence, the short story is almost invariably part of a 'polytextual' publication context that influences its reception, and in some cases its production, in manifold ways.[6] Magazines are of course a prime example of these polyphonic publication contexts that warrant a closer examination for their role in the dissemination, reception and development of the genre.

Yet, even if the relevance of a material approach in short fiction studies has been accepted on both historical and theoretical grounds, actual research on the short story's multiple publication contexts is still somewhat in its infancy. With the exception perhaps of the short story cycle, which has occasioned an expanding field of research since the late 1980s, the short story's various publication contexts have only received piecemeal critical attention. This is evident too in the two main multi-author publications in the field of short fiction studies that have appeared in recent years: *The Cambridge History of the English Short Story*, edited by Dominic Head, and *The Edinburgh Companion to the Short Story in English*, edited by Paul Delaney and Adrian Hunter.[7] Of the thirty-five chapters in Head's collection, only two deal with the short story's material publication contexts – the short story cycle and the avant-garde magazine *The Yellow Book*. The other chapters focus more conventionally on distinct historical periods as well as specific sub-genres of the English short story. While the editors of the more innovative *Edinburgh Companion to the Short Story in English* recognise the importance of the publication context with a separate section on 'Publishing the Short Story', the only chapter to investigate the periodical context reiterates the modernist emphasis of traditional short fiction studies by only considering the 'little magazines'. Clearly, more research is needed, into a larger cross-section of popular, mainstream and avant-garde periodicals, in order to gain a fuller understanding of the variegated interactions between the short story and British magazine culture.

The short story in periodical studies

This research can draw in part on the insights from periodical studies, which has benefited from both the material turn in literary studies and the increased digitisation of newspapers and magazines to develop into a vibrant discipline. Periodical research first emerged within Victorian studies, in recognition of the enormous expansion of the periodical press in the course of the nineteenth century and the prominent role it played in Victorian culture, politics and society. Victorian periodical studies has therefore developed as an interdisciplinary field in which literary studies, book history, cultural studies and history interact and overlap. If earlier approaches within the field tended to see the periodical as 'an empty vessel, a neutral medium for content that can be extracted and often analysed in a misleadingly decontextualized form', more recent scholarship has sought to conceptualise the periodical as an 'object of enquiry in its own right', a publication medium with its own characteristics, strategies and effects.[8]

The investigation of periodicals as autonomous (if fragmented) textual wholes also informs the more recent periodical turn within modernist studies. Here, research originated around the so-called 'little magazines' which played a crucial role in the modernist movement, by promoting avant-garde writing and art, disseminating new poetic ideas and engendering debate. From this focus on avant-garde magazines, the scope of modern periodical studies has since widened to include also more mainstream or middlebrow magazines of the modernist period, as witnessed by the impressive three-volume *Oxford Critical and Cultural History of Modernist Magazines*. This development is in tune with the geographical, temporal and non-canonical expansion of the 'new modernist studies'.[9] Nevertheless, as Patrick Collier notes in a recent assessment of modern periodical studies, the field remains heavily invested in highbrow and avant-garde modernism, thus limiting 'our understanding of cultural and aesthetic developments opposed to or uninterested in "making it new"'.[10]

Collier's call for an 'expansion of the *literary* field' in periodical studies, in a way that 'does not allow that field to be shaped excessively by modernism as a concept', has perhaps been heeded most in critical studies of women's magazines and the feminist press of the period.[11] In their study of the early twentieth-century feminist press, Lucy Delap and Maria DiCenzo advocate the substitution of 'modernity' for 'modernism' to more accurately assess these periodicals' use of literary texts.[12] In this, they draw upon Margaret Beetham's seminal study of women's magazines, *A Magazine of Her Own? Domesticity and Desire in the Woman's Magazine, 1800–1914*, which shows how the mixture of fiction, advertising and journalism in women's miscellanies since the nineteenth century has served to mediate the new social realities for women.[13] Beetham's broad consideration of the popular, middlebrow and occasionally highbrow fiction content of the women's magazines is also shared by more recent monographs in feminist periodical studies, such as Barbara Green's *Feminist Periodicals and Daily Life: Women and Modernity in British Culture* and Catherine Clay's *Time and Tide: The Feminist and Cultural Politics of a Modern Magazine*, as well as by the ambitious multi-volume *Edinburgh History of Women's Periodical Culture in Britain*.

Although feminist periodical studies have thus managed to open up the investigation of periodical literature beyond the confines of both Victorian serial fiction and modernist experiment, their primary concern is, of course, with the ideological, cultural and social functioning of the periodical as a whole rather than with the role of a particular genre within that whole. Indeed, to some extent, the focus of periodical studies – whether Victorian, modernist or feminist – on the periodical as an object of enquiry in its own right seems to preclude a consideration of a specific literary genre as proposed in this collection. Searching periodicals for their short stories seems tantamount to the decontextualised 'cherry picking' that periodicals scholars object to.[14] Still, in the 2015 special theory issue of the *Victorian Periodicals Review*, Dallas Liddle claims that 'periodicals scholars can and should devote more attention to the forms and patterns of genre'.[15] Since 'the periodical press was mediated by genres, organized by genres, and paid by genres', he argues, 'the last thing our scholarly subdiscipline can afford to do is to go on ignoring genre and privileging assumptions, theories, and methods derived from author- and work-oriented literary history'.[16] Although Liddle is primarily concerned with genres in journalism, his argument can also be applied to the genre of the short story. While previous literary histories tended to create the idea of an undistinguished – and indistinguishable – mass of magazine stories in which only a few, mostly highbrow, stories and authors managed to discriminate themselves, a closer consideration of the short fiction published in periodicals during the late nineteenth and early twentieth centuries reveals a functional system of discourse in which generic conventions are moulded in interaction with reader expectations, magazine policies and authorial intentions. Mapping these finely tuned generic patterns that emerged within British periodicals with regard to the modern short story is one of the central aims of this collection.

Historical context

The period covered by this book – from 1880 to 1950 – is generally recognised as a particularly prosperous and significant one in the history of the modern short story. For Ashley, it is the 'age of the storytellers', when numerous bestselling middlebrow and popular magazines entertained their readers with a large variety of short stories: ghost and gothic stories, romances and exotic stories, stories of crime and detection, adventure stories and war stories, historical romances, rural idylls and comic stories. Yet, the popularity of magazine short fiction also opened up myriad lucrative publishing opportunities for literary authors, while also avant-garde little magazines explored and promoted new aesthetics through experimenting with the form. This exceptionally large market for short fiction drew to an end, however, after the Second World War, as many magazines stopped publication (including, quite symbolically, *The Strand* in 1950) and readers increasingly turned to radio and, later, television for fictional entertainment.[17] While British authors have continued to write short stories and some magazines have continued to publish them, the genre had been on a downward trajectory since the late 1930s: in terms of popularity, lucrativeness and literary status, the short story became a 'minor' genre in the second half of the twentieth century; all the more important, therefore, to investigate the material, contextual and literary circumstances that made it such a 'major' genre more than half a century earlier.[18]

The factors that led to the periodical boom in the late Victorian era have been well documented by periodicals scholars: technological innovations reduced the costs of both paper and printing; a new royalty system and copyright acts created better conditions for authors; and the 1870 Education Act led to a significantly expanded readership. This resulted in an enormous expansion of the periodical press, with different titles addressing different sections of the reading public. Moreover, if earlier in the century periodicals offered fiction in the form of serialised novels (with the occasional Christmas tale or ghost story for special issues), in the course of the 1890s most periodicals made the transition to discrete, self-contained short stories. Critics have often pointed to the groundbreaking role *The Strand* played in this process, as it proudly announced its policy of publishing only self-contained short stories in January 1891.[19] If in its first volume, *The Strand* still published many translated stories by European authors; for Ashley this was the 'way the early *Strand* introduced British readers to the modern short story as such'.[20] British authors quickly followed suit and throughout the 1890s such bestselling authors as Arthur Conan Doyle, L. T. Meade, Walter Besant and Edith Nesbit regularly appeared in its pages. Following the success of *The Strand*'s editorial policy, most magazines made the transition from serial fiction to short stories, sometimes short story series, in the rest of the decade.[21] As a result, Chan notes, by the end of the nineteenth century, 'at least four periodicals included the words "short story" in their titles. And in 1897, for example, short stories were to be found in periodicals devoted to practically any subject from religion to cookery.'[22]

Nonetheless, it would be wrong to see *The Strand* as single-handedly responsible for the short fiction boom of the 1890s. Several other factors had prepared the ground for this success. First, the short story had already been on the rise internationally, with Alphonse Daudet and Guy de Maupassant in France, Nikolai Gogol and Ivan Turgenev in Russia, and Edgar Allan Poe, Herman Melville and Bret Harte in America. Inspired by these examples, further, British authors like Robert Louis Stevenson, Thomas Hardy and Rudyard Kipling started experimenting with the new form in magazine publications in the 1880s. The runaway success of Kipling's *Plain Tales of the Hills*, often considered the first short story collection, also contributed to the increased visibility of the genre. At the same time, *fin-de-siècle* movements of symbolism, decadence and aestheticism prompted writers such as Arthur Symons, Ernest Dowson and Henry James, but also New Woman writers like Olive Schreiner, George Egerton and Vernon Lee, to experiment with shorter forms in the late 1880s and early 1890s.[23] Consequently, as Baldwin has observed, 'by the time of *The Strand*'s insistence on individual stories, these movements and influences had collectively created a sense in England that the short story could and should be regarded as a separate genre with its own aesthetic principles and practices'.[24]

Still, *The Strand* did play an important role in consolidating the conventions that marked the new genre. In her study of *The Strand*, Chan claims that the magazine 'shaped the story as a mass-cultural form'.[25] With detective stories trained on a concluding revelation, Chan argues, the magazine popularised Edgar Allan Poe's characterisation of the short story in terms of a 'unique or single *effect*'.[26] From the detective story, these precepts were extended to the short story in general as an insistence on unity, compression, closure and plot. As Brander Matthews would put it in one of the first full-fledged poetics of the genre: '[t]he Short-story is nothing if there is no story to tell; – one might almost say that a Short-story is nothing if it has no plot'; and '[a] Short-story deals with a single character, a single event, a single emotion, or the series of emotions called forth by a single situation'.[27] As many magazines followed *The Strand* in its short story policy, these genre conventions quickly became the norm for short fiction published in most mainstream, popular and even literary periodicals – to such an extent that it would come to be known, disparagingly, as 'magazine short fiction' in the early twentieth century.

Indeed, although the magazine short story was certainly a modern form – with an emphasis on unity, brevity and condensation – its commercial success and tendency to the formulaic prompted a reaction from highbrow and avant-garde authors. Again, one periodical played a key role in this reaction: the first 'little magazine', *The Yellow Book*. Edited by American short story writer Henry Harland, *The Yellow Book* made the short story the spearhead of its aesthetic revolution. With Henry James's stories as his prime example, Harland argued that 'impression', rather than plot, should be the kernel of every short story: 'you start with an impression and you endeavour to express your impression with the greatest possible economy of means'.[28] In one of his editorials for *The Yellow Book*, written under the pseudonym of 'The Yellow Dwarf', Harland characterised the magazine's literary stories as 'delicate, distinguished, aristocratic', going on to claim, 'their touch is light, their movement is deft and fleet', 'they proceed by omission, by implication and suggestion' and use 'the demi-mot and the nuance'.[29] Although Chan sees *The Yellow Book*'s proto-modernist poetics as entirely the result of an elitist reaction against the middlebrow story popularised in *The Strand* and similar magazines, it is clear that the highbrow or avant-garde story too arose out of a convergence of factors: international models, the new aesthetic movements and the innovative experiments of particular writers. Nevertheless, *The Yellow Book* greatly enhanced the visibility of these developments, thus managing to style the short story 'as a difficult, artistic form, worthy of serious literary endeavour'.[30]

In short, by the end of the nineteenth century, two distinct models for the short story had emerged: the plotted story, which prioritised a tight plot, closure through surprise or revelation, and an authorial or objective narrative stance; and the plotless story, which privileged mood and psychology over plot, and worked through implication, ellipsis and suggestion to an open ending. Henry James outlined these distinctions in an 1898 article for the *Fortnightly Review* when he contrasted stories that provide the reader with 'adventure comparatively safe, in which you have, for the most part, but to put one foot after the other' until you reach a climax in the plot like 'the snap of the pistol-shot', and the plotless story that instead progresses through 'exposures' and 'glimpses', presenting the reader with an 'impression [...] of a complexity or a continuity'.[31] In both models, magazines played an important role in developing, debating and disseminating these generic conventions. And although *The Strand* and *The Yellow Book* have figured as convenient tags for these two story types, they were of course supplemented by other periodicals. Apart from *The Yellow Book*, the plotless short story also flourished in *The Savoy*, *The Albemarle*, *The New Age*, *The English Review* and many subsequent modernist little magazines, while the magazine short story of *The Strand* became the staple of such major monthlies as *The Windsor*, *Pearson's*, *Nash's* and *The Pall Mall Magazine*.

While the two short story models – and the magazines that published them – to some extent prefigure 'the great divide' that would come to characterise the modernist period, it would be wrong to draw all too strict dividing lines between the magazines, or the authors and stories they published. First, the multi-vocality and heterogeneity of periodicals makes it difficult to uniquely classify publications as 'lowbrow', 'middlebrow' or 'highbrow'. Moreover, as Dean Baldwin has shown in a survey of the periodical publications of some thirty representative authors, most writers published their work in periodicals that ranged across the spectrum from popular to literary and from mainstream to avant-garde.[32] Thus, bestselling middlebrow magazines played an important role in the careers of many now canonical literary authors, since 'they paid on average much higher prices than the highbrows and provided a writer with a far larger audience'.[33] Finally, the distinction between the plotted and the plotless short story too became less pronounced in the course of the twentieth century. On the one hand, the modernist emphasis on subjective narration, individual consciousness and epiphany became more widely accepted in the plotted story as well. On the other hand, literary writers also often deployed popular plots in their stories and generally moved away from excessive experiment as the century progressed.

What is important to emphasise, however, is that, from the 1880s onwards, the periodical press offered an extraordinarily rich, diversified and commercially viable market for short fiction. 'Periodical literature is a huge open mouth which has to be fed – a vessel of immense capacity which has to be filled,' Henry James noted somewhat disparagingly, while H. G. Wells recognised the positive effect on short fiction, observing that the 'nineties was a good and stimulating period for a short-story writer': 'Short stories broke out everywhere.'[34] For the first time, indeed, it became financially possible for writers to earn a living by writing short fiction and, for some time, writing stories was even more lucrative than novel writing.[35] Far from only resulting in formulaic magazine fiction, this situation gave rise to a veritable explosion of creativity in which writers across the literary spectrum turned to explore the possibilities of the form. Magazines were not only important for the development of the short story genre around the turn of the twentieth century, as several studies have shown, they also played a crucial role in the careers of individual authors such as Katherine Mansfield, Virginia Woolf and

Seán O'Faoláin.[36] Finally, as Catherine Clay has argued in a study of reader responses to short fiction in *Time and Tide*, the publication of short stories in periodicals enabled the reader a closer engagement with the form and content of literary texts than book publication traditionally allows for.[37] In short, the intertwined fates of the short story and the magazines during the period 1880–1950 resulted in a vibrant literary field defined by the interactions between authors, editors and readers as well as the interdependence of literary text, generic conventions and periodical context.

Theory and methodology

This investigation of the function and fate of the short story within a magazine context faces many challenges. Especially for a field like short fiction studies, traditionally trained on the analysis of short texts by a fairly small number of canonical authors, the sheer amount of material can seem overwhelming. Even if digitisation has facilitated access to this material, close reading techniques clearly no longer qualify for the analysis of the short fiction published in all but the most short-lived little magazine. So, what do we look for when reading a short story in its periodical context? How to interpret the co-textual and contextual framing of a given story within a particular magazine? How can we assess the periodical's editorial or ideological shaping of its component texts? Or how can we analyse the short story poetics of a mainstream, literary or avant-garde magazine? What is the relative importance of editorials, book reviews, short stories and other literary texts versus the journalistic content of a periodical? These and other questions have been dealt with by the few existing critical studies of short fiction and magazine context in a rather hands-on, pragmatic manner, yet a common theoretical framework or methodological toolset for these inquiries has yet to be developed.

Within the field of periodical studies, however, theoretical and methodological questions have been debated since the late 1980s, first within Victorian periodicals research and subsequently with regard to modernist magazines. The concepts and insights that have been developed about the genre or medium of the periodical text also offer useful concepts for the investigation of short fiction within periodicals. One of the first texts to present a theory of periodicals was Margaret Beetham's contribution to the 1989 special 'Theory' issue of the *Victorian Periodicals Review*, 'Open and Closed: The

Periodical as a Publishing Genre'. For Beetham, the tension between openness and closure in the periodical genre manifests itself in two ways. First, the periodical's 'heterogeneity of authorial voice and kinds of material' as well its engagement with the reader mark it as an open form, while the consistent, distinctive identity the periodical seeks to construct in order to attract readers gives it an aspect of closure as well.[38] Second, the periodical's 'particular relationship to time' generates tensions between closure and open-endedness:

> [e]very number of the periodical is the same in that it offers its reader a recognizable persona or identity and this is part of a recognizable pattern of contents and lay-out. But every number of the periodical is a new number which is different from all previous numbers. This means that each number must function both as part of a series and as a free-standing unit which makes sense to the reader of the single issue which gives the form its name and its distinctiveness as a literary or publishing genre. Although it has elements of the serial, the periodical is therefore not a true serial. It is both open-ended and end-stopped.[39]

Subsequent critics have further explored the generic characteristics that Beetham proposes here. The periodical's peculiarly time-bound nature, its mission to write to the moment, has been read as reflective of the cultivation of the 'time of the now' in modernity as well as of a predication on the 'new and on the very modern concept of advancement, of moving forward, of futurity'.[40] James Mussell has further elaborated on the periodical's pattern of repetition and variation – 'sameness and difference' – which is achieved through a 'formal continuity, repeated from the past and projected onwards into the future', thus providing the reader with 'a mediating framework whose purpose is to reconcile difference by presenting new content in a form already known'.[41] The polyvocality and heterogeneity of each individual issue thus functions as part of a more structured form, whose singular identity is serially reinforced through textual and visual means.

Ann Ardis has further theorised the periodical's multi-voiced nature in terms of a dialogic structure. The magazine's 'internal dialogics', she argues, pertain to 'the relationships among and between specific components of any given issue of the magazine, and the creation of meaning through these juxtapositions', while the 'external dialogics' refer to the magazine's 'discursive exchanges with other print media; the mappings of geographical (and temporal) space that they perform as they claim the territories that they report on, distribute copies to, take advertisements from'.[42] The periodical's engagement with other print media, with readers and writers, and the surrounding market and culture has also been theorised in terms of a periodical network, 'a chain of visible or material interactions among human and nonhuman entities'.[43] Drawing on earlier explorations of the reading communities that are constructed around certain periodicals, Fionnula Dillane emphasises the need to 'put affect and emotions back into these networks', as the 'periodical communicates successfully (and sometimes unsuccessfully) through structures of feeling'.[44]

Whereas Dillane uses insights from affect theory to analyse magazine texts, concepts from book history and textual materialism are more commonly used in periodical studies. Jerome McGann's claim that any text is 'a laced network of linguistic and bibliographic codes', with the latter referring to 'such matters as ink, typeface, paper, and various other phenomena which are crucial to the understanding of textuality', seems particularly useful for the study of the periodical context of short fiction, as does George Bornstein's additional concept of the contextual code.[45] Bornstein applies this concept to the placement of a poem in a collection, but it also pertains to the placement of a short story in a magazine issue. 'On the one hand,' Bornstein argues, 'such a contextual code is bibliographic in that it pertains to the physical constitution of the volume; on the other, the contextual code is linguistic in that it is made up of words.'[46] In their introduction to the *Oxford Critical and Cultural History of Modernist Magazines*, Peter Brooker and Andrew Thacker add another subset of codes to McGann's bibliographical codes: the periodical codes. These are 'at play in any magazine' and allow us to analyse 'a whole range of features including page layout, typefaces, price, size of volume, periodicity, use of illustrations, use and placement of advertisements, quality of paper and binding, networks of distribution and sales, modes of financial support, payment practices, editorial arrangements, type of material published'.[47] Some of these features belong to the periodical codes 'internal to the magazine', others concern its 'external relations', but together they reflect the magazine's ideology and construct the context for its individual component parts, including its short stories.

An interesting take on the ideological, rather than material, properties of the periodical is offered by Matthew Philpotts in his analysis of a magazine's 'habitus'. A literary periodical, he argues, 'exists not only as a literary-aesthetic text and a material production but also as a socio-cultural institution'.[48] Drawing on Pierre Bourdieu's sociological approach to literary texts, therefore, Philpotts claims that every literary magazine is marked by a common habitus, 'the defining ethos which unites the members of its "nucleus" and which acts as "a unifying and generative principle" for their cultural practice'.[49] At the same time, the editor of a literary magazine too has a 'personal habitus' that interacts with the institutional one of the magazine as a whole. Through a discussion of editorial practices at *The English Review* and *La Nouvelle Revue*, Philpotts distinguishes between three types of editorial habitus: a 'charismatic editorship', defined by the 'subordination of the common institutional habitus of the journal to the personal habitus of the editor'; a 'bureaucratic editorship', which is mostly concerned with the practical and commercial running of the magazine; and a 'mediating editorship', which can successfully mediate between aesthetic and commercial dimensions of the literary magazine.[50] Thus, 'editorial success' resides for Philpotts in 'as close an alignment as possible between these three dimensions of habitus – the personal, institutional, and the typological – or, to put it another way, between the editor, the periodical and the field'.[51]

Finally, periodical scholars too have observed that traditional hermeneutic methods for reading literary texts – methods which are trained on formal complexity, hidden meanings and textual ambivalence – fall short when one is dealing with the diversified plenitude of periodical texts. Some scholars recommend 'distant reading' techniques to deal with digital repositories of periodical texts, but for the study of a particular genre within a periodical context, Margaret Cohen's suggestions for 'surface reading' also seem particularly promising. In 'Narratology in the Archive of Literature', Cohen proposes a number of reading strategies for dealing with a large amount of non-canonical texts that defy the methods of close reading and attend instead to the features of textual surfaces. One such strategy is 'reading for patterns', where the aim is 'to define the horizon of possibilities that shape an individual text's construction and the range of variations with this horizon'.[52] Another is 'just enough reading': 'to read through a large body of texts looking for the configuration that provides a coherent pattern, rather than prolonging analysis until one has read exhaustively'.[53] A third reading strategy seeks to address 'the forgotten canon', based on the awareness 'that well-known texts may in fact be shaped by unrecognized, forgotten aesthetics'.[54] For our study of short fiction in a periodical context, this holds out the promise that surface reading of magazine fiction will uncover patterns, plots and generic conventions that will cast the canonical short stories published in different (or similar) magazines into a new light.

Chapter summaries

The chapters in this collection respond, directly or implicitly, to the theoretical and methodological approaches outlined above. While the aim of the collection is not to promote a common theoretical framework or uniform methodological approach, these essays, when taken together, suggest ways forward for scholars to examine how the modern short story form developed within and in response to the print contexts of magazine culture. Focusing on periodicals and magazines published across the British Isles in the period 1880–1950, the collection is necessarily selective; the sheer amount of relevant material across what Peter Brooker and Andrew Thacker have described as the 'vast hinterland' of magazines from this period that remain to be explored means that this collection cannot hope to provide an exhaustive, comprehensive account of the symbiotic relation between story-writing and magazine-publishing.[55] Instead, each of these essays presents a particular case study for consideration. Broadly chronological in organisation, the collection provides coordinates for mapping out the historical development of the short story in Britain from the late nineteenth century to the years following the end of the Second World War.

W. Somerset Maugham noted in his 1958 book *Points of View*, 'it can scarcely be denied that the rich abundance of short stories during the nineteenth century was directly occasioned by the opportunity which the periodicals afforded'.[56] The first three chapters in this essay collection examine this dynamic relation between the short story and magazine culture in the last two decades of the nineteenth century. Whitney Standlee and Elke D'hoker both provide correctives to the longstanding privileging of George Newnes's *The Strand* in academic accounts of the nineteenth-century story by turning attention instead to the female editors of magazines that either preceded or imitated *The Strand*. In the first chapter, Standlee focuses on *Atalanta* magazine, edited by L. T. Meade and founded four years prior to Newnes's magazine. Standlee charts the ways in which Meade consistently published stories by both existing and emerging female talent in *Atalanta*, as well as stories by male writers that challenged prevailing notions of femininity and aligned with the editorial emphasis on female education and agency. By paying attention to Meade's editorials and advice dispensed to women writers within the magazine, Standlee argues that *Atalanta* established the short story form as of vital importance in the increasing professionalisation of writing for women, paving the way for the many New Women contributors to *The Yellow Book*, as well as exercising a notable influence on later writers such as Virginia Woolf. Similarly, D'hoker focuses on one of the many magazines established in the late nineteenth century that were marketed to appeal directly to an expanding female readership. Envisioned as 'a female *Strand*' when it was founded in 1893, Annie S. Swan's *The Woman at Home* printed several short story series that looked to replicate the phenomenal success of Arthur Conan Doyle's Sherlock Holmes stories, which had been appearing regularly since 1891 in *The Strand*. Examining a range of short story series written by Swan for *The Woman at Home* from 1893 to 1918, D'hoker accounts for the specific narrative features of the short story series as a distinct form of publication, paying particular attention to periodicity and 'the pattern of repetition with variation' that distinguished the form from the serial novel, for example. Like Standlee, D'hoker also demonstrates how stories that were marketed to female readers in this period both reflected and promoted the social shift in women's roles, from domesticity to public, professionalised work, such as teaching, nursing and journalism. While conceding that many of the story series by Swan that were published in *The Woman at Home* were often moralistic in tone and conservative in message, D'hoker interprets the deferral of the marriage plot and the emphasis on female expertise in these stories as markers of 'modern' and 'progressive' form and content. Finally, David Malcolm provides a focused study of Hubert Crackanthorpe's short-lived periodical *The Albemarle*, published from January to September 1892. Malcolm recovers Crackanthorpe and his periodical from relative obscurity to demonstrate the ways in which short stories in this period occupied publication space alongside a range of other, miscellaneous content, including commentaries on socio-economic and political issues, articles on foreign affairs, poems, memoirs, travelogues, and so on. Analysing the eight short stories that were printed over the magazine's nine issues, Malcolm identifies a set of common themes that align with *The Albemarle*'s non-fiction items. In this way, his chapter highlights the value of returning short fiction to its original print contexts, refocusing our attention on how late nineteenth-century stories both reflected and constituted the social world in which they circulated.

The next two chapters provide original interpretations of two publications that have become central in our histories of early twentieth-century magazine culture: Ford Madox Ford's *The English Review* and John Middleton Murry's *Rhythm*. Annalise Grice surveys the consistent focus on working-class themes across contributions to *The English Review* in its first phase of publication under the editorship of Ford, from December 1908 to February 1910. Grice demonstrates that the journal was keenly attuned to social questions and concerned with class relations, and that this provided an apposite space for the publication of D. H. Lawrence's early stories 'Goose Fair' and 'Odour of Chrysanthemums'. In the course of her analysis, Grice also considers two little-known short sketches by Lawrence that were never published in his lifetime, and outlines Ford's own ideas about the *conte*, or what he termed 'the real short story'. These ideas about the short story form, promoted across Ford's monthly editorials, owed a clear debt of influence to Henry James and the stories published in *The Yellow Book* during the 1890s, and also highlight lines of continuity between the nineteenth-century European tradition of Maupassant and Balzac, for example, and the contemporary and regional English fiction produced by Lawrence. In the next chapter, Louise Edensor examines another magazine with which Lawrence was briefly associated, and which also drew inspiration from the literature, art and philosophy of continental Europe. Published from 1911 to 1913, *Rhythm* included one of the first printed uses of the word 'modernism' to describe literary and artistic experimentation, and it has since become synonymous with the modernist 'little magazine' in histories of the period. Edensor's chapter provides a welcome and original interpretation of *Rhythm* by shifting attention away from Katherine Mansfield's stories, which have been the focus of considerable attention in the existing scholarship, to the varied and diverse short fiction produced by other contributors to the magazine. Edensor interprets the apparent diversity of these stories, in both form and content, as in fact a sign of the underlying conceptual unity of *Rhythm*, in terms of its editorial focus and philosophical outlook. Relating these stories to the ideas of Henri Bergson, adopted and promoted by Murry, the editor of *Rhythm*, in early manifesto statements and essays, Edensor examines the ways in which story contributions to the magazine served to reiterate Bergsonian principles and concepts relating to time, creativity and spirituality. Just as Grice highlights the ideological conditioning of short story publication in the early twentieth century, Edensor demonstrates how individual stories, as well as the magazine-text as a whole, were shaped by particular editorial choices and intellectual preoccupations.

If the editor of *Rhythm* could write in 1911 (without a hint of irony) about 'the rational supremacy of art', declaring that art is 'eternal', 'the true and only expression of reality', and that 'the artist's vision is a moment's lifting of the veil', then by the 1920s such lofty ideas about art and the role of the artist were ripe for parody.[57] In her chapter, Emma West examines a particular sub-genre of short story that became popular in 1920s mass-circulation magazines such as *The Strand* and *The Royal*, 'the artist story'. The standard illustrated popular magazines that are the focus of West's chapter primarily published genre fiction and enjoyed a broad, mixed readership. West notes that the contents of such magazines 'were dominated by the publication of short fiction' and therefore 'constitute an almost unimaginably rich resource' for scholarship, but that such publications have not yet received the same kind of critical attention that has been afforded to modernist little magazines of the 1910s or the feminist magazines of the interwar period. Focusing on a particular and highly popular genre of story in these two competing publications (as West notes, stories that feature artists or writers as their protagonists were in vogue in 1921: in *The Strand*, there was typically an artist story in every issue; in *The Royal*, there were sometimes as many as two stories each month), West charts the ways in which short fiction reflected and responded to each magazine's wider stance on art, negotiating and comically commenting on the 'battle of the brows' that would continue to define the later 1920s and 30s. Examining stories by Joyce Cary (who had assisted with the editing of *Rhythm* as an undergraduate at Oxford) and Robert Magill, West also pays attention to the ways in which apparently light-hearted, humorous fiction served to reinforce the opposing gender politics of each publication: while these stories are strikingly similar in terms of content and theme, West highlights the ways in which genre conventions could be put to very different uses, for different effects, in different magazines. Another magazine published across the 1920s that regularly printed humorous genre fiction was *Eve*, which is the focus of Alice Wood's chapter. Founded in November 1919 and aimed at 'the women of to-day', *Eve* ran until April 1929; in this time, the magazine printed work by the likes of Winifred Holtby, Storm Jameson, Rose Macaulay and Edith Sitwell. In her chapter, Wood analyses stories by Elizabeth Bowen and Radclyffe Hall, as well as fiction by a range of lesser-known writers, in order to demonstrate 'the broad spirit of narrative play' that characterised the short stories printed in *Eve*. Like West, Wood explores the ways in which magazine fiction in this period often bolstered the political agenda of the publication in which it appeared; she examines how short stories in *Eve* 'probed new models of femininity and new models for heterosexual relationships' while retaining a conservative faith in nationalism, patriarchy and class hierarchy. This leads Wood to argue that the stories published in *Eve* were 'determinedly modern' without necessarily being 'modernist', sometimes 'playful in form' yet often promoting established ways of thinking and reinforcing existing social structures. Together, the chapters by West and Wood prompt us to reassess familiar critical categories, such as the 'middlebrow' or 'modernist', through which the literature of this period has frequently been organised and analysed. As West observes, 'magazines are heterogeneous, messy spaces' that place demands on the critic to re-evaluate the assumptions of existing literary history.

Inherent to a periodical's heterogeneous form are the 'internal' and 'external dialogics' that it cultivates, as theorised by Ann Ardis and discussed in the section above. The next two chapters in the collection illuminate the dialogic, conversational nature of periodical culture by examining either the internal relationships between different contributions to the same magazine or the external discursive exchanges between writers contributing to two separate publications. Examining *The London Mercury*, founded in 1919 and edited by J. C. Squire, Yui Kajita finds connections between two stories published in the magazine within three months of each other in 1925 that both feature a parrot, Walter de la Mare's 'Pretty Poll' and Elizabeth Bowen's 'The Parrot'. Looking beyond the obvious similarities in content and theme, Kajita finds echoes between these two stories that are only possible to discern when we pay close attention to the magazine context in which they appeared, arguing that discussions about literary form and aesthetics that *The London Mercury* helped to mediate shaped the intertextual conversation between the two stories. Kajita argues that the parrot call in each story, which figures language disassociated from meaning, highlights both writers' preoccupation with capturing 'impressions' and creating 'atmosphere' in their short fictions, which tend towards ambiguity and unresolved endings. Just as Kajita attends to the ways in which magazines help us to see 'writers as readers of each other's works', Saskia McCracken reveals how Virginia Woolf's reading of four essays by Aldous Huxley in *Nash's Pall Mall Magazine* shaped the revisions she made to a series of essays on London contributed to *Good Housekeeping* magazine in 1931–2. These comparisons are made possible by original archival research conducted by McCracken demonstrating that Woolf submitted the revised galley proofs for her series later than has previously been thought. Picking up on the description of these articles in *Good Housekeeping* as 'word pictures' and 'scenes', McCracken points to the generic instability and hybridity of Woolf's contributions, interpreting these essays as short fictions, in line with what Christine Reynier identifies as Woolf's 'ethics of the short story'. The ethical imperative of these texts, McCracken argues, is highlighted when we take into account the 'magazine format, ideology, illustrations, and advertisements' of *Good Housekeeping*, as well as the external discursive exchanges Woolf's contributions established with Huxley's essays on England in *Nash's Pall Mall Magazine*, published earlier in 1931. McCracken shows how Woolf's texts not only echo certain word choices and imagery in Huxley's essays, but also set out to resist his polemical style and authoritarian politics through hybrid, inconclusive form and non-didactic narratives that instead promote individual choice. The chapter closes with a discussion of a comic story published in *Good Housekeeping* satirising 'highbrow' writers that was accompanied by an illustration caricaturing Huxley and Woolf. This serves to illustrate the connections between these two writers, sustained by magazine culture, that the chapter elucidates. The next chapter in the collection continues the focus on Woolf, examining three stories she published in 1938–9 simultaneously on both sides of the Atlantic, in the American and British instantiations of *Harper's Bazaar*. As such, Dean Baldwin's chapter foregrounds another form of 'external' exchange made possible by magazines, between different nations and geographical sites, lines of connection that are the focus of Ardis and Collier's 2008 essay collection *Transatlantic Print Culture, 1880–1940*. Focusing on the target readership of *Harper's Bazaar* and the placement of Woolf's stories in each magazine issue, printed in juxtaposition with particular articles, illustrations, advertisements and a pervading commercial ethos, Baldwin argues that these stories stand in ironic contrast to the implied values of the magazine and its readership. In positioning these stories in the original print contexts, Baldwin identifies 'ironic tension[s]' that do not exist when we read the stories in later, book-form editions of Woolf's work. In particular, he argues that these stories, like *Harper's Bazaar* itself, served to deliberately insulate readers from the suffering of the Great Depression and the impending violence of another world war.

The short story form flourished during the years of the Second World War, appealing both to writers, who had seen the market for novels decimated by paper rationing, and readers, who were seeking brief moments of distraction at a time of anxiety. The next two chapters examine how magazine editors and writers responded to these contexts. Ann-Marie Einhaus focuses on the first five years of Cyril Connolly's magazine *Horizon*, established in December 1939.

Examining stories by Elizabeth Bowen and William Sansom, as well as discussing works by a range of other writers, Einhaus interprets the 'eclectic and erratic inclusion of short fiction' in the magazine (from popular comedy and old-fashioned yarns to soldier-tales and late modernist texts of psychological acuity and charged symbolism) negatively, on the one hand, as a sign that 'short fiction published in *Horizon* was not a central part of Connolly's editorial strategy' and positively, on the other, as emblematic of the 'diversity and strengths of wartime short fiction'. While peripheral to the editorial project of the magazine, the regular publication of short fiction helped to secure a diverse readership, Einhaus argues, making *Horizon* financially viable at a time when wartime paper shortages placed small-circulation magazines in a particularly precarious position. In the next chapter, Tessa Thorniley focuses on the other dominant magazine of the period, John Lehmann's *The Penguin New Writing*. Lehmann's magazine was very different to Connolly's: it had a much larger circulation; unlike the inconsistent political and ideological allegiances of *Horizon*, *The Penguin New Writing* was committed to representing the reality of ordinary, everyday, working-class life; whereas *Horizon* could seem remote, Lehmann's magazine actively sought out a broad readership; and, crucially, whereas Connolly did not privilege the publication of fiction, Lehmann made sustaining and developing the short story form a central pillar of his editorial mission. Thorniley charts this focused promotion of short fiction in Lehmann's magazine by analysing works by Bowen and Sansom, as well as Henry Green, Rosamond Lehmann, V. S. Pritchett, Graham Greene, Harold Acton and Zhang Tianyi, a wide-ranging list that speaks to the strength of short story writing and publishing in Britain in the years before the demise of both *Horizon* and *The Penguin New Writing* in 1950.

The final two chapters in the collection continue the focus on the 1940s, turning attention away from the wartime context and instead examining the history of magazine publishing in two of the United Kingdom's nations. Tara McEvoy analyses the short-lived Northern Irish periodical *Lagan*, published annually between 1943 and 1946. McEvoy explores the ways in which John Boyd's magazine, over its limited run of only four issues, sought to foster a 'vital tradition' of Ulster writing. She explores the ways in which short stories published in *Lagan* served to promote Ulster idiom 'as the basis for a new regional literature'. While regionalism could often be perceived as insularism, which perhaps contributed to the magazine's limited success, as McEvoy concedes, *Lagan* provided a 'cultural touchstone' for Northern Irish writers, proving influential for a postwar generation that included the likes of Seamus Heaney, James Simmons and Derek Mahon. McEvoy's chapter demonstrates the ways in which editors during this period often envisaged their magazines as forums for creating and sustaining communities. Likewise, Daniel Hughes analyses how *Wales* magazine, published between 1937 and 1949, sought to cultivate a 'home-grown modernist aesthetic' among a group of Welsh writers that included Dylan Thomas, Glyn Jones and Lynette Roberts. Unlike the promotion of regional idiolect in *Lagan*, *Wales* published English-language writing ghosted by the 'forgotten homely tongue' of Welsh. At the same time as *Wales* promoted a nationalist agenda, therefore, Hughes also demonstrates the ways in which the magazine looked beyond Wales: it made connections that reveal the 'intra-national' dimensions of modernism across the United Kingdom (printing advertisements for Hugh MacDiarmid's *The Voice of Scotland*, for example) and positioned Welsh literary experimentation within a European modernist tradition. Identifying its contributors as the heirs to the Welsh short story writer Caradoc Evans, for example, *Wales* also printed previously unpublished fragments by Franz Kafka, and stories by Dylan Thomas included in the magazine show the influence of Joyce, Proust and Baudelaire.

Conclusion

In 1922, that *annus mirabilis* of literary modernism, John Cournos and Edward J. O'Brien founded an anthology, *The Best British Short Stories*. With the stated aim of establishing 'a set of principles governing the art of the short story', Cournos and O'Brien's anthology was published annually until 1932, bringing together texts by British and Irish authors that in all cases had first been printed in a magazine.[58] These texts present a picture of the diverse, eclectic range of publications that carried short fiction in this period, from both sides of the Atlantic, as well as from both sides of the 'great divide' between 'popular' and 'highbrow' markets. In the third anthology alone, for instance, stories were selected from established periodicals such as *The New Age*, *The Nation and the Athenaeum*, and *The English Review*, small-circulation 'little magazines' such as *The Golden Hind*, *The Winter Owl*, and Ford Madox Ford's *Transatlantic Review*, mass-circulation journals such as *The London Mercury* and John Middleton Murry's *The Adelphi*, feminist weeklies such as *Time and Tide*, lifestyle and women's magazines such as

The Tatler and *Eve*, and standard illustrated popular magazines such as *The Illustrated London News*, *T. P.'s and Cassell's Weekly*, and *Nash's Magazine*. The *Best British Short Stories* anthologies provide a record of the astonishing array of magazines that published short fiction, indicating the degree to which 'the art of the short story' owed much to the enabling conditions for publication and reception created and sustained by magazine culture. Like the anthologies edited by Cournos and O'Brien, this essay collection can only hope to be selective; there are undoubtedly points of omission and more work that remains to be done, but in the range of publications, authors and genres covered in these pages we have tried to reflect something of the vibrancy and variety of British magazine publishing during the years 1880–1950, a print culture that conditioned and made possible innovations in the short story form.

Notes

1. For formalist studies of the short story, see May, *Short Story Theories* and *The New Short Story Theories*; Lohafer, *Coming to Terms with the Short Story*; Lohafer and Clarey, *Short Story Theory at a Crossroads*; Head, *The Modernist Short Story*.
2. Studies that have sought to locate the short story in specific national, historical or ideological contexts are, for instance, Awadalla and March-Russell, *The Postcolonial Short Story*; Einhaus, *The Short Story and the First World War*; Ingman, *A History of the Irish Short Story*; and Young, *Contemporary Feminism and Women's Short Stories*.
3. Comparing two histories of the short story in Britain makes this shift clear. In Clare Hanson's *Short Stories and Short Fictions, 1890–1980*, the modernist short story is very much the fulcrum of the history of the genre, but some twenty-five years later, in *The British Short Story*, the modernist short story is given only one in the twelve chapters that chart its history from the late nineteenth century to the present. Hanson, *Short Stories and Short Fictions*; Liggins et al., *The British Short Story*.
4. Chan, *Economy of the Short Story*; Ashley, *Age of the Storytellers*.
5. Abu-Manneh, *Fiction of the New Statesman, 1913–1939*; Einhaus, *The Short Story and the First World War*; Baldwin, *Art and Commerce in the British Short Story*.
6. Monfort, 'La nouvelle et son mode de publication. Le cas américain', p. 158.
7. Head, *The Cambridge History of the English Short Story*; Delaney and Hunter, *The Edinburgh Companion to the Short Story in English*.
8. Philpotts, 'A Return to Theory', p. 307.
9. Mao and Walkowitz, 'The New Modernist Studies'.

10. Collier, 'What Is Modern Periodical Studies?', p. 96.
11. Ibid. p. 104.
12. Delap and DiCenzo, 'Transatlantic Print Culture'.
13. Beetham, *A Magazine of Her Own?*
14. Faye Hammill et al. characterise periodical studies 'as a field that insists on the value of reading across full issues and multiyear runs of serial texts rather than cherry-picking individual items'. Hammill et al., 'Introduction: Magazines and/as Media', pp. vi–vii.
15. Liddle, 'Genre: "Distant Reading" and the Goals of Periodicals Research', p. 384.
16. Ibid. p. 397.
17. Baldwin, *Art and Commerce in the British Short Story*, p. 49; David Pringle and Mike Ashley, 'Introduction', in Ashley, *Age of the Storytellers*, pp. 1–16 (p. 16). See also Hewison, *Under Siege*, for a description of what he calls 'the grand slaughter of magazines' in Britain during the period (p. 11).
18. For theorisations of the short story as 'minor literature', see Hunter, *Cambridge Introduction to the Short Story*, pp. 138–41, and Maggie Awadalla and Paul March-Russell, 'Introduction: The Short Story and the Postcolonial', in Awadalla and March-Russell, *The Postcolonial Short Story*, pp. 1–14.
19. See Chan, *Economy of the Short Story*, pp. 5–7.
20. Pringle and Ashley, 'Introduction', p. 11.
21. Baldwin, *Art and Commerce in the British Short Story*, p. 44.
22. Chan, *Economy of the Short Story*, p. 8.
23. For an overview of these developments, see Liggins et al., *The British Short Story*, pp. 66–117; Hunter, *Cambridge Introduction to the Short Story*, pp. 20–42.
24. Baldwin, *Art and Commerce in the British Short Story*, p. 11.
25. Chan, *Economy of the Short Story*, p. 2.
26. Poe, 'Review of Twice-Told Tales', p. 61. It is worth noting, though, that Poe's precepts for the short story were themselves very much informed by economic motives and the material context of the magazines in which he sought to publish his short stories. See Chan, *Economy of the Short Story*, p. 15; Liggins et al., *The British Short Story*, pp. 2–3.
27. Matthews, *Philosophy of the Short-Story*, pp. 32, 16.
28. Harland, 'Concerning the Short Story', p. 6.
29. Harland, 'Dogs, Cats, Books, and the Average Man', p. 16.
30. Chan, *Economy of the Short Story*, p. 99.
31. Henry James, 'The Story-Teller at Large: Mr. Henry Harland', *Fortnightly Review*, 63 (April 1898), pp. 652–3.
32. Baldwin, *Art and Commerce in the British Short Story*, pp. 71–9. For a similarly wide range of publication options for the New Women writers of the 1890s, see D'hoker and Eggermont, 'The Short Fiction of New Woman Writers'.

33. Baldwin, *Art and Commerce in the British Short Story*, p. 69.
34. Henry James, 'The Science of Criticism', *The New Review*, 4 (1891), p. 398; H. G. Wells, 'Introduction to *The Country of the Blind, and Other Stories* (1911)', reprinted in Hammond, *H. G. Wells and the Short Story*, pp. 162–6 (p. 165).
35. Baldwin, *Art and Commerce in the British Short Story*, pp. 9–11.
36. See Mourant, *Katherine Mansfield and Periodical Culture*; Dubino, *Virginia Woolf and the Literary Marketplace*; Harmon, *Seán O'Faoláin: A Life*.
37. Clay, '"The Magazine Short Story and the Real Short Story'.
38. Beetham, 'Open and Closed', p. 97.
39. Ibid. pp. 97, 99.
40. Beetham, 'Time: Periodicals and the Time of the Now'; Turner, 'Periodical Time in the Nineteenth Century', p. 187.
41. Mussell, 'Repetition: Or "In Our Last"', pp. 347, 351.
42. Ardis, 'Staging the Public Sphere', p. 38.
43. Hensley, 'Network', p. 360.
44. Dillane, 'Forms of Affect, Relationality, and Periodical Encounters', pp. 8, 20. Early explorations of reading communities include Beetham, 'Periodicals and the New Media', and Delap, '*The Freewoman*, Periodical Communities, and the Feminist Reading Public'.
45. McGann, *The Textual Condition*, p. 13.
46. Bornstein, 'What Is the Text of a Poem by Yeats?', p. 179.
47. Brooker and Thacker, 'Introduction', p. 6.
48. Philpotts, 'The Role of the Periodical Editor', p. 41.
49. Ibid. p. 42.
50. Ibid. pp. 48–52.
51. Ibid. p. 62.
52. Cohen, 'Narratology in the Archive of Literature', pp. 59–60.
53. Ibid. pp. 60–1.
54. Ibid. p. 62.
55. Brooker and Thacker, 'Introduction', p. 4.
56. Maugham, *Points of View*, p. 150.
57. John Middleton Murry, 'Art and Philosophy', *Rhythm*, 1 (Summer 1911), pp. 9–12 (pp. 12, 9, 11, 9).
58. Cournos, 'Introduction', p. xiii.

Chapter 1

The 'wire-puller':
L. T. Meade, *Atalanta* and the Development of the Short Story

Whitney Standlee

The Strand magazine has been credited with creating, 'all by itself, a culture of the short story in Britain where none had theretofore existed'.[1] Launched in 1891, *The Strand* was indeed noteworthy for focusing its literary content on complete short works of fiction, and this editorial decision was unambiguously influential in changing the nature of popular literature and how it was consumed. Yet it was far from the first magazine to promote the short story as the quintessential form of periodical fiction: four years prior to the *The Strand*'s debut, L. T. Meade (Elizabeth Thomasina Meade Toulmin Smith) had begun editing *Atalanta*, a periodical aimed at adolescent and young adult female readers. From its first issue, Meade's magazine regularly featured short fiction in its pages, and during her tenure as its editor (1887 to 1893) it published on average ten stories per volume by existing and emerging (predominantly female) literary talent. Those whose short stories were printed in its pages included the professional fiction writers Edith Nesbit, Jean Ingelow, Frances Hodgson Burnett, Lanoe Falconer and Clemence Housman; winners of its scholarship competitions who went on to achieve greater fame included Angela Brazil and Evelyn J. Sharp. Through the medium of *Atalanta*, Meade also dispensed writing advice to her girl readers, who included not only Brazil and Sharp but also the young Virginia Stephen (later Woolf), and in doing so actively promoted both the short story form and the development of a proto-modernist literary aesthetic. This chapter will argue that Meade's editorship of *Atalanta* marks a significant milestone in the evolution of experimental short fiction, and that her publishing decisions and editorial advice were instrumental in encouraging future generations of women to play a central and increasingly professionalised role in the development of the short story as a literary form.

Women's writing, professionalisation and literary networks

Meade's promotion of women's literary professionalism was already well established by the time she came to edit *Atalanta*, but during the period of her editorship her public advocacy of women writers became recognisably more pronounced. It was during this time that she was at the forefront of a movement to create a more cohesive society of female writing professionals in London, and was centrally involved in London's 'Literary Ladies' dining club. As Linda Hughes asserts, this group was envisioned as a counterpart and rival to men's clubs such as the Savile, which 'were homosocial spaces that confirmed members' status as an elect by excluding undesirables, including women'.[2] Recognising that they were not only debarred from these spaces but also from the social and professional networks that such clubs facilitated, the group of women that adopted the sobriquet 'Literary Ladies' was founded with a view to facilitating cooperation and opportunity among women writers and editors in London. It featured among its members some of the most celebrated editors, journalists, biographers, poets and authors of fiction at the time, including Amy Levy, Alice Meynell, Katharine Tynan and Mona Caird, all of whom joined the group at its inception.

Meade was during that period not only the editor of *Atalanta* but also an established novelist with more than thirty published titles to her name. Eventually the author of well over two hundred novels for a variety of reading audiences, she was also a contributor to numerous periodicals, including *The Strand*, for which she would devise and author five highly popular series of short fiction in the 1890s. Yet despite the evidence of her many and varied literary accomplishments, in an interview with Helen C. Black in 1896 it was to her editorship of *Atalanta* that Meade referred as 'the greatest idea and achievement of her life'.[3]

In conversation with Black, Meade also described her typical working day as an author and editor: how she spent each of her early mornings at her home in the London suburb of West Dulwich composing fictional work before taking care of household duties before mid-day. She then travelled to *Atalanta*'s editorial offices in central London, where she worked from early afternoon until 7 PM. Returning home, she had dinner with her family before resuming work in her home office, correcting proofs until late at night. At that point in time, she noted, 'An eight-hours' day would have seemed very little work to me.'[4] Yet, while in this interview Meade is careful to underline her commitment to her family (she was married and the mother of three young children at the time), ultimately it was her career that took precedence. After all, it is not motherhood that Meade identifies as her greatest achievement, but *Atalanta*, and it was through *Atalanta* that her professional legacy and literary influence was established. In its pages she both nurtured writers of merit and helped to shape the future of literature by influencing the direction it would take through her choices of works to publish and editorial advice to dispense. It was also through *Atalanta* that Meade was eventually able to forge the types of powerful alliances between women that she and the group of 'Literary Ladies' in London had been seeking: via her magazine, she published and promoted female authors and fostered associations between them that led to greater professional influence for women in publishing more generally. The seeds of this type of power and impact develop recognisably in *Atalanta* over the course of Meade's editorship, and ultimately, two strands of thought pervade the magazine: those that encourage female agency and inter-female cooperation (or admonish the lack of it); and those that nurture, stimulate and even attempt to provoke readers into literary professionalism and creative innovation.

Atalanta and the development of the short story form

Early on during her editorship of *Atalanta*, Meade had spotted the popular potential of the short story. Through regular columns such as 'Reading Union' and 'School of Fiction', she dispensed professional writing advice to readers and promoted the writing of short fiction as a viable career option for women. By 1893 she was presciently directing those among her readers who aspired to be authors to 'turn their attention to the short complete story'.[5] Doing so, she argued, made good business sense: not only were magazines 'the best opening for the young writer', but also through publication in periodicals, short stories would be 'immediately presented to an assured public'.[6] In that same year, the short story writer Lanoe Falconer also advised *Atalanta*'s readers that their own stories should avoid excess detail, explanatory notes and didacticism:

> There are many things lawful, if not expedient, in the three-volume novel that in the short story are forbidden – moralizing, for instance, or comments of any kind, personal confidences or confessions [...] on that tiny stage where there is hardly room for the puppets and their manoeuvres,

there is plainly no space for the wire-puller. Even more cheerfully renounced those dreary addenda called explanations.[7]

Falconer's advice was both practical and prophetic. As Adrian Hunter notes, the short stories written by the generation of authors who preceded Falconer had varied little in tone, style and content from the novels of the period. Hunter asserts, for example, that Charles Dickens' short stories 'left little to the co-productive imagination of the reader: he *told* rather than *showed*, *stated* rather than *implied*, with the effect that his short stories, like those of his contemporaries Thackeray and Mrs Gaskell, seemed like "unused chapters of longer works"'.[8]

Elke D'hoker and Stephanie Eggermont meanwhile note in their exploration of women writers and the modern short story that 'in writing manuals and creative writing courses modernist short stories are staged as primary models and maxims such as "show, don't tell" or "every word counts" have become well-known mantras for aspiring writers'.[9] Falconer's conception of the short story can thus be seen not only to be insightful in advising *Atalanta*'s female readers to dispense with the realist conventions of the form, but also by describing what amounts to a modernist aesthetic. Meade's decision to include this type of advice in an article that runs to three pages and is centrally located in the volume situates her as an editor who was not only encouraging young women into the professions, but encouraging them into a specific profession, that of the short story writer, with a view to placing them at the forefront of the form's artistry.

As a seedbed of proto-modernist innovation, *Atalanta* is representative of the type of hybridity that D'hoker and Eggermont align with the development of the short story in the 1890s. Appearing in its pages are stories by authors of both sexes that experiment with and push the boundaries of form and content with mixed degrees of success. Meade, as the mediator of the magazine's content, is key: she decided which stories appeared and which themes and characterisations would be highlighted. In its focus on content for young female readers, *Atalanta* needed to appeal to those readers, divining their tastes and preferences. At the same time, the magazine's diverse content demonstrates that Meade recognised the diversity of its readership in its catering for a wide range of interests. Hence, the stories included in *Atalanta* range from the dismal and self-consciously political allegory to the sexually charged and morally ambiguous gothic tale. Yet it is significant that neither type of story fits comfortably within Victorian notions of childhood and femininity.

Instead, Meade recognised the burgeoning modernity of her readers, and sought to appeal to and direct it. If Victorian realism was, as D'hoker and Eggermont argue, the genre of 'reticence, truth and moral purpose', then the short stories published in Meade's *Atalanta* were, at their best, if not its antitheses, then at the very least its antagonists.[10]

The stories included in *Atalanta* by and large adhere to Falconer's advice by avoiding extraneous detail and sermonising. Eminently readable and generally written to a high literary standard, many feature proto-feminist content, celebrating the value of duty to others and promoting ideas of female strength, resilience and self-sufficiency. Viewed as a continuum, they can be seen to develop from tales aimed at passive readers whose minds and attitudes the magazine seeks to influence, to stories written with a view to challenging and invigorating readers who are already intellectually inquisitive. The first of the short stories to be published in *Atalanta*, Lady Lindsay's 'Lizzie's Pianoforte Class', from its inaugural issue, effectively illustrates Meade's early educative concerns. It features a young female protagonist who doubts her abilities and worries about the possibility of public ridicule when she is asked to take on a part vacated by another girl in a piano recital. Lindsay begins the tale by contrasting the joy with which Lizzie jumps into a stormy sea as others around her look on in fear with the young girl's terror at the prospect of striking the wrong notes at the piano recital in front of 'dreadful mammas who are going to sit and look on'.[11] In thus drawing distinctions between the freedom from dread and censure Lizzie enjoys out of doors, which allows her to thrive, and the antagonisms and ill-will characteristic of an older generation of women who oversee the interior spaces in which the young girl largely lives and moves, Lindsay highlights the damaging effects of the confinement and concomitant rivalry that mark women's lives. But a moment of epiphany the child experiences during the course of the recital leads to her recognition of the power inherent in cooperation and kindness: when she fears she might falter while playing the part originally assigned to her friend, Lizzie is reminded of the common saying that 'England expects every man to do his duty'.[12] This in turn moves her to wonder: 'Why not every woman, nay, even every child?' and ultimately to her act of inserting herself into a national narrative of cooperation from which, until then, she had been rhetorically excluded.[13] As a result she is able to fulfil her obligations and achieve her full creative potential. While ostensibly about the transformation of a single child, Lindsay's story can also be seen to confront and overturn wider discursive strategies that, whether purposefully or unintentionally, disregarded the importance (and even the existence) of women.

This model of female responsibility and capability is carried through to Arnold Hamlyn's 'A Jewel of Price', a story also noteworthy for anticipating the conversational style and mystery genre that would later become hallmarks of *The Strand*.[14] 'A Jewel' begins as a story about the career failure and relative poverty of its male narrator, but soon evolves into a tale concerning the unsolved theft of a valuable watch. Increasingly unconventional in tone and content as it progresses towards its denouement at a criminal prosecution trial, the story remains fascinating for Hamlyn's decision to make his narrator both ignorant of the solution to the mystery and responsible for the central crime (he has stolen the watch while sleepwalking). Meanwhile, its heroine is a twelve-year-old girl, Lettice, who takes the stand to testify on the narrator's behalf, exonerating him of guilt in the process. She does so with a dignity and self-possession that belies her years. Much attention is paid in the story to the protagonist's relative youth, but her sex is so little referenced as to prove inconsequential with regard to the unfolding plot. In line with this, in the story's final paragraphs the narrator describes the close friendship he has developed with Lettice over the years that have elapsed between the action of the story and his retelling of it, and reinforces the story's gender-blindness when he states that he has 'at this moment no dearer friend in all the world' than her.[15]

Frances A. Humphrey's 'Lost on the Prairie' offers an even more formidable challenge to prevailing notions of femininity. In Humphrey's tale a young American girl, Winifred, moves with her family from urban Massachusetts to a remote Kansas homestead. Narrated in its first half by its protagonist, the story demonstrates Winifred to be eminently capable of holding her own in the rugged conditions to which she has been relocated: among her many other athletic abilities, she rides her horse in races against her father and often wins. On the day in which most of the action occurs, she is left to care for her young brother, Dot, while her parents journey to the nearest town, fifteen miles away. Determined to fulfil the role she has been assigned as fully as possible, she leaves Dot alone outside in order to do some baking and housekeeping indoors. Fundamentally (and comically) unsuited to these tasks, Winifred takes far longer than she has anticipated to complete them:

> For first the fire wouldn't burn. Then after I had got that well going, I tipped over a pail of water into a pan of ashes, and made a mess on the

kitchen floor. And as our kitchen and dining-room and parlour were all one, I could not leave it, but had to clean it up carefully, and by that time the fire had gone down, and had to be kindled anew. [...] So after I had kindled the fire again I brought out the flour, and butter, and milk, and egg-basket. But by that time I was in such a hurry I hit my elbow and dropped the basket and there was another mess on the floor, and every egg smashed. But I cleaned that up, and then went out to the henhouse for more eggs, and there was the fire almost out again![16]

Detrimentally, these domestic pursuits are not only shown to be unnecessary but also cause her to neglect her far more imperative role as her brother's protector. Emerging from the house to find Dot has disappeared, she rides out on her horse to save him, but is pursued by wolves and forced to seek refuge in an abandoned cabin, where the wolf pack literally bays at the door. In the second half of the story, told through the medium of a letter written by her father to relatives in Massachusetts, we learn that local settlers have eventually found Dot and brought him safely home, and also of the rescue of Winifred, who has spent her time in the cabin protecting her frightened horse from the threat of the wolves, putting herself in mortal danger in the process. Though there is little didacticism in the story, the fact that the adventure of the ride and rescue is portrayed vividly and heroically, while the domestic duties the girl undertakes are likened to a childish game of pretending to fulfil a role she is entirely unsuited to, brings the girl closer to traditional Western heroes portrayed in the work of Humphrey's contemporaries H. Rider Haggard and Bret Harte than to conventional feminine heroines.

Meade's editorial choices continue to favour short stories that dwell on questions of morality and gender over the course of the next few issues of the magazine, yet some stories challenge the reader more than others. Susan Coolidge's fairy story, 'Etelka's Choice', for example, offers an intriguing variation on the Cinderella tale. In it, the main character, Etelka, is treated as a domestic servant and abused by her mother and brothers:

She spun and sewed, she cleaned the pots and pans, cooked the rye porridge and the cabbage soup, and rarely got a word of thanks for her pains [...] if she had refused or delayed to attend to their wants she would have got a rough word, a curse, or perhaps a blow. But Etelka never refused.[17]

When she subsequently meets fairies in the woods who have witnessed her suffering, they offer to grant her a choice of wishes: they will cast a spell so that when she dances, either flowers or gold coins will appear beneath her feet. Longing to experience the beauty of the flowers but believing that the gold will be of most help to her family, she prioritises duty over personal fulfilment and chooses the second option. But the members of Etelka's family are both greedy and undeserving and, after moving to the city, demand more and more material possessions from her without finding satisfaction. As their requests increase, Etelka is forced to dance until she is near death. Finally deserting her family (an unequivocally positive move in the context of the tale), she returns to the woods, where she seeks out the fairies and asks them to undo their spell. Unable to do so, they instead agree to alter it so that the wildflowers she originally longed for will appear when she dances. Etelka and her true love, the farmer Lepperl, are soon married, and through her dancing she transforms what was once his barren land into fields of colour and beauty. In demonstrating that Etelka (and the fairies) prioritise personal fulfilment over self-sacrifice and by dispensing with the materialist implications of the marriage motifs (such as marrying a monarch) which are prevalent in traditional European fairy stories, Coolidge can be seen to use the fairy-tale form as a means to query its moral conventions, and thus to attempt to establish a dialogue with readers about the purposes of such stories and how they might be rewritten for a new, more critically engaged audience.

Elizabeth Stuart Phelps' story 'The Toddlethwaite Prize' meanwhile offers a compelling complement to both Humphrey's and Coolidge's narratives by promoting the values of self-sacrifice but focusing instead on male characters. In this tale, a young student, Bob Gresham, sits up over the course of a long night to nurse a critically ill younger schoolmate, Teddy, who dotes on him and is doted on in turn. When pressed by a doctor to end his vigil at Teddy's bedside and get some rest, Bob replies, 'Teddy takes to me. I've got to stand by Teddy [. . .] I've *got* to.'[18] As a result, Bob is too tired the next day to recall the speech he has memorised for the Toddlethwaite prize competition, and which he was expected to win. When the sponsor of the prize learns of Bob's good deed, however, he awards Bob £100, twice the amount of the Toddlethwaite prize. The story is significant in this context for devaluing stereotypically masculine markers of success, such as the achievement of public glory, and instead rewarding those more commonly aligned with femininity, including nurture and selflessness.

In his more light-hearted 'The Talismans', which appears in the subsequent volume and also features a boys' school setting, Dr [Richard] Garnett creates a story that is simultaneously whimsical and thought-provoking, drawing on philosophical ideas to explore the nature and meaning of time. Again incorporating a male central character, Garnett's story can be seen to mark a shift in the tone and purpose of the short fiction published in *Atalanta*, with Meade from this point tending to publish stories that do not just defy the gendered status quo, but also experiment with the ways in which the short story can be used to convey ideas in a creative and original way. In 'The Talismans', Garnett dispenses with almost all extraneous detail, leading the reader through a series of mythical vignettes that are only revealed to be dream sequences in the story's final sentences. Beginning in a classroom where the subject of study is the philosophy of time, a student gradually loses interest in his tutor's lecture. The story then jumps to a mythical realm, where the student attempts to barter with the anthropomorphised figure of Time for an ancient treasure that will endow him with authority. Choosing as his prize Time's single lock of hair – the source of all Time's power – the student subsequently finds that by enfeebling the physical embodiment of Time he has also halted time, a prospect which turns out to be more problematic than he had anticipated. Specifically, a meteorologist reminds him that, '[r]ain being an agent of Time in the production of change, there can be no place for it under the present dispensation', and he at this point realises that the crops will soon wither in the sun and that fruit will never again ripen.[19] Featuring narrative ellipsis and playing with ideas of genre, Garnett's story is serious in tone but the effect is both humorous and educational. The enigmatic ending of the tale within the tale, in which time restarts because Time's hair has regrown, is clearly meant to provoke intellectual debate about the logic of time both in and outside the story. 'The Talismans' thus posits *Atalanta*'s readers as intelligent and active, encourages them to engage in thinking beyond the limitations of gender, and invites them to disentangle the various threads of a complex plot.

'The Talismans' signals a move towards the more radical literary and thematic experimentation that was to follow with Clemence Housman's 'The Were-Wolf', published in *Atalanta* in December of 1890. Housman, sister of the poet A. E. and the author/artist Laurence, and later a prominent figure in the women's suffrage movement, creates in this tale characterisations that not only question gender norms but also blur gender binaries. The story focuses on the repeated winter visits of a female character, 'White Fell', to an isolated farmhouse shared by twin brothers Sweyn and Christian and their extended family. Housman's choice of name for her main female character links her to a distancing or falling from sexual purity, and in line with this idea, White Fell's appearances increasingly endanger the family and disrupt the harmonious relationship the twin brothers have until then shared. Loved by Sweyn and designated a beast by Christian, who acts as the primary focaliser of the tale, she is noteworthy for her strength and athleticism, and intimations of something approaching non-heteronormative sexual desire are recognisable in Housman's consistent attention to White Fell's masculine attributes and Sweyn's explicit attraction to them. The story appears to be on the side of sexual convention when White Fell is described as

> a monstrous horror – a ghastly, deadly danger, set loose and at bay, in a circle of girls and women and careless, defenceless men – so hideous and terrible a thing as might crack the brain or curdle the heart stone dead.[20]

Her monstrosity is also conveyed through the acts of violence she commits, both of which transgress traditional female family roles. After acting as a nurturer to Rol, the youngest son of the family, she lures him away and presumably devours him; a similar fate befalls Trella, an elderly woman who has welcomed and treated White Fell as a daughter. But the story's extended ending, which consists primarily of a detailed description of a long race between Christian and White Fell through the snow, makes simplistic interpretations such as these problematic. Although White Fell kills Christian, she herself also dies in the effort and is turned into a wolf at the moment of her death. The next morning, Sweyn (not yet knowing what has occurred overnight) spots the two pairs of footprints in the snow and, thinking that Christian has pursued White Fell with a view to seducing or perhaps raping her, follows them with revenge in mind. When he finds both Christian's body and the corpse of a white wolf nearby, he comes to believe that his brother was right in his assumptions about the monstrosity of White Fell, and lovingly embraces the dead man. At this point in the narrative, there is much detailed description of the state of Christian's corpse, which is portrayed in the *Atalanta* illustration by Everard Hopkins with arms outstretched and feet crossed, the shadow of a cross looming over his left shoulder. This illustration not only fetishises Christian's physicality but also has obvious allegorical implications, which are made explicit in the story's closing lines, when Sweyn is described as realising that 'Christian had been as Christ, and had suffered and died to save him from his sins.'[21] This reference to Sweyn's, rather than White Fell's, sins complicates the placement of blame and, in line with this, the delineations of hero and villain roles in the story are never as clear as this statement makes them seem.

Scholars have suggested that 'The Were-Wolf' evidences a fear of female degeneration and non-traditional femininity, and such a reading is consistent with the story's early 1890s context, a point at which references to the New Woman were appearing with increasing frequency in newspapers and periodicals.[22] This interpretation is disturbed, however, by the description of White Fell dying 'causelessly – incomprehensibly', and through the evidence of Housman's own suffragist politics.[23] In its portrayal of a woman with needs that extend beyond traditional family roles, the story of White Fell – forced through circumstances over which she has no control to pursue illicit desires via elaborate disguise and under cover of darkness – can just as readily be seen as an allegorical tale about the danger of repressing women's access to power and suppressing the expression of alternative sexualities. Such a reading is made more explicit in Housman's subsequent full-length treatment of the tale, published by John Lane/the Bodley Head in 1896 and graphically apparent in illustrations by her brother Laurence which portray White Fell as a highly masculinised figure and, in the final image in the volume, show the twin brothers in a sexualised embrace.[24]

Though Meade would never again include a story quite as dense and disturbing as 'The Were-Wolf', in the ensuing volume of *Atalanta* she would for the first time publish a tale of her own. In combination with other works in the same volume including E. Nesbit's 'The Poor Lovers' and Evelyn J. Sharp's 'The Wraith of Turville', Meade's 'The Yellow Dragon Vases' continues to challenge traditional ideas about female identity, drawing attention to issues of sexual desirability, women's agency and the purposes of marriage. Critiques of capitalism and industrialism also feature alongside a questioning of class-based social hierarchies. These shifts in her choices of thematic and moral content attest to Meade's growing confidence not only in herself as an editor and tastemaker, but also in her readers. Thus we find that, in 'The Yellow Dragon Vases', financial problems within marriage are a central concern; so, too, is gender equality.[25] In Meade's tale, a wife receives the titular vases as her only inheritance from a wealthy and beloved aunt, after she has been ostracised by her family for marrying for love rather than money. The vases in the story act as a metaphor for the marriage itself: in her family's estimation the union between the woman and her husband is, like the vases, ugly and unwanted. In reality, both the marriage and the vases ultimately prove to be valuable. Their sale leads to financial solvency for the couple, whose affectionate and equable relationship is highlighted throughout the narrative.[26] The story also reinforces an idea that permeates *Atalanta*: the idea of remaining true to oneself, in both life and art. The admonishment to readers to 'be true' recurs nearly one hundred times over the course of *Atalanta*'s run, and is recognisable in the action and import of both the fiction and writing advice that Meade and her contributors mete out. Writing in 1893, for instance, Mabel Robinson would remind readers in her article 'The Novel with a Purpose' that fiction 'is not merely an interpreter', but that every writer 'who respects her art, her public, and herself, selects stories and characters and situations which are new as well as true, or which are made novel through being regarded from a new standpoint'.[27] In 'The Yellow Dragon Vases', Meade invites her readers to consider marriage and its purposes afresh, focusing on the benefits of affection rather than those of economics. The former, she indicates, will reap its own (often unexpected) rewards.

Likewise Nesbit's 'The Poor Lovers', told in the form of a fable, enacts an emphatic commentary on social inequity and gender roles within marriage. In this story, a young married couple moves to London to seek out work on equal terms – he as a poet, she as an artist. Nesbit's narrative makes it clear, however, that there are financial barriers facing these two hard-working people which preclude their access to artistic success: 'poetry is not marketable unless you are a lord', she writes, and 'pictures are not marketable unless you take a room in Bond Street, and hang the walls with sage-green satin, and give afternoon tea to possible purchasers'.[28] Debarred from his chosen profession by financial need, the husband instead becomes a reviewer of the poetry written by men who have made their fortunes through what Nesbit portrays as reprehensible capitalist exploits. The wife meanwhile becomes a painter of birthday cards and decorative fans (which presumably are sold to the wives of these self-same men). The couple are nonetheless 'foolishly happy' – until, that is, their only child dies and the husband loses his job.[29] Nesbit can find no way out of the psychological and financial distress they face other than their deaths – together, by drowning – which she portrays as a blessing bestowed on them by a fairy. An extended allegory for the state of society in general and the commercialisation of art in particular, 'The Poor Lovers' is one of Meade's boldest editorial choices, conveying as it does a recognisably socialist message in keeping with Nesbit's own Fabian politics.

Sharp's 'The Wraith of Turville', while far more conventional than Nesbit's tale, still manages to extend the ideas of gender and female agency developed in earlier volumes through its construction of a female protagonist, Lady Rilva, who is sexually desirable despite being 'very ugly indeed': Sharp describes her as 'only twenty-two years old, yet her face was white and drawn as if she had been twice that age, her back was bent with some deformity, and she walked with a slight limp'.[30] The story is most interesting for the manner in which it overturns the gender norms of the 'Beauty and the Beast' fairy tale in its various incarnations. In Sharp's variation on the tale, an evil father attempts to trick a rich man into marrying his daughter, Rilva, whom he has hidden out of sight. Yet Rilva manages to gain access to her potential future husband and, without revealing her true identity, uses her intelligence and kindness to win his love. When, due to his devotion to Rilva, he subsequently refuses to marry the master of the house's daughter, whom he believes he has not yet met, her father attempts to kill him by setting fire to the building in which he is lodged. Like White Fell in Housman's 'The Were-Wolf', Rilva is thereafter shown to be a physically powerful woman; like Christian in the same story, she saves the lives of others but is unable to save herself. Sharp's tale acts as both a complement to and a more radical variation on the themes of Housman's tale from just a year earlier: in 'The Wraith of Turville', bodily strength in the female is life-affirming rather than destructive, sexual attraction is predicated on morality and intellect rather than physical beauty, and the Christ-like saviour is female rather than male. Taken together, the strands of thought that emerge around the character of Rilva combine to create a new form of anti-feminine female heroine.

Meade's editorial legacy

The final volume of *Atalanta* to be edited by Meade, Volume 6, October 1892–September 1893, was also the first she was compelled to co-edit with Arthur Balfour Symington due to its amalgamation with *Victorian Magazine*. While the reasons for this merger were never publicly disclosed, the resulting publication, *Atalanta: The Victorian Magazine*, was marked by a discernible alteration in focus and intent, particularly in terms of its fictional content. For reasons that can only be conjectured, this combination of factors appears to have precipitated Meade's exit from *Atalanta*. If the change was, as might be guessed, brought about by Meade's decision to publish controversial fiction and flout gendered conventions both in her life and work, the result was nonetheless detrimental to the magazine overall.

As Janis Dawson asserts, '*Atalanta* continued to attract notable writers such as Ritchie, Molesworth, Sharp and Nesbit, though not in the numbers represented under Meade's editorship', and this first and only volume to be co-edited by Meade and Symington is notable for a lack of literary interest.[31] Of the short stories featured in it there are few that elicit further commentary: Mrs [Margaret] Oliphant's 'Mary's Brother' is a slight but well-told conventional romance; E. Nesbit and Oswald Barron's 'A Mercy by the Way, 1685' is a grim story of soldiers and poachers; Nesbit's solo effort, the fairy story 'A Rose by the Way', is a highly sentimental tale that by and large avoids the serious social commentary of 'The Poor Lovers'; and A. Hammond's 'A Justice of the Peace' features a female character who is gradually brought under the control of a male. The fiction in this volume perceptibly dilutes the magazine's earlier social and political themes, yet this change is mitigated by Meade's, Falconer's and Robinson's assertive and encouraging advice concerning the potential of the short story and readers' own professional practices and prospects.

Meade would follow her own directive by leaving *Atalanta* in 1893 to pursue more assiduously her career as an author of short fiction for literary periodicals. The development of the 'short complete story' would occupy a good deal of her attention for the next fifteen years and afford her an unprecedented level of popular success. Among her most prominent projects was the creation of a first short story series for *The Strand*, 'Stories from the Diary of a Doctor', co-authored with 'Clifford Halifax' (the pseudonym of Dr Edgar Beaumont). Running as they did alongside the 'Sherlock Holmes' series, these stories were immediately positioned as both rivals and literary equals to Arthur Conan Doyle's tales.[32] Meade would go on to write four further series of short fiction for the magazine.[33]

Conclusions

In 1865, Bessie Parkes noted in her *Essays on Women's Work* that the popular press afforded women a legitimate access to power: 'With the growth of the press has grown the direct influence of educated women on the world's affairs', Parkes wrote: 'Mute in the Senate and in the church, their opinions have found a voice in sheets of ten thousand readers.'[34] Although in Meade's time the majority of magazines continued to be owned and edited by men, a few maverick women were making inroads into periodical editorship and authorship, and influencing their readerships in important ways. One of those was undoubtedly L. T. Meade, who used her position as editor of *Atalanta* to promote the emerging form of the short story and encourage her readers not only to write them, but also to emulate her own exacting professional standards.

In her final, direct address to the readers of *Atalanta* in 1893, Meade issued a range of frank and firmly worded publishing advice that evidences the degree to which she was endeavouring to shape her readers into the writers of the future. 'Avoid hackneyed topics', she wrote in 'From the Editor's Standpoint', while directing aspiring authors, whom she referred to as 'fictionists', to be unfailingly professional in their approach by targeting specific publications and researching them thoroughly, timing submissions appropriately, remaining forthright and unapologetic when introducing their work to editors, and eschewing serial fiction in favour of the short story.[35] About the latter, she recommended beginning with 'a good, exciting incident', including 'plenty of movement' and being 'as terse and business-like as possible'.[36] First, she wrote, 'be fresh as regards *Subject*, second, be fresh as regards *Style*, third, fresh as regards *Idea*'.[37] To this she added:

> Whatever you are be true; write about things you know of; don't sit in your drawing-room and invent an impossible scene in a London garret. If you want to talk of hunger and cold and the depths of sordid privation, go at least and see them, if you cannot feel them.[38]

She closed with a parting wish: 'that you will succeed: and I hope to shake hands with you in spirit over the good work you have accomplished'.[39]

Meade's influence was both immediate and lasting, and her professional legacy is confirmed by the achievements of those who were known to be her readers. Angela Brazil, who was awarded a 'Highly Commended' in *Atalanta*'s first essay prize competition in November 1887, would go on to write fiction for girls that exceeded the popularity of Meade's own body of similar works, promoting the active, educated girl as a powerful agent for change. Evelyn Sharp, who as a young reader of *Atalanta* received a 'Commended' in its 'Original Christmas Story' prize competition in March 1888 and a Proxime Accesserunt award in the magazine's 1891–2 scholarship competition, became a prominent contributor of short fiction to *The Yellow Book*, the publication whose experimental literature has been widely acknowledged as the forerunner of modernism. Sharp's 'The Wraith of Turville' in many ways acts as a template and proving ground for some of her later literary experimentation: her story 'In Dull Brown', published in 1896 in *The Yellow Book*, for instance, retells the tale of the plain but desirable woman, incorporating the types of narrative ellipsis and impressionism that Meade's magazine had earlier advocated for the short story. 'In Dull Brown' places the reader in close proximity to its female protagonist's thoughts and feelings, allowing access not only to her quick mind but also to the degree to which her physical movements and prospects for professional and personal fulfilment are being constantly curtailed. Sharp also creates an unsettling ambiguity whereby the reader can never be fully certain of the veracity of the narrator's concluding belief that her lover has, over the course of a single evening, transferred his affections from her to her more conventional (and conventionally beautiful) sister. She thus artfully recreates in the reader similar psychological responses to those the character herself experiences, anticipating the techniques of literary modernism.[40] In terms of Sharp's development as a short story author, we can trace a direct line from the themes of 'The Wraith of Turville' to the advances on them in 'In Dull Brown', and thus from her reading of and writing for *Atalanta* to her experimentation and invention in *The Yellow Book*.

Meade's importance as an editor and influencer is clearly demonstrated if we turn our attention to Virginia Woolf, who kept two volumes of *Atalanta* in her personal library throughout her lifetime, despite the difficulty of doing so over a series of home moves and the bombing in 1940 of her successive residences at Tavistock and Mecklenburgh Squares in London. That Woolf held on to these volumes over a period of more than fifty years attests to their continued importance to her. Certainly, the volumes of *Atalanta* she retained (2 and 4) would have held personal memories for her, as both contained essays written by her 'Aunt Anny' (Anne Thackeray Ritchie), to whom she was very close, and who almost certainly introduced Woolf to the magazine at a young age. Yet these were not the only volumes of Meade's magazine to which Ritchie contributed, and Beth Rigel Daugherty argues that *Atalanta* was not just of sentimental value, but acted as the most important among many literary works that Ritchie bestowed on or shared with her niece.[41] In making this argument, Daugherty also draws attention to the fact that under Meade's editorship *Atalanta* actively challenged the gendered and professional status quo, and created links between young female readers that might not have been achievable otherwise. Because she was home schooled herself, Daugherty suggests, it would have been in the pages of *Atalanta* that the young and isolated Woolf became acquainted with some of the education that girls who attended school gained, not only in terms of curriculum and pedagogical 'how-to' articles, but also in terms of contact with other reading girls, if only through print. It showed her what women could do in publishing [. . .] Its conversational style and democratic inclusion of readers' responses through its discussion-oriented approach would also have provided Virginia Woolf with an early dialogic for her reviews and essays.[42]

Daugherty's argument can be taken even further: through the advice she dispensed in its many articles and regular columns on writing and publishing, Meade not only encouraged young female readers into the publishing industry, but also instructed and guided them in terms of literary style and genre, simultaneously pointing them in the direction of the short story as an emerging form and towards a method of writing that anticipated the later literary experiments in which Woolf herself participated so centrally. The evidence of Brazil, Sharp and Woolf alone is sufficient to suggest the profound effect Meade had on her readers and, through them, on the development of the short story form and the promotion of experimentation in both style and content. How many others she influenced is unquantifiable, but it is apparent that, in the community of readers she created through *Atalanta* and the confidence to experiment this instilled, Meade acted as a 'wire-puller' whose editorial decisions resulted in the emergence of women as prominent forces in both periodical culture and literary innovation more generally.

Notes

1. Chan, 'The Linked Excitements of L. T. Meade and . . .', p. 60.
2. Hughes, 'A Club of Their Own', p. 233.
3. Black, *Pen, Pencil, Baton and Mask*, p. 226.
4. Ibid. p. 227.
5. L. T. Meade, 'From the Editor's Standpoint', *Atalanta*, 6 (October 1892–September 1893), pp. 838–42 (p. 841).
6. Ibid. p. 838.
7. Lanoe Falconer, 'The Short Story', *Atalanta*, 6 (October 1892–September 1893), pp. 457–9 (p. 457).
8. Hunter, *Cambridge Introduction to the Short Story*, p. 10.
9. D'hoker and Eggermont, 'Fin-de-Siècle Women Writers and the Modern Short Story', p. 292.
10. Ibid. p. 298.
11. Lady Lindsay, 'Lizzie's Pianoforte Class', *Atalanta*, 1 (October 1887), pp. 32–8 (p. 33).

12. Ibid. p. 37.
13. Ibid.
14. Arnold Hamlyn, 'A Jewel of Price', *Atalanta*, 1 (April 1888), pp. 387–94 (p. 394).
15. Ibid.
16. Frances A. Humphrey, 'Lost on the Prairie', *Atalanta*, 1 (May 1888), pp. 427–32 (p. 428).
17. Susan Coolidge, 'Etelka's Choice', *Atalanta*, 1 (July 1888), pp. 558–66 (p. 559).
18. Elizabeth Stuart Phelps, 'The Toddlethwaite Prize', *Atalanta*, 2 (January 1889), pp. 263–7 (p. 264).
19. Dr Garnett, 'The Talismans', *Atalanta*, 3 (September 1890), pp. 753–6 (p. 755).
20. Clemence Housman, 'The Were-Wolf', *Atalanta*, 4 (December 1890), pp. 132–56 (p. 145).
21. Ibid. p. 156.
22. See, for example, Bourgault du Coudray, 'Introduction', and Purdue, 'Clemence Housman's *The Were-Wolf*'.
23. Housman, 'The Were-Wolf', p. 152.
24. John Lane/the Bodley Head was a publishing house known for its tendency to issue controversial and avant-garde works, and closely associated with New Woman writing through its publication of George Egerton's seminal collection of short stories *Keynotes* in 1893 and its decision to launch a *Keynotes* series of experimental fiction in the wake of the success of Egerton's volume. Housman also contributed to *The Yellow Book*, another prominent outlet for literary experimentation.
25. L. T. Meade, 'The Yellow Dragon Vases', *Atalanta*, 5 (December 1891), pp. 152–9.
26. This theme is also central to Katharine S. McQuoid, 'Madelaine Leroux', *Atalanta*, 4 (December 1890), pp. 182–91, and Mrs Walford, 'Three Feet of Obstinacy', *Atalanta*, 4 (December 1890), pp. 199–206.
27. F. Mabel Robinson, 'The Novel with a Purpose', *Atalanta*, 6 (October 1892–September 1893), pp. 778–82 (p. 779).
28. E. Nesbit, 'The Poor Lovers', *Atalanta*, 5 (January 1892), pp. 222–4 (p. 223).
29. Ibid.
30. Evelyn J. Sharp, 'The Wraith of Turville', *Atalanta*, 5 (September 1892), pp. 26–33 (p. 26).
31. Dawson, '"Not for girls alone"', p. 492.
32. Her short story series published in *The Strand*, all dealing with medical and scientific detection, were 'The Adventures of a Man of Science' (eight stories co-authored with Halifax, 1896–7), 'The Brotherhood of the Seven Kings' (ten stories co-authored with Robert Eustace, 1898), 'Stories of the Sanctuary Club' (six stories with Eustace, 1899) and 'The Sorceress of the Strand' (six stories with Eustace, 1902–3).

33. Edgar Beaumont, MD (1860–1921) had a general practice in Crystal Palace and according to his obituary in *The Lancet* was 'a surgeon to the Norwood Cottage Hospital [where] he kept well abreast of modern developments and never spared himself'. See 'Obituary: Edgar Beaumont, M.D. Durh.', *The Lancet* (12 November 1921), p. 1028. Meade's series was also recognised in its time as innovative and, more recently, has been credited with inventing the subgenre of the medical mystery. See Mitchell, *The New Girl*, p. 11.
34. Quoted in Showalter, *A Literature of Their Own*, p. 155.
35. L. T. Meade, 'From the Editor's Standpoint', *Atalanta*, 6 (October 1892–September 1893), pp. 838–42 (p. 838).
36. Ibid. pp. 839–40.
37. Ibid. p. 840.
38. Ibid. p. 841.
39. Ibid. p. 842.
40. Evelyn Sharp, 'In Dull Brown', *The Yellow Book*, 8 (January 1896), pp. 181–200.
41. Rigel Daugherty, '"Young writers might do worse"', p. 30.
42. Ibid. p. 33.

Chapter 2

The Short Story Series of Annie S. Swan for *The Woman at Home*

Elke D'hoker

The importance of *The Strand* for the development of the short story in Britain has been well documented in recent scholarship.[1] *The Strand*'s decision to publish only self-contained stories started off a major shift in the publication and consumption of magazine fiction and inaugurated the 'golden age' of the short story in the final decade of the nineteenth century.[2] Moreover, with Arthur Conan Doyle's first series of 'The Adventures of Sherlock Holmes' in 1891, *The Strand* also launched a new publication format: the short story series. Unlike the serialised novel which develops a single narrative across different instalments, the episodes in short story series are stand-alone stories, linked through the repetition of character, setting, and formula. In his autobiography, Conan Doyle prides himself on having single-handedly invented the form:

> it had struck me that a single character running through a series, if it only engaged the attention of the reader, would bind that reader to that particular magazine. On the other hand, it had long seemed to me that the ordinary serial might be an impediment rather than a help to a magazine, since, sooner or later, one missed one number and afterwards it had lost all interest. Clearly the ideal compromise was a character which carried through, and yet installments which were each complete in themselves, so that the purchaser was always sure that he could relish the whole contents of the magazine. I believe that I was the first to realize this and the Strand Magazine the first to put it into practice.[3]

The enormous success of the Holmes stories and *The Strand* can easily be measured by the successors they inspired. Stories of crime, detection and mystery proliferated, often in the form of series, for example Charles J. Mansford's 'Shafts from an Eastern Quiver' (1892), L. T. Meade's 'Stories from the Diary of a Doctor' (1893), and Arthur Morrison's 'Martin Hewitt, Investigator' (1894). The format of the short story series also branched out in other directions, with Conan Doyle's own 'The Exploits of Brigadier Gerard' (1894), Meade's 'Stories from the Diary of a Dressmaker' (1895), and Somerville and Ross's 'Stories of an Irish R. M.' (1899). Finally, the success formula of *The Strand* itself – an affordable, middle-class monthly featuring short stories and journalism on glossy paper with a lot of illustrations – was taken up by a host of imitators as well.[4]

One such imitator was *The Woman at Home*, subtitled *Annie S. Swan's Magazine*, which was launched in October 1893 to be 'a female *Strand*'.[5] Whereas *The Strand* was mainly aimed at male readers, *The Woman at Home* sought to address 'the great mass of middle-class women who are after all the feminine reading public', as Swan put it in her first 'Over the Teacups' column, which was to become a fixture of the magazine for more than fifteen years.[6] Like *The Strand*, *The Woman at Home* was a six-penny illustrated monthly which offered a mixture of non-fiction and fiction. Annie S. Swan, the popular Scottish novelist who had been invited to be the figurehead of the magazine, contributed a story to every issue, often as part of a short story series.[7] The opening series, 'Elizabeth Glen, M.B. The Experiences of a Lady Doctor', which ran from October 1893 to September 1984, proved a great success and Swan would continue to write stories and story series for the magazine until the end of the First World War. While the Elizabeth Glen series, and its sequel 'Mrs Keith Hamilton, M.B.', which appeared monthly between October 1895 and September 1896, have attracted some critical attention for their early representations of the woman doctor, Swan's other series have not yet been studied.[8] They are similar to the Elizabeth Glen series, not least in their depiction of a working woman as the central protagonist, but there are also interesting variations and developments across the series, which serve to qualify the critical verdict of the Glen stories as essentially conservative.[9] In this chapter, therefore, I propose to take a closer look at the different short story series which Swan wrote for *The Woman at Home* between 1893 and 1918, when her collaboration with the magazine ceased altogether.[10] Taking into account the specific narrative features of the short story series, I will investigate how Swan's depiction of professional women participated in the magazine's middlebrow negotiations of new female roles around the turn of the twentieth century.

The short story series

Even though Mike Ashley calls the short story series *The Strand*'s 'most crucial innovation in fiction', the form has not attracted much critical attention.[11] In periodical studies, it is mostly subsumed under the larger heading of serial literature or serialised fiction. In the recent surge of narrative theory on serialisation too, serials and series are often used as interchangeable terms. Nevertheless, as Raymond Williams observed in 1974, a serial is 'a dramatized action divided into episodes', whereas in a series 'the continuation is not of action but of character'.[12] Unlike the interwoven plotlines and cliff-hanger chapter endings of a serial novel, the story series offers episodic narratives, which can be read in random order, thus allowing new readers to come in at any moment, as Conan Doyle recognised. While the individual stories of a series are usually closed, the series as a whole is open and potentially endless. In practice, however, most story series achieve a more definite sense of closure through a concluding story, typically through the death, marriage, disappearance or retirement of the protagonist. This suggests that a narrative arc is never entirely absent in a short story series as even the most static characters and situations tend to develop over time. In other words, while it is important to recognise the short story series as a distinct literary form, the divide between the story series and the serialised novel constitutes perhaps more of a continuum than an absolute binary distinction.[13]

What does distinguish the short story series from the serial novel, however, is its dependence on a pattern of repetition with variation. Ed Wiltse notes about the Holmes stories, '[w]hile complete in itself, each story contains, like the genetic code in a cell, the formula for the complete series – a mystery and solution, the Holmes-Watson relationship, 1890s London, and Holmes's method'.[14] Umberto Eco puts it in more general terms as follows:

> [t]he series works upon a fixed situation and a restricted number of fixed pivotal characters, around whom the secondary and changing ones turn. The secondary characters must give the impression that the new story is different from the preceding ones while in fact the narrative scheme does not change.[15]

This pattern of repetition with variation is of course one of the prime attractions of the short story series, as readers can expect difference within the safe boundaries of the same. In this, the short story series shows itself very much in tune with the periodical context in which it typically appears. Periodical publication too is characterised by patterns of iteration and repetition, by the 'negotiation between sameness and difference'.[16] For, as Margaret Beetham argues, 'each number must function both as part of a series and as a free-standing unit which makes sense to the reader of the single issue'.[17]

In a similar way, the periodicity that is a basic feature of periodical publication has an impact on the reception of a short story series. The time lapses between episodes in serial storytelling, Frank Kelleter argues, allow for a 'particularly close entanglement of production and reception'.[18] This is made especially evident in cases where writers have made changes to serial narratives as a result of reader interaction – with Conan Doyle's own resurrection of Sherlock Holmes as a prime example. Yet, it also accounts for the greater affective investment in serial characters on the part of readers for whom the characters go on existing in the time lapse between serial instalments. Erica Haugtvedt notes:

> [s]eriality amplifies the speculative activity inherent in any construction of character by instantiating regular publication gaps during which audiences interpret and speculate [. . .] Serial character, then, depends upon the condition of temporal persistence – and seems realistic in this regard, even when serial character may not always share other traits of realist characterisation.[19]

For Haugtvedt, this explains why serial characters so often assume a transfictional dimension, which allows them to persist across instalments, translations and numerous adaptations. Again, Sherlock Holmes is perhaps the most famous serial character in this respect, but also Swan's serial protagonists seem to have invited a strong affective investment on the part of the readers of *The Woman at Home*.

Swan's working women short story series

All in all, Swan published ten short story series about working women in *The Woman at Home*; eight under her own name, and two under the pseudonym of David Lyall, which she had been using since 1895.[20] Apart from the two series about the lady doctor, Elizabeth Glen, these are 'Memories of Margaret Grainger, Schoolmistress' (October 1894 to September 1895); 'Miss Ferrar's Paying Guests'

(October 1897 to September 1898); 'Sister Ursula' (April 1900 to April 1901); 'The Journal of a Literary Woman in London' (May 1901 to May 1902); 'Anne Hyde, Travelling Companion' (November 1905 to September 1906); 'Hester Lane, Employment Agent' (October 1906 to September 1907); 'A Sister of the People', by David Lyall (October 1907 to September 1908); and 'The Consolation Bureau', about a journalist who writes an agony aunt column, also by David Lyall (November 1913 to September 1914). To this list could be added one further series, 'The Pioneers, Being Stories of the Woman's Cause' (October 1908 to July 1909), which offers stories of various women connected to the suffragette movement. Yet, as the series does not revolve around a central professional or working woman, it falls outside the scope of this discussion.

If in a serialised novel the events narrated in the instalments are 'cumulative' and 'have a persistent impact on storyworld', in Swan's short story series, the instalments describe separate incidents, involving secondary characters which mostly do not recur in subsequent stories.[21] The bibliographical codes of the magazine also distinguish these story series from the serial novels which *The Woman at Home* also published: the series title is in each story supplemented by a subtitle, a practice which also characterised the Holmes stories in *The Strand*. The instalments of a serialised novel, by contrast, are introduced by numbered but untitled chapter headings and sport the telling *'(to be continued)'* at the end of each chapter. At the same time, of course, the stories in the series are different from self-contained stories through the series title which is also prominently displayed as the header on every other page. Swan's series all amount to eleven or twelve instalments, which corresponds neatly with two six-issue volumes of the magazine.

Apart from these bibliographical codes, the series have many other characteristics in common as well. First, they all have a professional or working woman as the main protagonist: a doctor, two nurses (a hospital nurse and a nurse working in one of London's Christian Missions), a literary author and editor, an 'agony aunt', the principal of a girls' boarding school, an employment agent, a boarding-house keeper and a travelling companion. In some series, the protagonist is also the narrator of the stories; in others the stories are mediated by a first-person narrator, typically a friend of the protagonist. The individual stories relate incidents connected to the working life of the protagonist. Depending on the protagonist's profession, these are stories of patients, clients, pupils, customers or writers. They typically turn to the protagonist with a problem, which is then solved thanks to her sympathy, generosity and professional expertise. Depending on the setting, moreover, they concern different social strata. If the stories of Miss Ferrars, Margaret Grainger and Anne Hyde involve upper-class and upper-middle-class characters, the stories told by Sister Ursula from the St Dunstan's public hospital and Sister Mary from St Anne's Mission in West Ham typically concern lower-class or lower-middle-class characters. Other series, like 'Elizabeth Glen', 'Mrs Keith Hamilton', 'The Journal of a Literary Woman in London' and 'Hester Lane' feature stories across the social spectrum.

These different contexts notwithstanding, the same plotlines tend to recur across the different series: estranged family members are reunited, rebellious or impoverished girls find love, alcoholics are reformed, marriage problems are resolved, and so-called superfluous women find a new home. In general, the good characters are rewarded and the morally straying either die or are brought back to the right path. This is not to say that the stories are merely formulaic and without interest. To the contrary, several of the series would benefit a closer investigation for their representation of social problems, women writers and journalists, issues of race and nationality, and changing social norms. Still, the stories do run along traditional plotlines and contain a moralising tone. While the majority end happily, with domestic happiness attained or re-established, the stories that end in death also receive a moral glossing through deathbed reconciliations, a final repentance or religious acceptance.

As Wiltse notes in relation to the Holmes stories, the closure and independence of these single stories stand in tension with their interdependence as part of the series.[22] This interconnectedness in the series is realised primarily on the levels of setting, characters and plot patterns. First, the recurring setting foregrounds the unity of the stories, whether it is Miss Ferrars' boarding house, the parish of St Anne, St Dunstan's Hospital, Hester Lane's office, Elizabeth Glen's consulting rooms, or the newspaper offices of *The Sentinel* in Fleet Street. The stories typically start with a new 'case' arriving on the protagonist's doorstep, but the protagonists occasionally travel further afield to trace the problems of their 'cases' back to their origins in Britain, Ireland and even Barbados.[23] The interdependence of the stories is, secondly, the result of the recurring central protagonists: the working woman and a few of her close associates, whether family members or colleagues. Although the plot of the individual stories revolves around new characters each time, the protagonist takes centre stage in each story as the main confidante and helper of these characters. While she remains for the most part unaffected by the plot events of the individual stories, the majority of the series do work towards a form of narrative closure, typically through the marriage of the protagonist. This denouement is confined to the final story of the series, although some hints may be dropped in the stories immediately preceding the closing instalment. This does confer a sense of narrative progression to the stories, which serves to confirm Jason Mittell's observation that the difference between the story series and the serial novel involves a continuum rather than an absolute distinction.[24]

In the case of Elizabeth Glen, the final story puts an end to her successful medical practice because of her marriage to a Scottish peer. For Tabitha Sparks, this narrative closure suggests that, for Swan, marriage and medicine are irreconcilable and that the first, for a woman at least, should take precedence over the latter: 'if the professional success of the woman doctor upsets the forward motion of the marriage plot, her romantic reversal triumphantly restores it'.[25] Beetham too reads the ending as a 'return of the heroine to her traditional place', which is 'the result of two related forces, the demands of the romance fiction formula and the need to reassert the domestic nature of women'.[26] For Beetham, this romantic ending is part of the conservative domestic ideology of *The Woman at Home*, which sees women first and foremost as wives and mothers. In order to assess this reading of the Elizabeth Glen stories in the light of Swan's other story series, we need to take a closer look at the periodical that shaped both the production and the reception of these texts.

Balancing domesticity and women's work in *The Woman at Home*

William Robertson Nicoll, a 'prominent Free Church proprietor, journalist and editor', who had already successfully launched *Bookman* in 1891 and *The British Weekly* in 1886 with the publishing firm of Hodder and Stoughton, founded *The Woman at Home*.[27] He engaged two fellow Scots to run the magazine for him: Jane T. Stoddart, Nicoll's close associate at *The British Weekly*, became its editor and novelist Annie S. Swan its chief contributor and columnist. In *My Life*, Swan recalls Nicoll's proposal as follows:

> [o]ne day he [Nicoll] came to me with a rather startling proposition. He thought there was room for a new woman's magazine, and he wanted me to be associated with it – though not as Editor, where I should have been

a dismal failure (owing to the tendency to allow my heart to govern my head) but as chief contributor, and to have my name printed on the cover. For years the magazine was popularly known as *Annie Swan's Magazine*. Of course I was only too happy to agree, and thus began one of the most interesting chapters of my writing life.[28]

It would also prove to be one of the most prolific periods of Swan's career. She contributed one or two stories to every issue as well as occasional articles and biographies. In her 'Over the Teacups' column, moreover, she gave her opinion about current affairs and answered readers' letters. As Beetham notes, the title and the illustration of this advice column suggested 'a place where women could exchange confidences as equals and friends'.[29] Swan recalls the column as 'an instant and overwhelming success. The letters used to be sent from the office to my house, if not literally in sacks, at least in gigantic bundles'.[30] Because of the amount of letters received, 'Over the Teacups' developed an offshoot in a recurrent 'Love, Courtship and Marriage' column from April 1895 onwards, in which Swan gave advice on relationships in particular. The 'Teacups' column was the first in the 'Life and Work at Home' section at the back of the magazine, which was printed in smaller font and contained fewer illustrations. It was made up of a varying selection of a number of recurrent features on cooking, child raising, fashion, health and home furnishing, but it also contained a 'Women's Employments' column which gave quite practical information about jobs and professional training for women.

The presence of this column in the 'Life and Work at Home' section already hints at the mixed message of *The Woman at Home*. Although it aimed to address 'the woman at home', the 'woman in her own kingdom', as Swan puts it in the first issue, several of its features also represented or addressed working women.[31] The biographies and illustrated interviews often presented female high achievers such as writers, artists, philanthropists and activists even if the emphasis was typically on the subject's personal and domestic life, rather than her achievements.[32] Women's work was also the subject of debates, such as 'Should married women engage in public work?' and 'Is journalism a desirable profession for women?' in which different viewpoints were represented.[33] Moreover, as Beetham notes, one of the most persistent topics in 'Over the Teacups' was 'how to earn a living as a middle-class woman'.[34] If for Beetham, the tension between *The Woman at Home*'s domestic ideology and its attention to women's work is part of the 'heterogeneous form of the magazines [which] allowed contradictory discourses to coexist', Kate Krueger finds both united in the 'strong work ethic' of *The Woman at Home* and Swan's contributions in particular: '[b]y defining women as proven workers in the home, [Swan] reduces the stigma associated with working outside of it due to intellectual or economic need'.[35] Nevertheless, *The Woman at Home* also emphasises that woman's work in the home should always take precedence over any work or career outside of it. 'A woman's first duty is her home,' Swan notes in her response to the question, 'Should married women engage in public work?', adding: '[o]f that responsibility no one can entirely relieve her, though it is possible that it may be shared'.[36]

Let us now turn again to Swan's short story series to see how they deal with this tension between the working woman and the woman at home, between recognising the importance of paid, professional work for middle-class women and advocating the private sphere as woman's proper place. I will argue that Swan's ideological negotiation of these two positions is facilitated by the format of the short story series, which allows for a partial, character-based escape from the expectations of the marriage plot.

Framing the professional woman

In her reading of the Elizabeth Glen series, Tabitha Sparks notes that Swan 'averts the controversy of her female doctor by her distance from bodily specifics and medical or scientific information' and that 'her serene presence and sympathetic ministrations situate Elizabeth more as a nurse than a physician'.[37] It is true that medical or scientific knowledge is virtually absent in the series. 'It will not be very interesting for you to hear the details of my treatment,' Elizabeth Glen remarks in the second story, and this self-censure is kept up throughout.[38] Moreover, in so far as the stories have happy endings, these are not primarily the result of her professional expertise but rather of her committed and sympathetic care for her patients. Yet, this does not serve to downplay Glen's medical expertise, but rather to prove that the lady doctor is not just equal to the 'man doctor', but superior to him, because of her female sympathy. Indeed, it is precisely because Elizabeth Glen is willing to go beyond strictly medical care that she is able to truly help her patients. As the narrator notes, 'Elizabeth was a nurse *as well as* a doctor.'[39] In the story 'Norah Fleming', for instance, Glen helps an unhappy young mother by attending to her 'heart trouble' as well as her bodily complaints:

I always do my duty by the man doctor, as you call him, but I know very well that it is just in such cases that he makes his professional mistakes. He would have gone on exclusively treating poor little Norah Fleming's body, when the mind was at the bottom of it all the time. It was sympathy she wanted, and mothering, and loving understanding, for she was being worried and neglected into the grave.[40]

All of these the lady doctor generously provides. The other series too emphasise personal sympathy and care as the supplementary assets that a women can – and should – bring to a profession so as to really make a difference. Sister Ursula's success as a nurse, for instance, is shown to be the result of 'her power of personal sympathy', 'the gift [...] which crowned her life with conspicuous success', as it 'was possible for her to make all who sought her aid feel that their concerns were the only ones in the world for Sister Ursula as well as for themselves'.[41] Cordelia of 'The Consolation Bureau' feels that 'it was only when I gave myself, when it actually cost me something personally, that I did any good at the bureau', while Hester Lane often contrasts the personal and charitable approach of her employment agency to the purely mercenary concerns of 'the ordinary registry office', 'a cold, calculating business machine, intent upon merely selfish ends'.[42]

In general, Swan's working women are generally able to help other people – boarders, patients or the poor – by going beyond the call of duty in their professional contexts and helping them solve their personal, domestic or marital problems. As a result, the professional expertise of the protagonist is not often instrumental to the plot development. Some exceptions to this, however, can be found in 'The Memories of Margaret Grainger' and 'The Journal of a Literary Woman in London'. In 'Kathleen', the happy ending is due to Grainger's 'new department at Fleetwood', namely 'the teaching of household management down to the smallest detail', while in 'The Mite' and 'A Revolting Daughter', some wayward pupils are set on the right path thanks to Grainger's progressive educational principles with regard to discipline and punishment.[43] The plots of 'An Omnibus Acquaintance' and 'What Price a Soul' hinge on the literary woman's ability to recognise literary talent even in the unlikeliest of places, while in 'Wanted – A Conspiracy' she is able to expose a literary hoax by her correct assessment of a novel which other reviewers have praised to the sky.[44] Yet even in stories where the professional expertise of the protagonists is not instrumental to the plot of the individual stories, the authority, competence and success of these working women is highlighted in a variety of other ways.

In the framework of Swan's story series, the professional context and status of the protagonist is foregrounded strongly. This framework is typically sketched in the opening story, but then reactivated in the introductory paragraphs of each subsequent story. The concluding paragraph often returns to this frame, as the protagonist reflects on what these events have meant for her career, her worldview or her life. The exemplary nature of the protagonist's work is repeatedly stressed in these introductions, by means of the high esteem in which it is held or the financial profits it brings. In 'Miss Grainger', for instance, parents come to her because '[her] establishment has been highly recommended to [them]' or because they 'have heard so much of [her] wise guiding and judicious training', while in 'A Sister of the People', a fellow nurse praises Sister Mary as 'the chief cornerstone' of the Christian mission, whose 'fame [. . .] has spread as far east as Beddoes Street'.[45] Material success is emphasised in 'Hester Lane, Employment Agency' when, by the tenth story, Hester is able to employ an office boy and an assistant as well as move to larger premises, which have 'every comfort and convenience necessary for the conduct of a first-class business'.[46] Elizabeth Glen's professional success too is measured by the speed with which she has been able to build up a thriving practice: '[s]he had got to that stage in her profession when you always found two or three people in her waiting-room during her consulting hours', the narrator notes on one occasion, and when taking a ride with her friend, she explains: '[p]rosperous days had come to Dr. Glen, and the carriage was paid for out of her own professional earnings'.[47]

Apart from her professional success, the authority of the working woman is often emphasised as well. Sister Mary is said to have 'great power over the people', having considerable charisma as well as 'the diplomacy of the most able statesman'.[48] In 'Rachel Waters', Miriam Carter, the literary woman, proves her professional authority by successfully managing a recalcitrant and jealous sub-editor.[49] And Sister Ursula notes how 'the whole concern seems to move like clockwork under my direction – it belongs to me, and I do it'.[50] One of Margaret Grainger's pupils tells her headmistress, 'you were perfect [. . .], keeping us in our places and making us stand in awe of you, though we were never afraid'.[51] Grainger herself does 'not flinch' when her authority is challenged. 'Are you sure you can maintain order and discipline in a large establishment like this?', a sceptical parent asks. To which Grainger responds, '[t]hat I have been at the head of it for seven years, Mrs. Bellamy, surely proves some degree of fitness'.[52] Given the greater controversy over the female doctor at the time, these challenges to the protagonist's authority are even more explicit in the Glen series. As the doctor notes, 'the prejudices to be overcome against women doctors, even today, my dear, are tremendous'.[53] Most of the stories, therefore, show how Glen is able to surmount or face down these challenges, proving her true value and authority as a doctor. At the same time, the stories occasionally draw ironic attention to the performative nature of professional behaviour. When challenged about her age and sex, Elizabeth Glen responds with 'all the dignity [she] could command' and gives '[her] orders in a quick, decisive way, which favourably impresse[s] them'. She concludes, wryly, 'I know that my prompt action saved my reputation.'[54] Surprised by an early client on a wet morning, similarly, Hester Lane notes: 'I had just time, as I heard her step on the stair, to get my wet things hustled into the cupboard and assume my most business-like air.'[55]

Swan does not make light of the difficulties and hardships of the working life either. The protagonists are always busy, often tired and invariably hard-working, which is in tune with the strong work ethic Swan advocates throughout *The Woman at Home*. Moreover, most of the series describe the professional context of the protagonist with a degree of realism that is sometimes lacking in the plots of the individual stories. The 'Sister Ursula' series, for instance, gives a detailed description of the hospital, with its struggle for funds, shortage of staff, camaraderie among the nurses, and very hard work.[56] In many stories, moreover, Ursula is shown to struggle with the 'Matron' of the hospital, who 'ruled us all with a rod of iron'.[57] In the 'Sister of the People' series too, the work done by the Christian missions in London's East End is accurately evoked. The greatest detail can be found in the professional context of the 'Literary Woman' stories, where the narrator-protagonist, Miriam Carter, is not just a well-respected novelist, but also editor for 'a great weekly newspaper' in London.[58] She rides to work 'in the City-Atlas Omnibus', struggles through too many submissions ('for every article we wanted we received at least a hundred'), has to deal with a difficult publisher ('for some unaccountable reason our circulation had gone down two consecutive weeks, and Lascelles wanted to know the cause') and is a regular guest at literary dinners and soirées.[59]

In different ways, in short, the frame of the short story series manages to establish the protagonist as a credible, well-respected and likeable professional woman. Especially for the professions which were still very much a male preserve – journalism, medicine, business – Swan also takes care to emphasise the genteel and feminine qualities of her protagonists. In 'Elizabeth Glen', she seeks to remove the stigma of the 'mannish' lady doctor and to counter the belief, voiced by one character, that medical study would 'rob [a woman] of that exquisite womanliness'.[60] Both Cordelia from 'The Consolation Bureau' and Miriam from 'The Literary Woman' are often confronted with the stereotype of the bluestocking. 'You don't look that sort of person [. . .] a person employed by a newspaper,' a client tells Cordelia: 'I imagined a long, lank woman with cheap clothes and perhaps an eyeglass. Why, you look quite the lady.'[61] In 'Hester Lane', to give a final example, Swan sets out to correct the stereotype of the cold-hearted businesswoman. Hester's mother, who disapproves of her daughter's career, admits in the final story, 'you've done splendidly, and you've never got hard or unsympathetic'.[62]

In the other series too, the protagonists are gentlewomen, whose professional authority, hard work, high moral principles and altruistic care make them both perfect heroines and clear examples for the readers of *The Woman at Home*. Because of the iterative format of the short story series, moreover, the protagonist's admirable qualities and her professional context are repeated again and again. Similarly, as we have seen, the periodicity of serial publication stimulates a reader's affective involvement with the heroine, who seems to assume an even greater 'reality' in the eyes of the reader. Swan also actively fostered the illusion that her working women were real persons. Beyond the precise London locations and the credible professional context of the stories, the authorial personae of Swan and David Lyall also appear in several series to vouchsafe for the truth of the incidents and the reality of the heroine.[63] Small wonder then that readers of *The Woman at Home* wrote letters to Swan asking 'for the address of Elizabeth Glen, and also some authentic particulars regarding that lady and her work', which she dealt with in 'Over the Teacups'.[64] In a metafictional feedback loop, she even refers to these letters in the stories themselves when she tells her friend, 'I have ever so many letters asking for your address, and I believe I am right in withholding it. So long as I wrap you in a veil of mystery, my readers regard you with a proper mixture of awe and respect.'[65]

In short, the frame structure and repetition-with-variation pattern of the short story series contributes considerably to the strong profile of the working woman in these stories. Even if the individual episodes are concerned with romantic or domestic problems, the iterative insistence on the very real professional context in the series' frame serves to put the working woman at the centre of attention. In this way, the series succeed in making these working women acceptable heroines, even for the middle-class housewife targeted by *The Woman at Home*.

Postponing the marriage plot

In a discussion of TV series, Robyn Warhol claims that '[t]he serial form defies the dominant "marriage plot" governing so much of popular fiction', due to 'its structurally mandated impulse to defer indefinitely'.[66] In Swan's short story series too, the marriage plot is avoided or deferred for the main protagonist, but not indefinitely. Instead, the periodical practice of bringing serialisation to an end after a two-volume run demands a form of closure that can only be realised, it seems, by means of a return to novelistic plotting, through the marriage or, more rarely, death of the heroine. It is important to stress, however, that the marriage plot is deferred, and even openly defied, for much of the short story series. First, it is quite striking that the protagonists of the stories are all in their thirties or even forties, well beyond marrying age by Victorian standards, and that they have therefore worked in a professional context for many years. Second, their pursuit of paid work is explicitly justified in the stories, either by references to financial hardship or to professional ambitions. Miss Ferrars and her sister start taking in 'paying guests' because of financial misfortunes, while Margaret Grainger and Anne Hyde are left 'unprovided for' by their improvident fathers.[67] Sister Ursula, on the other hand, turns to nursing because 'personal sorrow [. . .] caused her to abjure the world and give herself literally for the service of others', while the literary woman and her sister, an illustrator, pursue artistic ambitions.[68] Elizabeth Glen also speaks of her 'desire to be a doctor, and to live a more useful and a fuller life' than as a married woman.[69] And even though these ambitions are deflected as the desires of 'headstrong youth', they are echoed by Hester Lane, who is reluctant to give up her business in order to emigrate with her mother and sister: '[w]as I ready to leave it all and return to the quiet of household ways, and the thousand petty but all-important trifles with which women fill their days?'[70] Third, the marriage plot is typically only introduced in the final story, even though hints about the protagonist's tiredness or unhappiness may be introduced in the penultimate one. In the introductory paragraphs to Glen's 'A Commonplace Tragedy', for instance, the narrator notices 'a change in our friend': '[s]he was more thoughtful and subdued, and sometimes had a far-off, contemplative look on her face'.[71] With these and similar remarks, Swan builds up narrative tension that will find resolution in Elizabeth Glen's marriage in the final story and her concomitant decision to give up her professional career.[72] Most series follow this pattern of a quite sudden closure through marital bliss, even though in some later series, marriage and work are presented as less mutually exclusive than in the Glen stories. Sister Mary continues to lead the Christian mission together with her vicar-husband and the 'Journal of a Literary Woman in London' ends with 'I have never quite given up my outside work.'[73]

The 'Memories of Margaret Grainger, Schoolmistress' series forms an early exception to this pattern, since Grainger never marries. As she proudly announces in the opening story: 'I am an old maid, and I have no history. I have never even had a romance. I suppose I have always been too busy.'[74] More than any other series, indeed, the Grainger stories set out to prove that a perfectly happy, full and useful life can be lived outside of marriage. This is demonstrated both through the figure of Margaret Grainger herself – whose sympathetic care for her pupils is rewarded by the many friends with whom she can spend her holidays – and through some of the stories themselves, which emphasise that nothing is worse for a young girl than marriage at all costs.[75] Since Grainger neither marries nor dies at the end of the series, no novelistic emplotment is introduced to bring the series to a close. Instead, it ends rather abruptly, with the protagonist-narrator noting: 'With poor Adelaide Brand's mistake my memories, for the time being, must be brought to a close.'[76] The 'for the time being' suggests that the schoolmistress could have gone on recounting incidents from her 'long and busy life', that the story series could run on indefinitely.

By contrast, the second Elizabeth Glen series, 'Mrs Keith Hamilton, M.B.', shows the format of the story series to be much less suited to the life of a married woman. Resurrected by popular demand, Elizabeth Glen, now the wife of a Scottish landowner and M.P., again shares some incidents from her life with her friend 'Annie' and the reader. Yet, it quickly becomes clear that the life of the married woman sits uncomfortably with the repetitive structure of the short story series. In one story, Elizabeth Glen records a case from her previous career; in a few others she uses her medical knowledge to help a tenant family on her husband's estate. Yet other stories revolve around her new projects: setting up a hospital in Scotland and a boarding house for shopgirls in London. For, as is repeatedly emphasised, Elizabeth 'is really lost for want of something to do' and has an 'intense desire to find some useful and satisfying outlet for her energies'.[77] Yet these incidents and projects disrupt the format of the series as they extend over two or more instalments before being abandoned again. Moreover, the frame story – Elizabeth's friendship with 'Annie', the authorial persona – takes up more and more space as the two women debate the importance and value of philanthropy. In the eleventh instalment, the series is brought to a sudden close with Elizabeth becoming a mother. In terms of format and structure, in short, 'Mrs Keith Hamilton, M.B.' is quite unsuccessful as a short story series, moving closer to the episodic novel. It is not surprising, therefore, that Swan would not again be tempted to 'revive' one of her heroines.[78] Instead she preferred to stage always different working women and different professional contexts, since they seemed best suited to the repetition-with-variation structure that the short story series demands.

Conclusions

Although there are undeniably conservative elements to Swan's short story series – their romantic plots, moralising tone and domestic focus – I would argue that the progressive elements outweigh these. Aided by the repetitive and open structure of the short story series, the stories create professional and working women who do not conform to the type of the mannish, and even man-hating, 'advanced woman', who was perceived as a threat by men and women alike. Instead, Swan's heroines combine authority, agency and professional expertise with 'womanly' and maternal qualities, which makes them acceptable, and even exemplary, heroines to the reader of *The Woman at Home*.[79] If Swan still feels the need to explain these women's particular reasons for turning to paid work or a career, she also shows how they enhance the profession, and truly help others, by topping professional expertise with the strongly gendered qualities of 'sympathy and service'.[80] In this way, the short story series participate in *The Woman at Home*'s middlebrow negotiation of the new female roles and feminine ideals that were being debated at the time. Given the difficulties which more progressive New Woman writers also had with representing these roles and ideals in fiction, it is particularly interesting that Swan does succeed in making these working women plausible fictional heroines as well. That she does not do this in the form of the popular novel – still too wedded to the marriage plot – but in the form of the short story series testifies to the flexibility, hybridity and modernity of the form, closely bound up as it is with the vibrant periodical culture of the turn of the twentieth century.

Notes

1. See Baldwin, *Art and Commerce in the British Short Story*, p. 41; Chan, *Economy of the Short Story*, pp. 1–51; Ashley, *Age of the Storytellers*, pp. 1–2; Liggins et al., *The British Short Story*, p. 30.
2. H. G. Wells, 'Introduction to *The Country of the Blind, and Other Stories* (1911)', reprinted in Hammond, *H. G. Wells and the Short Story*, pp. 162–6 (p. 165).
3. Conan Doyle, *Memories and Adventures*, p. 90.
4. Ashley, *Age of the Storytellers*, pp. 1–2.
5. Jane Stoddart, quoted in Ashley, *Age of the Storytellers*, p. 231.
6. Annie S. Swan, 'Over the Teacups', *The Woman at Home*, 1.1 (October 1893), pp. 62–4 (p. 62).
7. Annie S. Swan became Mrs Burnett-Smith after her marriage, but she kept her maiden name for her writing.
8. See Beetham, *A Magazine of Her Own?*, pp. 171–2; Sparks, *The Doctor in the Victorian Novel*, pp. 142–9; and Krueger, '*The Woman at Home* in the World'.
9. See Beetham and Sparks in particular; Krueger argues that Swan uses a 'tactical conservatism'; Krueger, '*The Woman at Home* in the World', p. 517.
10. In 1909, after a change in publishers and the resignation of Jane Stoddart as main editor, Swan's name was dropped from the magazine's title page. In 1918, it was rebranded as *The Home Magazine*. See Ashley, *Age of the Storytellers*, pp. 233–4.
11. Ashley, *Age of the Storytellers*, p. 186. Ed Wiltse also suggests that critics have failed 'to register the impact of [Doyle's] generic innovation in the field of serial narrative'. He argues that the 'invention of the short story serial or series [. . .] based on continuous characters and setting was not only, as Doyle perceived, a very clever innovation in magazine marketing, it was a watershed moment in the history of narrative, one with crucial implications for twentieth-century fiction, film, radio, and especially television'. Wiltse, '"So Constant an Expectation"', p. 106.
12. Williams, *Television*, pp. 56–7.
13. See Jason Mittell, who makes similar observations with regard to episodic vs serialised TV series. Mittell, 'Operational Seriality and the Operation of Seriality', p. 232.
14. Wiltse, '"So Constant an Expectation"', p. 108.

15. Eco, 'Interpreting Serials', pp. 85–6.
16. Mussell, 'Repetition: Or, "In Our Last"', p. 351.
17. Beetham, 'Open and Closed', p. 99.
18. Kelleter, 'Five Ways of Looking at Popular Seriality', p. 13.
19. Haugtvedt, 'The Victorian Serial Novel and Transfictional Character', p. 413.
20. Swan recalls in her autobiography how 'Sir William [Nicoll] said to me: You have never got justice done to your work. They've set you in a groove. Let us create a new writer in the *British Weekly*. So David Lyall was born. The secret was well kept for a great many years, and until now I have never openly acknowledged my part in the harmless plot.' Swan, *My Life*, pp. 95–6.
21. Mittell, 'Operational Seriality and the Operation of Seriality', p. 231.
22. Wiltse, '"So Constant an Expectation"', p. 108.
23. The story series of 'Anne Hyde, Travelling Companion' is an exception to this rule, as the protagonist travels all over Europe and the US, in the footsteps of her different employers. As a result, this series also lacks the repetitive plot pattern that is developed in the other series.
24. Mittell, 'Operational Seriality and the Operation of Seriality', p. 232.
25. Sparks, *The Doctor in the Victorian Novel*, p. 140.
26. Beetham, *A Magazine of Her Own?*, p. 172.
27. Brake and Demoor, *Dictionary of Nineteenth-Century Journalism in Great Britain and Ireland*, pp. 64, 79, 456.
28. Swan, *My Life*, p. 80.
29. Beetham, *A Magazine of Her Own?*, p. 161.
30. Swan, *My Life*, p. 81.
31. Swan, 'Over the Teacups', 1.1 (October 1893), p. 62.
32. Beetham, *A Magazine of Her Own?*, pp. 161–2.
33. Lady Laura Ridding et al., 'Should married women engage in public work', *The Woman at Home*, 4.8 (November 1895), pp. 110–14; Mrs Jack Johnson et al., 'Is journalism a desirable profession for women?', *The Woman at Home*, 9.6 (March 1898), pp. 534–8.
34. Beetham, *A Magazine of Her Own?*, p. 169. See also Krueger, '*The Woman at Home* in the World', pp. 520–1.
35. Beetham, *A Magazine of Her Own?*, p. 140; Krueger, '*The Woman at Home* in the World', p. 520.
36. Ridding et al., 'Should married women engage in public work', p. 114.
37. Sparks, *The Doctor in the Victorian Novel*, p. 143. In this, Sparks also notes, the Glen stories resemble Samuel Warren's *Passages from the Diary of a Late Doctor* (1830–7), which also focused on the personal and domestic life of patients rather than their medical conditions.
38. Annie S. Swan, 'Elizabeth Glen, M.B. The Experiences of A Lady Doctor. II. A Shadowed Life', *The Woman at Home*, 1.2 (November 1893), pp. 91–9 (p. 93).
39. Annie S. Swan, 'Elizabeth Glen, M.B. The Experiences of A Lady

Doctor. VI. John Ransome's Love Story', *The Woman at Home*, 1.6 (March 1894), pp. 412–21 (p. 413). My italics.
40. Annie S. Swan, 'Elizabeth Glen, M.B. The Experiences of A Lady Doctor. V. Nora Fleming', *The Woman at Home*, 1.5 (February 1894), pp. 348–56 (p. 350).
41. Annie S. Swan, 'Sister Ursula. Stories of Hospital Life. I. The Little Old Lady', *The Woman at Home*, 14.1 (April 1900), pp. 672–81 (p. 674).
42. Lyall, *The Consolation Bureau*, p. 50; Swan, *Hester Lane*, p. 87. As I was unable to access both of these series from *The Woman at Home*, I am quoting from the book publications instead.
43. Annie S. Swan, 'Memories of Margaret Grainger, Schoolmistress. V. Kathleen', *The Woman at Home*, 3.6 (March 1895), pp. 481–90 (p. 484); Annie S. Swan, 'Memories of Margaret Grainger, Schoolmistress. VIII. The Mite', *The Woman at Home*, 4.4 (July 1895), pp. 251–60; Annie S. Swan, 'Memories of Margaret Grainger, Schoolmistress. III. A Revolting Daughter', *The Woman at Home*, 3.4 (January 1895), pp. 345–55. The title of this story is an ironic reference to the debate sparked by Mrs Crackenthorpe's 'The Revolt of the Daughters' in *The Nineteenth Century*. See Beetham, *A Magazine of Her Own?*, p. 135.
44. Annie S. Swan, 'The Journal of a Literary Woman in London. III. An Omnibus Acquaintance', *The Woman at Home*, 16.4 (July 1901), pp. 322–31; 'The Journal of a Literary Woman in London. VII. What Price a Soul', *The Woman at Home*, 15.4 (January 1902), pp. 377–84; 'Journal of a Literary Woman in London. IV. Rachel Waters', *The Woman at Home*, 16.5 (August 1901), pp. 487–95; 'Journal of a Literary Woman in London. IX. Wanted – A Conspiracy', *The Woman at Home*, 15.6 (March), pp. 587–94.
45. Annie S. Swan, 'Memories of Margaret Grainger, Schoolmistress. II. A Touch of Colour', *The Woman at Home*, 3.2 (November 1894), pp. 92–100 (p. 92); Swan, 'Kathleen', p. 483; David Lyall, 'A Sister of the People. VIII. Mrs Traddles', *The Woman at Home*, 25.2 (May 1908), pp. 163–70 (pp. 163–4; 170).
46. Swan, *Hester Lane*, p. 86.
47. Swan, 'Nora Fleming', p. 346; Swan, 'A Shadowed Life', p. 92.
48. Lyall, 'Mrs Traddles', pp. 164, 170.
49. Swan, 'Rachel Waters'.
50. Swan, 'The Little Old Lady', p. 675.
51. Annie S. Swan, 'Memories of Margaret Grainger, Schoolmistress. VI. The Pride of Killoe', *The Woman at Home*, 4.1 (April 1895), pp. 12–22 (p. 13).
52. Swan, 'A Revolting Daughter', p. 345.
53. Swan, 'A Shadowed Life', p. 93.
54. Ibid. pp. 92–3.
55. Swan, *Hester Lane*, p. 46.
56. The third story, 'Shabby Genteel', revolves around a case of 'hospital

abuse' whereby well-off patients pretend poverty in order to be treated for free at the hospital, which relies on voluntary subscriptions to relieve the poor. Annie S. Swan, 'Sister Ursula. Stories from Hospital Life. IIII. Shabby Genteel', *The Woman at Home*, 14.3 (June 1900), pp. 852–60 (p. 852).
57. Swan, 'The Little Old Lady', p. 676.
58. Swan, 'An Omnibus Acquaintance', p. 322.
59. Ibid.; Swan, 'What Price a Soul', p. 377.
60. Annie S. Swan, 'Elizabeth Glen, M.B. The Experiences of A Lady Doctor. XII. Her Own Romance', *The Woman at Home*, 2.6 (September 1894), pp. 397–405 (p. 400).
61. Lyall, *The Consolation Bureau*, p. 41.
62. Swan, *Hester Lane*, p. 104.
63. In the two 'Elizabeth Glen' series, Glen tells her stories to her friend, a writer named Annie, who is clearly an alter ego of the novelist. In the 'Sister Ursula' series, a similar authorial figure introduces these stories as 'a series of separate incidents treated in full detail, each complete in itself, forming a complete and vivid picture of hospital life', which were among 'the immense mass of papers' left to her by her friend Ursula after her death, with a little note: 'To be used by my friend in THE WOMAN AT HOME, if desired'. Swan, 'The Little Old Lady', pp. 671–2. In 'The Consolation Bureau', the first chapter is told by 'David Lyall', who then hands over to his friend, the agony aunt Cordelia. Winnie Chan finds this type of frame narration a common practice in *The Strand* as well and argues that '[f]ar from undermining the stories' credibility, the painstaking documentation of their mediation is supposed to enhance their authenticity'. Chan, *Economy of the Short Story*, p. 35.
64. Annie S. Swan, 'Over the Teacups', *The Woman at Home*, 1.6 (March 1894), pp. 466–8 (p. 468).
65. Annie S. Swan, 'Elizabeth Glen, M.B. The Experiences of A Lady Doctor. IX. Barbara', *The Woman at Home*, 2.3 (June 1894), pp. 175–83 (p. 175).
66. Warhol, 'Making "Gay" and "Lesbian" into Household Words', p. 382.
67. Swan, 'A Revolting Daughter', p. 344.
68. Swan, 'The Little Old Lady', p. 671.
69. Swan, 'Her Own Romance', p. 398.
70. Swan, *Hester Lane*, p. 101.
71. Annie S. Swan, 'Elizabeth Glen, M.B. The Experiences of A Lady Doctor. X. A Commonplace Tragedy', *The Woman at Home*, 2.4 (July 1894), pp. 270–8 (p. 270).
72. I disagree therefore with Krueger's claim that Glen's 'vacillation' between marriage and medicine runs throughout the series. It is really only introduced in the final few stories. Krueger, '*The Woman at Home* in the World', p. 518.

73. Annie S. Swan, 'The Diary of a Literary Woman in London. XI. The Common Way', *The Woman at Home*, 18.2 (May 1902), pp. 150–7 (p. 157).
74. Annie S. Swan, 'Memories of Margaret Grainger, Schoolmistress. I. A Passing Shadow', *The Woman at Home*, 3.1 (October 1894), pp. 24–33 (p. 24).
75. 'A Passing Shadow', for instance, ends with the following summary of her pupil's life: 'She devoted herself to him till his death, and though often asked to marry, she has elected to remain single, and is likely so to remain now, being a middle-aged woman, whose hair is tinged with grey. But I know of no life, married or single, so crowded with blessed usefulness as that of Judith Sale. She is the steward of great wealth, which is used for the furtherance of every good and noble work.' Swan, 'A Passing Shadow', p. 32.
76. Annie S. Swan, 'Memories of Margaret Grainger, Schoolmistress. XI. A Bitter Mistake', *The Woman at Home*, 4.6 (September 1895), pp. 432–42 (p. 441).
77. Annie S. Swan, 'Mrs. Keith Hamilton, M.B. More Experiences of Elizabeth Glen. IV. Ida Falconer's Wedding', *The Woman at Home*, 5.4 (January 1896), pp. 349–58 (p. 349); 'Mrs. Keith Hamilton, M.B. More Experiences of Elizabeth Glen. V. On the Brink', *The Woman at Home*, 5.5 (February 1896), pp. 413–23 (p. 412).
78. At the beginning of the series, the authorial narrator says to her friend, 'You were an even greater favourite than Margaret Grainger and had to be revived sooner or later.' Annie S. Swan, 'Mrs. Keith Hamilton, M.B. More Experiences of Elizabeth Glen. II. An American Heiress', *The Woman at Home*, 5.2 (November 1895), pp. 129–38 (p. 129).
79. In her first 'Over the Teacups' column, Annie Swan announces precisely this type of heroine as more suited to the tastes of the 'modern' reader of the *The Woman at Home*: 'The reader of to-day no longer sympathises with the heroine who melts into tears on the smallest provocation, but prefers a more robust personality who strikes out a path for herself.' Swan, 'Over the Teacups', 1.1 (October 1893), p. 63.
80. Lyall, *The Consolation Bureau*, p. 53.

Chapter 3

Hubert Crackanthorpe and *The Albemarle*: A Study of Contexts

David Malcolm

It has long been argued that short fiction should be read in context, although it is often not considered in this way, being read rather as discrete and isolated texts.[1] The appropriate context is usually understood as that of the cycle or collection of which an individual story is part. But, as Mary Louise Pratt suggests, another type of codicological study is possible, one that considers short stories in the context of the individual edition of a journal, or, indeed, in that of a run of issues of a journal, or specific set of journals, in which it appears. The scale of such an undertaking is of course daunting, but Hubert Crackanthorpe's involvement with *The Albemarle* presents a manageable and fruitful case study of the interaction between short fiction and journal publication in the late nineteenth century. Crackanthorpe was an important if nowadays somewhat forgotten figure in the world of English short fiction in the early 1890s. Under Crackanthorpe's editorship and that of his co-editor, W. H. Wilkins, *The Albemarle* ran for only nine numbers, from January to September 1892, and, thus, the material, at around 400 pages of text, is not unmanageably large. It is hoped that the approach suggested in this chapter may find development in studies of other, longer-lasting journals.

The editors and the journal

Hubert Crackanthorpe may not be well known among literary scholars and readers today. In the 1890s he was seen as a substantial writer of great promise, by those disposed to admire his work; by many others, however, Crackanthorpe was seen as a controversial figure within a disreputable and corrupt generation of authors.[2] A member of an intellectual, literary, legal and very wealthy family, he died, under mysterious and somewhat melodramatic circumstances, in 1896 at the age of only twenty-six. This life is well documented – as far as it is possible to do so – in David Crackanthorpe's study *Hubert Crackanthorpe and English Realism in the 1890s,* and in Jad Adams's essay 'The Drowning of Hubert Crackanthorpe and the Persecution of Leila Macdonald'.[3] In a short career, Crackanthorpe published two collections of short fiction, *Wreckage: Seven Studies* (1893) and *Sentimental Studies and A Set of Village Tales* (1895). *Vignettes: A Miniature Journal of Whim and Sentiment* (1896) is a collection of observations of landscapes and urban settings that prompt reflections of an existential and social nature. *Last Studies* (with an introduction by Henry James) was published posthumously in 1897. In addition, Crackanthorpe's work, before being collected, was published in periodicals such as *The Albemarle* and *The Yellow Book*. His work is marked by its openness about sexual matters, its observation of the seamier sides of English life, and its considerable range of social and geographical settings. Crackanthorpe has a particularly bleak view of male–female relationships. His approach to women's dilemmas is often remarkably perceptive and sympathetic. Reviewers identified him as an English Maupassant and sometimes an English Zola.[4]

Contemporary responses to Crackanthorpe's work were often negative. An anonymous reviewer of one of his stories wrote in 1894: 'The gutter is celebrated in prose by Mr Crackanthorpe, a young man who, when he writes of depravity, which he usually does, leaves nothing to the imagination. By the weak he is called "strong", by the strong – but what do the strong reck of Mr Crackanthorpe?'[5] Another commentator wrote in 1897: 'I am not at all surprised at the tragic death of Mr Hubert Crackanthorpe. No young man, or old one for that matter, could write such morbid, loathsome stories as he wrote and have a sane mind.'[6] For many other contemporaries, however, Crackanthorpe's death deprived English literature of a potentially great writer who had already achieved much. For example, in January 1897, writing in *The Star*, Richard Le Gallienne called Crackanthorpe 'something like the Chatterton of the English novel'.[7] Lionel Johnson saw in his work '[a] brief record of accomplishment, but all the finer, the firmer, the more successful for its very scantiness'.[8] The American scholar William Peden sums Crackanthorpe up thus: 'Of the lesser-known fiction writers of the nineties [. . .] the most talented, the most important and the most undervalued is Hubert Crackanthorpe.'[9] His reputation may rise in the future. Indeed, Adrian Hunter devotes three insightful pages to

Crackanthorpe's work in *The Cambridge Introduction to the Short Story in English*.[10]

Crackanthorpe's co-editor on *The Albemarle* was W. H. Wilkins, a writer even more obscure than Crackanthorpe. *The Dictionary of National Biography* of 1912 provides some information on him. Wilkins wrote romantic novels under the pseudonym W. H. de Winton and became a historian and biographer of historical royal personages in the late 1890s. He was also associated with the wife of Sir Richard Burton and helped to edit texts by and about the celebrated explorer and orientalist. In addition, Wilkins was involved in anti-immigration politics in the early 1890s, while he was co-editing *The Albemarle*. His text *The Alien Invasion* (1892) is a politically engaged piece arguing for 'some moderate and judicious restriction of the influx of the destitute and worthless of other countries', by which the author means largely Central European Jewish and Italian immigrants.[11] Wilkins contributed an essay on 'The Alien Question' to volume 2, issue 1 of *The Albemarle*.

It is tempting to suggest that Crackanthorpe may have been primarily responsible for the literary aspects of *The Albemarle*, while Wilkins was responsible for the social and political material. There is, however, no documentation to support this argument. Further, Crackanthorpe came from a very politically savvy and engaged family, and there is no reason to assume that he was not fully engaged in the non-literary side of the enterprise.[12] In addition, as his list of publications indicates, Wilkins clearly had literary ambitions of his own.

Not much has been written about *The Albemarle*. There is no mention of the journal in a basic archival source like Alvin Sullivan's *British Literary Magazines: The Victorian and Edwardian Age, 1837–1913* and no references appear in the *Victorian Periodicals Review*. Writers about Crackanthorpe, such as Franklin Fisher and Adams, skim over his period as an editor. David Crackanthorpe, however, devotes some seven pages to discussing *The Albemarle*.[13] He writes that the magazine was financed substantially by Crackanthorpe's father, Montague Crackanthorpe, and that he and Crackanthorpe's mother, Blanche, used their political and social connections among the Liberal and progressive elite of the 1890s to obtain articles for the journal. The magazine is described by David Crackanthorpe as 'a rather haphazard synthesis of artistic, political, and social elements', with, however, 'a lively tone' and 'elegant presentation'.[14] The journal ran from January to September 1892. Its nine issues were priced at six pence.[15] It ceased publication without the slightest warning with the issue of September 1892. Indeed, that issue ends with the usual list of authors who have promised to write for *The Albemarle*. There is, however, no customary note of important contributions to the following edition. David Crackanthorpe writes that the journal had been 'a notable success while it lasted'.[16] Certainly, *The Albemarle* regularly published its own array of positive press comments from many parts of the United Kingdom. David Crackanthorpe suggests that it ceased publication as 'no doubt an agreed limit of funds had been reached', which I take to mean that Montague Crackanthorpe had decided to discontinue his family's backing of the enterprise.[17] There has been no substantial analysis of the contributions to *The Albemarle* or of the role of short fiction in it. What follows is an attempt to fill this gap.

Short fiction in *The Albemarle*

The Albemarle carried eight short stories over its nine numbers. Before I proceed to look more closely at them, I will make two qualifications. One short story – 'An Awkward Will' by the Earl of Desart – appears in brief instalments of three to four pages each over three numbers of the journal, volume 1, issues 4–6. Thus, in fact, every number contains some short fiction, and the final number, volume 2, issue 3, contains two pieces. A second qualification is that the majority of non-fiction items that can be classed as memoir, impressions or travel writing – six out of seven – are narratives, and, thus, although they are not stories, they are technically close to the fictions published in *The Albemarle*. They are, however, clearly marked as non-fiction.

The first two numbers of the journal contain two stories that are studies of lower-class urban life with an emphasis on the sordid and ugly aspects of that existence. In volume 1, issue 1, F. Mabel Robinson's 'A Unit' presents the brief life of a workhouse child. The protagonist is born in the workhouse, spends his life in it, and dies there early and miserably. I will discuss this story and its context in more detail below.

The same type of narrator as in 'A Unit' (omniscient and linguistically more formal than the characters, who all speak a marked urban dialect) recurs in 'Weekly Payments: A Humble Tragedy' by Alice Fleming in volume 1, issue 2. The story recounts the failure of Jessie Chaplin's attempts to attain some slight embellishment of her home and her life. She buys an oval looking glass on terms of deposit and weekly payments. Her young husband George is a plumber who has an accident and dies. All the money Jessie can raise must go to pay for a decent funeral. She cannot meet the payments for the glass, and has to sell it (and she still owes money on it) to pay for George's proper burial. Faced with financial disaster and moral humiliation, she commits suicide in the Thames. The focus is on the petty shifts and petty sums that are important in such a lower-class life as the Chaplins', on its sordid circumstances and its precariousness.

Crackanthorpe's first contribution to the fiction of the periodical is in volume 1, issue 3. It takes the form of a short story, 'He Wins Who Loses', which the author did not reprint. It is a tale of *mésalliance*, a type of story material that Crackanthorpe later frequently employed in his fiction. The social environment could scarcely be more different from that of the preceding stories. Mrs Hayward has been married for three years to John Hayward of Coatbridge Hall, J. P. and Deputy Lieutenant of the County of Suffolk, a man of substance and social standing, and thirteen years older than she. Kate Hayward – from an urban, artistic and intellectual background – finds her life with him dull and uninspiring. A visit from an artistic and aristocratic friend of her husband, Lord Flamborough, leads to an almost instantaneous elective affinity between the two. Flamborough writes proposing friendship; Mrs Hayward declines; Flamborough leaves the country and becomes a better painter for his experience of loss. Crackanthorpe's second contribution to *The Albemarle* comes five numbers later in volume 2, issue 2. 'Dissolving Views' (which Crackanthorpe reprinted as 'Dissolving View' in his collection *Wreckage*, published in 1893) is again set among the very well heeled. However, the male protagonist Vivian Marston, a philanderer, has enjoyed a liaison with the lower-class Kit in the past. Through a letter appealing for help, she returns to his life. She is ill; she has had a child; she is in dire need. Marston seeks her out in a squalid part of London, only to discover she and the child have recently died. His response is one of relief, and his charmed and comfortable life proceeds without interruption. This is a much darker *mésalliance* text than 'He Wins Who Loses', although technically both are similar in that they employ a third-person narrator, who, however, closely follows the protagonist's consciousness, at times employing free indirect speech. This technique is much used by Crackanthorpe in his fiction published elsewhere.

The complexities of male–female relationships are at the centre of two other fictions in later numbers of *The Albemarle*. Lionel Johnson's 'A Commentary on Love' in volume 2, issue 1 largely takes the form of a dialogue between an unnamed man and a woman. They have been lovers in the past. Marriage is financially impossible; they have decided to wait. No longer able to watch life slip by her, the woman has married a dull but wealthy person. The story charts their last conversation – weary, hopeless and sad – in an ugly, sordid city street, surrounded by noise, harsh flaring streetlight and indifferent bustle. The ending is open and closed simultaneously. The woman returns to the man's house, but finds him not at home. Is he ignoring her? Has he really gone out? Has he killed himself in despair?

There is no doubt about the corrosive despair at the end of George Douglas's 'A Deathbed Vigil', subtitled 'Leaves from an Autobiographical Fragment: 1830', in volume 2, issue 3. The narrator, Tom Hedley, a county gentleman of an old and impulsive family in Northumberland, seeks to marry the younger and lovely Phillis Gray. Before the wedding, she disappears. Her body is found some months later in a moorland pool. Hedley mourns deeply, but his suffering is increased when, by virtue of a series of circumstances, he hears the deathbed ravings of his friend Binny Clennel, who has clearly been Phillis's lover, and, it seems, has betrayed her.

Two stories lighten the mood of the fictional offerings in *The Albemarle*. These are the Earl of Desart's three-part story 'An Awkward Will' in volume 1, issues 4–6, and Lionel Johnson's 'Mors Janua Vitae' in volume 2, issue 3. The former is a piece of social comedy with supernatural elements. Charlie Robledon, a young gentleman of limited intellectual abilities and ambitions, but decent and well liked for his kindness to an Indian holy man, is granted the power to have his wishes realised. Unaware of this, the young man precipitates a series of untoward social occurrences: for example, the staid older members of his gentleman's club behave in an unseemly fashion, a working-class lady encumbered with children and packages magically becomes a director of a train company, a group of card sharps play an honest game (which Charlie wins), and an austere aristocratic lady leap-frogs over her husband's back. Charlie's intended, the lovely and intelligent Queenie of Congleton Hall, works out the truth and has Charlie renounce his gift, which he is most willing to do, thus eliminating a threat to the social order.

Johnson's 'Mors Janua Vitae' (his second contribution) is one of the most interesting texts among those published in *The Albemarle*. Narrated in the first person by an unnamed character-narrator, it is an account of the life of Sir John Purchas, scion of an old Catholic family in England, who realises his quest for life's meaning in the

Catholic Church and its exalted mysteries. I will discuss this story and its context in more detail below.

Four general observations can be made about the stories in *The Albemarle*. First, they are not a homogeneous group in terms of form. Narration runs through a technical gamut of third-person omniscient point of view, and first-person narration. However, the language of narration is always formal and relatively sophisticated, although characters in some texts may use non-standard language. Second, the stories are diverse thematically: the first two stories, 'A Unit' and 'Weekly Payments', focus on the lives of the poor; four stories (Crackanthorpe's two contributions, Johnson's 'A Commentary on Love' and Douglas's 'A Deathbed Vigil') deal with incompatibilities in male–female relationships; Desart's text is a social comedy; and Johnson's 'Mors Janua Vitae' is a fictional spiritual biography. While some stories take up dark and socially controversial themes – the lives of the poor, adultery, the breakdown of love – others are much more soft-edged, including Crackanthorpe's 'He Wins Who Loses' and Desart's 'An Awkward Will'. Johnson's 'Mors Janua Vitae' has no substantial social or moral concerns, but focuses on the spiritual. In fact, there is a thematic progression in the sequence of stories in *The Albemarle*, from naturalistic social observation in 'A Unit' and 'Weekly Payments', through morally and socially traditional sentiment in 'He Wins Who Loses' and whimsical social comedy ('An Awkward Will') to much darker tales of *mésalliance* and adultery ('A Commentary on Love', 'Dissolving Views' and 'A Deathbed Vigil'), which are not without controversial aspects and social criticism, to Johnson's asocial spiritual piece. Apart from the first two stories, the texts' *milieux* are relatively well heeled. There is a clear thematic movement towards the moral, emotional and spiritual lives of the better off. All narrators in the stories, however, employ a language that is educated, relatively formal, and sophisticated. 'A Unit' and 'Weekly Payments' are about the poor and unfortunate, but the characters are seen from a much higher-class perspective.

Third, the stories conform to categories of avant-garde stories that recur throughout *fin-de-siècle* short story writing. Thus, 'A Unit' and 'Weekly Payments' belong among the naturalist texts offering a slice of sordid lower-class urban life that were part of avant-garde writing in the 1880s and 1890s.[18] Arthur Morrison's *Tales of Mean Streets* (1894) exemplifies this kind of text. Hopeless, disturbing and controversial accounts of disastrous male–female relationships are the stuff of *fin-de-siècle* fiction. Crackanthorpe made a speciality of them throughout his brief oeuvre, as did George Egerton in

Keynotes (1893) and *Discords* (1894). Also relevant here is the work of Ella D'Arcy; for example, the stories included in *Modern Instances* (1898), such as 'At Twickenham' or 'A Marriage'.[19] Pieces of social comedy like Desart's 'An Awkward Will' have a long tradition, and are scarcely innovative in the early 1890s, although the supernatural element is unusual at this time. Saki's much more subversive *Beasts and Superbeasts*, a collection that combines social comedy with the supernatural, was published over two decades later in 1914. However, the combination of social comedy and the supernatural was not unknown in the 1890s: see, for example, H. G. Wells's 'The Temptation of Harringay' from *The Stolen Bacillus and Other Incidents* (1895). Johnson's 'Mors Janua Vitae' conforms, almost programmatically, to the plotless, psychological, Jamesian story which Hunter discusses.[20]

Fourth, the authors of the stories are not well known. Johnson and Crackanthorpe (especially the former) became much better known, but *The Albemarle* editors appear to have been interested in the work of persons within the world of literature, in all cases competent, but mostly with reputations still to make. The fact that Alice Fleming has to be designated as Rudyard Kipling's sister is an indication of her relative obscurity. The Earl of Desart, although now largely forgotten, was a well-known author and stands out in the company of the others. However, whether the choice of authors was motivated by policy or necessity is impossible to determine.

Contexts

What is the codicological context, the performative environment, of these fictional texts? What internal dialogues are set up over the range of pieces published in *The Albemarle*? Depending on how one calculates the figure, *The Albemarle* over its nine numbers contains ninety-four contributions, eighty-five of them written. The uncertainty is produced by the fact that one article in volume I, issue 1 on 'The Primrose League' consists, in fact, of two contributions, by writers who take very different views of the institution. Nine contributions consist of artwork, in the form of lithographs, attached to the journal.

One can identify two principal groups of contributions: those that are primarily political (in a broad sense) in their focus, and those unconnected with politics directly (visual art, poetry, reviews, fiction). There is also an intermediate group concerned with broad cultural issues, something like contemporary and past *mœurs* and cultural practices. This group could be included in either of the first two.

The first large political group includes contributions about British domestic politics, about foreign affairs, about broad social-economic issues and about women's issues. Contributions about British domestic politics are around fifteen in number; one, 'A Liberty Election Address', in volume 2, issue 1, because of its abstraction from the realities of political life, could be included among social-economic issues or even the contributions on social practices and *mœurs*. Those on British domestic politics range from Ben Tillett on 'Labour Questions' in volume 1, issue 1, through Herbert Gladstone on 'The Liberal Party and the Labour Question' in volume 1, issue 2, to those on less central political issues, such as 'The True Jacobitism' in volume 2, issue 1. Labour issues are prominent; R. B. Haldane's 'The Eight Hours' Question' in volume 1, issue 5 is an example. The focus is primarily that of the Liberal Party, although there is an attempt to strike a political balance in some essays. The co-editor W. H. Wilkins is allowed to ride his own political hobby-horse in an essay on 'The Alien Question' in volume 2, issue 1, in which he advances a polemical complaint about masses of unskilled and destitute aliens, who are flooding into Britain, causing severe economic distress to a settled working class. Fifteen out of eighty-five written contributions can be included in this political group.

Foreign affairs are a recurrent concern of contributions, although these are highly eclectic. For example, Sir Charles Dilke's piece on 'Foreign Affairs and Home Defence' in volume 1, issue 1 is a Liberal criticism of Conservative neglect of Britain's defences, and an interesting example of invasion fears in the late nineteenth century. Other contributions deal with a variety of topics, such as the politics of a small Indian state and free trade. Only six contributions can reasonably be seen as dealing with foreign affairs, and the interest of the editors of *The Albemarle* in the topic seems sporadic and eclectic.

Nine or ten essays (depending on how one allocates 'A Liberty Election Address' in volume 2, issue 1) deal with what may be called miscellaneous social issues. These include, for example, an article on 'Fox-Hunting' in volume 1, issue 2, and one on the distribution of wealth and the role of the state in alleviating indigence, 'A Social Problem' in volume 1, issue 6. Three contributions focus on educational issues: 'Greek at Public Schools' in volume 1, issue 1; 'The Education Question' in volume 1, issue 2, which concerns religious instruction in primary schools; and 'The Postponement of the Oxford

Terms' in volume 1, issue 3. It is notable that two out of three essays deal with what can only be called the elite end of English education, and the third is a well-meaning, if rather conservative, appeal for more religious instruction within the state education system.

Connected but distinct from these essays are four articles directly devoted to women's issues; for example, 'The National Training and Education of Women' by Susan, Countess of Malmesbury in volume 1, issue 5. These all adopt a critical stance toward the current disposition of gender roles. For example, 'L'Eternal Feminin: Girls and Their Mothers' by Elizabeth Holland Hollister in volume 1, issue 6, takes issue with the consequences of the marriage market and female conditioning to fulfil repressed and repressive social roles within relatively well-off families.

It is worth noting here that twelve contributions in *The Albemarle* have women authors, Elizabeth Holland Hollister being the author of three. Despite an interest in women's issues in the journal, women writers do not write on political or foreign affairs, except for Miss Meresia Nevill's half-piece on 'The Primrose League' in volume 1, issue 1 and Ethel St Clair Grimwood's essay on 'Manipur before the Revolution' in volume 1, issue 3. Women largely contribute pieces on women's issues and two stories, one by Miss F. Mabel Robinson in volume 1, issue 1, and another by Alice Fleming (née Kipling, Rudyard Kipling's sister, as the editors of *The Albemarle* remind their readers) in volume 1, issue 2.

There is a group of seven articles that cannot be called either directly political or literary, theatrical, or artistic. It is a mixed bag: for example, 'Dinner Giving; Not by Double Entry', a jocular piece on dinner-party conventions, *faux-pas* and *longueurs* by Elizabeth Holland Hollister in volume 1, issue 4. Another such essay is on 'Mediæval Medicine' in volume 2, issue 2.

Besides the short stories, a second large group of contributions establishes the artistic credentials of *The Albemarle*. Most notable among these are the lithographs that are attached to every issue. These reproduced work by highly respected artists of the 1890s. Of these, the best-known today are J. McNeill Whistler, Walter Sickert, Frederic Leighton, Henri Fantin-Latour and Philip Wilson Steer. Even the other artists, Charles H. Shannon, Marcus Stone, W. B. Richmond and James Hayllar, although perhaps less well-known today, were figures of some substance in the artistic world of the 1890s. However, unlike Aubrey Beardsley's work for *The Yellow Book*, the lithographs of these artists were unlikely to provoke serious controversy, and they appear not to have done so.[21]

Also, there belongs within the fundamentally non-political group of pieces a set of essays that can be understood as memoir pieces, impressions and travel writing. These include a piece on 'Cafés' in Paris in volume 1, issue 1 and 'The Evolution of a Village' in volume 1, issue 6, in which R. Cunninghame Graham writes an anti-industrial, anti-capitalist fable about the modernisation of an Irish village (indeed, this text could easily be taken as a story). 'The Head of the River', a narrative about a fishing competition, could also be included in this set, although like 'The Evolution of a Village', it could also be seen as a story. Most of these texts are narratives, and certainly have features in common with narrative fiction of the time: tales of exotic travel, stories of hunting and fishing expeditions and exposures of the destruction of rural life.

Apart from its short stories, the literary aspect of the journal is emphasised by the presence of eight poems in the nine-month run: Stafford A. Brooke's 'Stone Walls', in volume 1, issue 2, about a death in the workhouse; 'La rose du bal' by Selwyn Image, in volume 1, issue 3, a text celebrating transience and delicate femininity; Richard Le Gallienne's 'Orbits' and 'Dissipabitur Cappanis' by Herbert P. Horne, in volume 1, issue 5, linked pieces on transience and love; Lewis Morris's 'The Soul in Nature', in volume 1, issue 6, a poem about transience and transcendence; 'Poppies' by Edmund K. Chambers, in volume 2, issue 1, another text on death and melancholy abandonment; Ernest Dowson's 'To One in Bedlam', in volume 2, issue 2, a sonnet focused, once again, on the lost and melancholic, with transience at its centre; and 'Quis Multa Gracilis' by H. Smith Wright, in volume 2, issue 3, a version of Horace's Ode 1.5, full of motifs of fleeting love and sad evanescence. These poems are a cohesive group. All are written in traditional metrical patterns and are very regular. The subject matters, as one can see from the above, are repeated: death, unhappy love and impermanence. Classical models recur. Apart from Dowson, and, perhaps, Le Gallienne, the writers are not noted poets (Selwyn Image is known for other things, such as his association with the Arts and Crafts movement and being the first Slade Professor of Fine Arts at Oxford, and Crackanthorpe may have been a private pupil of his).[22] A rather self-indulgent melancholy suffuses all the poems. They fit in with the norms of much *fin-de-siècle* verse.

The largest set of literary-cultural pieces in *The Albemarle* is made up of reviews, impressions of celebrated writers, dialogues on aesthetics and writing on the visual arts. There are seventeen of these. For example, in volume 1, issue 1, there is a review essay on 'Mr

Henry James as a Playwright' by Crackanthorpe himself; in volume 1, issue 2, Crackanthorpe gives an account of an interview in Paris with Émile Zola, and George Douglas writes a very positive review of 'Mr Thomas Hardy's "Tess of the D'Urbervilles"'. In volume 1, issue 3, Maurice Barrès writes in French of 'Les beautés de l'interview'. In volume 1, issue 5, there is an appreciation of the character and achievements of 'Monsieur Renan', a piece, 'Hornpipes in Fetters', on English theatrical legislation, and a discussion of 'Modern French Art'. Indeed, art, above all French art, is the focus of six contributions over the run of the journal. The French writer Paul Bourget is the subject of an appreciation in volume 2, issue 2. There are fictional dialogues on art and criticism in volume 1, issue 6 (by Crackanthorpe) and in volume 2, issue 1 (by Edward Delille). George Bernard Shaw has a robust piece on Shelley and his reception in volume 2, issue 3 ('Shaming the Devil about Shelley'). The pieces on literary topics are cosmopolitan and broad-minded.

As in most journals, there is in *The Albemarle* an abundance of non-discursive, non-lyric and non-narrative material that enfolds or permeates the contributions. What follows is an attempt to discuss some aspects of this material. The title of *The Albemarle* immediately carries associations with it. It is the name of a street in Mayfair, a fashionable part of London. The celebrated Brown's Hotel is still on that street. It was the name of a well-known club (the real notoriety of which was to come later in 1895 in connection with the Wilde trials). Albemarle is an aristocratic English name of some antiquity. Clearly, there was a marginal fashion in the 1890s for journals with grand-sounding titles: *The Strand* is certainly fashionably metropolitan, but *The Savoy* is distinctly high-class. One has to say, however, that *The Savoy* and *The Albemarle* were both very short-lived ventures. The distinctly proletarian and colloquial-sounding *Tit-Bits* lasted from 1881 to 1984.

The Albemarle regularly included two to four pages of advertising in the front and at the end of each number. For example, volume 1, issue 1 carries an opening advertisement for the 'Rock Life Assurance Company', giving details of claims, security, profits and investment and leasehold policies. Two pages of advertisements at the end of the number bring to readers' attention Messrs Windover and Clark of 70 Hatton Gardens, who specialise in what can only be called luxury metal goods: silver-mounted silk umbrellas, solid-gold opera glasses and electro-plated 'entré' [sic] dishes, some of which are described as 'REALLY MARVELLOUS VALUE', take a full page. Then follows a single composite page advertising the services of: Sun Life; The Fine

Art Insurance Company, Ld. [sic]; the Economic Fire Office, Limited; Fuller's American Confectionery, Novelties for Christmas in Great Variety; and William Buszard of Oxford Street, maker of wedding cakes, prices from one to sixty guineas. It would take up too much space in this essay to list all the advertisers, although the modern reader surely finds them charming, amusing and strangely decorous. But the important thing to note is that the kinds of advertisements are consistent: well-funded insurance and investment companies, luxury goods, publishers, and in several numbers, German table water, solid and respectable literature and texts focusing on the issues of the day, as well as books on general political, historical and philosophical issues. Other aspects of *The Albemarle* confirm the configuration of the journal's implied reader as well off. Many articles quote widely from Greek and Latin without helpful glosses; one essay is even entirely in French; the emphasis of the journal is on politics, social mores, the visual arts, concerns of a well-educated, socially concerned but well-heeled bourgeoisie. I am not sure if the implied audience is male, but the class identification of that audience is beyond dispute. An analysis of the language of articles reveals a formality and sophistication of both lexis and syntax which matches that of the short fiction in the journal.[23]

Part of the codicological, performative or dialogic context of fiction must be the matter that surrounds a particular short story, and where in a sequence of contributions that story occurs. Because numbers are not entirely homogeneous, there are varying shades and nuances in the contexts of stories. However, if we look at the first number of *The Albemarle*, we can see a complex, and surely semantically loaded, interweaving of contributions. F. Mabel Robinson's 'A Unit' is a dark story about poverty and marginality. It gives an account of the life and death of 'Arry, a workhouse child, without parents, without even a full name. He has a number (hence the title of the story), No. 59 from birth to the time when he is confined to the workhouse hospital, when he becomes No. 15. He is unloved, subject to unsavoury diseases and to the hostility of his peers. His health declines and he dies unvisited, neglected and alone but for attendant officials. The story aims to reveal the sufferings of the poor and outcast, and does so in a moving manner.

However, there are features of the text that mitigate any social criticism. First, the narrative is not just logical and chronological (and, thus, traditional, if not conservative in the 1890s), but also works through summary. Most of 'Arry's life and death is presented in terms of typical events and passages of time. These events are not explored in any detail, but with a detached concision. Further, the narrator, while setting out a degraded world, is detached from that world. The narrator has privileged insight into 'Arry's mind (how she has this is not explained) and, indeed, a close knowledge of the other workhouse children. She sees them as a collective, not as individuals, and 'Arry as a typical member of a group. Such generalisation, in fact, undermines the complaint of the text. The workhouse authorities see 'Arry as a unit, but the narrator makes him less than individual too. In any case, the narrator employs a lexis and syntax that is not 'Arry's; indeed, 'Arry never speaks for himself in the text. It is also worth noting of the narrator that, while focusing on the exclusion of the poor from love and humane treatment, she does not see her child characters in a positive light. 'Arry spends a great deal of time thinking of malicious vengeance that he can take on a fellow orphan who has harmed him. He is a degraded figure and in that he is typical.

The dialogic context of 'A Unit' is complex. Whistler's lithograph that opens the number is of a street scene with children, presumably in a lower-class district of London. The front advertising material is as I have noted above (the Rock Life Assurance Company). Dilke's quasi-interview on 'Foreign Affairs and Home Defence' is followed by a piece on the teaching of Greek in public schools; a double contribution, far from entirely negative, on the conservative Primrose League; Mrs Lynn Linton's essay on 'Echoes' (which argues for a kind of universal intertextuality *avant la lettre*); and Ben Tillett's essay on 'Labour Questions'. 'Cafés', a reminiscence of Parisian life, comes next, and then we have Robinson's dark story. There follows a review of J. A. Froude's study of Catherine of Aragon and Crackanthorpe's review of Henry James's work as a playwright. There is also an appeal for support for the East London Church Fund, to help pay for the salaries of Anglican clergy in unfashionable parts of the capital. The luxury advertising noted above follows that.

Thus, one could argue that the short story by Robinson occurs in a context of political and social issues that, to a degree, echo its bleak subject matter: Whistler's lithograph and Tillet's essay. But it is also wrapped up in quite different concerns, much more orientated toward the social and intellectual concerns of the high bourgeoisie. The luxury and bourgeois advertising is in dissonance also with Robinson's story. Further, the short story forms only a small part of a number full of non-fictional and often non-literary material. Other issues of *The Albemarle* are configured somewhat differently, but a similar overall intellectual, moral, social and political pattern is reproduced throughout.

The context of short fiction in later numbers of *The Albemarle* is both similar and somewhat different. I have selected two other numbers for closer analysis. Volume I, issue 4 contains the first of three instalments of the Earl of Desart's story 'An Awkward Will'. It is a humorous piece of social satire about a young, undistinguished, wealthy young man, Charlie, who discovers that his wishes magically come true. Towards the end of the story, both Charlie and his fiancée work out what is going on and why, and put a stop to it. Yet in the first part, the protagonist does not understand his new power. He can, without knowing it, make respectable persons behave in extravagant ways that go against their character and social standing. He wishes the club bore to go to Jericho (presumably a euphemism for hell). The gentleman, who has never shown any disposition to travel before, does so. Charlie, vexed at a Club Committee decision, wishes that the members would go to the devil. He and others in the club are shocked when an archdeacon, a financier, and an aristocratic philanthropist start to drink magnums of champagne, plan a louche evening on the town and use appalling language. The saturnalian aspects of the story material are developed in later parts. However, despite the social and moral upheavals engendered by Charlie's new power, the overall configuration of the text is a conservative one. The narrative is linear, and the narrator is omniscient. The setting in part one is the Thomas Club in London; characters are drawn from the upper strata of society. In his lexis and syntax, in literary and cultural allusions, the narrator is at one with this world.

The story is in close accord with its context. It concludes the number, which begins with a lithograph, 'Willow-Willow', by the well-known and establishment artist Marcus Stone, RA. At the start, too, a lithograph by the very well known and respectable Sir Frederick Leighton, PRA, is promised in the next number. The majority of the essays in the journal are conservative and establishment-orientated in tenor. 'The Lesson of the County Council Election' is a conservative (indeed, a Conservative) critique of Progressive, Liberal policies and electioneering. The essays on 'The New Jacobitism' and 'Dinner-Giving' are similar in social orientation, while the travel piece 'To Kustendil' aims to demonstrate the bravery and dedication of the Bulgarian royal house and the devotion of the Bulgarian people to it. Even the essay on 'The Influence of Photography on Art' is a defence of traditional painting and drawing in the face of challenges from photography. There are certainly essays promoting reform – David Lloyd George on 'Welsh Disestablishment', on state provision for the poor and old and on revising criminal sentences – but these promote reform within the status quo. Front material advertising Macmillan editions of Tennyson and Dickens is typical of *The Albemarle* and clearly orientated toward a well-off middle-class reader of (in the 1890s) traditional literary taste. Rear advertising is similar: co-editor W. H. Wilkins's alarmist and racist *The Alien Invasion* is there, as are advertisements for a first-class private hotel at a London SW address, insurance and investment companies, a high-class furniture and decoration business (Frederick H. Grau) and Mudie's Select Library. Any tension between story and context noted in volume 1, issue 1 is absent here. Socially and intellectually the number is coherent and cohesive.

Volume 2, issue 3 was the last number of *The Albemarle*. In it, the short fiction again is substantially consistent with its codicological context. Lionel Johnson's 'Mors Janua Vitae' is, at eight pages, one of the two longest freestanding stories published in *The Albemarle* (the other is Crackanthorpe's own 'He Wins Who Loses' in volume 1, issue 3). Johnson's story is one of the most interesting and most challenging texts in the run of the journal. The story material concerns the childhood, youth and old age of Sir John Purchas. Belonging to an old English rural family, the protagonist sees his father, a devotee of arcane scholarship, commit suicide in his presence. After an education and spiritual upbringing by a scholarly and benign Catholic priest, Purchas travels the world, deeply impresses those he meets, though they cannot quite say how, and eventually finds emotional, intellectual and spiritual satisfaction by becoming a Catholic priest. The horror of his father's death and, indeed, the enigma of death itself are solved for Purchas by the doctrine and beliefs of the Catholic Church. He triumphs over mortality at the story's end.

The narrative of this text is complicated, certainly by the standards of the stories in *The Albemarle*. It is recursive, inasmuch as it starts with a sight of Purchas now as an elderly priest, and concludes with the same moment. In between, the narrative moves in a linear fashion, but with significant ellipses. Much space is given over to Purchas's father's intellectual torment and suicide, and to the protagonist's education at his hands and at those of his tutor. After Purchas decides to go off into the world, narrative information becomes much more exiguous; however, this is understandable, given the vagueness of Puchas's actions. Indeed, at one point the narrator notes all the adventurous experiences Purchas does not have. Even Purchas's becoming a Catholic priest is presented as a *fait accompli* and the process of decision and joining is not shown.

Narration, too, has complex aspects. The text is narrated by an anonymous figure, about whom the reader knows little, except that he, too, becomes a Catholic, has a brother who becomes a priest, and encounters Purchas at various points in his life. The 'I' of the first-person narration is, however, very prominent. He sees the old priest and he is fascinated enough to recount his life and its circumstances. The times of each encounter are given. How the narrator gains insight into and knowledge of the protagonist's mind is obscure, but he indicates that he and others know it. Both the narrator and those whom he addresses are clearly conversant with arcane lore and classical texts. The Latin in the text is not translated for the reader. The narrator also deploys a lexis and syntax that are complex and sophisticated. Although the addressee of the text is not gendered, the world that the narrator presents is entirely male. Purchas's mother is influential but long dead, and the story is rooted in male figures (the protagonist, his father, his tutor, the narrator and the narrator's brother). It is clear that the narrator greatly admires the protagonist and finds both him and his life beautiful. 'Mors Janua Vitae' is a compelling and complex text about a strangely fascinating figure, whose spiritual journey is mysterious but intriguing.

George Douglas's 'A Deathbed Vigil' is a much more traditional and conventional story. Its story material – a mismatched couple, a local squire and a girl from somewhat lower in society, a seduction by the squire's close friend, an abandonment, a suicide, a death-bed revelation – belongs to melodrama and is full of the conventions of that type of text. The story is subtitled 'Leaves from an Autobiographical Fragment' and is dated 1830. The narrator and protagonist Tom Hedley falls deeply in love with Phillis Gray. She accepts him for his position, but before they can be married she is seduced and abandoned by Hedley's best friend Binny Clennel. On his deathbed, after a hunting accident, he reveals all to Hedley in his fevered ramblings. Hedley keeps the secret of his betrayal. It is a grim story of deceit and corruption beneath a handsome surface. But that revelation of deceit and selfishness is not given any political resonance in the text. Nor is it psychologically very surprising or profound (Crackanthorpe did much better himself with similar material in his rebarbative and surprising 'Anthony Garstin's Courtship', published in 1897 in his collection *Last Studies*). As a whole, the story seems old-fashioned, and the '1830' time setting is appropriate.

The fiction in volume 2, number 3 of *The Albemarle* is consistent with the non-fictional contents. Only one essay stands out against an overall conservative configuration. That is George Bernard Shaw's rambunctious defence of Shelley as an atheist and a revolutionary ('Shaming the Devil about Shelley'). 'The Logic of Painting' questions the value of impressionism (still controversial in some circles in 1892) in painting. 'The Gathering' is a narrative celebrating the upper-middle-class and aristocratic sport of deer stalking. 'Stray Leaves from the Black Forest' discusses the pros and cons of two German holiday resorts for the wealthy and the extremely wealthy. 'Electioneering in Greece' indicts Greek democracy for destroying the country's finances; the autocratic Ottoman Empire is favourably compared to it. The poem in the number, a version of Horace's Ode 1.5, 'Quis Multa Graciles', is elegant, metrically regular, rhyming, and archaic in language and syntax. It is a languid pastiche of Tennysonian diction.

Front and back matter are equally orientated toward a conservative readership. The lithograph is by James Hayllar, a popular painter of genre and historical scenes, pictures of children and portraits of royalty. German table water and Wilkins's *The Alien Invasion* are both advertised before the contributions. At the back of the number, the services of an Oxford Street dentist, a novel by Wilkins and the usual insurance companies are promoted; Grau's frame-making business and Robbins's gold- and silver-plating business are also advertised. Only Johnson's 'Mors Janua Vitae', with its resolute spiritual focus, stands at an odd angle to the upper-middle-class concerns and attitudes implied across this issue of the journal.

Conclusions

Four conclusions can be drawn with regard to the role of short fiction in *The Albemarle*. First, short fiction does play an important role within this publishing venture, as one might expect in the 1890s. Every issue has a story, on one occasion two. In addition, a significant number of essays are narratives as well, although the genre markers in the texts indicate that they are to be read as travel pieces or non-fiction sporting narratives. Second, that short fiction is, however, immersed within a mass of different material. It is only a small part of a *mélange* of diverse items, very often of a political nature. The arguments of the political material accord well with the albeit vague social conscience of Robinson's 'A Unit', Fleming's 'Weekly Payments' and the harsher perspective of Crackanthorpe's 'Dissolving Views', but less well with the other quite apolitical stories. The largest group of articles (seventeen) is concerned with art and literature, but these are pieces of criticism or reviews. Third, the radical import of some of that fiction (of the pieces by Robinson, Fleming, Johnson and Crackanthorpe) must surely be attenuated by the nature of the implied readership and of the advertising material of the journal. Luxury silver goods and confectionery sit uncomfortably against the darker aspects of the fiction in *The Albemarle*. The implied reader of the journal is clearly highly educated in a traditional upper-class manner (the assumption of a knowledge of one modern and two classical foreign languages surely suggests this). The abrasive aspects of some of the short fiction are somewhat defused by the very traditional, fixed-form lyrics, with their sensuous melancholy, that weave throughout the issues of the journal. Perhaps the central figure, and focaliser, of Crackanthorpe's 'Dissolving Views' – extremely rich, living in the lap of refinement and luxury, sorry for the young woman whose life he has ruined but glad to escape any further unfortunate entanglement with her – is cruelly representative of the suggested reader of *The Albemarle*. However, it must be noted that some of the fiction (the contributions by Desart – in three numbers – and Douglas) fit in very well with their context. In addition, there is little that is innovative in the fiction in *The Albemarle*. The grim subjects of 'A Unit' and 'Weekly Payments' are well within the norms of *fin-de-siècle* writing. Technically, texts are conservative – they have linear narratives, omniscient narrators and sophisticated lexis and syntax on the part of those narrators. Exceptions are the extensive use of free indirect speech in Crackanthorpe's 'Dissolving Views' and the narrative complexities of 'Mors Janua Vitae'. A final conclusion that one can draw from the codicological contexts, performative contexts and internal dialogics of *The Albemarle* is that short fiction was – ultimately – rather peripheral to the venture, even though a short story writer was one of the editors. Political and social non-fictional contributions to *The Albemarle* substantially outweigh short stories. That conclusion, to a degree, stands at odds with established literary-historical wisdom, but it seems to be the case. Of course, perhaps that lack of fiction is one reason why *The Albemarle* ceased publication after nine numbers.

Notes

1. Pratt, 'The Long and the Short of It'. See also: Malcolm, *British and Irish Short Story Handbook*, pp. 42–7; Liggins et al., *The British Short Story*, p. 15; Beetham, 'Open and Closed', p. 97. The issue of the

context of short fiction within a journal or journals is also discussed in Ardis, 'Staging the Public Sphere' (pp. 34, 38) and Pong, 'The Short Story and the "Little Magazine"', pp. 80, 84.
2. I discuss such views of Crackanthorpe in the 'Introduction' in Malcolm, *Hubert Crackanthorpe: Wreckage Seven Studies*, pp. vii–xxxix (pp. vii–xii).
3. Crackanthorpe, *Hubert Crackanthorpe and English Realism*, and Adams, 'The Drowning of Hubert Crackanthorpe'.
4. See Fisher, 'Hubert Crackanthorpe', p. 61; Hunter, *Cambridge Introduction to the Short Story*, p. 34. For further discussion of Crackanthorpe's work, see Malcolm, *British and Irish Short Story Handbook*, pp. 101–2, 191–3.
5. Quoted in Fisher, 'Hubert Crackanthorpe', p. 61.
6. Quoted in Crackanthorpe, *Hubert Crackanthorpe and English Realism*, p. 145.
7. Quoted in Adams, 'The Drowning of Hubert Crackanthorpe', p. 8.
8. Johnson, *Poetry and Fiction*, pp. 12–13.
9. William Peden, 'Foreword', in Crackanthorpe, *Hubert Crackanthorpe and English Realism*, pp. vii–xi (p. vii).
10. Hunter, *Cambridge Introduction to the Short Story*, pp. 34–6.
11. Wilkins, *The Alien Invasion*, p. vii. See, especially, chapters 3 and 4.
12. Crackanthorpe, *Hubert Crackanthorpe and English Realism*, pp. 7–10. Both Hubert Crackanthorpe's mother and father were persons of pronounced, well-known and controversial political–social views.
13. Ibid. pp. 46–53.
14. Ibid. p. 46.
15. Shafquat Towheed is wrong when he gives the price as six shillings. Towheed, 'Reading the Life and Art of Hubert Crackanthorpe', p. 52.
16. Crackanthorpe, *Hubert Crackanthorpe and English Realism*, p. 57.
17. Ibid. p. 57.
18. A useful account of this kind of story and responses to it (and not just with regard to Crackanthorpe's work) is in Greenslade, 'Naturalism and Decadence'.
19. See Adrian Hunter's discussion of Egerton's and Crackanthorpe's work, as well as that of Ella D'Arcy, in Hunter, *Cambridge Introduction to the Short Story*, pp. 36–8.
20. See Hunter, *Cambridge Introduction to the Short Story*, pp. 33–4.
21. For an account of the controversy about Beardsley's artwork for *The Yellow Book*, see Beckson and Lasner, '*The Yellow Book* and Beyond'.
22. Crackanthorpe, *Hubert Crackanthorpe and English Realism*, pp. 36–9.
23. Margaret Beetham argues that the entire congeries of the material in a periodical serves to constitute its reader. She writes that: 'The reader is addressed as an individual but is positioned as a member of certain overlapping sets of social groups: class, gender, region, age, political persuasion or religious denomination – to name only the most

important. This positioning is effected by all aspects of the periodical: price, content, form and tone. The periodical, then, may offer its readers scope to construct their own version of the text by selective reading, but against that flexibility has to be put the tendency in the form to close off alternative readings by creating a dominant position from which to read, a position which is maintained with more or less consistency across the single number and between numbers.' In Beetham, 'Open and Closed', p. 99.

Chapter 4

'It is astonishing how little literature has to show of the life of the poor': Ford Madox Ford's *The English Review* and D. H. Lawrence's Early Short Fiction

Annalise Grice

The importance of *The English Review* for the development and exposure of modernist fiction in the Edwardian period has been securely established. From as early as 1930 Ezra Pound helped to consecrate Ford Madox Ford's contribution to the field of magazine publication, declaring *The English Review* in its earliest years 'the most brilliant piece of editing I have known'.[1] Ford published the literary lights of the period (including Joseph Conrad, Henry James, W. B. Yeats, Arnold Bennett, Vernon Lee, Violet Hunt, May Sinclair and John Galsworthy) together with a younger generation of newcomers (D. H. Lawrence, Ezra Pound and Wyndham Lewis). Described by Cliff Wulfman in 2009 as 'a fountainhead of modernism' with markedly 'Edwardian concerns', *The English Review* is now recognised for the way it combines distinctive fictional writing with social, political and cultural commentary.[2] As John Attridge observes, however, critical discussions of its political content have 'tended to be summary' and have been used to conduct a general overview of the publication.[3] While Attridge insightfully explores the contributions of the 'bloc' of New Liberal essayists in the magazine (notably J. A. Hobson, H. W. Nevinson and H. N. Brailsford) to propose shared correspondences with Ford's political viewpoints, his analysis does not consider the literary content of *The English Review*. This chapter argues that a reading of the spread of contributions to *The English Review* under Ford's editorship from December 1908 to February 1910 reveals that the publication was keenly concerned with social questions in relation to the working class. Much of the short fiction published in *The English Review* dramatises the concerns expressed by cultural commentators in its political pages, but the fictional representation of the working class is often from the perspective of a middle-class observer, and/or focuses largely on the lives of beggars, orphans, prisoners, fallen women and 'vagrants'. Whilst we must not underestimate the heterogeneity of periodicals, we can observe editors seeking to create an ideological identity for their publication by aiming to offer a complete reading experience in terms of the way individual stories, sketches and serialisations work alongside editorials, poetry, essays and reviews. Accordingly, this chapter considers the complexity of Ford's politics as stated in *The English Review*, examines his aesthetics and explores the emphasis Ford placed on the absence of technically accomplished English short story writers in the Edwardian literary marketplace. It surveys the extent of material dealing with working-class themes in *The English Review* before using the case study of D. H. Lawrence's early short fiction, comprising stories and little-known sketches. When Lawrence (then a Croydon schoolteacher) first visited the offices of *The English Review* in September 1909, Ford identified an opportunity to advise a young writer with the potential to fill what he called a 'lacuna' in the marketplace for social realist fiction dealing empathetically – and without condescension – with daily life in a working-class community.

'The functions of the arts in the republic': Ford's aesthetics

Before outlining the range of short fiction contributions to *The English Review* and Lawrence's place within them, it is first necessary to examine the ideological identity of the magazine and Ford's editorial and aesthetic principles. Ford affirmed that the function of the creative writer was to stimulate broader intellectual debate and his monthly periodical was to be devoted to the arts, to letters and ideas. He maintained that he founded *The English Review* as a successor to the *fin-de-siècle Yellow Book* (a name derived from the bindings of controversial French novels), and did so in order to publish Thomas Hardy's poem 'A Sunday Morning Tragedy', which had been rejected elsewhere because it raised the contentious issue of social attitudes towards illegitimacy among the poor and its tragic consequences, a woman's death after a botched abortion. Another account states that the magazine was founded in order to serialise H. G. Wells's novel of a slowly declining Edwardian England, *Tono-Bungay: A Romance of Commerce* (both works appear in the first number in December

1908).⁴ It has been observed that *The English Review* emulated influential high Victorian reviews such as the *Fortnightly Review* (founded in 1865) and the *Contemporary Review* (1866) together with a French model, Alfred Vallette's *Mercure de France* (1890), a journal which was of 'crucial importance' to Ford's conception of his own endeavour.⁵ Mark S. Morrisson argues that Ford's modelling of *The English Review* on the *Mercure de France* is representative of a wider impulse in early British modernism to 'enter into what we would now call the public sphere'.⁶ While the creation of a counter-public sphere would be the aim of the artistic avant-garde 'little magazines' founded in the second decade of the twentieth century, such as *Rhythm* (1911–13) and *BLAST* (1914–15), *The English Review* operates at the transition point from mainstream Victorian and Edwardian literary reviews to coterie little magazines and does not fit straightforwardly into the category of the 'modernist magazine'. This is due in part to its similarity to Victorian precedents, its serious tone and formal, consistent style in terms of layout, its extensive length and physical size, the intended appeal to a broad, intellectually enquiring audience and the avoidance of antagonism or confrontation to provide a permissive discursive space.

Paul Peppis finds that *The English Review*'s aim to instil in its readers a 'critical attitude' is a position derived from Matthew Arnold's ideal of the 'critical spirit'.⁷ Arnold believed that the English literary critic should study foreign thought and look to the French academy as the model of an elite literary institution, which may account in some part for the cosmopolitanism of *The English Review* and Ford's insistence on the supremacy of French writing. According to Peppis, Ford makes efforts to resurrect Arnold's mid-Victorian model of literary liberalism in which 'culture' is considered to be of greater import than politics for the way it promotes in the individual a mindset of self-development or self-realisation. As if to mimic this hierarchy, the 'highest' art form, poetry, is placed at the forefront of *The English Review*, followed by other literary content. Of course, many writers held no active political agenda when writing. Authors would frequently submit older, previously unpublished work to a magazine and pieces would often be published purely pragmatically in order to bulk out its pages, but the ideological identity the editor attempted to fashion for the publication often affected how the literary content was received. The creative work is contextualised by the socio-political ideas which follow and *vice versa*: the articles inflect and inform the reading of the literature, which gains an enhanced socio-political colouring when read alongside articles by prominent economists, politicians and social scientists (such as Hobson, Nevinson and Brailsford, who contributed journalistic articles to Liberal weeklies such as the *Speaker* and the *Nation*). Hobson also blended his political ideas with literary critical writing in his essay 'The Task of Realism', which was published alongside Sidney Webb's 'The Economic Aspects of Poor Law Reform' in the October 1909 number. Hobson announced that *The English Review* devotes itself to 'the view that experiments in collective self-consciousness' by a new movement of realists are 'a means of accelerating and directing the "urge of the world" towards human enlightenment and well-being'.[8] D. H. Lawrence took note of Hobson's rousing argument and advertised *The English Review* to his friends in October 1909 as 'the best possible way to get into touch with the new young school of realism'.[9] Essays in *The English Review* are authored not just by journalists and social scientists but by those well known for writing short descriptive sketches, such as R. B. Cunninghame Graham, a former MP who was pro-suffrage and anti-imperialist and founded the Scottish Labour Party with Keir Hardie in 1888. His article 'Aspects of the Social Question' is included in the first number, alongside the notorious Welsh 'supertramp' and nature poet W. H. Davies on 'How it feels to be Unemployed' and an article by Ford's close friend, the sceptical Tory mathematician Arthur Marwood, who outlines a State Insurance scheme for the 'labouring man' and his home ('A Complete Actuarial Scheme for Insuring John Doe against all the Vicissitudes of Life'). Ford adopts a patrician tone in his editorials and although his first editorial emphasises the disinterestedness of *The English Review*, which 'sets boldly upon its front the words "No party bias"', much of the content is broadly left-leaning in nature.[10]

The editorial section is given the general title of 'The Month'. It is a transitional section that physically separates the literary content from the 'Political and Diplomatic' articles but combines discussion of literary and topical affairs. The editorial acts as a critical intervention that remarks on the contemporary state of literature, often giving close attention to literary form and style while also addressing key concerns raised by the essayists and book reviewers in the remainder of the magazine. An asterisk appended to the first editorial, entitled 'The Functions of the Arts in the Republic', refers readers to a footnote which states that the editorial will include 'either informal notes on subjects of the day [. . .] or more studied articles upon political or diplomatic topics'. Roughly one third of the content is given over to political articles, but Ford makes clear that the 'main section of the Review is devoted strictly to *Belles-lettres*'.[11] Ford elevates the status of literature as having the potential to enlighten and educate the populace. The reader of *The English Review* is invited to look for connections across different kinds of texts – literary and journalistic – and must negotiate the varied public discourses into which the journal intervenes.

As 'The Functions of the Arts in the Republic' makes clear, however, for Ford the greatest writers engage with the public sphere with subtlety and understatement. Ford has a clear idea of the quality of fiction he hopes to print yet expresses scepticism about finding writers who are capable of fulfilling such high standards in England, 'the country of Accepted Ideas'.[12] Setting out a tripartite hierarchy which approximates critical categories still in debate today (the lowbrow, middlebrow and highbrow), Ford's first editorial defines three classes of literature: the 'inventive', the 'factual' and the 'imaginative'. Those who are 'merely inventive' have 'functions in the Republic nearly negligible': they 'divert', 'delight', 'tickle' and 'promote appetites'. Despite their superficiality, however, they are able to tell a good story.[13] The 'factual' writers deprive their work by their tendency to provide a more statistical or sociological analysis, 'because no collection of facts and no tabulation of figures can give us any sense of proportion'.[14] According to Ford, the greatest artists fall into the 'imaginative' category, comprising those who 'stimulate' and 'awaken thought' by recording life in their own terms, by which he means writers who put forward 'the expression of his view of life as it is, not as he would like it to be'. About Henry James, Ford writes that 'whatever his private views may be, we have no means of knowing them. He himself never appears, he never buttonholes us, he never moralises'. James refrains from

> drag[ging] round his pictures of life so as to make it appear that, if the social state were what he desires it to be, all would be well with the world. We rise from extremely protracted readings of his works with the feeling that we have assisted at a great number of affairs.

The greatest writers, then, are 'intent merely to register' and leave the reader in an active self-reflective or analytical mode of thought without having been subject to evangelism or instruction.[15] Despite his mid-Victorian Arnoldian inheritance, Ford's editorials demonstrate his responsiveness to new writing and outline aesthetic ideals that approach those we now term 'modernist'.

The 'blank misery of our Anglo-Saxon sense': French influences on modern short fiction

Magazines such as *The English Review* provided a forum for and shaped conversations about the short story form. According to the *Oxford English Dictionary* the first usage of 'short story' occurs in 1877 (by *The Independent*) but the term was still used indiscriminately in the early twentieth century; even then Ford reaches for French terminology to better describe the form he is after. French models for the development of short fiction were influential in Britain from the 1880s, when writers such as Gustave Flaubert and his protégé, Guy de Maupassant, began to be translated into English. Maupassant, known as the 'French Chekhov', was the author of some three hundred short stories from 1880, the year he published his immensely successful 'Boule de Suif' in *Les Soirées de Médan*, a collection of six naturalist short stories on the subject of the Franco-Prussian war by authors including Émile Zola and Joris-Karl Huysmans. Maupassant's stories were speedily translated into English from 1887 and Flaubert's *Trois Contes* (*Three Tales*, 1877) appeared in translation in his *Complete Works* (1904). The short story in France had been shaped by editorial policies in magazines such as the *Revue de Paris* and the *Revue des deux Mondes* (both founded in 1829) that relied on shorter length fiction and writers had to adapt to the requirement for an economical *dénouement*. Within a short period in France the genre attained a level of prestige that would rival the novel until the renewal of interest in forms such as the *roman-fleuve* (such as Honoré de Balzac's *La Comédie humaine* and Zola's *Rougon-Macquart* series) and the *roman psychologique* (for example, Marcel Proust's *À la recherche du temps perdu*).

The development of the English short story had been hindered by the predominance of the social realist novel, which provided a large canvas for extended discussions of cause and effect. Ford adopts a strong position on the fortunes of the English short story and in his editorial for the September 1909 number he directs a call to action at aspiring English writers:

> [T]he Englishman appears to be almost incapable of producing the real short story – the *conte*. He has not the technical skill necessary for getting the best out of his subject, and, his especial genius being what is called 'getting an atmosphere', he is utterly incapable of getting an atmosphere in a few words.[16]

The term *conte* is derived from the French *conter*, 'to relate', and Ford uses it here to refer to a narrative of approximately 30–40,000 words in length: a tale, which is shorter than a novel but longer than a typical short story. This 'beautiful' form has 'practically no place for publication in England at all now [. . .] the magazines will not print it since it is too short to be a serial, and too long to go in in one or two instalments'.[17] Ford's distinctions are slippery: he equates the *conte* with the 'real short story' in an article in which he sets out to discuss the commercialisation of the novel. The difficulty of distinguishing between *conte* and *nouvelle* has been debated in theories of the modern short story, as well as in the period. Allan H. Pasco observes that *nouvelle* 'seems to be used primarily as a generic term to cover such subcategories as *conte*, tale, anecdote, and so on, [. . .] *conte* maintains a strong association with its oral routes'. The debate might remind us of the older distinction between the novel and the romance.[18] Like Maupassant, who used *nouvelle* and *conte* interchangeably, Henry James elides the distinctions and also uses French terminology, referring most frequently to the *nouvelle*, which was his ideal form since he found its indeterminate length liberating. James extols the virtues of the *nouvelle* in the 'Prefaces to the New York Edition' of his works which were dictated to his secretary between 1906 and 1908. In the Preface to 'The Lesson of the Master', he shares Ford's condemnation of the dull 'Anglo-Saxon sense' in matters of literary form:

> It was under the star of the *nouvelle* that, in other languages, [. . .] such studies on the minor scale as the best of Turgenieff's, of Balzac's, of Maupassant's, of Bourget's, and just lately, in our own tongue, of Kipling's, had been, all economically, arrived at – thanks to their authors, as 'contributors', having been able to count, right and left, on a wise and liberal support. It had taken the blank misery of our Anglo-Saxon sense of such matters to organise [. . .] the general indifference to this fine type of composition. In that dull view a 'short story' was a 'short story', and that was the end of it. Shades and differences, varieties and styles, the value above all of the idea happily *developed*, languished, to extinction, under the hard-and-fast rule of the 'from six to eight thousand words'.[19]

James had himself received 'wise and liberal support' from Henry Harland at *The Yellow Book* when his long short story 'The Death of the Lion' was published in its first number, followed by 'The Coxon Fund' in the second and 'The Next Time' in the sixth. Given our sense that *The English Review* was a fountainhead of early British modernism, we might find it confusing that Ford should want the English to write 'tales' – that is, the term conventionally used for Victorian short fiction which was much longer than the 'modern short story'. However, taking James (countryman of perhaps the most influential practitioner of the short story, Edgar Allan Poe) as his model of the pre-eminent imaginative artist who looked to nineteenth-century French and Russian predecessors provides an indication of the ways in which Ford felt that foreign influence could beneficially invigorate English literature. If a writer like James favoured the longer short form, then that was an indication to Ford of its distinction and he was willing to make room for it in his journal. Since the novella was a happy medium between the novel and the short story, it seemed to Ford a more suitable shorter form for the English pen, which was used to writing expansively. Ford's own porous terminology indicates the indeterminacy about distinctions between shorter forms of fiction in this period and he adopted an eclectic or purposefully *laissez-faire* attitude to the contributions in *The English Review*, giving authors the creative freedom to submit for publication writing of varying lengths. Fiction in *The English Review* ranges from short sketches to short stories, stories in translation (such as Leo Tolstoy's 'The Raid', translated by Constance Garnett) and serialisations of longer works including Ford's *A Call: The Tale of Two Passions*, which appeared in *The English Review* in four parts from August to November 1909 before it was published as a single-volume novel in 1910. In the same August 1909 number, for example, 'Les Saltimbanques' by Wyndham Lewis (described by Louise Kane as a 'short sketch' and totalling 5,423 words) was published alongside James's 'Mora Montravers', which was serialised across the August and September numbers; at 24,405 words it is more a novella than a short story.[20]

'Pictures of life': depicting the poor

Practically, as Ford observes, short fiction suited busy modern lives in which 'the amount of time the public can, or will give to reading is now entirely taken up'.[21] Since modernity is characterised by a lack of true intimacy but innumerable 'social contacts', fictional form in the new century has to change with the times and in 1908 'it is no longer a matter of long letters but of the shortest notes'.[22] Following Ford's argument, well-crafted short fiction is better suited to the condition of modernity, with features such as the epiphany or moment of revelation, the event, the use of symbolism, slice of life and irresolution offering the reader a glimpse of lives rarely encountered. The ability to write with economical suggestion or implication rather than directly stating meaning became the basis of modernist experimentation in the short story form, which lacks the space for extended moralisation traditionally occupied by the novel or epic poem and has the capacity to be more impersonal than the lyric or sonnet. For Ford, 'the finest class of work is that in which every superfluous word is meticulously excised'.[23] In terms of the content of short fiction in *The English Review*, many of the contributions reveal Ford's interest in urban experience in Edwardian England, but he actively sought writers with knowledge of working-class life. Immediately following Ford's first editorial is his essay subtitled 'The Unemployed', which discusses the rigidity of class barriers and proposes literature as a solution for understanding class difference. 'It is astonishing how little literature has to show of the life of the poor,' Ford muses, 'of the thousands of books that pour upon us day by day and year by year, the percentage which gives us any insight into the inner workings of the poor man's mind is either infinitesimal or non-existent.'[24] Ford provides us with an indication of the intended readership of *The English Review* when he speaks of the poor as if he and his readers are of one mind, sex, class and political persuasion:

> the poor are breaking in on us everywhere. They break in on us as we drive through the streets. We see them in their knots, in their bands, at street corners [. . .] We drive past these broken knots with a touch of fear [. . .] We are the men whose hearts bleed for them – but how, if passing through the streets they catch us afoot, shall we be able to escape from them? [. . .] With pity, with fear, or with music – in a hundred ways – the poor man is breaking in on us.[25]

Max Saunders identifies the 'coexistence of usually opposed views' in Ford's writings (coincident, perhaps, with the turbulent world of politics under Edward VII). Despite considering himself 'by temperament an obstinate, sentimental and old-fashioned Tory', Ford often takes up positions which are anathema to the Tory party.[26] Here, he conveys some empathy for the poor but is dogged by the feeling of 'pity' aroused in him. He emphasises the fleeting nature of the modern subject's interactions with his fellow man; the repetition of 'breaking in', 'fear' and being caught 'afoot' suggests that transgression and the threat of sudden violence or uprising is associated with 'these broken knots' of humanity. Short stories often draw attention to what tends to be disregarded, neglected or considered incomprehensible, such as the ordinary and the everyday, the regional, the domestic, the lives of children, the non-human and the marginalised or outcast; as Adrian Hunter observes, the form, if 'handled right, is able to embody an experiential condition of modernity – a sense of chronic uncertainty, historical sequestration and social isolation'.[27] If English short fiction has historically been considered a minor genre in comparison to the novel, and magazines as ephemera of transient interest, short fiction in magazines offers a fitting form and embodiment for Ford's investigation into the 'hundred ways' the lives of the impoverished are momentarily encountered and cast aside.

In his first editorial Ford discusses the few examples of literature he knows that reveal the lives of the working class (which is, of course, an expansive and complex category). He cites 'only the two Bettesworth books' and W. H. Davies's *The Autobiography of a Super-Tramp* (1908), the latter of which is not, however, an account of 'a man who makes his living by working with his hands'.[28] *The Bettesworth Book: Talks with a Surrey Peasant* (1901) are sociological memoirs by George Bourne, a pseudonym for George Sturt, the proprietor of a wheelwright's shop. The 'peasant' in question, Bettesworth, was Bourne's gardener, and the book contains vivid short sketches of Bettesworth's life as a day-labourer married to an ailing wife. But an even better representative of the fiction Ford wishes to read is Stephen Reynolds's novel *A Poor Man's House* (1908), set in the cottage of a Devonshire fisherman. Reynolds works across forms, blending autobiographical reportage with fiction. Ford remarks on Reynolds's romantic background as a university-educated former science student who turned away from a secure middle-class profession among 'what he calls contemptuously "[t]he cultured classes"' in order to live among and document the lives of the poor.[29] Although it offers a genuine and sympathetic portrayal of an industrious community, Ford implicitly acknowledges that as a latecomer to the locale Reynolds's perspective on the fishermen's lives is inevitably that of an outsider.

John Galsworthy's short story 'A Fisher of Men' also appears in the opening number of *The English Review*. Galsworthy uses his skills as a dramatist to mimic West Country dialect in the story, which depicts the tragic downfall of a poor country clergyman who treats his parishioners like disobedient children and is shunned by them. Originally antipathetic to the clergyman's plight, the reader is gradually won over by his loneliness and despair and it is the faceless mass of provincial villagers who appear culpable for his decline when he is taunted and turned out of church. In the August 1909 number a review of C. F. G. Masterman's prominent treatise on political reform, *The Condition of England*, by 'E. R.' (initials probably chosen in reference to the magazine title) again mentions the 'Bettesworth books', Reynolds and Galsworthy – together with H. G. Wells's *Kipps*. *The Condition of England* gives Masterman's experiences and observations of the social conditions of the London poor and contributes to the zeitgeist of works on this subject.[30] St John Hankin's short story 'A Man of Impulse', which appeared in the June 1909 number, is just such an example. This story is narrated by a snobbish middle-class fellow, Richard Maxwell, who prevents a poor, drunken elderly man from committing suicide by drowning in the River Thames. He begins to regret doing so when the beggar repeatedly returns to him as if, having rescued this 'shabby-looking fool', Maxwell is responsible for his continuing wellbeing.[31] Although it could be read as a satire of class stereotypes, the story gives the overall impression that readers should beware of altruistic acts that bring one into contact with the poor and serves to emphasise and reinforce barriers between the classes rather than to break them down.

H. M. Tomlinson's 'A Shipping Parish' (6,381 words) and J. E. Malloch's 'Cheap Lodgings' (3,221 words) in the September 1909 number are examples of works which might be better described as observational short sketches rather than creative stories; they straddle the literary content and the journalistic articles. The distinction lies less in the length of the work and more in terms of its content, specifically perceptions of fictionality ('sketch' has connotations with a brief outline, rough drawing or written account, or a single scene in a revue dealing with topical matters, sometimes with a degree of satire). 'Cheap Lodgings' largely uses dialogue to dramatise a slice of life in a grimy London lodging house that is filled to the rafters with twenty-five inhabitants. It takes the perspective of Lilian, a thin, pale woman with cigarette-stained hands who has fallen on hard times. Tomlinson's sketch (or 'chronicle', as his narrator terms it) of the London Docklands pokes fun at

> [t]hose bright and eager young men anxious for social service, who come down to us to learn of the 'people of the abyss' – for we are of the East End of London – and to write about us, never seem to have been able to make anything of us.[32]

Sketches such as these respond to Ford's call for fiction about the unknown lives of his poor contemporaries.

D. H. Lawrence, Ford and *The English Review*

Lawrence recognised that Ford was attempting to spark debate about the status of modern literature in England and to define a new literary aesthetic, but he would also have been alert to the publication's political content. Lawrence's interest in socialism was at its peak in 1908; during his studies at University College Nottingham he was a founder member of the 'Society for the Study of Social Questions' and that year gave a paper to the Eastwood Debating Society (of which he was also a member) entitled 'Art and the Individual', which discussed 'social problems with a view to advancing to a more perfect social state'.[33] He read *The English Review* from its inauguration and as a member of the National Union of Teachers was eligible to receive reduced subscription rates. 'The coming of the *English Review* into our lives was an event, one of the few really first-rate things that happen now and again in a lifetime.'[34] These are the words of Jessie Chambers, Lawrence's childhood sweetheart and the young woman who provided the basis for the character of Miriam in Lawrence's third novel *Sons and Lovers* (1913). It was Lawrence who presented the Chambers family with the first number of *The English Review* and they were 'delighted' with the publication; Chambers's description indicates its aura of masculine authority:

> The very look of it, with its fine blue cover and handsome black type, was satisfying. Father thoroughly appreciated it, and we decided to subscribe to it amongst us [. . .] what a joy it was to get the solid, handsome journal from our local newsagent, and feel it was a link with the world of literature.[35]

With a cover price of 2s 6d, subscribing to the monthly *Review* was no small consideration for a working-class family, but while they were economically poor (certainly in relation to members of Ford's class), the Chambers family were intellectually aspirational. It was to Jessie and the Chambers family that Lawrence fled to escape the conflicts of home, and together with friends they exchanged books and literary conversation which often responded to the content of *The English Review*. In March 1909 Lawrence writes to a correspondent, 'I have just finished Wells' *Tono-Bungay* – in the *English Review*. Do you take the *Review* – if not, then you ought. At any rate, you *must, must* read *Tono-Bungay*.'[36] And again in May: '[r]ead *Kipps*, *Love and Mr Lewisham*, and read, *read*, *Tono Bungay* [sic]; it is a great book'.[37] He asks the same correspondent in November whether she is taking *The English Review*, and advises her to read the works of a range of its prominent contributors: Bennett, Galsworthy, J. M. Synge and George Moore.[38] In October, he had described the publication to a friend as 'very fine, and very "new" [...] There you will meet the new spirit at it's [sic] best' and he tells her to pay close attention to the short fiction printed in its pages, stories which 'you would find nowhere but in the *English*'.[39] Lawrence repeatedly writes of his wish to see a staging of Galsworthy's three-act play *Strife*, which was reviewed positively in the fifth number of *The English Review* (April 1909).[40] Lawrence wrote his first play, *A Collier's Friday Night*, that autumn; as its title suggests, it drew directly on the everyday life of the mining community he knew so intimately. In *Strife*, prolonged strike action at a Tin Plate Works on the Welsh–English border results in factory workers and their families facing destitution and forces confrontation between the company chairman and strikers. The reviewer, 'L.', comments that '[t]he only disappointing thing about Mr Galsworthy's play on the 9th was that the audience consisted so entirely of intellectuals. One would wish it to be within the reach of and to be appreciated by all classes.'[41] Published alongside the review is Bennett's short story 'The Matador of the Five Towns', which charts the excitement of a First League football match between the local 'Five Towns' Knype Club and their rivals Manchester Rovers, and is part of a series of stories Bennett produced documenting the everyday lives, dialect and speech patterns of residents living in the pottery manufacturing towns of the East Midlands he knew from his youth. Much of the short fiction Lawrence was reading in Ford's *English Review*, then, had modern, regional, communal concerns, frequently portraying an individual life lived within that community and often using a form of semi-biographical observational realism.

Given the ethos of *The English Review* it is not hard to imagine why Lawrence was taken up by Ford and members of his inner circle in autumn 1909, and considering his attentive reading of the magazine Lawrence may have intuited what kind of writing Ford might accept. But it was Chambers who noticed that the editor of *The English Review* was on the lookout for new writers and in June 1909 she had carefully selected, copied out and sent to Ford a batch of Lawrence's poems, together with a covering letter which explained that Lawrence was a young man 'who would be very grateful for any recognition'.[42] Jessie was strategic in her choice of poems, placing 'Discipline' (a poem narrated by a Lawrence figure, a pensive young schoolteacher) at the top of the page, hoping that it 'might attract the

Editor's attention'.⁴³ Ford's response in August was promising but non-committal: he advised Jessie to tell Lawrence to '"come and see me some time when he is in London [and] perhaps something might be done"'.⁴⁴ The meeting at *The English Review* offices, 84 Holland Park Avenue, occurred in early September when Lawrence returned to his Croydon lodgings for the start of the teaching term. Immensely enthused, he told a correspondent that Ford 'says he will be glad to read any of the work I like to send him'.⁴⁵ Lawrence's first poetry sequence was published in the 'Modern Poetry' section that opened the November 1909 number, comprising five of the poems Jessie originally sent for Ford's consideration.⁴⁶

This rather romantic narrative of Lawrence's entry into London literary society through the pages of Ford's prestigious *English Review* has been frequently (if often inaccurately) documented. Before the Cambridge University Press edition of the *Letters and Works of D. H. Lawrence*, which helped to establish an authoritative chronology of the dates of composition of Lawrence's texts, critics tended to follow the account Ford gave in his 1937 book of memoirs *Portraits from Life* that it was the short story 'Odour of Chrysanthemums' (dealing with the death of a miner) that Jessie sent to him, and which he immediately recognised as a work of 'genius'.⁴⁷ In fact, this story was not begun until December 1909. Ford, himself fond of acclaiming his role as a paternal literary talent scout, has been seen as the greatest influence on Lawrence's emergence and the driving force behind his 'turn' to working-class realism, and it is therefore unsurprising that he wanted to put on record that the very accomplished 'Odour of Chrysanthemums' – rather than a sequence of proficient and modern but (by the standards of the 1930s) consciously literary poetry – was his first experience of Lawrence's writing. However, there is evidence to support Ford's claim that, 'intent on exploring the lives of artisans', he urged Lawrence to write on 'workingman' themes.⁴⁸ Perhaps prompted by Ford's claim that September that the English are almost incapable of writing atmospheric short stories, over the next three months Lawrence worked on short fiction he hoped might be published in the *Review*.

Lawrence revised the regional story 'Goose Fair', which he had originally written collaboratively with fellow schoolteacher Louie Burrows (later his fiancée). Gaining its title from the October fair held annually in Nottingham, the story depicts class tensions amid the decline of the region's lace and hosiery industry in the late 1870s; the workers blame the downturn on reduced foreign trade due to the Franco-Prussian war of 1870–1. This allusion may have reminded readers (and Ford) of those very successful naturalist short stories written by Maupassant et al. At this time Lawrence had 'a great admiration for French literature' and knew Maupassant's *Tales*; his first short story collection was entitled *The Prussian Officer and Other Stories* (1914), which may have enhanced associations with Maupassant's collection on the Franco-Prussian war, *Boule de Suif et Autres Contes de la Guerre*.[49] In 'Goose Fair' these tensions are explored by way of a blaspheming 'country girl' who wearily leads her bedraggled geese to market at the fair, together with an examination of the mismatched relationship between Lois Saxton and Will Selby, the teenage children of lace factory owners. In contrast to the goose girl, Lois is a young woman of 'superior culture', a reader of John Ruskin's *Sesame and Lilies* (1865) who models herself 'in the true fashion of romance'. Her suitor is far less refined but similarly performative: speaking 'with his lip curling up on one side' he has 'a drawling speech with ironically exaggerated intonation'.[50] Will's father is a self-made man and has no inherited wealth – unlike Lois's father – but Selby's factory is just one of many competitive businesses which (in the words of one 'grey old manager') '"spring up like mushrooms as big as a house side"'.[51] Lois's father suspects that Will is responsible for setting fire to his father's warehouse in order to claim the insurance money, and having witnessed the tragic scene of the gutted premises remarks that Selby seemed '"fair struck down, fairly shrunken, like any common man"'.[52] In the morning after the fire Lois asks the family parlourmaid to accompany her through the streets to find Will, and they encounter 'swarthy, thin-legged men' pushing barrels of water towards the marketplace, 'gipsy women' and a 'trembling, drink-bleared man'; Lois goes 'on her way accepting the grim tragedy of life'.[53] She finally locates a shamefaced Will with her brother Jack, and to Will's embarrassment Jack tells her that they had been part of a group of boys who bullied the country girl and her geese the night before and that the girl had hit Will, giving him a black eye. Lois delivers 'her own blow' by informing Will that the community suspects he caused the fire and he is 'utterly cast down' at the wrongful charge.[54] Lois is both alarmed by and attracted to Will's sense of daring and their differences bind them, with Lois being prepared to rise above her father's social snobbery against the Selbys and to rally in defence of her lover.

'Goose Fair' was the first short story by Lawrence published in *The English Review*, appearing in February 1910. The combination of an urban, regional setting and the subject of class tensions, economic instability and human interactions in the face of ill circumstances fitted neatly alongside Ford's previous selections of short fiction for the magazine. And yet it was still a rather middle-class story, focused largely on the genteel Lois. Lawrence had direct, background experience of the working-class life that Ford wished to hear about, but in this story he was imitating the kind of fiction he read in *The English Review*, which often tended to focalise discussions of the poor through a middle-class narrator. This is understandable given his lack of publishing experience: he had only begun writing in spring 1905 and his first publication, a short story entitled 'A Prelude', was printed in the *Nottinghamshire Guardian* at Christmas 1907 under the name of Jessie Chambers.

After several meetings with Ford, who prompted Lawrence to use his observational skills to break new ground by writing about the mining community he knew, Lawrence wrote a new story, 'Odour of Chrysanthemums', which (in the heavily revised version published in *The Prussian Officer and Other Stories*) became one of his most highly regarded stories and one which we would now have little difficulty terming 'modernist'. The 1909 version which I will discuss here, however, was more sentimental in tone. 'Odour of Chrysanthemums' was revised and set in proof for publication in *The English Review* by March 1910, by which date Austin Harrison had replaced Ford as editor. In July Harrison asked Lawrence to 'cut it 5 pages' but in September Lawrence reports that the magazine is 'full up of prose', having a backlog of contributions.[55] In March 1911 Lawrence and Harrison met in person to speak about further revisions to the story, which prompted Lawrence to make improvements to it (cutting out, for example, the original prominence of the children's chatter at the start), and it did not appear in *The English Review* until June 1911.[56] Contrary to perceptions that short stories were quick money-spinners for authors – and that editors such as Harrison were commercially rather than artistically minded – in the case of this story, even though Ford had accepted it immediately, the process from manuscript to print took eighteen months and Harrison's suggestions arguably enhanced its quality.

Writing 'Odour of Chrysanthemums' ('a story full of my childhood's atmosphere') demanded of Lawrence a deeper analysis of his own responses to his provincial working-class upbringing than he had ever attempted before.[57] It was the beginning of a line of autobiographical realist works Lawrence would produce alongside his other interest in romantic middle-class 'literary' writing, exemplified by stories such as 'The Virtuous' (revised as 'A Modern Lover' from late December 1909 to the spring of 1910). Lawrence based the plot of 'Odour of Chrysanthemums' on a family account of the death of his uncle James in a mining accident and the story is told from the perspective of his pregnant wife, who is given the name Elizabeth Bates. The couple already have two young children and the story focuses on the minutiae of their daily domestic life as they await the return home of the father from the coalface. Throughout the day Elizabeth thinks of the poor state of their marriage and the unhealthy living conditions they endure inhabiting a damp cottage situated beside the colliery railway line. As the time shrinks away, Elizabeth feels increasingly concerned about her husband's whereabouts and the tragic news finally arrives that he has been asphyxiated by a fall of coal. Colleagues bring in his body to be washed by Elizabeth and her weeping mother-in-law and their shared 'sense of motherhood' is emphasised, along with a rather falsely expressive sense of her conflicting emotions: 'She was content, so content, and she loved him. How she had loathed him, loathed him!'[58] It is this epiphanic ending that Lawrence was to revise most extensively over the next five years, to bring Elizabeth's individuality and inner thoughts into clearer focus as she tries to determine how she will carry on for the sake of the children. Lawrence not only provided Ford with a slice of life insight into the poor man's world, but attempted to recreate with fidelity and empathy the emotional responses of working-class women to their domestic circumstances. Providing a sensitive analysis of 'Odour of Chrysanthemums' in *Portraits of Life*, Ford writes of Lawrence as an 'imaginative' writer who

> knows how to open a story with a sentence of the right cadence for holding the attention. He knows how to construct a paragraph. He knows the life he is writing about in a landscape just sufficiently constructed with a casual word here and there. You can trust him for the rest.[59]

Ford founded *The English Review* at a time of 'progressive alliance' in Liberal–Labour relations; between 1906 and 1914, successive Liberal governments passed a vast amount of social legislation which responded to the most critical needs of the working class.[60] These reforms included the establishment of a school meal programme (1906) and a school medical service (1907), the eight-hour day for miners (1908), as well as reformed structures of welfare bureaucracy and improved working conditions in factories (1909).[61] These issues provide contexts for much of the subject matter of the short fiction that Lawrence produced in 1909: early work which was not always technically innovative, but certainly topical and appropriate for inclusion in *The English Review* under Ford. Buoyed by Ford's interest in his work, Lawrence began to write with a new sense of purpose. Although they were never published, two little-known short sketches based on his full-time day job as an elementary schoolteacher in Croydon, 'A Lesson on a Tortoise' and 'Lessford's Rabbits', along with an unfinished fragment entitled 'Two Schools' (relating to his time at the British School in Eastwood, Nottinghamshire) are likely also to have been written as potential contributions to *The English Review*; paper analysis demonstrates that these manuscripts also date from the winter of 1909.[62] Lawrence may have taken Ford's advice to write about what he knew to mean that the editor would also be interested in observational reports of his full-time occupation as a junior schoolteacher, a lower-middle-class profession which brought him into contact with children from poor urban backgrounds (Ford had, of course, just published Lawrence's schoolteacher poems 'Discipline' and the 'Dreams Old and Nascent' sequence). The short sketches are similar in documentary style to those written by the aforementioned Tomlinson and Malloch. 'A Lesson on a Tortoise', for example, is written in the first person and framed as if the reader has no knowledge of the strains of a teaching day. The narrator describes a Nature Study class in which the group of thirty schoolboys are tasked to draw a live tortoise. They are a 'difficult, mixed class [. . .] consisting of six Gordon Home boys, five boys from a fairly well-to-do Home for the children of actors, and a set of commoners [. . .] poor lads who hobbled to school, crippled by broken enormous boots'.[63] By referring to the Gordon Home boys, Lawrence preserves the real title of the Croydon Gordon Boys' Home run by the Church of England Society for Providing Homes for Waifs and Strays. The Gordons are 'crop haired, coarsely dressed lads, distrustful, always ready to assume the defensive' but 'willing, and would respond beautifully to an appeal'; the 'actors', on the other hand, 'were of different fibre', some 'polite and obedient, but indifferent, covertly insolent and vulgar'.[64] The sketch uses dialogue to dramatise a class argument about the theft of four erasers from the stationery cupboard and the narrator's enervated attempts to pinpoint the culprit, who turns out not to be one of the Gordon Home boys, but the class assistant-monitor, Ségar, who is one of the actors and a 'fine, handsome lad'.[65]

'Lessford's Rabbits' similarly indicates the nuances in social class distinctions that Lawrence and the working-class communities he describes are so alert to. The schoolteacher narrator describes his responsibility for administering free school breakfasts to the eligible children in his care, boys 'dressed in mouldering garments of remote men', girls 'with their rat-tailed hair' and infants, 'quaint little mites'.[66] The Kellett family, 'pinched and pared thin with poverty' are too proud and sensitive to 'partake of charity meals', and few of the parents would 'submit to the indignity of the officer's enquiries'.[67] The Lessford of the title is a boy 'skilled in street lore' who appears to consume prolific quantities of bread; on closer inspection he is found to be concealing food under his jersey.[68] The narrator gradually learns that he has been raising broods of young rabbits on the allotments and fattening them on the school's bread before selling them to the greengrocer at eightpence each. The sketch ends when Lessford and his friend Halket lose the rabbits and suspect that someone has stolen them. Lawrence warmly dramatises the entrepreneurial exploits of these young boys and his writing responds to the contemporary political context of social analysis and reform.

Considering Ford's interest in a range of Edwardian concerns and his founding of *The English Review* as a forum for wide-ranging intellectual and literary discussion, Attridge's description of him as an 'impressionist sociologist' seems apt.[69] In announcing itself as a place for 'imaginative' writing to appear alongside social questions directed at a broad audience, the impulse of this magazine is to engage with the public sphere to promote a movement for collective social good. Ford draws together a range of viewpoints and subjects interesting to an urbane metropolitan readership, from the regional and provincial to the cosmopolitan and transnational. Ford and his magazine shaped conversations about and showcased variations in the short story form – from the sketch to the short story and the *conte* – providing a venue for writers such as James to publish the longer short fiction that he favoured. In speaking out about the paucity of working-class fiction in the marketplace and the lack of good short story writers in England, Ford provoked writers such as the young Lawrence to develop and extend his writing in the genre and to respond to the social questions that *The English Review* sought to address. Lawrence's interaction with Ford in September 1909 gave him access to London literary circles and proved to be crucial for the establishment of his writing career. Correspondingly, for Ford, Lawrence was a young English writer who could be trusted to create an 'atmosphere' in a short story and document little-known lives across a wide spectrum of the working class, from orphan boys to miner's wives, country girls and ruined tradesmen. There is a reciprocal relation between the short story genre and magazine culture, and read in context, short fiction in *The English Review* under Ford is shaped by a combination of the publication's high literary ideals and sociological commitments.

Notes

1. Ezra Pound, 'Small Magazines', *The English Journal*, 19.9 (November 1930), pp. 689–704 (p. 693).
2. Wulfman, 'Ford Madox Ford and *The English Review*', pp. 227–8.
3. Attridge, 'Liberalism and Modernism', p. 169.
4. Ford, *Return to Yesterday*, p. 385. Wulfman offers alternative accounts of why Ford founded *The English Review* in 'Ford Madox Ford and *The English Review*'.
5. Mark S. Morrisson has discussed how Ford was inspired by the *Mercure de France* in *The Public Face of Modernism*, pp. 17–53. My quotation is taken from Morrisson's earlier essay, 'The Myth of the Whole: Ford's *English Review*, the "Mercure de France", and Early British Modernism', p. 513.
6. Morrisson, 'The Myth of the Whole', p. 513.
7. Peppis, *Literature, Politics and the English Avant-garde*, pp. 23–4. See also Arnold, 'The Function of Criticism at the Present Time'.
8. J. A. Hobson, 'The Task of Realism', *English Review*, 3.11 (October 1909), pp. 543–54 (p. 554).
9. Lawrence, *Letters, Volume I*, p. 139.
10. Ford Madox Ford, 'The Functions of the Arts in the Republic', *English Review*, 1.1 (December 1908), pp. 157–60 (p. 159).
11. Ibid. p. 157.
12. Ibid. p. 160.
13. Ibid. p. 159.
14. Ibid. p. 160.
15. Ibid. p. 160.
16. Ford Madox Ford, 'The Critical Attitude: The Two-Shilling Novel', *English Review*, 3.10 (September 1909), pp. 317–23 (p. 321).
17. Ibid. p. 321.
18. Pasco, 'On Defining Short Stories', p. 413.
19. James, *The Art of the Novel*, p. 220.
20. Kane, 'Pre-War Writing', p. 8.
21. Ford, 'The Critical Attitude', p. 322.
22. Ford, 'The Functions of the Arts in the Republic', p. 160.
23. Ford, 'The Critical Attitude', p. 320.
24. Ford Madox Ford, 'Political and Diplomatic: The Unemployed', *English Review*, 1.1 (December 1908), pp. 161–4 (pp. 162–3).
25. Ford, 'Political and Diplomatic', pp. 161–2.
26. Ford writes this of himself under the pseudonym 'Didymus', *English*

      Review, 4.15 (February 1910), p. 544. See also Saunders, *Ford Madox Ford: A Dual Life*, p. 250.
27. Hunter, *Cambridge Introduction to the Short Story*, p. 3.
28. Ford, 'The Functions of the Arts in the Republic', p. 163.
29. Ibid.
30. E. R., 'Review', *English Review*, 3.9 (August 1909), pp. 182–4 (p. 183).
31. St John Hankin, 'A Man of Impulse', *English Review*, 2.7 (June 1909), pp. 485–99 (p. 485).
32. H. M. Tomlinson, 'A Shipping Parish', *English Review*, 3.10 (September 1909), pp. 200–13 (pp. 213, 200).
33. Lawrence, *Study of Thomas Hardy and Other Essays*, , p. 223.
34. E. T. [Jessie Chambers], *D. H. Lawrence*, p. 156.
35. Ibid. p. 156.
36. Lawrence, *Letters, Volume I*, p. 119.
37. Ibid. p. 127.
38. Ibid. p. 142.
39. Ibid. p. 139.
40. Ibid. pp. 138, 140.
41. 'L.', 'Drama', *English Review*, 2.5 (April 1909), pp. 144–7 (p. 147).
42. E. T., *D. H. Lawrence*, p. 158.
43. Ibid. p. 157.
44. Ibid. p. 158.
45. Lawrence, *Letters, Volume I*, p. 138.
46. These poems were 'Dreams Old and Nascent: "I. Old"; "II. Nascent"'; 'Discipline'; and 'Baby-Movements: "I. Running Barefoot"; "II. Trailing Clouds"'. See D. H. Lawrence, 'Modern Poetry: A Still Afternoon', *English Review*, 3.12 (November 1909), pp. 561–5.
47. Ford, *Portraits from Life*, pp. 70–89.
48. Ibid. p. 83.
49. E. T., *D. H. Lawrence*, pp. 105–7.
50. D. H. Lawrence, 'Goose Fair', *English Review*, 415 (February 1910), pp. 399–408 (p. 401).
51. Ibid. p. 403.
52. Ibid. p. 405.
53. Ibid. p. 406.
54. Ibid. p. 408.
55. Lawrence, *Letters, Volume I*, pp. 156, 172.
56. Ibid. p. 246.
57. Ibid. p. 471.
58. Since the Modernist Journals Project currently only reproduces numbers of *The English Review* under Ford's editorship, I take my quotation from the most widely accessible text: Lawrence, *The Prussian Officer and Other Stories*, pp. 204–5. This critical edition, edited by John Worthen, reproduces the extant manuscript fragment of the 1909 ending to the story under discussion here.

59. Ford, *Portraits from Life*, pp. 70–89.
60. On this alliance, see Bernstein, 'Liberalism and the Progressive Alliance'.
61. See Peppis, *Literature, Politics and the English Avant-garde*, p. 26.
62. Andrew Harrison makes this suggestion in Harrison, *The Life of D. H. Lawrence*, p. 42, following John Worthen, who undertakes paper analysis to date the stories to winter 1909. See the Introduction to Lawrence, *Love Among the Haystacks and Other Stories*, p. xxv. This volume reproduces the sketches in full.
63. Lawrence, *Love Among the Haystacks and Other Stories*, p. 16.
64. Ibid. p. 17.
65. Ibid. p. 20.
66. Ibid. p. 22.
67. Ibid. p. 23.
68. Ibid.
69. Attridge, 'The Saddest Tory', p. 799.

Chapter 5

Rhythm and the Short Story

Louise Edensor

Rhythm, a magazine described by its editor John Middleton Murry as '"The Yellow Book" of the modern movement',[1] ran for fourteen issues from June 1911 until March 1913, initially as a quarterly and then as a monthly magazine. In her introduction to the magazine on the Modernist Journals Project website, Carey Snyder summarises how *Rhythm* was a publication 'most notable for its visual arts' that 'actively engaged in defining, disseminating, and promoting an early version of modernism'.[2] Indeed, the editors of *Rhythm* could boast that they were the first magazine to feature art by Pablo Picasso, Henri Gaudier-Brzeska and André Derain.[3] Along with original drawings by notable artists, essays, reviews and poetry, *Rhythm* also published short stories, including over its fourteen-issue run thirty-three short stories by both well-known and new writers.

There has been little critical interest in the short stories published in *Rhythm*, though, with some scholars dismissing the stories because they 'rarely match[ed] that of the artwork' in quality.[4] Angela Smith argues, in her work on Katherine Mansfield's relationship with *Rhythm*, that the magazine's main concern was to prioritise heterogeneity over homogeny, an expression of its Bergsonian principles, but her argument is confined to Mansfield's fiction and the essays and artwork of the magazine, dismissing the other short stories as 'generally lacklustre'.[5] In this chapter, I will redress this imbalance in order to show how the short stories in *Rhythm* form a fundamental part of the magazine in exemplifying its underlying Bergsonian principles through their variety and diversity. The short stories represent a rich tapestry of aesthetic approaches, narrative techniques and experimentation with style, contributing a fundamental element to the magazine's 'rhythmic form'.[6] *Rhythm*'s manifesto garnered criticism for being vague but I will show how this speaks to the editor's need to demonstrate heterogeneity in the magazine's output and how the short stories represent a principal element in achieving this goal.

Within the scope of this chapter, it is only possible to examine a small selection of stories. I have, therefore, chosen narratives from across the magazine that are representative of the diversity of the literary output of *Rhythm* and that best illustrate how the concerns of the editors are narrativised. In June 1912, Katherine Mansfield joined Murry as co-editor of the magazine. The stories by Mansfield published in *Rhythm* have received considerable critical attention, and her relationship with Murry and his magazine is already well documented. My study in this chapter, therefore, concentrates on those stories written by other writers so as to cast another light on the magazine. From volume 1, I examine the three key articles written by Murry and Frederick Goodyear, along with two short stories by Arthur Crossthwaite, to argue that the aims for *Rhythm* must be amassed by reading the volume as a whole. I will show how those aims and the plots of the two short stories are closely aligned. From volume 2, I analyse five short stories: 'The Holy Man' by Frank Harris, 'On the Dogger Bank' by Gerda Morgan, 'The Blue Peter' by Gilbert Cannan, 'The Look-Out Man' by Richard Curle and 'The Little Town' by J. D. Beresford. These stories reveal how Mansfield and Murry together develop the magazine, gathering regular contributors and increasing the diversity and experimentation of its output. Overall, I will show how the short stories of *Rhythm* can be aligned with Murry's original conceptualisation for the magazine, as outlined in his and other contributors' essays in the early issues. By using samples of some of the short stories published, I will illustrate how they form an important element of the magazine and should be counted with equal importance to the essays, poems and artwork. I will also demonstrate how the underlying Bergsonian principles of the magazine created a space of artistic freedom within *Rhythm*'s pages, its goal a heterogeneous environment which would not be confined by 'a narrow aestheticism'.[7]

Volume 1: Numbers 1 to 4

The first volume of *Rhythm* (issues 1 to 4) seems to feature an eclectic mix of essays and drawings, stories and poems. However, closer scrutiny reveals how each entry has a symbiotic relationship with other contributions, becoming an expression of the magazine's vision. Early criticism of *Rhythm*, by its rival paper, *The New Age*, concentrated on Murry's manifesto 'Aims and Ideals', in the first issue of the magazine, in which he presents a series of grand yet indefinite statements about the nature of art and its relationship with *Rhythm*. Indeed, Arnold Bennett (writing under the pseudonym of Jacob Tonson) remarked how the mission statement of *Rhythm* 'flaps in the vague'.[8] As Smith remarks, however, *Rhythm* bases its art on achieving heterogeneity, the idea stemming from Bergson's concept of a 'heterogeneous multiplicity' in human perception.[9] In approaching this Bergsonian principle, providing a firm literary policy would have been counterproductive. Laurence Binyon, writing in issue 4, confirms this, saying, 'for us it is infinitely difficult, in seeking rhythm, not to impose it' because 'a rhythm imposed is no rhythm [...] rhythm is subtle and natural, unendingly various'.[10] The apparent vagueness of the manifesto, coupled with the eclectic mix of publications, then, spoke to the magazine's desire to develop a truly creative space free of restrictions. I will show, by examining the first volume of *Rhythm* as an ensemble, how the manifesto must be understood not simply from Murry's single article but from a more holistic view of the volume as a whole. With reference to two short stories, Arthur Crossthwaite's 'Ennui' and 'A Railway Vision', I will examine how connections can be made between the various pieces that make up the first volume as they each express the magazine's ambitions, contributing towards its intertextuality whilst simultaneously demonstrating the magazine's rhythmic heterogeneity.

The purpose of the first volume of *Rhythm* is to establish itself as a magazine with its own concept of art, and each published article, story, poem or drawing expresses part of, or illustrates, that concept. In order to examine how the contributions in the first volume are illustrative of *Rhythm*'s ambitions, I read them in relation to three key texts in the first issue: Frederick Goodyear's 'The New Thelema', Murry's 'Art and Philosophy' and the final piece of issue 1, Murry's 'Aims and Ideals'. The opening and closing articles in issue 1, by Goodyear and Murry, express the formulation of art as a struggle in which man must embrace change. Goodyear, in his article entitled 'The New Thelema', proclaims that modernity is synonymous with change, man having at last embraced such change as his 'greatest friend and ally', finding stability, ironically, in 'the principle of flux itself'.[11] Goodyear advocates that art must, henceforth, reflect man's conception of the world as unstable, yet this is the very aspect of the world man has now learned to accept as the impetus for the creation of art.[12] The perception of the world in 'flux' can be recognised as fundamental to Bergsonian principles, and Murry's interest in

Bergson was explicit in the magazine. In 'Art and Philosophy', Murry highlights how 'the philosophy of Bergson [. . .] is the open avowal of the supremacy of the intuition, of the spiritual vision of the artist in form, in words and meaning'.[13] For Bergson, our true experience of sensations is immediate and heterogeneous and he calls this our immediate consciousness or 'la durée'. The states of consciousness we experience represent 'a succession of qualitative changes, which melt into and permeate one another, without precise outlines, without any tendency to externalize themselves in relation to one another'; in other words, they are perceived, like music, as a continuous stream.[14] This Bergsonian concept of perception seems to be what Goodyear refers to as the 'flux'.

The very first short story featured in *Rhythm*, 'Ennui' by Arthur Crossthwaite, engages with Goodyear's ideals for the creative process and the artist's need to 'embrace the flux' by attempting to represent a moment of perception of the world from a single viewpoint. Chris Mourant has argued convincingly that the short stories penned by Arthur Crossthwaite in *Rhythm* are likely to be stories by Murry himself.[15] Writing under a pseudonym was, perhaps, an attempt to suggest that there were more contributors to the magazine than in fact existed, but it also symbolises the magazine's heterogeneous nature by using a variety of literary forms to expresses the aims for the magazine. These interconnections between essays, poems and short stories provide a sense not just of heterogeneity, but also of the 'rhythmic form' of Smith's comment as various publications create a patina of repeated ideas.[16] Repetition is evidenced as a cornerstone of rhythm in an article by C. J. Holmes in issue 3 where he remarks that 'repetition is necessary' but mechanical repetition becomes inexpressive, it is only in the 'unequal qualities', the heterogeneous elements, that true rhythm is expressed.[17] The intertextuality of *Rhythm*, its ability to explore 'one art form in terms of another' is, then, fundamental to its concept of rhythm, and the short stories of the magazine form part of that rhythm.[18]

'Ennui' is a very short narrative with clear connections to the decadent movement, the concept of ennui itself being a common trope; however, the fast-paced energy of the short sentences also reflects Goodyear's reference to the 'flux' described above. For example:

> The raucous laugh of a woman stabs. The door crashes and snaps. For a moment a familiar tune lulls the tingling nerves – only to awake with a sense of ennui unutterable. The nervous laugh of the women, the hard clink of the glasses, the quick rattle of conversation, hammer insistently,

ennui, ennui. Not a minute passes unconscious. Every day, every moment bears a torture of its own.[19]

The syntax generates an almost breathless narrative with pithy sentences patterned by repetition: 'Red ribbon in the hats of the women. Red velvet on the pillars. Red in the insipid frescoes. Red the tiny spots of matches that fester on every table.'[20] The imagery suggests a bombardment of sense impressions, clattering onto the narrator's consciousness as the protagonist is immersed within the 'flux'. The story seems to subvert the concept of ennui – a moment of desperate inertia and boredom – by describing it in terms of fervent activity, in the sights and sounds perceived by the narrator. The concept of ennui is personified as it 'stares in the red and the black and the white' and oxymoronic statements add to the confusion: 'each movement jerks with the spasm of a lifeless thing'.[21] The narrator lies in his state of ennui, silent and still, but cannot escape his own perception of the sights and sounds around him. The flux of reality defies ennui and the narrator's description of it creates art, reinforcing Goodyear's idea that the creative process lies in the ability to embrace the flux.

The capability to disrupt the concept of inertia, or ennui, in Crossthwaite's story connects to a further article in the magazine written by Murry, entitled 'Art and Philosophy'. In this article, Murry adds to Goodyear's ideas by expressing how the very nature of art is to 'disengage the rhythms that lie at the heart of things', suggesting that the creation of art involves actively causing disruption and instability.[22] In articulating the creative process, Murry uses the rhetoric of battle, as 'art sweeps onward, and by its forward march alone has its being', suggesting that it is art's continuous struggle to move ahead that creates the disruption.[23] A sketch that accompanies the article reinforces Murry's ideas. Beneath the essay is a drawing of a monkey, barely keeping ahead of a tiger chasing behind. This underscores the notion that, in *Rhythm*, art is imagined as a constant contest to move forward, dogged, perhaps, by those of a more primitive nature. The motif of the chasing tiger is repeated twice in issue 2, where it frames a poem; it is also present above the announcements of issue 3 and illustrates Mansfield's story 'Sunday Lunch' in issue 9. The repetition of the drawing functions to provide unity across the magazine (a rhythm), and serves as a reminder to the reader of Murry's conceptualisation of art as a struggle.

For Murry, however, striving to advance in art is not synonymous with breaking with the past. He is careful to outline that whilst art 'seeks an expression that is new', it is 'new because it holds within itself all the past [...] thrusting from the vantage ground that it inherits'.[24] Volume 1 contains artworks by new artists at the cutting edge of the avant-garde, such as sketches by Picasso, or articles that call for a new attitude towards art such as 'A Plea for Revolt in Attitude' by Holbrook Jackson. However, these are intermingled with essays, poems and stories that actively engage with movements of the past. The poem 'Sic Transit' by Rhys Carpenter in issue 1, for example, depicts a war of the 1600s and references a painting by George Frederic Watts from 1891 of the same name; two stories by Hall Ruffy, 'The Death of the Devil' in issue 1 and 'The Superman' in issue 3, play with the tropes of the decadents, as Faith Binckes has comprehensively illustrated; and a number of essays discuss artists of the recent past, such as Michael Sadler's articles on Vincent Van Gogh and Paul Gauguin.[25] The short story by Murry discussed above is illustrative of how the artist 'looks to the past to create in the present', looking back at decadence and forward towards emergent modernisms.[26]

The final article of issue 1, Murry's 'Aims and Ideals', features the much-quoted statement: '"Before art can be human again it must learn to be brutal."'[27] These words reverberate through another short story penned by Arthur Crossthwaite (Murry), 'A Railway Vision', published in issue 3.[28] In the story, the homodiegetic narrator is travelling by train, sitting comfortably as he falls into a reverie about the paintings in the galleries of Paris that he has visited recently. He remembers one painting in particular, 'Les Boxeurs' by André Dunoyer de Segonzac, a sketch of which is printed in the following issue of *Rhythm*.[29] The narrator dreams 'of the Salon D'Automne, and the beginnings of the promise of a new and mightier art of something more brutal, more vital', echoing Murry's words from issue 1 of *Rhythm*.[30] It is the baseness, the primitive nature of boxing, that the narrator finds fascinating. He remarks how a duel 'is a matter of pinpricks and honour too easily satisfied', losing the 'brute force behind the skill', but in boxing there is 'a great primeval instinct satisfied'.[31] He advocates that a return to the more primitive is preferable over the aristocratic and it is in this very primitiveness that the art resides.

The narrator explains how the 'promise of something more brutal, more vital' relates explicitly to art, asking: 'has art yet found anything more subtle than the relation of one body to another [...] I see why the fight in the ring is not external to art, why great art could find no better field for its searching vision'.[32] The brutality in modernity does not create art, the 'insane machine-made slaughter by a hair trigger', but instead it is 'shrewd blows, straight from the shoulder, direct without disguise' that is artful.[33] Here, life is pared back, 'stripped to the buff', creating an artform that is 'more vital'.[34] The narrator concludes, 'give me a fight – a brutal sketch in a few sudden lines and I will show you Art, the Art of Essentials'.[35] Like 'Ennui', Murry uses the short story form to contribute to the rhythmic elements of the magazine, creating an intertextual dialogue between the essays, the artwork and the short stories.

The articles by Goodyear and Murry frame the first issue of *Rhythm*, enveloping its pages in its philosophy and encouraging the reader to consume the intervening pages as the substance of the philosophical and aesthetic ideals of the magazine. The two short stories examined illustrate how closely connected the entries of the first volume were to those aims and ideals. I will continue this close reading of stories in *Rhythm* into the second volume to show how, as the contributors to the magazine increase, the stories remain closely aligned with the magazine's underlying Bergsonian philosophies.

Volume 2: Numbers 5 to 14

With Mansfield as co-editor, Murry gathers together a band of regular contributors as well as attracting some new writers, increasing the variety of contributors. Regular contributors include Wilfrid Wilson Gibson, who contributes a poem to almost every issue; Francis Carco writes both French short stories and participates, with Tristan Derème, in a regular article, 'Lettres de France'; and Gilbert Cannan produces a regular essay, 'Observations and Opinions', along with numerous short stories, dialogues and reviews. Towards the end of volume 2, *Rhythm* begins to attract emergent writers who Murry describes as having 'some measure of reputation', such as Frank Swinnerton, Walter de la Mare, J. D. Beresford and also D. H. Lawrence, who writes a review for the Literary Supplement of issue 14.[36]

Despite the increase in contributors, the short stories continue to be reflective of Murry's ambitions for the magazine. One of Murry's key ideas is that *Rhythm* should be 'the rhythmical echo of the life with which it is in touch', finding 'art in the strong things of life'. He advocates that 'in its pity and its brutality it shall be real'.[37] Many of the stories in volume 2 address Murry's concerns by taking their inspiration from life's hardships; for example, Gilbert Cannan's 'The Midwife' in issue 6, which takes the form of an anti-romance, being a story of unrequited love in the life of a woman whose job involves both birth and death. There is also Murry's short story 'The Little Boy' in issue 7, a tale of child abuse; and 'The Wedding Ring' by Lascelles Abercrombie in issue 12, which is about a man who expresses grief for his dead wife in an argument over the wedding ring she wore. The drawings and sketches also reflect the 'life with which it is in touch' by depicting everyday scenes such as images of saucepans and fruit by J. D. Fergusson in issue 8, and an image of a woman ironing by R. Ilhee in issue 14, intermingled with drawings of naked women, faces and the dancers at the Ballet Russes.[38] The magazine aims to capture the totality of life, whether it be high art or the everyday.

The stories discussed below feature a variety of subject matters and aesthetic approaches, speaking to the desire for the artists of *Rhythm* to be unconfined by any 'narrow aestheticism'.[39] The tales include a parabolic retelling of an older story, a sea adventure that uses acute insight into inner consciousness to create suspense and mystery; a narrative exploiting temporal references to explore the inner and outer life of a lonely bank clerk; the story of a disorientated railway worker at the mercy of his own imagination and an enigmatic tale of a journey to a new town that provides a glimpse of 'something other'. Each of the stories provides evidence of how the creative space within the pages of *Rhythm* was designed to express Murry's concept for *Rhythm* of individual creativity but with an underlying unity. In his joint statement with Mansfield, 'The Meaning of Rhythm', he explains that 'art is individual; the artist is individual. Their unity is ultimate and unassailable. It is the essential movement of life. It is the splendid adventure, the eternal quest for rhythm.'[40] In the discussion below, I relate each of the stories to some element of the underlying principles for *Rhythm*, either from Bergsonian philosophy or from Murry's essays, to illustrate the unity and rhythmic form of the magazine of which the short stories are a fundamental part.

Frank Harris's tale 'The Holy Man (after Tolstoi)' [sic] is one of the first short stories to appear in volume 2. It is published in issue 5, and has been identified as a retelling of Tolstoy's narrative 'The Three Hermits' of 1886.[41] Frank Harris was a prolific writer and editor, much admired at the time by Murry and Mansfield, who praise his achievements in the 'Notes' section of issue 5, remarking that he is 'the greatest English master of the short story'.[42] 'The Holy Man' is a parabolic tale that updates a nineteenth-century narrative to encompass more modernist concerns with religion and doctrine, and is in line with Murry's discussion of art and religion in the first volume of *Rhythm*. Murry states explicitly in his article 'Art and Philosophy' in issue 1 that the 'only creed which is of and for this world can give us art; for then it is art. Art is against religion or religion itself.'[43] As highlighted above, Murry further advocates that 'Bergson's philosophy is an open avowal [. . .] of the supremacy of the intuition, of the spiritual vision of the artist in form, in words and meaning.'[44] Harris takes Tolstoy's criticism of religion in 'The Three Hermits' and turns it into a narrative illustrative of spirituality, not through religion but through intuition; in so doing, the story supports Murry's ideals for creative art.

The story concerns a travelling Bishop who alights upon a 'Holy Man' ignorant of Christianity. The Bishop explains the gospels to the Holy Man and is delighted with his response and his enthusiasm for the teachings. The Bishop tries to teach the Holy Man the Lord's Prayer and promises to send back a priest who can work with the Holy Man to disseminate Christian doctrine. The Bishop and his attendants return to their boat and discuss their meeting. The two priests are dismissive of the Holy Man, considering him arrogant, but then they observe the Holy Man walking towards them on the water. He has come to ask the Bishop to help him remember the words of the Lord's Prayer, which he claims he has already forgotten. Surprised by the Holy Man's abilities, the Bishop remarks: 'I don't think I can teach you anything about Jesus the Christ.'[45]

Harris's tale differs from Tolstoy's in a number of ways. Tolstoy's narrative is a didactic parable used to expound Christian ideology by retelling an old legend popular at the time in the Volga district of Russia.[46] It is a critique of organised religion and in particular, its practitioners. His tale features a 'Holy Trinity' of hermits on the island, visited by an arrogant Bishop who humbles himself by learning the true meaning of Christianity. Harris's Bishop, however, is the son of a count, known for his 'sincerity and gentleness', whose lack of arrogance is illustrated by how 'the honours paid to him seemed to increase his lovable qualities'.[47] Harris secularises Tolstoy's story by creating a trinity of travellers rather than holy men on the island. In 'The Three Hermits', the three holy men come to represent the Holy Trinity: Father, Son and Holy Spirit. However, in Harris's tale the label 'holy man' is a misnomer and he is simply an old man with 'silver hair and beard' and eyes that are 'clear, blue and steady'.[48] His status as 'Holy Man' is designated not by his teachings but simply by his actions and the respect paid to him by the members of his community. Harris problematises the religious aspects of the story by eliminating the 'power of three', representative of Christian doctrine, opening up the interpretative framework to a consideration of other theories and philosophies. These might have included popularised notions of the 'Superman' or the achievement of higher forms of consciousness attained not through spiritual means but other, earthlier, pathways. The Holy Man's abilities in Harris's tale are achieved intuitively, rather than through any kind of religious teaching; as such, the story supports Murry's ideas, outlined above, about Bergsonian intuition being more attuned to the 'spiritual vision of the artist'.[49]

In discussing the modernists' relationship with religion, Pericles Lewis acknowledges that 'secularization became a basic tenet of twentieth-century sociology', but he cautions that the modernists' relationship with religion is one of some complexity.[50] Rejecting the idea that the modernists believed that 'the only alternative to the monotheistic God is a secular worldview', he establishes that the 'modernists were not the devout secularists that many critics portray; instead, they were seeking through their formal experiments to offer new accounts of the sacred for an age of continued religious crisis'.[51] Harris's retelling of Tolstoy's parable would seem to support Lewis's point by depicting a Holy Man with exceptional, superhuman qualities, qualities previously explained by Christian doctrine, who has no formal knowledge of any kind of religion. His experience in the story is nevertheless one of some kind of spirituality and the depiction of the Bishop as gentle and kind would suggest that the spiritual experience, with or without religion, depends upon individual intuition, an idea more attuned to the aesthetic and creative ideals of *Rhythm*.

As discussed above, one of Murry's key concerns was that *Rhythm* should be 'the rhythmical echo of the life with which it is in touch', finding 'art in the strong things of life' and in 'brutality'.[52] Throughout the volume, this is exemplified by stories of everyday realities and brutalities. One such example from volume 2 is Gerda Morgan's narrative 'On the Dogger Bank', a semi-plotted story that depicts the everyday existence of men aboard a trawler ship. Angela Smith has argued that what attracted the Rhythmists initially to certain art forms was 'the return to the barbaric' and Morgan's literary depiction of the basic lifestyle of trawlermen 'on dogger bank', a fishing area in the North Sea often subjected to brutal weather, seems aligned with that attraction.[53] 'On the Dogger Bank' is the only short story Gerda Morgan contributed to the magazine and I have been unable to find any reference to her as a writer. The name may have been a pseudonym of one of the other contributors to *Rhythm* or, as the narrative is set near Sweden, Morgan could have been a Swedish writer, now forgotten in British literary history.[54]

The story may have been inspired by the painting 'On the Dogger Bank' by William Clarkson Stanfield, which depicts a ship tossed mercilessly by the wind and rain, the trawlermen desperately trying to hold the sails and survive the storm.[55] 'On the Dogger Bank' is a third-person narrative of trawlermen on a ship. Two have been suffering from food poisoning and one has died. The story opens with the burial at sea of the dead man, Gustave. It depicts the hardships of the life of the trawlermen on board the 'Karin', metaphorically referring to the natural rhythm of life and death through the motion of the boat that lurches on the sea: 'The "Karin" rolled over very far; she paused, and then slowly she rolled back again. Then again she rolled over very far, and again she rolled back again.'[56] Within the narrative there is the suggestion of a sinister undercurrent, borne out of the brutality of the trawlermen's harsh existence. It is implied that the young boy, Jan, who works as general servant to the others, may have poisoned the two older trawlermen, driven by his exhaustion and the savage conditions on board. This is revealed through careful control of the narrative point of view, evoking ambivalence and obliquity, a technique that would later become a hallmark of the modernist short story.

The story takes place over just one day and is told almost exclusively from the point of view of one character, Karl. The diegesis is scant, but the reader is given the impression of a plotted narrative through the division of the story into three sections. In part I, Gustave is buried; in part II, Karl fantasises, delusional from his poisoning; and in part III, Karl recovers. With its concentration on the psychological facets of one character, though, the story is reminiscent of the modernist plotless narrative.[57] The heterodiegetic narrator of 'On the Dogger Bank' is omniscient but unobtrusive, and frequently the narrative point of view is 'delegated' to Karl.[58] Access to Karl's consciousness allows for both analepsis and prolepsis, so that Karl's relationship with his dead shipmate can be revealed and the individual perspective of the life at sea can be realised. The harsh reality of life on board ship means that Karl and Gustave were 'cold and wet often' but nevertheless 'content to work hard day and night' in the fifteen years that they have been at sea together.[59] Stricken himself by food poisoning, Karl cannot attend the burial above deck and in his delirium fantasises the burial for himself:

> He thought he could see Gustave floating stiffly down through the cold sea, through the haunts of all the familiar fish. How they would turn, and flick their tails, and dart away in fright! Then he saw him an oblong

bundle, lying at the bottom; it scarcely rested there, but lay half floating, sometimes touching the ground, then lifting again a little, as the currents swayed it to and fro.[60]

Although indicated by attributive signs ('he thought', for example), which makes the transition less smooth, the focalisation and free indirect discourse give the reader access to Karl's consciousness and his fear that he will be buried alive: 'suppose there was a mistake, he thought, and they tied a man up like that before he was dead!'[61] The fantasy also subjects Gustave to the rocking of the ocean even in death. The motion of the ship is depicted throughout the narrative, unifying the three sections, connecting Karl's movement in and out of consciousness, the shifts in narrative perspective between the external and internal focalisers and the rhythm of life and death aboard the ship.

Despite their long relationship, Karl's reaction to Gustave's death is unemotional; he is simply 'thankful that Gustave's moans had stopped' and in the final lines of the story Karl thinks only 'Gustave's gone.'[62] Karl's reaction to Gustave's death is juxtaposed to his desperate need for the sustenance delivered by Jan. Having had nothing but 'water and bread for three days' he 'sip[s] some of the coffee eagerly' as he thinks simply, 'Gustave's gone.'[63] His visceral needs are prioritised and juxtaposed to his thoughts of Gustave's absence, revealing that the harsh environment in which they live has conditioned them to feel little beyond their own basic needs.

The barbarous nature of the trawlermen's life is reinforced through the character of the boy, Jan, who it is implied may have attempted to kill the others. Throughout the story, the reader is divested of access to Jan's consciousness so that the revelation that he 'thought there might be two buryings' remains enigmatic.[64] It is suggested that Jan may have poisoned his fellow trawlermen with the fish that 'smelt villainously' left by Karl's side, to give himself some relief from his harsh existence.[65] This is not made explicit, however, and so the reader is left wondering at the moral ambivalence of the tale. Morgan's tale sits well within the pages of *Rhythm*, a tale with its concentration on the raw existence of life at sea, an example of a narrative that is 'the rhythmical echo of the life with which it is in touch'.[66]

Gilbert Cannan's short story 'The Blue Peter', published in issue 10, is also a tale of the everyday, but in a much less brutal environment, and serves as an example of a narrative in tune with Murry's interest in Bergson. Cannan is now a largely forgotten British novelist and dramatist who, by 1912, had already published three novels.

'The Blue Peter' is an anti-adventure story that depicts a lowly bank clerk who harbours a secret inner life as an adventurer on the high seas. The juxtaposition of the outer world of the bank clerk (who is never named), and his inner world echoes Goodyear's words from the first issue of *Rhythm* that the 'external is but a shell where the internal liberty may inhabit'.[67] This dichotomy, depicted in the story through focalisation that gives the reader access to the protagonist's inner consciousness, resonates with Murry's words from issue 1, that 'the artist's vision is a moment's lifting of the veil'.[68]

The protagonist of the story is depicted as a man of routine and habit, which is illustrated through the repetition of temporal references: it has been 'forty years' of living with his mother in the same house; 'forty-five years' that he has worked as a bank clerk; and 'twenty years' that he has walked the same route to work, arriving at 'four minutes past nine'. The narrator advises that '[e]verything that he did between half-past eight and five was as purely mechanical as sleeping, or eating or dressing'. Symbolically, however, when at home and away from the crushingly dull world of work, the bank clerk is free from these temporal constraints where 'the clock ticked monotonously, but he never heard it'.[69] The depiction of temporality in the narrative aligns it with the magazine's Bergsonian roots. Bergson identifies two concepts of time: 'le temps' and 'la durée': the first, clock time and the second, a more personal account of time. This dichotomy is illustrated in the story in the contrast between the character's life during the day, which is driven by 'la temps', and at night, driven by 'la durée'.[70] Although these concepts of time are not explicitly discussed in the magazine, Murry's interest in Bergson is well documented, Antony Alpers remarking, for example, how 'the influence of Bergson on Murry's thinking was profound'.[71] The adoption of temporality as the frame for the narrative, beginning and ending with time references, aligns the story with Murry's conceptualisation of the magazine's underlying principles, particularly in relation to individuality: the concept of duration being an individual concept of time.

At the weekend in his bedroom 'scant and bare', the protagonist imagines himself the 'master of many ships', which is revealed through his fantasies.[72] The narrative moves seamlessly between external detail and inner consciousness, referencing geographical markers to illustrate the dichotomy between the protagonist's inner and outer worlds. For example:

On the mantelpiece were a schooner, a cutter and a yawl. On a cupboard by the window was a steamer that, in a swaggering moment, he had bought for a yacht, but he never believed in steamships and he had turned her to base traffic as a tramp. She never had any luck and was always in dirty weather, and her profit being small, he had cut down her expenses to a minimum. She was very dirty. Her bow had been stove in in the bath and she was never really seaworthy again.[73]

The mixture of external detail (the mantelpiece, the cupboard and the bath) frames the fantasy elements of the protagonist's imagination (the dirty weather, the small profit and the broken bow). Each year the bank clerk toils on his ships: 'every winter, the brig, the schooner, the cutter and the yawl were put in dry dock, and thoroughly overhauled. They needed new masts or new rudders, or anchor chains or deck timbers.' He maintains a captain's log for each ship, fantasising about the 'great many characters [that] passed in and about the bedroom'. In the log he records the imagined journeys of the ships and the perils they encounter: 'cholera, plague, enteric, mutiny, lascar crews frantic with opium, typhoon, fire, water in their bulkheads'.[74] The bank clerk has read scholarly books and novels about ships and 'the lives of learned men' and each year, on his two weeks' holiday when he travels by ship, 'his whole attention [was] concentrated on criticizing the navigation', his knowledge as extensive as the 'learned men' he so admires.[75]

The only actual plot of the story revolves around a quarrel between the protagonist and his mother over a proposed house move to Deal so that he may live out his retirement watching 'the ships going by, coming and going from all parts of the world'.[76] When his mother refuses, the clerk destroys all but one of his ships, sulking in his room for days. The narrative ends with a return to the routine of its opening, the bank clerk entering the doors of the bank at 'four minutes past nine'.[77]

The final page of the narrative is illustrated by the drawing of a ship by Anne Estelle Rice and the reader is left with the firm impression that even this dream of escape – the life in Deal – would have been a life of inertia and disengagement. The bank clerk had no intention of working on the ships in actuality but only wished to observe them from afar. Cannan's narrative is a polished examination of the art versus life dichotomy, revealed through the inner workings of a single character's consciousness. The protagonist retains the sacredness of his fantasises and the story suggests that the inner world of art (imagination) is too delicate to be sullied by the real world of monotony and routine.

A further example of the use of revelation through inner consciousness is Richard Curle's story 'The Look-Out Man', which appeared in issue 11. Richard Curle was a writer of travel narratives, now remembered, primarily, as a friend and biographer of Joseph Conrad. 'The Look-Out Man' uses the traditional plot of the accident narrative, so popular in the nineteenth century, to illustrate the psychological effect of a sinister fog on the psyche of an individual character. The main character, John Turnbull, is employed on the railway as a look-out man, who has to warn his co-workers of approaching trains and safeguard them from accidents. As a dense fog descends around the workers, Turnbull becomes disorientated, neglecting his duties, which causes the death of the rest of the crew. In a fit of despair, he commits suicide, drowning himself in a deep pool of water nearby. Curle updates the stock disaster narrative (for example, Charles Dickens' 'The Signalman') to explore more modernist concerns with individual perception. The story becomes illustrative of Bergson's concept of a 'heterogeneous multiplicity' in which successive states of consciousness overlap and interpenetrate, in this case causing the main character to misjudge his surroundings and cause a disaster.[78]

'The Look-Out Man' is almost entirely focalised from John Turnbull's point of view and his perception of events is coloured by his dislike of his job and his relationship with his co-workers. Driven by his self-absorption and disgruntlement, Turnbull becomes neglectful but perceives that the fog, which he sees in increasingly sinister terms, causes his forgetfulness. When initially warned by the signalman to be careful, Turnbull feels snubbed and remarks, 'what could they teach him – pack of interfering fools!'[79] He does not want to leave the other men to work as the look-out man, feeling that he 'was always the one to be set to do the dirty things'.[80] As the narrative becomes focalised from Turnbull's point of view his perception of the fog shifts and becomes more sinister as his disgruntlement with his job grows. He becomes 'conscious of a depressing influence in the air [. . .] as though one were alone in a wilderness full of some secret evil', perceiving that there was 'unfairness wherever you looked! It was a rotten world, and no mistake!'[81]

As the 'fog was growing worse every minute', Turnbull becomes self-absorbed: 'what did they go and build railways in a place like this for? And why should he be made to stand about in the cold with a lot of silly flags?' His immersion in his own thoughts causes him to forget his job as he tries to recall 'a duty to perform which he had forgotten'.[82] In the instant that the train approaches, Turnbull remembers that he has failed to set detonators on the line. He believes that the fog has muffled any sound, and this is the reason he has not heard the train. He tells himself that he would have heard cries had there been an accident. In a deeply ironic passage, the reader witnesses Turnbull convincing himself that he has lived up to the expectations placed upon him: 'You had to do your duty or you weren't any good! Yes, he liked men who stuck to their posts, men like himself, men whom people trusted.'[83] As he tries to convince himself that all is well, the fog again engulfs him: 'It seemed like a gigantic, resistless force pressing on to him, silent as death, sinister as a blind evil face.'[84]

In the final lines of the story, Turnbull fantasises about the enmity of his fellow workers: 'he was not an imaginative man, but he suddenly knew by intuition that round that corner all four of the faces were now turned towards him, and he could have sworn that they were all really staring at him with eager and glittering eyes' because 'dead men reproach you'.[85] His fantasy leads to hysteria and he imagines the eyes of the men 'on the end of stalks, going zig-zag, zig-zag'.[86] In his despair he jumps into 'a hole full of black water'.[87] Turnbull's singular perception of the fog as sinister, a figment of his own imagination, and his dislike of his duties, which preoccupies his thoughts, leads to the eventual disaster. The malevolence of the fog is not real and is created by Turnbull, highlighting how perceptions are individual and, therefore, selective. Throughout the narrative, the depiction of Turnbull's inner consciousness reveals how his feelings volley between self-confidence and his increasing fear of the fog, and this becomes illustrative of how nuanced successive states of consciousness can become. For Turnbull, the Bergsonian 'heterogeneous multiplicity' of his perception leads to disaster as he becomes consumed by his own inner thoughts, which colour his perception of reality.

The last story I examine is J. D. Beresford's 'The Little Town', which was published in the final issue of *Rhythm* and later collected in Beresford's short story collection *Nineteen Impressions* (1918). Beresford was a writer of science fiction stories, as well as ghost and horror stories. He is known to have been interested in psychology and attended meetings organised by *The New Age* editor, A. R. Orage. In the introduction to *Nineteen Impressions*, entitled 'The Other Thing', Beresford discusses a glimpse of something otherworldly that is achieved only in moments:

> The mesh of the net is very fine; so fine that even when the eye of the would-be observer is pressed close to this apparently impervious web, nothing can be seen. It is true that the scientist who habitually adopts this

method of peering is occasionally visited by an impression of something bright beyond, something that shines. But he hardly ever records that impression. It is so elusive; and it comes only at those times when he is not deliberately seeking it.[88]

Beresford juxtaposes scientific enquiry, rational and reasonable, with that of a momentary glimpse of something 'other' through 'the mesh of the net'. This recalls how the metaphor of a net or mesh was common currency in discussing Bergson's concept of intuition. Murry himself, in describing Bergson's ideas, explains how 'the philosophies which would explain the universe are by their own nature debarred from touching its one great reality. They are but barren jugglings with worthless counters. As water through the meshes of a sieve, Life slips through their iron technologies.'[89] Murry's enigmatic statement echoes that of T. E. Hulme writing for *The New Age* in 1909. Hulme translates Bergson's philosophy as 'conceiving the constructs of logic as geometrical wire models and the flux of reality as a turbulent river [...] you cannot hold water in a wire cage, however minute the mesh'.[90] Beresford's short story can also be linked to Murry's interpretation of intuition. Murry states in issue 1 of *Rhythm* that 'artistic intuition must turn away from the practical. Art turns to regard the things of daily life with the eyes of heightened reason; and in the moment of intuition once more to behold and make actual, though for a moment, the great continuity.'[91] In 'The Little Town' Beresford will address his idea of a moment's glimpse of something, 'an instant's separation', by depicting an ordinary journey that leads to a singular revelation for the main character, an enigmatic instant that is not explained to the reader.[92]

'The Little Town' is the most perplexing among the stories published in *Rhythm*. It follows an unnamed narrator as he visits a new town. As he arrives by train, he remarks: 'This adventure into unknown country was immensely exciting. It was discovery. I gave up my strained enquiry into the world beyond, and let my imagination wander out into mystery.'[93] The mystery encompasses an 'interminably long' walk down a hill and the narrator tells us, 'it was not what I expected to find, yet the reality, when I came upon it, was so inevitable that I believed it to be the thing I had always anticipated'.[94] The narrator's efforts to give up his 'strained enquiry' lead to his discovery, replicating Beresford's idea above that the fleeting sight of something cannot be achieved when the 'would-be observer is pressed too close'. It is only when the narrator allows his imagination freedom that he finds 'the thing [he] had always anticipated'.

The thing that the narrator finds is 'an impossibly grotesque' marionette show that appears to have no discernible structure, and he is unable to 'disentangle some meaning, some story, some purpose from the apparently aimless movements of these tiny dolls staggering about their gigantic setting'.[95] The narrator realises that the 'rustics' of the audience twitch and move as if trying to 'influence the dolls in contradictory ways', as the narrator hears their 'impatient groans and suppressed groans of despair', all feeling they could 'work the unseen wires far more efficiently'. The narrator considers the 'actions of the dolls [were] so infantile, so contemptibly purposeless'.[96] When the show ends and the narrator tries to leave, he takes the wrong staircase and discovers the puppeteer, who is 'still going on in the same aimless, inexplicable manner'. The narrator marvels at the dexterity of the old man working the dolls and how he 'could see no wires, no connection between those mesmeric hands and the tottering figures'. He finally acknowledges that he can 'at last discern some purpose in the play . . .'[97] The ellipses suggest a train of thought, perhaps a momentary glimpse of something else. The purpose or meaning found by the narrator is not communicated to the reader.

Throughout the short story Beresford withholds information from the reader to create a narrative that is inconclusive and oblique. Several questions arise that go unanswered. For example, the narrator can obtain no certain information about the little town before he visits, but it is not clear why; the train passes over 'an interminable bridge' where there is no water or viaduct, so its purpose remains unclear; the walk into the town is as 'interminable' as the bridge but the journey back takes only 'ten minutes', and the plot and the execution of the marionette show, without wires for the dolls, remains equally mysterious.[98] Beresford himself acknowledged, in the introduction to *Nineteen Impressions*, that the story remains enigmatic even to him:

> At the best I could only say that if the story meant anything at all – and I was not the least sure whether it did or not – it meant that under the stress of such an excitement of the discovery of an unknown town, a man might be moved to dream of the shadow of some relation between himself and the impersonal; that he might in fact, achieve the moment's separation which reveals the apparently commonplace as a vision of wonder.[99]

Presaging the revelatory moments or epiphanies of later modernist stories by writers such as Katherine Mansfield and Virginia Woolf, Beresford attempts in his story to depict something otherworldly, something intuitive beyond the reasonable and rational. It is not clear whether he had Bergson in mind when he wrote the introduction to *Nineteen Impressions*, but the story sits well with Murry's thoughts and ideas for the magazine and demonstrates how experimental the fiction of *Rhythm* had become by the final volume.

Conclusion

I have shown in this chapter how the first volume of *Rhythm* was largely choreographed to present the magazine's purpose and ambitions by whatever means – articles on art, many drawings and sketches that illustrated other contributions, essays and short stories. Murry wrote many of the pieces in volume 1 himself, either under his own name or using a pseudonym, contributing poems, criticism, short stories and essays. Reading the contributions as a composite, guided by Murry's and Goodyear's essays, serves to highlight how the disparate entries can be viewed as a consolidated whole with a common purpose. In volume 2 the number of contributors increases, but the connection between the underlying principles of the magazine and the short stories remains clear.

Each of the short stories examined here contributes something vital to the expression of the concept of 'rhythm'. The intertextuality of the entries published in *Rhythm* speaks to the magazine's fundamental concentration on Bergsonian heterogeneity; despite their variety, each entry contributes to the magazine's unity. The dialogue between the published pieces, essays linked to artwork or stories, creates the rhythmic form of the magazine.

Notes

1. Murry, *Between Two Worlds*, p. 157.
2. Snyder, 'Introduction to *Rhythm* and *The Blue Review*', <https://modjourn.org/introduction-to-rhythm-and-the-blue-review/> (last accessed 1 September 2020).
3. Ibid.
4. Tomalin, *Katherine Mansfield: A Secret Life*, p. 99.
5. Smith, *Katherine Mansfield: A Literary Life*, p. 81.
6. Ibid. p. 83.
7. John Middleton Murry, 'Aims and Ideals', *Rhythm*, 1.1 (1 June 1911), p. 36.

8. Jacob Tonson [Arnold Bennett], 'Books and Persons', *The New Age*, 9.14 (3 August 1911), pp. 327–8 (p. 327).
9. Bergson, *Time and Free Will*, p. 90.
10. Laurence Binyon, 'The Return to Poetry', *Rhythm*, 1.4 (1 March 1912), pp. 1–2 (p. 1).
11. Frederick Goodyear, 'The New Thelema', *Rhythm*, 1.1 (1 June 1911), pp. 1–4 (p. 2).
12. James, *Principles of Psychology*, p. 25.
13. John Middleton Murry, 'Art and Philosophy', *Rhythm*, 1.1 (1 June 1911), pp. 9–12 (p. 9).
14. Bergson, *Time and Free Will*, p. 104.
15. Mourant, *Katherine Mansfield and Periodical Culture*, p. 152.
16. Smith, *Katherine Mansfield: A Literary Life*, p. 83.
17. C. J. Holmes, 'Stray Thoughts on Rhythm', *Rhythm*, 1.3 (1 December 1911), pp. 1–3 (p. 2).
18. Smith, *Katherine Mansfield: A Literary Life*, p. 77.
19. Arthur Crossthwaite [John Middleton Murry], 'Ennui', *Rhythm*, 1.1 (1 June 1911), p. 22.
20. Ibid. p. 22.
21. Ibid. p. 22.
22. Murry, 'Art and Philosophy', p. 12.
23. Ibid. p. 9.
24. Ibid. p. 10.
25. For a discussion of the decadent tropes adopted in 'The Death of the Devil' and 'The Superman' see Binckes, *Modernism, Magazines, and the British Avant-Garde*, pp. 49–50.
26. Murry, 'Art and Philosophy', p. 12.
27. Murry, 'Aims and Ideals', p. 36.
28. Arthur Crossthwaite [John Middleton Murry], 'A Railway Vision', *Rhythm*, 13 (1 December 1911), pp. 32–4.
29. A. Dunoyer-Segonzac, 'Les Boxeurs', *Rhythm*, 1.4 (1 March 1912), p. 22.
30. Crossthwaite [Murry], 'A Railway Vision', p. 32.
31. Ibid. p. 34.
32. Ibid. p. 33.
33. Ibid. p. 33.
34. Ibid. p. 34.
35. Ibid. p. 34.
36. Murry, *Between Two Worlds*, p. 238.
37. Murry, 'Aims and Ideals', p. 36.
38. J. D. Fergusson, 'Untitled', *Rhythm*, 2.8 (1 September 1912), p. 144; R. Illhee, 'Drawing', *Rhythm*, 2.14 (1 March 1913), p. 461.
39. Murry, 'Aims and Ideals', p. 36.
40. John Middleton Murry and Katherine Mansfield, 'The Meaning of Rhythm', *Rhythm*, 2.5 (1 June 1912), pp. 18–20 (p. 20).

41. Mourant, *Katherine Mansfield and Periodical Culture*, p. 117.
42. John Middleton Murry and Katherine Mansfield, 'Notes', *Rhythm*, 2.5 (June 1912), p. 36.
43. Murry, 'Art and Philosophy', p. 10.
44. Ibid. p. 9.
45. Ibid. p. 10.
46. McGee, 'Feature', <http://thebluegrassspecial.com/archive/2010/november10/leo-tolstoy-one-hundred.php> (last accessed 1 September 2020).
47. Frank Harris, 'The Holy Man', *Rhythm*, 2.5 (June 1912), pp. 2–10.
48. Ibid. p. 4.
49. Ibid. p. 9.
50. Lewis, 'Modernism and Religion', p. 249.
51. Ibid. p. 251.
52. Murry, 'Aims and Ideals', p. 36.
53. Smith, *Katherine Mansfield: A Literary Life*, p. 77.
54. One of the characters in the tale, Jan, refers to his childhood in Sweden, and the names of the other characters are common in Sweden.
55. The date of this painting is recorded as both 1846 and *c.* 1890–1910. Similarly, the title of the work is recorded as both 'On the Dogger Bank' and 'A Dutch Dogger carrying away her Sprit'.
56. Gerda Morgan, 'On the Dogger Bank', *Rhythm*, 1.5 (June 1912), pp. 24–30 (p. 28).
57. See Hanson, *Short Stories and Short Fictions*, p. 5.
58. Bal, *Narratology*, p. 162.
59. Morgan, 'On the Dogger Bank', p. 27.
60. Ibid. p. 28.
61. Ibid. p. 28.
62. Ibid. pp. 27, 30.
63. Ibid. pp. 29, 30.
64. Ibid. p. 30.
65. Ibid. p. 27.
66. Murry, 'Aims and Ideals', p. 36.
67. Goodyear, 'The New Thelema', p. 2.
68. Murry, 'Art and Philosophy', p. 9.
69. Gilbert Cannan, 'The Blue Peter', *Rhythm*, 2.10 (1 November 1912), pp. 238–41 (p. 238).
70. Wildon Carr, *Henri Bergson*, p. 34.
71. Alpers, *The Life of Katherine Mansfield*, p. 134.
72. Cannan, 'The Blue Peter', p. 238.
73. Ibid. p. 239.
74. Ibid. pp. 238–9.
75. Ibid. p. 239.
76. Ibid. p. 240.
77. Ibid. p. 241.

78. Guerlac, *Thinking in Time*, p. 66.
79. Richard Curle, 'The Look-Out Man', *Rhythm*, 2.11 (1 December 1912), pp. 293–300 (p. 294).
80. Ibid. p. 294.
81. Ibid. pp. 294–5.
82. Ibid. p. 295.
83. Ibid. p. 296.
84. Ibid. p. 297.
85. Ibid. pp. 299, 298.
86. Ibid. p. 300.
87. Ibid.
88. Beresford, 'The Other Thing', p. ix, <https://archive.org/details/nineteenimpressi00bereiala/page/xiv/mode/2up> (last accessed 1 September 2020).
89. Murry, 'Art and Philosophy', p. 9.
90. T. E. Hulme, 'New Philosophy', *The New Age*, 5.10 (1 July 1909), pp. 198–9 (p. 198).
91. Murry, 'Art and Philosophy', p. 12.
92. Beresford, 'The Other Thing', pp. xii–xiii.
93. J. D. Beresford, 'The Little Town', *Rhythm*, 2.14 (1 March 1913), pp. 440–5 (p. 440).
94. Ibid. pp. 441–2.
95. Ibid. p. 443.
96. Ibid. p. 444.
97. Ibid. p. 445.
98. Ibid.
99. Beresford, 'The Other Thing', p. xiv.

Chapter 6

For Love or Money: Popular 1920s Artist Stories in *The Royal* and *The Strand*

Emma West

In his landmark study *The Age of the Storytellers: British Popular Fiction Magazines, 1880–1950,* Mike Ashley introduced a generation of scholars and collectors to dozens of all-but-forgotten popular magazines, from *Hutchinson's Story Magazine* and *Cassell's Magazine* to *The New Magazine* and *The Grand Magazine*.[1] Ashley termed such periodicals Standard Illustrated Popular Magazines, characterised as they were by a standard size (240 × 165 mm); copious pen-and-ink, wash or occasionally photographic illustrations; and large circulations, typically in the hundreds of thousands. Following its publication, and the introduction of online databases such as *Galactic Central*, one might have expected to see a renaissance in popular magazine studies, but such titles remain understudied, both in short fiction and periodical studies.[2] *The Strand*, described by Ashley as the 'grandfather' of the genre, has received some attention, but such studies have tended to focus on Arthur Conan Doyle's Sherlock Holmes stories.[3] Celebrity contributors aside, few critics have analysed how the majority of short fiction worked in magazines such as *The Royal, The London, Lloyd's, Pearson's* and *The Windsor*. There are of course exceptions, such as work by Dean Baldwin, Winnie Chan and Kate Jackson.[4] Yet the number of such studies is disproportionate to the sheer volume of standard illustrated popular fiction magazines published in Britain from the 1890s through the interwar period. To date, modern periodical studies has been dominated by a focus on 'little' or modernist magazines, largely from the 1900s or 1910s (*Blast, Rhythm, The Little Review*); in the interwar period, recent studies have focused on feminist or women's magazines (*Time and Tide, Vogue, Harper's Bazaar, Good Housekeeping*), leaving this huge field largely untapped. With their broad and mixed readership, mass circulations, middlebrow (often genre) fiction and dearth of well-known or avant-garde contributors, standard illustrated popular magazines appear to be deemed less worthy of sustained critical attention.

Such a critical blind spot is all the more surprising given that these magazines were dominated by the publication of short fiction: typically five to seven complete stories within one monthly issue and often a running serial or serialised novel. The January 1921 issue of *The Royal*, for instance, contained seven complete stories, plus the first instalment of John Galsworthy's *To Let*, the fifth novel in the popular Forsyte saga. For anyone interested in short fiction from the 1880s to the 1950s, standard illustrated popular magazines constitute an almost unimaginably rich resource. A single magazine like *The Strand* published around 4,500 stories between 1891 and 1950: such a wealth of material opens up possibilities for all kinds of analysis and modes of reading, from distant readings utilising new technologies to trace patterns in short fiction, to comparative studies of how different magazines presented a single author's work. Given that so many authors published in a range of titles – we could think of Baroness Orczy, the prolific romantic author and creator of 'The Scarlet Pimpernel', who published short stories in *The Royal*, *Pearson's*, *Cassell's* and *The Grand Magazine*,[5] or the thriller writer Edgar Wallace, who published short fiction in *The Windsor, The Strand, Mystery Magazine* and *The Weekly Tale-Teller* – there are huge opportunities for future studies exploring fiction in popular fiction magazines.

In this essay, I seek to explore how a magazine's brand identity and editorial practices affected its fictional contents. In order to do so, I focus on stories within a single genre across several issues of two leading fiction magazines, *The Strand* (1891–1950) and *The Royal* (1898–1930). Across the years 1920–1, I examine five stories within a sub-genre popular during the early 1920s – the artist story – by writers ranging from the hugely popular Morley Roberts and 'Sapper' (H. C. McNeile) to the all-but-forgotten Christine Castle. These stories all feature artists or writers as their protagonists, but the fate of the artists and the tone in which this fate is described differs widely. By reading these stories in the context of their host publication, I consider the extent to which the stories were shaped both by the magazine's intended readership and the publication's wider stance on art, as indicated by their editorials and accompanying non-fiction pieces.

Art and the artist story in *The Strand* and *The Royal*

The artist story was in vogue in *The Strand* and *The Royal* during 1921. In *The Strand*, there was typically an artist story in every issue; in *The Royal*, there were sometimes as many as two stories each month. There are many possible reasons for this brief burst in popularity. Francis Baily, editor of *The Royal* from 1912 to 1927, argued in his autobiography that in the aftermath of the Great War a 'kind of unnatural gaiety pervaded everything, partly because people were trying to forget the anxieties of the war and [. . .] reading matter became very gay'.[6] In the early 1920s, the artist story was the perfect vehicle for all kinds of gaiety, not least because artists had been behaving in increasingly ridiculous ways since the 1909 publication of F. T. Marinetti's 'Manifesto of Futurism'. As William C. Wees points out, Edwardian literary and artistic scenes were disappointingly respectable, dominated by the mediocre Royal Academy and 'conventional' authors such as Galsworthy, George Bernard Shaw and Arnold Bennett. The modernists, on the other hand, were like grist to the tabloid mill.[7] Columnists in the *Daily Mirror*, in particular, took delight in the outrageous exploits of the Futurists et al., to the extent that Futurism became a byword for anything absurdly modern or outré.[8] Despite this comic potential, artist stories published in *The Strand* and *The Royal* in the early 1920s relied less on the exigencies of the modernist artist and more on the existential dilemma between art and life rehearsed in short fiction of the 1890s.[9] Yet although modern art is rarely mentioned in these stories, the excesses of the avant-garde may have inspired popular writers to adapt the Romantic stereotype of the starving artist for 1920s audiences wanting something more substantial than wartime 'fluff'.[10] This was, after all, the beginning of the interwar 'Battle of the Brows', in which anyone suspected of having highbrow sympathies became an acceptable figure of fun.[11]

One archetypal example of the comic artist story is Morley Roberts' 'Brown of Boomoonoomana', published in *The Strand* in March 1921. Although largely forgotten today, Roberts was an extraordinarily prolific short fiction writer, novelist, traveller and biologist, described by Storm Jameson in her 1961 biography as the 'Last Eminent Victorian'. From the 1890s onwards he published stories in a range of publications, including the *Windsor*, *Lady's Realm*, *Saturday Evening Post* and *Black and White*, but his main outlet was *The Strand*. From 1901 to 1922 he was one of the magazine's 'most popular contributors', publishing thirty-eight stories in total.[12] 'Brown' was Roberts' second-to-last *Strand* story: it can therefore be read as a culmination of his long association with the magazine, revisiting one of his favourite themes, namely that of struggling Bohemian artists and writers. Markus Neacey notes that in the late 1880s Roberts 'led a struggling Bohemian existence in Chelsea lodgings, spending his days in nearby artist studios for warmth and companionship'; this experience inspired early short stories such as 'The Bronze Caster', originally subtitled 'A Study from Life' on its publication in *Macmillan's Magazine* in January 1891.[13] Thirty years later, Roberts was still revisiting his early formative experiences in 'Brown of Boomoonoomana', this time with a comic bent and a three-part structure characteristic of so many popular artist stories from this period.

First, the naïve yet pretentious artist-protagonist is introduced. Eustace Rankine is a quintessential starving artist, obsessed with the Romantic poets, to whom he likes to compare himself: '"I don't believe there's a single butcher or grocer in the King's Road who would have helped Keats, or a coalman who would have given Shelley a scuttle of coals for his *Ode to Night*."'[14] Convinced that geniuses cannot 'make money till they are dead', Eustace's straitened circumstances set up the story's second part: the crisis, in which the protagonist must decide whether to sacrifice his artistic ideals in pursuit of something more prosaic (usually love or money).[15] Cut off by his rich Australian uncle for refusing to give up his writing, Eustace goes without food for three days before he steals a shoulder of mutton hanging in a butcher's window in desperation. A madcap chase ensues, with Eustace being pursued around the streets of London by the butcher and a policeman (Figure 6.1). As can be seen in Frank Gillett's illustration, this chase becomes the story's focal point: two of the three illustrations accompanying the story feature the shoulder of mutton, and the third one portrays the policeman searching for the mutton. There is little in these illustrations to remind us that Eustace is a writer, save perhaps his 'artistic' floppy bow tie.[16] As in many popular artist stories from this period, the fact that the protagonist is an artist or writer is immaterial to the plot: the character simply needs to be open to ridicule while remaining sympathetic. Indeed, the resolution to such stories often disregards artistic dilemmas in favour of a romantic dénouement. There is no romantic subplot in 'Brown', but there is a happy ending: through a convoluted series of events related, inevitably, to the mutton, Eustace is reunited with his long-lost uncle and his allowance is restored.

"Next moment Eustace was running round the corner with the butcher and the constable after him."

Figure 6.1 Frank Gillett's illustration accompanying Morley Roberts's story 'Brown of Boomoonoomana'. © British Library Board, *The Strand*, March 1921.

'Brown' features all the key characteristics of the popular 1920s artist story. It uses a standard three-part structure of introduction, crisis, resolution, and it features three character types essential to the genre: an idealistic artist protagonist whose ambition outstrips his (and it is always his) talents, a friend or friends with whom he can rail against the unfairness of the system, and a level-headed woman who compels him to produce art which can make money (in this case, Eustace's landlady). Such stories are undeniably formulaic, but what interests me is how authors adapted this formula for publication in standard illustrated fiction magazines. In recent years, critics such as Sean Latham and Robert Scholes, Ann Ardis, Patrick Collier and Chris Mourant have described magazines as 'multi-vocal texts', heterogeneous spaces which could accommodate divergent views and styles; this polyvocality also characterises the 1921 issues of *The Strand* and *The Royal* explored here.[17] At times pure fantasy, at others social satire, the stories surveyed below adapt the artist story's same basic structure of set-up, crisis and resolution to create a variety of effects: providing entertainment, fuelling aspiration, undermining highbrow pretension or setting out a nostalgic vision of postwar Britain. And yet despite these differences in tone and desired effect, the short stories within this sub-genre are more similar than dissimilar: by and large, these stories share the host magazine's broader stance on art and its cultural and gender politics. While it is an oversimplification to suggest that each standard illustrated popular magazine communicated a distinct, singular and stable message, those writers wishing to support themselves by publishing short stories in such magazines had to adapt their fiction to each periodical's brand identity and desired readership, however complex and ambiguous that message or that readership might have been.

This need to adapt was especially the case, I would like to suggest, for lesser-known authors. It is significant that the one artist story from this period that diverges significantly from its host magazine was the French actress Sarah Bernhardt's story 'Love Wins', published in *The Strand* in January 1921. Bernhardt's story follows Arlette d'Ormange's efforts to recover her playwright husband's script, stolen by the villainous Monsieur Courleville. Despite her husband's lack of faith in her, Arlette and her New Woman sister Georgia outsmart Courleville when Arlette poses as his typist.[18] Bernhardt's proto-feminist message appears at odds with the rest of the magazine, yet the appeal of Bernhardt's first short story was surely such that she could have written a piece as radical as Marinetti's 'Manifesto of Futurism' and it still would have been accommodated within *The Strand*. The magazine clearly used Bernhardt's celebrity to maintain its readership: it placed the story at the front of the magazine, introducing it as 'a new departure which will excite great interest' and promising 'other stories from her pen which we shall publish in early numbers'.[19] In contrast, artist stories published without fanfare and written by authors working at a level below 'big-name' contributors like Arthur Conan Doyle, P. G. Wodehouse, Ethel M. Dell or Agatha Christie appear more of a piece with the host magazine's other fictional and non-fictional contents. In what follows, I consider two artist stories by precisely such authors: 'On the Line: An Academy Story', by T. Joyce (Joyce Cary), published in *The Strand* in May 1921, and Robert Magill's 'Gossamer for Goddesses', which appeared in *The Royal* in January 1921. Despite each story's apparent similarities – both revolve around young artists trying to make enough money to marry their respective love interests – the style, tone and above all the treatment of female characters diverge in ways that tally with the host publication's broader ideology on art and their target audience.

The *Strand*'s attitude towards art can be summarised by what J. B. Priestley, in a 1926 article for *The Saturday Review*, termed 'Broadbrow': those 'who do not denounce a piece of art because it belongs in a certain category but only ask that it shall be well done, shall have in it colour, grace, wit, pathos, humour or sublimity'.[20] Priestley's references to 'colour', 'wit' and 'humour' neatly describe both the tone and content of fiction and non-fiction pieces on art in *The Strand* of the early 1920s. In 1921, there was a trend for articles on caricaturists and illustrators – on Fougasse, Dulac and Phil May – all of which coincided with the appearance of W. Heath Robinson's humorous cartoons from August of the same year.[21] These articles are united by the same desire to have humorous art taken seriously: each fights real or imagined objections from the highbrow, who threatens to dismiss such art as light and inconsequential. The persistent argument that art can be at once humorous and possess artistic value may have been rather self-serving: *The Strand* itself had a reputation for humorous short fiction through its longstanding partnership with P. G. Wodehouse, whose stories it had published regularly since February 1910. Yet the defence of broad- or middlebrow values seems genuine: although *The Strand* contained no editorials, its non-fiction articles depict popular or vernacular forms of art as pleasurable and accessible. Fine art is not covered, but there is a piece on scene painting in February 1921 and two articles by Winston Churchill on 'Painting as a Pastime' in December 1921 and January 1922.[22] Churchill's claim that '[j]ust to paint is great fun. The colours are lovely to look at and delicious to squeeze out' summarises the tone of *The Strand*'s artistic output: as long as it is not taken to extremes, art can bring joy and humour into the reader's life.[23]

It is in this context of a dual appreciation for popular art and a scepticism of anything highbrow that Joyce Cary's '"On the Line": An Academy Story' appeared in May 1921. Written under the pseudonym T. Joyce, 'On the Line' was the first of only three stories that Cary published for *The Strand*, yet it captures the magazine's scepticism for anyone who takes their art (or themselves) too seriously. For years, the story's protagonist, the painter Mark Roberts, derides the Royal Academy as 'a museum of artistic incapacity, "the mummy-case of painting"', until one of his paintings is accepted and he begins to visit the Academy nearly every day.[24] On one such visit, Mark is delighted to discover his estranged sweetheart Jean South apparently engrossed in his painting, only for it to transpire that she was using it as a looking-glass to check whether she had a smut on her nose. 'On the Line' is a strange story: it is a romantic comedy, but one without warmth for any of its characters. Like Morley Roberts, Cary had some experience of artistic circles: he trained as a painter at the Edinburgh School of Art from 1907 to 1909 and while at Oxford reportedly 'spent a lot of time' editing the little magazine *Rhythm* for his lifelong friend John Middleton Murry.[25] Yet the affection for even the most inept of artists we see in Roberts' 'Brown' is absent from 'On the Line'. Mark's denunciations of the Royal Academy as a 'limbo, an exploded relic of the Dark Ages, a moribund institution for the support of the Old Men – a picture shop-for the provinces' serve only to set him up for the inevitable fall when Jean describes his painting as a 'portrait of a boot-hole', a 'slab of blackness' whose only redeeming feature was that one could see one's reflection in it.[26] The story reads less as a piece of fiction invested in the characters than as one interested in bringing its (anti)heroes down to size. Such a message seems surprising given Cary's own artistic ambitions and involvement with *Rhythm*, but this incongruity lends weight to the notion that writers felt pressure, whether explicit or implicit, to adapt their fiction to suit the target publication.

Where Cary's 'On the Line' works to lampoon its artist protagonist, artist stories in *The Royal* adopt a much gentler form of satire. Artists are figures of fun, but the humour is softer. In his editorial for February 1922, subtitled 'Are Poets Human?' Francis Baily ponders why the verses he receives always follow the same formula:

> The amateur poet is never cheerful, never individual. He generally writes about a flower, the wind, a river, or the sea, and it is always a decrepit flower, a mournful wind, a mistaken river (often complete with suicide's body), and a pitiless sea.[27]

Despite all of the marvellous subjects available in modern life, from motor-buses to vacuum cleaners, amateur poets 'dig from the depths of their souls the repressed instincts, complexes, inhibitions, and all the rest of it, which cripple their lives, set them out in verse, and send them to me'. Instead of writing a diatribe about the state of modern poetry, Baily transforms his frustration into comedy, describing himself as 'the great human safety-valve, through whom thousands avoid nervous breakdown and melancholia. Some day your children will lay a tribute of flowers (faded) at the foot of my statue in the Cromwell Road.'[28] Bad poets are made ridiculous, but the humour stops short of an attack: with his characteristic lightness of touch, Baily makes himself (and not the amateur poet) the target for the editorial's joke.

Baily's affectionate tone is echoed in the magazine's other artist stories, most notably Robert Magill's January 1921 romantic comedy 'Gossamer for Goddesses'. Magill was a prolific short fiction writer during the 1920s. He contributed to *Pearson's Weekly*, *Hutchinson's*, *20-Story Magazine* and *The Passing Show*. He had a particular talent for comic short stories, publishing in *The New Magazine*, whose tagline was 'A Magazine of Humour and Romance' and *Gaiety*, subtitled 'A Magazine of Humour'. These bright, cheerful publications struck a similar tone to Baily's *Royal*, as exemplified in 'Gossamer'. Like Cary's 'On the Line', the plot revolves around the protagonist, the artist Edgar Pritchard, and his attempts to earn enough money to woo his love interest, the businesswoman Pauline. In many ways, Edgar is a typical artist – he is bad with figures and even worse with money, lacks common sense, and is incapable of sticking to a work schedule – but equally

> Edgar was not a little bit like the usual impression of an artist, with long hair, and an atmosphere of having breakfasted on rose-clouds instead of eggs and bacon. He was short and dapper, neatly dressed, liked pickles, and was a keen motor-cyclist.[29]

Similarly, Edgar's artistic ideals subvert the stereotype of the starving artist suffering for his work. Edgar has no qualms about producing art – in his case sketches for serials in illustrated magazines – for money. In a humorous sequence of events, it is discovered that Edgar's sketches contain beautiful designs for dresses, but when he is offered a job by a department store owner as a dress designer he cannot produce designs on demand: 'all he could do was to produce some weak and hashed-up mixtures of the old ideas'.[30] It is only when the owner asks him to illustrate a mock version of a magazine serial that Edgar begins 'to produce some really new designs in women's clothing'.[31] The story thus presents a gentle satire on the process of artistic production and the genesis of inspiration: it takes the ancient notion that artists cannot produce great works to order, but only as inspiration strikes, and gives it a modern twist. Edgar is a new breed of (commercial) artist. 'Gossamer' follows the same three-part structure of introduction, crisis and resolution as 'Brown', yet the crisis comes not because Edgar refuses to create commercial work, but rather because he cannot create commercial work without some creative thinking from the department store owner.

If 'Gossamer' is a satire, then, it is a 'delicate' Horatian satire, designed to 'laugh men out of their follies'.[32] Edgar is made absurd, but his flaws are relatable ones: he is guiltier of procrastination than he is of pretentiousness. The humour comes from exposing universal 'follies', such as composing a wildly over-ambitious schedule only to fail at it miserably, not by wounding the arrogant artist. As such, the story collapses the distance between artists and the reader, much as Baily seeks to do in his editorials. The February 1922 editorial leads readers through the process of commissioning, designing and printing illustrations for the magazine's short fiction, demystifying the creative process.[33] Baily cannot resist throwing the occasional barb at his artists, especially on the subject of timekeeping, but the piece is a celebration, not a denigration, of the professional, commercial artist. In his editorials, Baily repeatedly debunks the notion of the artist or writer as a genius with innate talent: 'No one was born a great writer. The great ones had to make perfect, through practice, their latent gift.'[34] Baily himself writes that he is 'only too anxious to help the promising beginner with advice, encouragement, even money' so as to bring the dream of becoming a successful artist or writer one step closer.[35] Like the heroes of stories such as 'Gossamer', with a little perseverance and guidance, it is possible for readers to produce art and make money at the same time.

The short fiction published in *The Royal* and *The Strand* thus not only echoes but also helps to construct each magazine's stance on art. In the context of the Battle of the Brows, in which contributors to *The Strand* sought to defend and legitimise middlebrow literature and art, artists are the butt of the joke: in 'Brown' and 'On the Line', the magazine's readers are invited to laugh at rather than with the fictional protagonists. In *The Royal*, artist stories play with stereotypes of the artistic temperament, but in 'Gossamer' and Baily's editorials, the gentle gibes are outweighed by a celebration of the professional commercial artist: a career made accessible for *The Royal*'s aspiring lower-middle-class readers. In the section below, I explore the effect of each magazine's intended audience on its short fiction in more detail so as to argue that changing readerships after the First World War made it unlikely that artist stories like 'On the Line' would have appeared in *The Royal*. In particular, I examine the representation of female characters in the artist stories already discussed, alongside two short stories about writers: 'White Hyacinths' by Christine Castle, published in *The Royal* in February 1921, and 'God's Truth' by 'Sapper' (H. C. McNeile), which appeared in *The Strand* in January 1921.

Comedy and comfort: The role of the reader in *The Strand* and *The Royal*

In his 1966 biography of *The Strand*, former editor Reginald Pound wrote that

> the middle-classes of England never cast a clearer image of themselves in print than they did in *The Strand Magazine*. Confirming their preference for mental as well as physical comfort, for more than half a century it faithfully mirrored their tastes, prejudices, and intellectual limitations. From them it drew a large and loyal readership that was the envy of the publishing world.[36]

Pound's depiction gets to the heart of this publishing phenomenon: under the forty-year editorship of Herbert Greenhough-Smith, it was a magazine 'as solid and polished as the mahogany in [its publisher] Sir George Newnes's office'.[37] It concentrated on 'readability': short stories by 'proficient', 'pedestrian' writers whose 'feet were planted squarely on a common ground, where the surface was solid and familiar'.[38] Christopher Pittard observes that 'the term [Newnes] used most frequently to describe his periodicals was "wholesome," and its various synonyms'.[39] Similarly, Kate Jackson argues that readers sought 'reassurance' in *The Strand*'s pages.[40] This readership was predominately male: as Pound points out, although 'posing as a family magazine, *The Strand* primarily appealed to men', in particular the 'paterfamilias [. . .] still all powerful in the domestic circle'.[41] Although several successive generations grew up with the magazine, it essentially courted the same types of readers, if not the same readers, throughout its life: male, conservative and middle class.

In contrast, *The Royal*'s readership, and thus its contents, changed dramatically during the 1910s as a result of the First World War.[42] As Baily notes in his autobiography, 'since the war women have formed the bulk of magazine readers, whereas before the war they were mostly men'.[43] For *The Royal*, this meant a shift from pre-war adventure stories to 'emotional adventure appealing to women'.[44] Women not only constituted the magazine's new target audience: they were also featured more prominently in the magazine as contributors, whether of short fiction or articles on 'women's topics'. One representative series of articles was a four-part series on 'aspects of modern life' by the infamous romantic novelist and screenwriter Elinor Glyn, beginning with 'How I Would Bring Up a Girl' from

January 1921.[45] In it, Glyn argues that 'girls should be encouraged to be as attractive and beautiful and sensible as it is possible to be with each particular temperament'.[46] Beauty is important, but so is the ability to think independently and critically. The well-raised girl 'does what she pleases, because her mind is so trained that she can decide for herself the best'.[47] It is an exaggeration to say that all the articles were written for or by women – *The Royal* was still a general-interest, family magazine, which also included pieces aimed at men and children – but Glyn's emphasis on female independence and critical thinking is representative of much of the magazine's fiction and non-fiction from the postwar period.

I do not want to draw too simple a parallel between *The Strand* and *The Royal*'s readers and the characters depicted in the artist stories published in each magazine. Nevertheless, the female characters in 'On the Line' and 'Gossamer for Goddesses' give an insight into each magazine's intended readership. In 'On the Line', Jean South is a woman without any ideas or interests of her own: her thoughts centre around her appearance and her love life. When asked for her opinion about the pictures in the Royal Academy exhibition, she defers to Mark, remarking that '"I'm not much of a critic, am I?"'.[48] The narrator implies that Jean's lack of confidence in her own critical judgement has been caused by Mark's repeated tirades on the shortcomings of the Royal Academy, yet the narrator himself draws the same conclusion on the following page: 'She was, in short, preoccupied with affairs which may or may not be more important than art, but will always be more interesting to young women.'[49] Although made for comic effect, this patronising assumption that women are not interested in art is reinforced by the story's conclusion, in which the narrator observes that 'it does not matter in the least to an artist what his wife thinks of his pictures. Because, whatever she thinks, she will always say that every one of them is better, much *much* better, than the last' (emphasis in the original).[50] The role of the woman – interchangeable with the role of the wife – is reduced to mere sycophancy. Such a conclusion recalls John Ruskin's quintessentially Victorian portrait of womanhood in 'Of Queen's Gardens', in which he argues that a woman's 'great function is Praise'.[51] Here Jean reassures Mark in much the same way as *The Strand* offered 'comfort and security' to its readers: by invoking Victorian, if not eternal, values, Cary presents a balm for those made anxious by campaigns for female suffrage and the rise of the New Woman.[52]

Female love interests like Jean South rarely appeared in the postwar *Royal*. Although its fictional female protagonists were seldom artists, they were almost always successful professionals, whether typists, filing clerks or movie stars. Even those without a profession knew their own mind: both the fictional and non-fictional women depicted within its pages had agency over their actions, whether in their love life or their career. Magill's heroine Pauline is a quintessential example: she is a businesswoman who owns and manages her own dress shop. After becoming 'quite good pals' with Pauline at their motor-cycle club, Edgar attempts to propose:

> 'I want to – say, have you ever thought how useful a man would be around the place?'
> 'A *man*?' she said. 'Poof! This is a modiste's, not an ironmonger's. Or do you suggest he should stand outside all day in buttons and drag in possible customers?'[53]

Pauline's no-nonsense response reveals her as a typical New Woman, but Edgar mistakes her dismissive attitude for a lack of interest in romance. When he repeats his proposal, Pauline rebuffs him: '"You silly boy," she said, smiling. "Do you think because I am what they call a business woman that I don't want wooing?"'[54] This nuanced depiction of modern women and their desires is typical of the postwar *Royal*: in his July 1921 editorial, Baily writes that his female readers have, since the war, 'cast forth luv from their books and magazines, replacing it with love'.[55] Postwar romantic fiction was newly populated by strong female characters who wanted both romance and equality in their relationships. Equality is the key word in 'Gossamer': Edgar's eventual success as a dress designer only matters because he is able to enter into a partnership with Pauline, both as her husband and her business partner (Figure 6.2). In Helen McKie's illustration, Edgar becomes a modern knight in shining armour/well-cut suit, wooing Pauline by saving her business and thus allowing her to continue in a profession that she loves.

In these artist stories, the representation of female characters could not be further apart: Pauline has agency, ideas and ambition; Jean is uncertain over anything but her desire to see more looking-glasses in picture galleries. Reading these stories in context of their host publications, each one gives us an insight into the magazine's intended readership, whether a new breed of professional young women or an established and loyal readership wanting the solace of Victorian values and gender politics. To conclude, though, I would like to complicate this simple distinction by considering two artist stories which have more in common: 'God's Truth' by 'Sapper'

He went back to Pauline. . . . "I know!" he said, bursting in on her. "I'll go and ask old Harridge to lend it to me." [*Page* 244, *col.* 2.]

Figure 6.2 Helen McKie's illustration accompanying Robert Magill's story 'Gossamer for Goddesses'. © British Library Board, *The Royal*, January 1921.

(H. C. McNeile), which appeared in *The Strand* in January 1921, and Christine Castle's 'White Hyacinths', published in *The Royal* the following month. In both stories, the male writer protagonists are thrown into crisis when their love interest questions the type of art they produce. In 'God's Truth', Ruth Bannister tells Basil Milward that she hates his short stories '[b]ecause they're so cruel; because they're so true'.[56] Instead of the truth, women 'want what ought to be the truth – beauty, love, kindliness. We want to see visions and dream dreams. We want to forget. Don't you see?'[57] Almost the same exchange appears in 'White Hyacinths', in which Desirée Foster tries to persuade Dicky Whitney that neither editors nor readers want his stories with unhappy endings: 'people who are sick and sorry and sad like to forget it in a story where all the dreams come true, and both live happily ever after – oh, Dicky, can't you see?'[58] Both men resist the idea of altering their fiction: for Basil, the 'truth was all important; to sacrifice it for a sugar and spice effect struck him as cowardly – worse still, as being false to his art'.⁵⁹ Dicky feels a similar frustration with any reader, or editor, who told him otherwise: 'The editor, in Dicky's cheerfully expressed opinion, was an ass. Art was Art, and Truth was Truth, and no pitiful caterer to a Fool Public could alter that.'⁶⁰ Regardless of their beliefs, however, Dicky and Basil ultimately change their mind – and the tone of their fiction – for love, moving away from cynicism to idealism and from tragedies to potboilers.

The similarities between the two artist stories are striking, but more interesting is how each writer takes the same set-up and uses it to entirely different effect. In 'God's Truth', financial pressures mean that Basil has lost his earlier idealism, but his encounter with Ruth forces him to reconsider his life:

> 'Men *do* want ideals,' he said, gravely. 'More than ever to-day. But because they realize all too early in life that what you said is the truth – that ideals don't give you bread and butter – they forget them. They fold them up and put them away [. . .]. You made me take mine out. I – I – want help to make them fit.'⁶¹

Ruth rehabilitates Basil, helping him to recover his lost ideals and, in doing so, to write fiction that combines artistic integrity with financial stability. As such, the story vindicates the middlebrow values perpetuated by *The Strand*, despite the fact that McNeile was himself viewed more as a lowbrow than a middlebrow writer during this period. Lise Jaillant argues that, in the years following the Great War, McNeile was seen as a 'lightweight', a 'mere entertainer': perhaps Basil Milward's attempts to slough off his existing literary reputation and produce something more worthy were based on McNeile's own experiences – or at least his aspirations.⁶² Whatever his public perception, the conclusion to McNeile's story nevertheless provides the 'comforting sense of stability and continuity in a changing world' that *The Strand* offered its readers.⁶³ It is no coincidence that Ruth and Basil first meet in a glade, interrupted only by a brook that 'gurgled and bubbled its way through the heat of the summer afternoon' and a 'blackbird pouring out his song ecstatically'.⁶⁴ This is a mythical, nostalgic vision of an England, and a way of life, that has been lost. Ruth, whose family owns the land, represents an opportunity for Basil to recapture traditional English values: 'by God, Hastings,' Basil exclaims, 'it was like a breath of one's own childhood to hear her talk. The old simplicity came back—'.⁶⁵ In 'God's Truth', the artist story is mobilised to express McNeile's conservative, heteronormative vision of postwar reconstruction, one in which pure and idealised women offer damaged men physical and ideological salvation.

Christine Castle's 'White Hyacinths' offers no such nostalgia or reassurance. Indeed, Castle adapts the plot and structure used by McNeile to create a self-referential parody of artist stories such as 'God's Truth'. Desirée and Dicky break up when Dicky refuses to change the unhappy ending to his magnum opus, 'Blue Roses', yet his brutally realist approach to short fiction is vindicated when he wins first prize and £500 in a story competition. Upon receipt of the winnings, Dicky is reconciled with Desirée, and, as she points out, their story appears to have a happy ending. In the story's last few lines, however, Dicky blanches, realising with horror that the 'five hundred would not last for ever'. Concerned, Desirée asks him what is wrong:

> 'What are you frowning about?' asked Desirée, and Dicky kissed her again, this time between the eyes.
> 'I have an idea,' he said grimly, 'for a potboiler.'[66]

This clever dénouement subverts reader expectations by not providing (or at least complicating) a happy ending. The ending might be happy for Desirée, who gets both her man and her own way, but it is decidedly unhappy for Dicky, who is forced to abandon his ideals in order to keep Desirée supplied with bouquets of white hyacinths. Indeed, the placement of Dicky's kiss and his grim tone suggest that the inspiration for the potboiler might run along the lines of 'suffering artist kills demanding wife'. With this final twist on the anticipated happy ending, Castle satirises not just the figure of the artist or even artist stories but magazine short fiction more broadly. In *Art and Commerce in the British Short Story*, Dean Baldwin explores the constraints placed upon writers of short fiction by editors and publishers with a preference for a 'cheerful tone, sympathetic characters, moral propriety and conventional plot'; by self-consciously playing with these conventions, 'White Hyacinths' invites its readers to share the story's metafictional joke.[67] It creates the impression that Castle, and by extension *The Royal*, had faith in its readers: they are not passive consumers of formulaic fiction but rather intelligent and critical readers. To borrow a term from Pierre Bourdieu, the story's ideal reader would have enough 'cultural capital' not only to identify the archetypal features of an artist's story, but also to understand when it was being subtly satirised. Through his editorials, Baily consistently sought to give his readers a sense of agency and ownership over the magazine and its contents: publishing clever, metafictional artist stories like 'White Hyacinths' constituted a key part of his editorial strategy, with humour reinforcing a sense of community between *The Royal*'s readers and its producers.

That is not to say, however, that every story published within the pages of *The Strand* or *The Royal* toed the magazine's line: as we have seen, magazines are heterogeneous, messy spaces, with short stories as likely to subvert the title's values as to uncritically regurgitate them. With its self-referential play on the ubiquitous happy ending, 'White Hyacinths' is a case in point. Yet this air of subversion, the sense of peering behind the curtain or of being brought into the joke, itself came to define the postwar *Royal*. It is possible to discern a difference, even if a very small one, between the 1921 artist stories in these rival publications, whether in each piece's tone, style or moral (or lack thereof). Indeed, it is often easier to identify differences between pieces published in *The Strand* and *The Royal* than it is to find tonal or ideological similarities between short stories published within the same magazine. McNeile's nostalgic, conservative 'God's Truth' constructs a very different philosophy of art and vision of the world than Roberts' madcap and irreverent 'Brown', in which Literature is really just a backdrop for a caper involving a stolen shoulder of mutton. Yet it is these artist stories' female characters, in particular, which expose the difference between a magazine with a dynamic young editor (Baily was just eighteen when he became the editor of *The Royal* in 1912) responsible for a postwar reorientation towards young women, and a conservative magazine with an established male readership under the tenure of an editor who had already been in post for three decades. In my introduction, I noted that many short fiction writers from this period typically wrote across half a dozen or more magazines, but it is interesting to note that none of the writers discussed here published in both *The Strand* and *The Royal*. This lack of crossover may be a coincidence, but it also suggests that Greenhough-Smith and Baily published writers and stories that would appeal to different readers and prompt different responses. In this essay, I have used artist stories as a way into the complex relationship between short fiction writers, the stories they produced, and the magazines in which those stories were published, but the possibilities for future studies into short fiction in standard illustrated popular magazines are almost infinite. In the words of *The Times*'s 1949 obituary for *The Strand*, the popular fiction magazine 'still offers endless enchantment' for readers and critics alike.[68]

This research was supported by the Arts and Humanities Research Council (grant number 1071124).

Notes

1. Ashley, *Age of the Storytellers*.
2. See Stephensen-Payne, *Galactic Central*, <http://www.philsp.com> (last accessed 1 September 2020).
3. See, for instance, Cranfield, *Twentieth-Century Victorian*, and Ashley, *Adventures in the Strand*.
4. See Baldwin, *Art and Commerce in the British Short Story*, Chan, *Economy of the Short Story*, and Jackson, *George Newnes and the New Journalism*.
5. See Dugan, *Baroness Orczy's* The Scarlet Pimpernel.
6. Baily, *Twenty-Nine Years' Hard Labour*, p. 155.
7. Wees, *Vorticism and the English Avant-Garde*, pp. 9–11, 38–41, 107–8.
8. Representative *Daily Mirror* headlines include 'The Futurist Tea-Party' (17 February 1914), p. 7; 'How Would a Futurist Diet' (26 May 1914), p. 5; and 'Futurist Guardrooms?' (2 November 1915), p. 12.
9. See D'hoker, 'Artist Stories of the 1890s'.
10. Baily, *Twenty-Nine Years' Hard Labour*, p. 157.
11. See Brown and Grover, *Middlebrow Literary Cultures*.
12. Neacey, 'Introduction', p. 11.
13. Neacey, 'Introduction', p. 18; 'The Bronze Caster' is reprinted in *Selected Stories*, pp. 29–40.
14. Morley Roberts, 'Brown of Boomoonoomana', *The Strand*, 61.363 (March 1921), pp. 207–19 (p. 216).
15. Ibid. p. 210.
16. In a December 1919 diary entry, Anaïs Nin associates a 'floppy bow tie' with artists. See Nin, *Linotte*, p. 389.
17. 'Multi-vocal texts' is Chris Mourant's term: see Mourant, *Katherine Mansfield and Periodical Culture*, p. 5. See also Patrick Collier's discussion of the 'polyvocal' *John O'London's Weekly*, '"Quite ordinary men and women": *John O'London's Weekly* and the Meaning of Authorship', in Collier, *Modern Print Artefacts*, pp. 94–140.
18. Sarah Bernhardt, 'Love Wins', *The Strand*, 61.361 (January 1921), pp. 3–12.
19. Ibid. p. 3.
20. Priestley, 'High, Low, Broad', p. 166.
21. 'The Humorous Art of "Fougasse"', *The Strand*, 61.365 (May 1921), pp. 461–4; 'Dulac as Caricaturist', *The Strand*, 61.366 (June 1921), pp. 528–32; Arthur Lawrence, 'Phil May: Some Unpublished Drawings', *The Strand*, 62.369 (September 1921), pp. 235–40; and W. Heath Robinson, 'The Home-Made Car', *The Strand*, 62.368 (August 1921), pp. 178–82.
22. Reginald Pound, 'Fifty Years of Scene Painting: An Interview with

Mr. Joseph Harker', *The Strand*, 61.362 (February 1921), pp. 173–8, and Winston Churchill, 'Painting as a Pastime', *The Strand*, 62.372 (December 1921), pp. 535–44, and 63.373 (January 1922), pp. 13–20.
23. Churchill, 'Painting as a Pastime' (December 1921), p. 543.
24. T. Joyce [Joyce Cary], '"On the Line": An Academy Story', *The Strand*, 61.365 (May 1921), pp. 454–60 (p. 454–5).
25. See Fisher (ed.), *Joyce Cary Remembered*, p. 52.
26. Joyce [Cary], '"On the Line"', pp. 457, 459–60.
27. F. E. Baily, 'Mr. Editor – His Page', *The Royal*, 47.280 (February 1922), p. 277.
28. Ibid. p. 277.
29. Robert Magill, 'Gossamer for Goddesses', *The Royal*, 45.267 (January 1921), pp. 239–44 (p. 239).
30. Ibid. p. 243.
31. Ibid. p. 243.
32. Griffin, *Satire*, pp. 6–7.
33. Baily, 'Mr. Editor' (February 1922), p. 277.
34. F. E. Baily, 'Mr. Editor – His Page', *The Royal*, 45.270 (April 1921), p. 439.
35. Ibid. p. 439.
36. Reginald Pound, *The Strand, 1891–1950* (London: Heinemann, 1966), p. 7.
37. Ibid. p. 65. Greenhough-Smith was editor of *The Strand* from 1891–1930.
38. Ibid. p. 105.
39. Pittard, '"Cheap, Healthful Literature"', p. 2.
40. Jackson, *George Newnes*, p. 92.
41. Pound, *The Strand*, p. 70.
42. West, 'Cover Stars and Covert Addresses', pp. 88–9.
43. Baily, *Twenty-Nine Years' Hard Labour*, p. 156.
44. Ibid. p. 156.
45. Elinor Glyn, 'How I Would Bring Up a Girl', *The Royal*, 45.267 (January 1921), pp. 212–17. The other titles in the series were 'How I Would Bring Up a Boy' (February 1921, pp. 284–9), 'How I Would Educate a Husband' (March 1921, pp. 392–6) and 'How I Would Educate a Wife' (April 1921, pp. 462–6).
46. Glyn, 'How I Would Bring Up a Girl', pp. 212–13.
47. Ibid. p. 217.
48. Joyce [Cary], '"On the Line"', p. 457.
49. Ibid. p. 458.
50. Ibid. p. 460.
51. Ruskin, 'Of Queen's Gardens', p. 101.
52. Jackson, *George Newnes*, p. 88.
53. Magill, 'Gossamer for Goddesses', pp. 239–40.
54. Ibid. p. 240.

55. F. E. Baily, 'Mr. Editor – His Page', *The Royal*, 46.273 (July 1921), p. 179.
56. 'Sapper' [H. C. McNeile], 'God's Truth', *The Strand*, 61.361 (January 1921), pp. 72–9 (p. 74).
57. Ibid. p. 74.
58. Christine Castle, 'White Hyacinths', *The Royal*, 45.268 (February 1921), pp. 290–7 (p. 295).
59. 'Sapper' [McNeile], 'God's Truth', p. 73.
60. Castle, 'White Hyacinths', p. 291.
61. 'Sapper' [McNeile], 'God's Truth', p. 79.
62. Jaillant, 'Sapper, Hodder Stoughton, and the Popular Literature of the Great War', pp. 140, 158.
63. Jackson, *George Newnes*, p. 90.
64. 'Sapper' [McNeile], 'God's Truth', p. 72.
65. Ibid. p. 76.
66. Castle, 'White Hyacinths', p. 291.
67. Baldwin, *Art and Commerce in the British Short Story*, p. 93.
68. Anon., 'Farewell to the "Strand"', *The Times* (14 December 1949), p. 5.

Chapter 7

Fiction for the Woman of To-day: The Modern Short Story in *Eve*

Alice Wood

In 1919, the London publishers of *The Sphere* and *The Tatler* launched *Eve*, a new magazine for women. *Eve* was edited (at least initially) by the editor of *The Tatler*, Edward 'Teddy' Huskinson, and was conceived as a sister publication to that weekly society paper.[1] The new magazine drew its name from *The Tatler*'s well-loved column 'The Letters of Eve', which depicted the amusing exploits of its frivolous upper-class heroine and was written by Olivia Maitland-Davidson with the distinctive illustrations of Annie Fish ('FISH').[2] *Tatler*'s fictional Eve gained such popularity in wartime that she spawned four books and a series of short films, *The Adventures of Eve* (1918), starring Eileen Molyneux.[3] *Eve* capitalised on this success while expanding the character of 'Eve' far beyond Davidson and Fish's column. 'Whereas in the *Tatler*, Eve spoke with one voice and bore one image,' as Elizabeth M. Sheehan has observed, 'in *Eve* she appears in different guises.'[4] 'Eve' appeared in the title of many of the magazine's routine features – including 'Eve and her Car', 'Eve in her Garden', 'Eve at the Play', 'Eve at Golf' and 'Eve Goes Shopping' – and was voiced by two regular columns, 'And Eve Said unto Adam' and 'Eve in PARadISe', each offering a gossipy, satirical account of society news, fashions and events, the former from London/England and the latter from Paris. This elastic persona – representing the young, smart, modern, wealthy, female socialite in all her guises – was positioned as both the magazine's central consciousness, directing its content (while concealing its male editor), and the collective consciousness of its audience, epitomising their interests and aspirations. 'It is the sincere wish of "EVE" that this, her first number,' the November 1919 issue asserted, 'should prove to be a milestone marking the foundation of a long and lasting friendship between you, fair reader, and herself.'[5] In January 1921, in 'Eve and Her Books', the magazine's readers themselves were framed as 'ultra-modern Eves, so frank and so free'.[6]

This chapter explores short fiction in *Eve* that was directed, as was the magazine as a whole, to 'the women of to-day'.[7] In print from November 1919 to April 1929, *Eve* began life as a high-class woman's monthly and moved to weekly publication in March 1920. Priced at a shilling and printed on large glossy paper, *Eve* targeted an affluent, leisured audience of upper- and middle-class women, though it claimed to address 'the woman of taste [. . .] whether rich or poor'.[8] On 2 March 1921, the magazine merged with the more established *Lady's Pictorial*, in circulation since 1881, and the *Women's Supplement* of *The Times* to become *Eve: The Lady's Pictorial* (for simplicity, this chapter uses the short title *Eve* throughout). With the amalgamation of these three papers, an editorial statement 'To Our Readers – Old and New' declared the aim of *Eve*'s editor 'to produce a clean, healthy English paper' catering 'for the woman of to-day and to-morrow who is interested in sports and in the open-air life, and yet retains live mental interests and a knowledge of affairs intimately connected with woman's domestic life'.[9] This eclectic mix of content, ranging from fox hunting and golf to arts and the home, was characteristic of *Eve* throughout its ten-year run. In 1926, the magazine absorbed another long-running periodical, the *Gentlewoman*, before, in 1929, being itself absorbed within the monthly *Britannia and Eve* following a merge with the current affairs journal *Britannia*.[10] During its decade of publication, *Eve* supplied its readers with society and celebrity news, fashion and beauty advice, fiction, recipes, home decoration ideas, travel tips and reviews of art, books, dance, theatre, music and cinema, including commentary on modernist experiments in the arts, all lavishly illustrated with a central colour photogravure supplement in most issues. Billed as 'The New Paper for the New Woman', the magazine profiled and celebrated not only aristocratic women and debutantes but also women who had achieved success in a variety of public and professional fields, including writers, actresses, dancers, singers, university graduates, politicians and sportswomen.[11] Its regular book columns attended to texts debating modern ideas about gender roles, love, courtship and sex – such as Havelock Ellis's *Little Essays in Love and Virtue* (1922) – as well as contemporary experiments in literature, including Virginia Woolf's sacrifice of plot for 'mental "atmosphere"' in *To the Lighthouse* (1927).[12] Woolf's writing appeared directly in *Eve* when her essay 'The Waxworks at the Abbey' was published in the magazine in May 1928, as did the writing of other modernist and middlebrow authors such as Elizabeth Bowen, Winifred Holtby, Storm Jameson, Rose Macaulay and Edith Sitwell.[13] This chapter chiefly turns attention to short fiction by less well-known writers in *Eve*, however, through which we might contextualise literary experiments in the magazine by writers better known today. By surveying dissident stories by familiar and forgotten authors, I seek to demonstrate the broad spirit of narrative play that characterised the fiction printed in this self-consciously modern magazine.

'In its exuberance and its determination to break with the past', Cynthia L. White has observed, '*Eve* embodied the spirit of the "roaring twenties".'[14] The magazine was closest to and rivalled *Vogue* (UK) in its fusion of society and fashion content, but *Eve* was lighter in tone, more frivolous in outlook and less uniformly polished in design. The inclusion of fiction also significantly distinguished *Eve* from *Vogue*, which published virtually no fiction in the same period. In contrast, *Eve* typically printed one or two short stories in each issue, sometimes accompanied by an instalment from a serialised novel. The magazine's bumper Christmas numbers, in the tradition of many nineteenth-century periodicals, were packed with extra fiction by celebrity authors, such as D. H. Lawrence and Edith Wharton. Regular issues of *Eve* printed stories of variable quality from new and emerging writers alongside fiction by popular household names such as E. M. Delafield and Stephen McKenna. As well as commissioning professional writers, *Eve* invited and published contributions from readers through essay and fiction competitions. Genre fiction abounded: detective stories, romance fiction and weird tales were common. The magazine specialised in witty, intentionally modern short stories, which evoked and satirised contemporary social mores or literary styles.

As the emphasis on contemporaneity in its framing of its audience suggests, *Eve* was avowedly modern in outlook: debating new models of femininity, new ideas about psychology and sexuality, changing gender relations and modernist aesthetics. Yet, at the same time, the magazine upheld traditional conservative values such as respect for aristocracy and marriage. Vike M. Plock has identified how *Eve*'s 'miscellaneous columns effectively negotiated a possible tension between tradition and modernity by alternating the occasional approval of progressive outlooks with a thinly veiled promotion of patriarchal standards and nationalist viewpoints'.[15] Plock aligns *Eve*'s outlook with Alison Light's notion of 'conservative modernity' as 'the dominant mood' in interwar Britain, when radical shifts in gender identities and the restructuring of English nationalism were entwined with 'a conservative embracing of modernity, shaped by the experience of dislocation after the First World War'.[16]

Eve's positioning as 'a clean, healthy English paper' – in contrast to 'papers of a similar type' that 'lean too much upon American and Parisian ideas' – indeed reflects conservatism and the magazine's unshakeable faith in nationalism, patriarchy and class hierarchy, as well as conveying its editor's desire to market *Eve* as a superior alternative to *Vogue*.[17] This tension between modernity and convention was reflected too in the magazine's short stories, which ranged from formulaic and conservative plots to experimental and subversive narratives. This chapter argues that *Eve* provided a productive space for short stories by women writers that, in more or less radical ways, probed new models of femininity and new models for heterosexual relationships. My focus here is fiction that is determinedly modern without being modernist, that enabled *Eve*'s readers to explore alternatives to patriarchal gender norms and marriage.

New femininities/new relationships

Eve's first number included a brief fictional sketch humorously caricaturing the magazine's ideal female reader. Billed as 'A Little Story by V. M.', 'Aramintha and the Ancients' functions as internal advertisement as well as entertainment and was evidently written specifically for publication in the magazine.[18] Set in Paris in 1919, the story introduces its title character crossing the Pont de la Concorde wearing a 'smart frock' and clasping her 'copy of EVE'.[19] Aramintha is presented as the kind of woman that *Eve* imagines as its audience, or rather, she is the feminine ideal that *Eve* imagines its readers will admire and aspire to emulate. Young, beautiful, financially comfortable, fashion-conscious, pleasure-seeking and somewhat irreverent in outlook, Aramintha makes the crowds 'envious' when she passes with 'her dainty figure', 'her slim ankles in cobweb silk' and her 'vanity bag [...] monogrammed in gold'.[20] As she hurries towards the Champs-Elysées to purchase a fur coat she has seen in the latest issue of *Eve*, the narrative breaks into free indirect discourse to describe how:

> She *wanted* THAT COAT! That most gorgeous fur coat! It had haunted her for ... hours! (Aramintha was accustomed to rapid realisations.) Ever since she had bought the current copy of the paper she carried so preciously and had seen its glossiness and exquisite silhouette in the centre of the furrier's page she had ardently desired THAT COAT.[21]

The sudden shift into Aramintha's thought processes using expressive punctuation, italics and upper-case letters for emphasis (it is clumsily done) recalls narrative techniques associated with the recent psychological trend in fiction. This parallel further boosts *Eve*'s perceived modernity by suggesting the magazine's contact with avant-garde aesthetics just as A. E. Johnson's essay on 'The Russian Ballet' does in the same issue.[22] As Aramintha considers the economies necessary to afford the fur coat – 'No more taxis! [...] No more white gloves' – and determines to '*walk* home—and boil a modest egg on a spirit-lamp', she stumbles upon a hotel offering a four-course lunch for the 'incredible' price of four francs.[23] Inside, she is watched as she eats by three men at a nearby table, 'prosperous-looking old souls' whom the story names 'the three Ancients'.[24] Aramintha imagines herself with three such 'rich and generous' uncles and how that would empower her shopping in the 'vast showrooms of the rue de la Paix'.[25] The three men each send over a card appealing for her acquaintance, at which Aramintha is 'insulted' at first, but then, thinking 'it was, perhaps, *rather* flattering', writes on each card with amusement 'Outside Ramilions, 5.30' just 'to see if they'd be there'.[26] By four o'clock, we are told, 'for this is a fairy story', Aramintha is gaily reunited with her beau, a soldier named Henri, who has now suddenly returned for ten days' leave with the happy news that his 'old and entirely objectionable' uncle Gustave has died, presumably – the narrative urges us to infer it – fulfilling the role of the 'rich and generous' uncle in death by leaving Henri money.[27] Thus the story closes at 5:33pm at the allotted place as 'three faithful and punctual Ancients' see Aramintha pass by looking 'gorgeously happy, and happily gorgeous', but Aramintha does not see them as she is 'busy gazing at her reflection ... in Henri's eyes'.[28] Drawing on modern narrative methods, this promotional sketch depicts a markedly modern model of femininity that is impetuous, chic, conspicuously materialistic and eschews automatic deference to men or elders. Yet, this version of the modern girl is utterly dependent on traditional social and economic structures. The narrative closes with the glib assertion that '[t]his is a moral story', but if it conveys any message beyond endorsing *Eve*'s modernity and the value of its fashion pages, it is seemingly that the postwar leisured classes can behave frivolously and without moral scruples precisely because they are the beneficiaries of inherited wealth.[29]

This hedonistic model of femininity, and the hedonism of modern relationships more broadly, is presented as a consequence of the Great War by another short story published in *Eve* in March 1920.

The narrator of Jean Anderson's 'Incidental Music' posits that 'after the drab, crimson-flecked horrors of the front', a 'fierce need of easy pleasures, of lights and music' has sent young and old 'in greedy quest of enjoyment'.[30] This story depicts a couple who are 'married and modern', 'young, good-looking, wealthy', and pass their time socialising with others, meeting only at mealtimes and '[u]sually at other people's houses'.[31] Ted and Mary have 'both done their bit during the war' and now are each so concerned that the other 'should have "a good time"' that they have drifted apart, neglecting each other and their young son 'somewhere in the far-off nursery of a far-off wing'.[32] In this satirical and moralistic tale, a servants' strike forces the couple together to care for their son, who asks that his parents come 'of'ener' to his nursery so that he can see them 'really-trooly' instead of only in 'their photographs at house parties and dances' in 'the tattered copies of "The Tatler"' piled on his book-shelf.[33] The story's implied censure of the glamour and decadence of contemporary high society reverberates with the society and gossip pages of *Eve*, companion to *The Tatler*. *Eve*'s society content included photospreads showing notable personages at play, although usually engaged in desirable upper-class leisure activities – such as hunting, skiing or holidaying on the Riviera – rather than dancing. Discussions of fashionable nightspots and the latest dance crazes were reserved for the magazine's gossip columns, 'And Eve Said unto Adam' and 'Eve in PARadISe', which maintained an ironic, tongue-in-cheek distance from all their subject matter through the humorous monologue of their frivolous fictional narrators. In 'Incidental Music', both Ted and Mary feel jealousy as they watch each other dance with other partners, though they quickly suppress it. The couple's reconnection with their son is sentimentally depicted as the tonic they need to break the cycle of their unhappy revelries. After an afternoon of 'gaily riotous' games and having 'discovered that romping with a small boy is the most strenuous sport in the world', Ted and Mary pass the evening together 'joyously, tenderly' and are finally reunited as they step into 'the rosy warmth' of Mary's boudoir with confessions of their loneliness and the realisation that neither they nor their son need be lonely anymore.[34] Anderson's story explains, and to some extent excuses, the postwar hedonism associated with the generation who came to be known as the 'Bright Young Things', but also critiques the behaviour of these '[p]oor, punished, toyless, grown-up children'.[35] 'Incidental Music' closes with a conservative view of marriage and child-rearing, suggesting that Ted and Mary will be more fulfilled by living quietly and companionably together with an active role in raising their son.

Eve published a good deal of amusing, light-hearted and sometimes risqué short stories of this type, depicting changing gender roles and the perceived contemporary trend for increasingly casual romantic and sexual liaisons among the younger generation. Marthe Troly-Curtin's 'The Ukulele Lovers', printed in *Eve* in February 1928, like Anderson's 'Incidental Music', portrays the radical possibilities of modern relationships, but ultimately deems them unfulfilling and reverts to a more traditional view.[36] Troly-Curtin was a novelist and regular named contributor to *Eve*, author of the routine column 'Salted Almonds' and occasional reviewer for the early column 'Eve and her Books'. 'The Ukulele Lovers' presents one scene, the interactions of an unnamed couple in a nightclub, narrated by a spectator from a nearby table. Its narrator is anonymous, but her/his subjective view and close proximity to the couple suffuses the story, which begins when '[t]he night (though sophisticated) was still young' as it is 'barely two'.[37] '[T]he term "barely" springs to my pen,' we are told, 'suggested, perhaps, by the backless frock with the *obi* bow of the woman at the next table'.[38] Considerable space is given to describing the appearance of this '"woman," [. . .] really quite a girl under her make-up', who is an exaggerated embodiment of the flapper fashions of the day, with 'a delicate terra-cotta' complexion, '*puce*' lips, her hair 'shorn almost to the skin', and a 'corsage, modestly high in front', that 'allowed you, nevertheless, to count her ribs from the opening under her arms'.[39] 'She was incredibly thin, delightfully decadent, and absurdly attractive', the narrator reflects: 'But had she been ten years younger and belonged to poor parents, the N.S.P.C.C might have had something to say about her emaciated condition'.[40] The young woman's waif-like appearance and shorn head evoke the subversive androgyny and gender fluidity of dress and hair styles in this period, which were routinely profiled in *Eve*'s fashion pages with sketches of impossibly long, thin female bodies with cropped or shingled hair in the straight, loose-waisted dresses and tailored skirt-suits popular at this time. Her male companion similarly challenges conventional gender stereotypes by holding 'a long cigarette-holder', while 'she contented herself with a small cigar'.[41] The narrator informs us that the couple 'spoke very little, danced a lot and drank a great deal', until the woman takes out 'a beautiful little fan from Paris, a reproduction of a Watteau scene' depicting '[s]hepherds in tender blues [. . .] playing the lute with silly and delightful amorousness' to 'shepherdesses in rose-coloured paniers, lazy and idyllic', among 'a dream landscape of pastel hues'.[42] In response to this 'sweetly pretentious pastoral', the woman asks her partner why he can't take her to the countryside, to which he responds scornfully: 'Well, you don't mean to say you'd like to sit on the grass the whole day like all those blighters in the fan, doing nothing, listening to me for hours playing the ukulele!'[43] Somewhat crestfallen, she remarks that it 'must have been rather fun living in those days—with the men putting themselves out to fascinate you, and saying nice things'.[44] 'The Ukulele Lovers' briefly explores the subversive potential of more fluid gender norms and less restrictive codes of courtship and sexual behaviour, but ends with sentimental longing for the stable gender roles and established courtship rituals of a mythical bygone age. As these 'two youthful, serious skeletons' take to the dance floor again, the narrator sees 'in the girl's eyes a sort of hungry look – a wistfulness' and speculates about what she really wanted; 'could it be . . . *Romance?*'[45]

This suggestive narrative appeared in the mid-February 1928 Valentine's Day issue of *Eve*, which featured a cartoon on its front cover captioned 'Shades of St. Valentine!' Like the fan in Troly-Curtin's story, this cover sentimentalises the courtship rituals of the past with an image of a couple in eighteenth-century dress; the man kneels in a blue tail coat with an arrow in his chest and a bouquet of roses by his side before a coquettish woman in a pastel pink, full-skirted, puff-sleeved dress, while Cupid watches from above with his bow. Inside the issue, the theme of romance was picked up and debated by a range of features. Just as 'The Ukulele Lovers' conveys longing for a traditional model of heterosexual courtship, a two-page article on 'Unromantic Miss 1928' by Norman Venner similarly despairs that 'Blushing, Innocence, Sweet Lavender, petticoats, white gloves, love-letters, girlishness' all seem to be things of the past for the 'modern young woman'.[46] Venner's essay voices 'the deepest possible admiration' for the 'hard-headed' young woman of 1928, who is 'frank and open', 'hides nothing – or very little', 'is capable of friendship' and 'can do a job of work in a way which makes a number of men I know quite nervous'.[47] Yet, despite his praise of the modern business girl and professional woman – from the girl 'who works in an office' to the woman with 'a B.Sc Honours' and 'a post in an industrial chemist's works' – Venner cannot comprehend how, without embracing romance, these women will marry and why they would not wish to.[48] In contrast, Richard King's column 'Talking about Books . . .' in this Valentine's Day issue, opens with the reflection: 'Whatever may be said against the greater freedom, even the laxity, of life in this post-war world, this at least is in its favour – very rarely nowadays do you see what I can only call the "tragedy of the unmarried daughter".'[49] King welcomes women's right to work and make their own way in life, whether or not they marry, and the end of the middle-class practice of keeping a girl 'at home to be a companion to her parents, [. . .] guarded from any real contact with the world'.[50] Troly-Curtin's story participates in this lively issue-wide discussion of new models of femininity, new relations between the sexes, and the changing position of marriage in postwar British society. Indeed, the latter portion of 'The Ukulele Lovers' appears on the same page as the last paragraph of King's book column, in which his earlier progressive outlook is tempered by a glowing review of R. Brimley Johnson's *A Study of Jane Austen* that declares Austen's novels, with their central themes of courtship and marriage, 'one of the endless joys of life'.[51] The radical alternatives this story presents to strictly delineated gender identities and early marriage can be safely explored in the context of this issue's wider debate of modern relationships, which overwhelmingly leans – as does Troly-Curtin's story at its close – towards conservative yearning for committed monogamy and a revival of romance.

Despite the wealth of public and private roles opening up to women in the interwar period, women's domestic identities as wives, mothers and housekeepers remained a central concern for women's magazines at this time. In May 1923, *Eve* published a short story titled 'An Ideal Home' by Jan Struther, penname of Joyce Anstruther, better known for her 'Mrs Miniver' column for *The Times*, her novel of the same name, and the Hollywood film adaptation of this book from 1942.[52] Struther's story provides a much more satirical perspective on the middle-class housewife than *Mrs Miniver*, gleefully poking fun at the contemporary ideal of the modern industrious homemaker. Driven by the marketing strategies of manufacturers of household goods and appliances, women's domestic labour was recast in this period as skilled work requiring expert knowledge, good management and, crucially, up-to-date specialist equipment. Drawing on '[t]he rhetoric of scientific management and industrial rationalisation', as Judy Giles has identified, interwar housewives were framed as modern rational planners and efficient household managers, whether doing their housework alone or with the aid of paid domestic staff.[53] This framing was most evident in the new range of domestic consumer magazines emerging 'for middle and lower-middle class consumption' in the wake of the First World War – often termed service magazines, of which *Good Housekeeping* (launched in Britain in March 1922) is a prime example – but it was also visible in *Eve*'s occasional features for the hostess and home decoration pages, and in the magazine's advertisements for domestic appliances.[54] The Western Electric Domestic Clothes Washer advertised in *Eve* in December 1922, for example, promised to clean clothes 'in double quick time' and bring 'efficient working' to the home, while an advertisement from the General Electric Company in *Eve* in September 1923 positioned electricity as 'the silent servant in the home' which makes 'housework [. . .] no longer drudgery', advocating the use of the company's 'Magnet' electrical appliances, including an iron, kettle and toaster, 'to reduce living costs, overcome the domestic problem, and still have more time to yourself'.[55] Struther's 'An Ideal Home' satirises this commercial discourse and the era's prizing of domestic efficiency. This humorous tale depicts Emily Murple, a practical woman to whom '[n]othing out of the ordinary ever happened', until she attempts to save her marriage by modernising her home through a trip to the Ideal Home Exhibition at Olympia, an annual event first held in 1908.[56] Emily is ill-suited to her husband Geoffrey, 'a nice man' but 'a dreamer', and their marriage is 'a failure' due to their incompatible temperaments.[57] 'Being matter-of-fact', Emily decides their unhappiness 'must be something to do with the housekeeping', because 'men, she had always understood, were perfectly contented so long as they were perfectly comfortable' and so 'evidently [Geoffrey] must need better food and better service' and 'she must run the house in a better way'.[58] With money scarce and 'a larger staff [. . .] out of the question', Emily decides 'to lay out a little on labour-saving appliances, and try to increase efficiency'.[59] She heads to the Ideal Home Exhibition, where she views all manner of ridiculous labour-saving devices, from 'a combination coal-scuttle and meat-safe' to 'a patent mincing-machine-musical-box' that emits 'popular tunes from one end and sausage-meat from the other' when its handle is turned.[60] The story descends further into farce as Emily falls asleep inside a show cottage where she awakes to find herself locked in the exhibition overnight and is drawn into conversation with a collection of talking household appliances. After a vacuum-cleaner, gas-stove, saucepans and cutlery beg Emily to 'buy us [. . .] buy us, and your home will be perfection', Struther's story shifts from the absurd to the sentimental as a more 'subtle voice, full of secret laughter and boundless understanding and whimsicality' assures her that what her marriage needs cannot be bought in a catalogue.[61] Returning home with her labour-saving goods the following morning, Emily is surprised to find her husband gone and wonders how 'she had failed him', not realising it was a 'Sense of Humour' that she spoke with (or dreamt) in the Ideal Home show cottage and that she so sorely lacks.[62] This short comic story challenges the dominant domestic ideal and consumer culture upheld by commercial women's magazines of the period, but does so through an equally conservative endorsement of good humour and understanding as the saviour of any marriage.

Elizabeth Bowen's 'Making Arrangements', printed in *Eve* in November 1925, offers a darker portrayal of marital relations.[63] Bowen had published her first collection of short fiction in 1923, but had yet to publish a novel when *Eve* welcomed this story into its 1925 Christmas number with an editorial caption describing it as a 'finely drawn character study [. . .] brimful of atmosphere'.[64] 'Making Arrangements' presents another married couple who are ill-suited in temperament; in this case the husband, Hewson Blair, excels at dealing with practical details while his wife, Margery, is flighty and amusing. At the story's opening, Margery has blithely left Hewson for 'a young man' called Leslie and written to her husband requesting that he 'make all arrangements, [. . .] like getting the divorce and sending [her] clothes on'.[65] The letter is written in a light, confident tone that assumes Hewson's cooperation, secure in the knowledge that he will 'manage it all beautifully'.[66] If our sympathies are initially directed to the cuckolded husband wronged by his narcissistic wife, this allegiance is challenged as the story unravels. 'Hewson never conceived or imagined, but he intended', the narrator explains, and Hewson had chosen Margery because 'he had always intended to marry an amusing wife – a pretty little thing with charm' that would be 'becoming to him'.[67] Brief flashbacks to their life together reveal the lack of affinity between them. Hewson is preoccupied with his social status and the good opinion of others, far above the emotional life of himself or his wife. Indeed, Hewson is so unaccustomed to emotion that in the days following Margery's departure he is not 'sorrowful, venomous, or angry', but busies himself with making new arrangements for his housekeeping.[68] This equanimity ends, however, when Hewson enters his wife's bedroom to select her clothes for packing and the story takes a gothic turn. Opening the wardrobe door, he is startled as '[f]rom the dusk within, cedar-scented and cavernous, Margery leapt out at him'.[69] Haunted by her presence while surrounded by her things, he snatches one of Margery's dresses from the wardrobe and, apparently inexplicably, tears it. Only when Hewson anticipates her anger at the torn dress does he begin to feel his own fury. After ripping the dress 'effortlessly from throat to hem', he looks down at all her dresses laid out before him and imagines they possess 'the irrepressible palpitation of that vitality she had infused into them'.[70] The intense description that follows of Hewson's interactions with his wife's dresses suggests both bodily violence and a sexual encounter. As the clothes 'lay there dormant', he 'bent and touched' and 'brought down his two outspread hands slowly', turning his attention 'with dilated eyes' to a dress that 'lay stretched out and provocative and did not resist him'.[71] Hewson's simultaneous desire to touch the dresses and to 'crush, and crush, and crush' them is evidently fuelled by repressed emotion and suggests the complex interplay between power, control and sexual violence.[72] Usually acting only with intention, Hewson loses command of himself as he attempts to reassert his control and authority over his absent wife through the symbolic domination and destruction of her clothes. Hewson's actions, we are to understand, and perhaps also his wife's departure, stem from flawed expectations of marriage and the characteristically English suppression of feeling and desire. Bowen's sardonic narrative supplies a robust critique of middle-class repression, often a target for scorn in *Eve*, and of the conservative construct of marriage as a practical arrangement through which to gain or maintain social status, rather than a romantic and sexual union.

In 'The Scarecrow', published in *Eve* in September 1923, Radclyffe Hall critiques the pervasive social forces that stifle compassion, creativity and emotional and intellectual freedom.[73] Ostensibly a ghost story, 'The Scarecrow' follows in the tradition of nineteenth-century supernatural and weird tales exploring Victorian preoccupations with spiritualism and madness as well as cultural anxieties about changing gender relations and female sexuality – all themes picked up by this narrative. Hall's reputation chiefly rests on *The Well of Loneliness* (1928), famous for the scandal and obscenity trial prompted by its lesbian subject matter, though she was the author of a wide body of work including a volume of short stories, *Miss Ogilvy Finds Herself* (1934). Jana Funke notes that 'Hall is not generally known for her short fiction', though 'numerous short stories are among Hall's unpublished works'.[74] 'The Scarecrow' appears in Funke's 2016 edition of Hall's unpublished writings; its discovery in *Eve*, also traced by Plock, notably suggests the possibility that Hall published other stories in lesser-studied periodicals where they have yet to be found. Funke has observed that Hall's short fiction 'covers much ground in terms of style and genre', combining elements of realism, fantasy, fable and the gothic, while maintaining a focus on 'outsiders and outcasts, lost and lonely individuals looking for meaning and purpose and striving for a sense of connection and belonging in the world'.[75] Hall's *Eve* story depicts the spirit of a vagabond poet who died friendless and alone, now trapped in the physical form of a scarecrow that has been dressed in his coat and hat. In life, the poet was said to be mad, the narrative tells us, because he was 'always friendly to beasts and birds'.[76] Ostracised by his community because his emotional openness and compassion deviated from social expectations of behaviour, the poet sought solace in nature and in the company of animals and birds before dying from starvation while sheltering in a barn. After death, the scarecrow/poet continues to speak to passing creatures – a field mouse, an owl and a rabbit – and is visited by a young girl, daughter of the owner of the barn in which the poet died, who is also called mad because she speaks with animals. Hall's story draws attention to society's cruel treatment of individuals who do not conform and, as will be shown shortly, affirms the value of these outsiders and the creativity and freedom they represent.

The notion of freedom was central to *Eve*'s conception of modern femininity, whether in relation to new modes of courtship, the adoption of less physically restrictive dress styles, or women's right to education and entry into the professions. A few pages away from Hall's story with its emphasis on the imaginative power and liberating potential of nature in this 19 September 1923 issue, for example, *Eve* printed two photographs of 'the Muriel Abbott dancers taking an early morning dose of *joie de vivre* in a delectable sea-side haunt much favoured by holiday-making Americans'.[77] Wearing short, loose, lightweight dresses, the young women move freely on the beach and in the water, throwing balls and pulling a fishing net. Such images of young female dancers at play or holding graceful poses in nature, including photographs of the Margaret Morris Summer Schools, featured in both *Eve* and British *Vogue* in this period, during which the natural movement in contemporary dance – epitomised by the style of Morris and Raymond and Isadora Duncan – was frequently held to exemplify the new physical, intellectual and sexual freedoms associated with modern femininity.[78] Yet, elsewhere, *Eve*'s portrayal of what its editor termed 'the open-air life' was inherently bound to more conservative values.[79] An image inset within the second page of 'The Scarecrow' shows four women on a riverbank, dressed stylishly in country suits as they pose facing the camera. The photograph's caption reads: 'A pause in fishing operations at Invercauld, on the Dee', and names from left to right, 'Miss Viola Meeking, Lady

Somers, Mrs. Wilfred Ashley and Lady Caroline Agar', informing us that Miss Meeking 'owns Richings Park in Buckinghamshire' and 'is Lady Somers's elder sister'.[80] In this photograph, and *Eve*'s many society snapshots in every issue, the image offers the reader a glimpse into the apparently carefree private lives of their subjects, but the caption emphasises that their public social role, usually defined by aristocratic title, parentage, marriage or ownership of property, underpins their value and remains ever important. The elevation of the women's activity to 'fishing operations' in this caption reflects *Eve*'s framing of leisure as a formalised, professional occupation for the wealthy, which conveys the extent to which, within the confines of polite society, an individual's interactions and conduct, even at rest or play in nature, are not free but are structured by rigid codes of behaviour. 'The Scarecrow' implicitly condemns these rigid social codes through its sympathetic treatment of the poet and the girl who visits him. 'Everyone is mad', says the scarecrow/poet, 'only some of us are madder than others'.[81]

In Hall's story, animals talk back, answering the scarecrow/poet when he asks first the field mouse and then the owl, before finally the girl, whether they know him and can tell me 'who I am'.[82] The use of patterning and repetition and the presence of talking animals evokes several narrative genres – a religious fable, children's story, or fairy tale – while the text also brings 'the barriers between the known and the unknown' to 'the brink of collapse' in a manner typical of the gothic uncanny.[83] The scarecrow's face takes on the physical characteristics of the poet, with his cheeks 'sunken as though from hunger' and 'his blue eyes [. . .] cloudy from many dreams', to such an extent that a passing doctor who attended the poet's body exclaims: 'By God! that scarecrow looks real [. . .] I thought, I thought – but it must have been the moonlight.'[84] The theme of entrapment runs throughout the narrative, from the scarecrow/poet's opening declaration that he 'can feel but [. . .] cannot move', to the sheepdog who is 'always chained' and the girl who fears her father 'will lock [her] away'.[85] Like the poet, the girl is also portrayed as too rare to survive in the cruel earthly world in which individual sensibility and behaviour must conform to social convention. She escapes incarceration at the end of the story only through death. Addressing the scarecrow as her 'beloved', she begs him: 'take me away [. . .] to the place where you go when the moon sets, to the place where no one is mad or sane, or angry or cruel, or sorrowful, any more'.[86] Funke has described this story's ending as 'a reconciliatory Christian salvation narrative' informed by Hall's subversive Catholic belief.[87] The girl lifts her hair to the scarecrow/poet's cheek and 'command[s]' him to look into her eyes, whereupon, perceiving God there, he is momentarily 'made whole' and takes her in his arms, leaving her body to be found 'dead on the ground, at the foot of a scarecrow'.[88] This story's alignment of female agency and sexuality with the divine is highly unorthodox. The girl herself seemingly occasions her own and the poet's salvation, acting as a conduit for God through the awakening and assertion of her desire for the poet. Evoking the macabre and the sublime, instinct, imagination and the power of nature, 'The Scarecrow' owes much to the eighteenth-century gothic, which is here fused with a religious vindication of the individual's right to freedom of thought, emotion and sexual expression in a manner that is as strikingly modern as the story's blending of narrative genres.

Conclusions

With its spirited negotiation of modern attitudes and art forms, *Eve* offered a receptive vehicle for writers of short fiction that was formally inventive, disruptive of conventional values, or illustrative of modern trends in behaviour, relationships and intellectual fashions. My analysis in this chapter has shown how short stories in *Eve* often probed new dissident possibilities for women while maintaining a distanced, ironic stance on modern models of femininity and new modes of courtship through humour or by reverting to a more conformist view in conclusion. Throughout its decade of publication, *Eve* embraced and debated modernity from a position of conservatism that was underpinned by deeply ingrained respect for class hierarchy and patriarchal heterosexual marriage. The magazine's eclectic content explored new opportunities opening up to women in the interwar period, changing views on sex and relationships and the experimental movement in the arts alongside reflecting core interests in the English aristocracy and domestic life. This chapter has demonstrated that *Eve* presented women writers of different kinds – emerging/established, populist/intellectual – with a productive space in which to engage with contemporary debates surrounding shifting gender roles and social mores as well as to experiment with narrative conventions and techniques. Fiction published here was often modern in subject and playful in form without being overtly modernist or securely middlebrow. *Eve*'s short stories for 'the woman of to-day' give twenty-first-century readers a window onto the conservative modernity of the 1920s and the formal diversity of magazine fiction from this era, unsettling some of the familiar assumptions and critical categories through which we analyse and organise the literature of this period.[89]

Notes

1. Early issues of *Eve* disclosed in small print on their internal cover that the magazine was 'edited by the Editor of "The Tatler"' (see November 1919, December 1919 and February 1920). This declaration was dropped when *Eve* moved to weekly publication in March 1920, after which the identity of the magazine's editor was withheld.
2. 'The Letters of Eve' column appeared in *The Tatler* from 1914 until 1920 and made 'FISH' a household name. Fish also produced covers for *Vanity Fair* in this period and illustrated for *Eve*, *Vogue*, *Harper's Bazaar* and other periodicals in the 1920s; see Mark Bryant, 'Fish, (Harriet) Annie [Anne] (1890–1964)', *Oxford Dictionary of National Biography*, Oxford University Press, 25 May 2006, <https://www.oxforddnb.com/view/10.1093/ref:odnb/9780198614128.001.0001/odnb-9780198614128-e-57152> (last accessed 1 September 2020).
3. *The First Book of Eve* has been digitised by the *Internet Archive* and is available at <https://archive.org/details/firstbookofeve00fish/page/n0> (last accessed 1 September 2020). Davidson's 'Letters of Eve' for *The Tatler* were reproduced in three further books (bibliographic details drawn from the British Library catalogue): *The New Eve: Drawn by Fish. Written and designed by Fowl* (London: John Lane, 1917): O. M. Davidson, *The Letters of Eve* (London: Constable & Co., 1918); and *The Third Eve Book: Drawn by Fish. Written and designed by Fowl* (London: John Lane, 1919). On *The Adventures of Eve* (1918), produced by J. L. V. Leigh for Gaumont, see Cook, *Early British Animation*, pp. 38–40. Other sources date these short films to 1920, but Cook's book includes an image of an advertisement for *The Adventures of Eve* from 1918 which seems to support his dating.
4. Sheehan, 'Now and Forever?', p. 134.
5. Editorial, *Eve*, 1.1 (November 1919), p. 1.
6. Marthe Troly-Curtin, 'Eve and her Books', *Eve*, 4.47 (27 January 1921), pp. 112, iv (p. 112).
7. Editorial caption, *Eve*, 1.1 (November 1919), p. 1.
8. Editorial, *Eve*, 1.4 (February 1920), p. 109.
9. The Editor, 'To Our Readers – Old and New', *Eve: The Lady's Pictorial*, 4.52 (2 March 1921), p. 259.
10. The character of *Eve* shifted when the magazine was subsumed in *Britannia and Eve*, initially marketed as a magazine for men and women. On *Britannia and Eve*, see Parkins, '"Eve Goes Synthetic"', pp. 139–52.

11. Editorial subheading, *Eve*, 1.3 (25 March 1920), p. 73.
12. Colin Gray, 'A Quiet Corner', *Eve: The Lady's Pictorial*, 9.116 (24 May 1922), p. 235; Richard King, 'Talking about Books . . .', *Eve: The Lady's Pictorial*, 29.377 (1 June 1927), pp. 504–5, 540 (p. 505).
13. On Woolf's 'The Waxworks at the Abbey', in *Eve: The Lady's Pictorial*, 33.428 (23 May 1928), p. 429, see Pollentier, 'Virginia Woolf and the Middlebrow Market'. On the presence of modernist and middlebrow women writers in *Eve* see Plock, '"A Journal of the Period"'. On the broader contexts of modernism in *Eve* see Alice Wood, *Modernism and Modernity in British Women's Magazines*.
14. White, *Women's Magazines 1693–1968*, p. 94.
15. Plock, '"A Journal of the Period"', p. 29.
16. Light, *Forever England*, p. 11. See Plock, '"A Journal of the Period"', p. 29.
17. The Editor, 'To Our Readers', p. 259.
18. V.M., 'Aramintha and the Ancients', *Eve*, 1.1 (November 1919), pp. 25, iv (p. 25). The identity of 'V.M.' is unknown.
19. Ibid. p. 25.
20. Ibid.
21. Ibid.
22. A. E. Johnson, 'The Russian Ballet', *Eve*, 1.1 (November 1919), pp. 6–7.
23. V.M., 'Aramintha and the Ancients', p. 25. Emphasis in original.
24. Ibid. p. iv.
25. Ibid.
26. Ibid.
27. Ibid.
28. Ibid.
29. Ibid.
30. Jean Anderson, 'Incidental Music', *Eve*, 1.1 (11 March 1920), pp. 14–15 (p. 14).
31. Ibid.
32. Ibid.
33. Ibid. p. 15.
34. Ibid.
35. Ibid. p. 14.
36. Marthe Troly-Curtin, 'The Ukulele Lovers', *Eve: The Lady's Pictorial*, 32.414 (15 February, 1928), pp. 323, 341.
37. Ibid. p. 323.
38. Ibid.
39. Ibid.
40. Ibid.
41. Ibid.
42. Ibid.
43. Ibid. p. 341.

44. Ibid.
45. Ibid.
46. Norman Venner, 'Unromantic Miss 1928', *Eve: The Lady's Pictorial*, 32.414 (15 February 1928), pp. 306–7.
47. Ibid.
48. Ibid. p. 307.
49. Richard King, 'Talking about Books . . .', *Eve: The Lady's Pictorial*, 32.414 (15 February 1928), pp. 313, 315, 341 (p. 313).
50. Ibid.
51. Ibid. p. 341.
52. Jan Struther [Joyce Anstruther], 'An Ideal Home', *Eve: The Lady's Pictorial*, 13.165 (2 May 1923), pp. 143–4. See Nicola Beauman, 'Placzek, Joyce Anstruther [*pseud.* Jan Struther] (1901–53)', *Oxford Dictionary of National Biography*, Oxford University Press, 3 October 2013, <https://www.oxforddnb.com/view/10.1093/ref:odnb/9780198614128.001.0001/odnb-9780198614128-e-39183> (last accessed 1 September 2020).
53. Giles, *The Parlour and the Suburb*, p. 117.
54. White, *Women's Magazines 1693–1968*, pp. 93–4.
55. Advertisement for Western Electric Clothes Washer, *Eve: The Lady's Pictorial*, 11.147 (27 December 1922), p. ii; 'The Silent Servant in Your Home', advertisement from The General Electric Co., Ltd., *Eve: The Lady's Pictorial*, 24.185 (19 September 1923), p. ix.
56. Struther, 'An Ideal Home', p. 143.
57. Ibid.
58. Ibid.
59. Ibid.
60. Ibid. pp. 143–4.
61. Ibid. p. 144.
62. Ibid.
63. Elizabeth Bowen, 'Making Arrangements', *Eve: The Lady's Pictorial*, 23.298 (20 November 1925), pp. 4–5, 7, 19, 88.
64. Editorial caption for Bowen, 'Making Arrangements', p. 4.
65. Bowen, 'Making Arrangements', p. 5.
66. Ibid.
67. Ibid. p. 7.
68. Ibid. p. 19.
69. Ibid. p. 7.
70. Ibid. p. 19.
71. Ibid.
72. Ibid.
73. Radclyffe Hall, 'The Scarecrow', *Eve: The Lady's Pictorial*, 14.185 (19 September 1923), pp. 366–7.
74. Funke, 'Introduction', p. 2.
75. Ibid. p. 3.

76. Hall, 'The Scarecrow', p. 366.
77. 'The Sands of Enchantment', *Eve: The Lady's Pictorial*, 14.185 (19 September 1923), p. 369.
78. See, for example, 'A Silhouette of Youth', *Eve: The Lady's Pictorial*, 23.296 (4 November 1925), pp. 262–3, a photograph by Fred Daniels of five bare-footed Margaret Morris pupils holding balancing poses in a 'frieze-like silhouette' between two trees with the sea and Antibes in the distance.
79. The Editor, 'To Our Readers', p. 259.
80. 'Catch as Catch Can', *Eve: The Lady's Pictorial*, 14.185 (19 September 1923), p. 367.
81. Hall, 'The Scarecrow', p. 367.
82. Ibid. p. 366.
83. Punter, 'The Uncanny', p. 130.
84. Hall, 'Scarecrow', pp. 366–7.
85. Ibid. pp. 366–7.
86. Ibid. p. 367.
87. Funke, 'Introduction', p. 16.
88. Hall, 'Scarecrow', p. 367.
89. The Editor, 'To Our Readers', p. 259.

Chapter 8

Calling Parrots in Walter de la Mare and Elizabeth Bowen: A Communion in *The London Mercury*

Yui Kajita

'The big orange *London Mercury* was the dominating magazine', writes Elizabeth Bowen in 'Coming to London', a reminiscence of her life between 1919 and 1922.[1] When she first arrived, she 'haunted the fringes of literary London'.[2] Soon, however, the novelist and critic Rose Macaulay pulled her into the company of its central players. Bowen met Naomi Royde-Smith, then editor of the *Saturday Westminster Gazette*, and began to frequent the two women's evening parties in Kensington. Such gatherings were drawn from personal friendships as much as networks formed by the periodical culture of the time. Bowen vividly recalls the 'sense and atmosphere' of those evenings – though little of the actual words of the conversation – and how she came into contact with eminent writers: 'Inconceivably, I found myself in the same room as Edith Sitwell, Walter de la Mare, Aldous Huxley.'[3] The writers she names here were all current or future contributors to *The London Mercury*. This magazine was established by J. C. Squire in November 1919 and continued to run, albeit in a different form, until April 1939. Bowen herself would soon publish a short story in this magazine, which reveals a significant intersection between her work and that of de la Mare.

Critics rarely make associations between de la Mare and Bowen. Writers such as Henry James and Virginia Woolf are prominent in studies of Bowen as her sources of influence, but de la Mare, when he is mentioned at all, is a fleeting presence.[4] For Bowen, however, he was a remarkable figure in the development of the English short story, as well as a writer with a singular voice. In a letter to Alan Cameron on 19 January 1923, she wrote: 'There is something perfectly distinctive and different about the de la Mare sentence, written or said.'[5] In 'The Short Story in England' (1945), she argues that D. H. Lawrence is 'our finest short story writer':

With him I should place Kipling, Somerset Maugham, Aldous Huxley, William Plomer and Katherine Mansfield. But here, I fear, I risk being controversial. Walter de la Mare's position is indefinable: he belongs more than half, always, in the poetic province.[6]

The same essay theorises the short story as an art form which 'promised to do in prose what had, so far, only been done in poetry' – in other words, to isolate 'some perhaps quite small happening', and to emphasise 'its significance by giving it emotional colour'.[7] In light of her view, de la Mare's short stories, immersed in the 'poetic province', can be said to embody this crossing over from poetry to prose. Whenever she mentions him, she is consistently attentive to the individual style and poetic quality of his prose. In her preface to Cynthia Asquith's anthology, *The Second Ghost Book* (1952), she notes how de la Mare's story reveals a 'poetic element' of 'ghostliness'. 'Fear has its own aesthetic', she writes, 'as Le Fanu, Henry James, Montague James and Walter de la Mare have repeatedly shown'.[8] Indeed, in Bowen's 'The Back Drawing-Room' (1926), which unsettles the ghost story's aesthetic, one character imagines something beckoning, '[d]eep from out of the depths of those dark windows', and another character immediately links this image to de la Mare's poetry.[9] Bowen likely had in mind his numerous ghostly writings, especially the poem 'The Listeners' (1911) and the short story 'Out of the Deep' (1923). In the former, a traveller's knocking is answered only by the silence of the phantom listeners; in the latter, a man obsessively listens for something that might clamber up, in response to his calls, from the depths of his empty house. Bowen engaged with de la Mare's work both in her critical essays and short stories, and it is clear that she held his writing in high esteem. Among the twenty-six stories she selected for *The Faber Book of Modern Stories* (1937), de la Mare's 'Physic' (1936) features alongside those by Lawrence, James Joyce, Frank O'Connor and others.

In *The London Mercury*, de la Mare and Bowen each published a short story featuring a cryptic parrot within three months of each other. De la Mare's 'Pretty Poll', which appeared in the April 1925 issue, concerns a mesmeric parrot and a man's desperate search for the original of its voice. Bowen's 'The Parrot', published in July 1925, is about a fugitive parrot and a girl's attempt to catch it.[10] Given Bowen's appreciation for de la Mare's work and her familiarity with *The London Mercury* as the 'dominating magazine' in the 1920s, the echoes between the stories may not be coincidental. Reading them together reveals a more fundamental affinity between the stories and their authors. The stories deal with themes that preoccupied both writers, such as the ambivalence of morality, the anxiety of suicide and the psychological condition of longing. Moreover, they illuminate their author's attention to the evolving form of the short story and demonstrate how short stories may participate in literary criticism through their implicit metafictional concerns.

The London Mercury provides a context that turns de la Mare's and Bowen's stories into possible companion pieces. By choosing to publish them in close proximity, the magazine enabled this communication. The stories also draw attention to an interesting tension between their authors' poetics and that of other contributors to the magazine by subtly challenging some of the assumptions about prose fiction, particularly about narrative endings, that are presented in the magazine. This chapter will first delineate the textual and thematic links between the two stories, then explore how the context of The London Mercury – its presentation; its interactive community of contributors and readers; and its self-professed position as an arbiter of taste, committed to protecting and advancing literature and culture – plays a role in this intertextual communication between the two stories, influencing our interpretation. The magazine's characteristics, I argue, spurred on de la Mare and Bowen to engage with questions of genre and form in their own stories.

The two tales

Although de la Mare rose to prominence as a poet's poet in the early twentieth century, his earliest forays into the literary profession in the late 1890s were through publishing short stories in periodicals.[11] His short stories became widely known just as Bowen was starting her literary career. When their first collections appeared in 1923 – de la Mare's *The Riddle and Other Stories* and Bowen's *Encounters* – they were reviewed on the same page in *The New Statesman*, for which Squire had been literary editor until the end of 1919.[12] In 'Pretty Poll', collected in his third volume of short stories, *The Connoisseur and Other Stories* (1926), de la Mare presents a story within a story. On a late summer evening, what begins as a conversation about the institution of marriage among Judy, a married woman, Stella, her taciturn friend, and Tressider, a satirical bachelor, turns into Tressider's tale about his friend who became obsessed with a parrot. The friend, Bysshe, is a London flâneur who thinks he suffers from indigestion. One day, he buys a parrot at Leadenhall Market, drawn to it by a strange, nondescript sound: 'A kind of call-note which appeared to have come out of the cage.'[13] Bysshe soon discovers that it has two voices. One is vitriolic, sounding 'as if out of some vast hollow, dark and subterranean'.[14] The other is seraphic: an ethereal aria, 'abjectly beautiful'.[15] Helplessly possessed, Bysshe searches in vain for the original of the angelic voice. Minnie Sturgess, who was as good as engaged to Bysshe, calls the bird 'Pretty Poll' at first.[16] Eventually, she wrings its neck out of restless jealousy – though the narrative only implies the act with a handkerchief bound clumsily around her hand. What becomes of Bysshe is left unsaid. The story comes to a close as Tressider grows tired and disinterested from the exertion of telling his tale.

Bowen's 'The Parrot' was collected in her second book, *Ann Lee's and Other Stories* (1926), when she was beginning to gain more recognition. The story, she recalls in the preface to the 1951 edition, was inspired by 'the sunny tossing chestnut-tree, waxy with blossom, at the corner of our road'.[17] It seems to pick up where de la Mare's story left off – or rather, it seems to imagine a part of the story that was not imagined by his. 'The Parrot' begins with the bird's escape. Eleanor Fitch, a young companion to the parrot's elderly owner, Mrs Willesden, scrambles to capture it before her employer awakens. The parrot, in an ungainly flight, lands in the Lennicotts' garden. Mr Lennicott writes supposedly scandalous novels and lives with a woman whom the fastidious neighbours suspect is only called 'Mrs'. Eleanor dreads becoming contaminated by their 'wickedness', but when she takes Mr Lennicott's hand to climb on the roof to catch the parrot, she experiences 'a magical interlude': she has 'shared a roof and breasted the clouds' with him.[18] As soon as she is back on the ground, however, the fear returns, and she takes the back way to avoid being seen with the Lennicotts. When she lies to Mrs Willesden that she had caught the parrot all by herself, the bird emits a cry like a cock's crow.

Although the incidents, tones and narrative speed of the two stories differ, Bowen's story is clearly linked to de la Mare's through the parrot's calls. Her parrot, bought at an auction in London and nicknamed 'Pretty Polly', only utters inane cries.[19] It would 'mutter "Poll, Po-oll, Pol-pol-pol" for hours, in an ecstasy of introspection', or say, simply, 'Lead, kindly Light'. If one tried to elicit a reaction from it, 'it would blink at one in a smoulder of malevolence, and say, "Minnie? Minnie! Tom? Minnie!"'[20] At the end, it beats its wings and cries in a hoarse voice: 'Minnie, Minnie, *Minnie?*'[21] There is no character named Minnie in Bowen's story, and the story never elucidates what these utterances mean. The 'smoulder of malevolence' and the parrot's gestures are puzzling, for they are unaccountable, disproportionate to their object. It is as if someone named Minnie had once abused the parrot; the bird sounds hoarse, as if Minnie had clutched at its neck. Bowen's story plays with the slightly uneasy sense that the parrot has a past unknown to its current owners, as in de la Mare's story. Such connections make the reader wonder whether Bysshe's parrot had narrowly escaped from Minnie Sturgess's hands and flown into Bowen's pages – at least, in Bowen's imagination. The motley vocabulary of her parrot includes John Henry Newman's hymn 'Lead Kindly Light', which gives yet another sign that she might have been inspired by de la Mare's writing, since this hymn had an exceptional significance for him.[22] In both stories, hymns give a slight glimpse of the parrots' past lives: Newman's hymn in Bowen's, and 'Hold the Fort' in de la Mare's.

The affinity between the stories can be felt not only through these verbal connections, but also through overlapping thematic concerns. Hermione Lee notes Bowen's talent for suggesting a 'constant sense of peril'; comparably, Dylan Thomas remarks that de la Mare's 'subject, always, is the imminence of spiritual danger'.[23] The parrot stories present moral predicaments without resolving them. In de la Mare's story, the parrot is the source of possible contamination. The danger of the parrot insinuates itself into the narrative, when Bysshe begins to listen intently:

> There was no response. And he had again almost forgotten the presence of the parrot when, hours afterwards, from the gloom that had crept into its corner, there softly broke out of the cage [. . .] a low, slow, steady gush of indescribable abuse.[24]

The narrator frustrates the reader's expectation by delaying the 'response', pulling it back just enough to impart an offbeat rhythm. The winding sentence does a kind of double take – a characteristic feature in de la Mare's writing – as the parrot's call comes 'from the gloom', then 'out of the cage'. There is a slight jarring sensation in 'softly broke'. The sentence slows down, building the tension, with the internal rhyme and alliteration in 'low, slow, steady'. The sense of spiritual danger emanates from something that lacks moral agency; the parrot's voice is described as sheer evil, yet it is unconscious of what it speaks. There is also something off-kilter about Bysshe. Tressider mentions Bysshe's 'queer harmless habits', which is exemplified by his 'odd and esoteric taste in books'.[25] Rather than a moral judgement on Bysshe's self-destruction – culminating, perhaps, in suicide – and Minnie's murder of the parrot, the reader is left with Tressider and Stella's sudden apathy, and Judy's ineffectual comment that the newborn baby she had been sewing a shirt for has 'ventured into a rather difficult world'.[26]

The Lennicotts, like Bysshe, are judged by their literary taste. Eleanor expects to find 'moral obliquity' in them, based on the rumours of Mr Lennicott's 'improper', 'terrible books'.[27] When she ventures into their forbidden house, a suffocating, almost maddening sense of moral danger assails her. It is expressed in sensory stimuli: the place is 'heavy' with the scent of lilac, and the house's 'shadows and scents were surcharged for her, every contact was intolerably significant'.[28] A crucial element of the Lennicott's 'wickedness' lies in the suspicion that Mr Lennicott had attempted suicide. Mrs Willesden treats them as a taboo, but still gossips: 'it was all very, very sad [. . .] sin was becoming, alas, very prevalent'.[29] When he climbs up on the roof, Eleanor worries whether she would be compromised by having to appear at an inquest. As if she guesses her thoughts, Mrs Lennicott nonchalantly assures her that 'Trotsky never killed himself'.[30] When this story was written, suicide was still stigmatised as a sin: 'only one degree less criminal than the murder of another', as a *Fortnightly Review* article put it in 1921.[31] The problem of suicide haunts de la Mare in numerous works, such as *The Return* (1910), 'Promise at Dusk' (1919) and 'The Green Room' (1925). The idea of suicide had left a lasting impression on him when, as a child, he overheard a conversation about someone who poisoned himself with strychnine; comparably, Bowen recalls talking about suicide in her schooldays.[32] Although Bowen's 'The Parrot' never names the crime, the hint of suicide makes the sense of peril more tangible and disquieting. Where the story draws the line of 'moral obliquity' is slightly complicated by Mrs Lennicott's offer of figs and Eleanor's reluctant refusal, as if she is tempted by the forbidden fruit of Eden. Eleanor seems to have realised that her idea of 'sin' – or rather, Mrs Willesden's idea of sin that she accepts as her own – cannot be maintained in good faith. But there is no outward change in her behaviour after the incident. The perturbation she feels is articulated only in the parrot's hoarse, meaningless cry, ending in 'a note of regret and bewilderment'.[33]

Aesthetic debates in *The London Mercury*

If 'Pretty Poll' and 'The Parrot' are encountered separately, tracing their connections might stop here. An important factor in the communication between them, however, is the shared context of their first publications in *The London Mercury*. The magazine's position, composition, and the discussions about literature that it mediated can be seen to shape the conversation between the two stories. In November 1919, when the First World War was still a raw memory, Squire began *The London Mercury* on a bold note. His 'Editorial Notes', which opened the first issue and became a staple feature of each number, show that he was conscious of this historical moment. He claims that the magazine emerges out of an urgent need, in the face of the recent 'crisis' and the uncertainty of the future: 'The more intense the troubles of society, [...] the more obvious is the necessity for periodicals which hand on the torch of culture and creative activity.'[34] Remarkably, he emphasises the duty of shining a light on 'new works of the imagination' and of protecting the 'spirit' of humanity on none other than the periodical.[35] The orange cover of the magazine – adorned with the refined, robust profile of Mercury – and the high quality of the printing commanded attention as much as his heralding of this new 'torch of culture'. *The Athenaeum* announced its arrival as an 'important addition' to London literary journals.[36] The *Saturday Review* expressed anticipation: 'In spite of these increasing worries of printing and paper, and the mastery of advertisement, new contributions to literary criticism and *belles lettres* are promised shortly.'[37] Squire's purpose, in his own words, was to 'publish the best "creative work" that [the magazine] could obtain, to criticise new books and old, and to minister to the other needs of the British reader and the British book-collector'.[38] As he specifies in an interview in *The Observer*, he sought to provide a 'journal with definite critical standards', in which 'the best contemporary critics [could] express their opinions on literature and the arts'.[39]

In 1922, the anthologist J. E. Wetherell wrote about Squire that 'no living poet has a wider influence on the literary views and tendencies of his age'.[40] Squire gained traction in the world of literary journalism through regular contributions to *The New Age*, which established his reputation as a master of parody in verse, and through his critical essays in *The New Statesman*, for which he was the first literary editor from 1913.[41] With his personal charisma, Squire was able to gather over 1,000 subscribers in advance of the first issue of *The London Mercury*; by 1921, circulation had risen to 10,000, and by 1926, over 12,000.[42] Compared to *The English Review* – which was also sold for half a crown for each monthly issue but never gained much more than a circulation of 1,000 under Ford Madox Hueffer's editorship from 1908 to 1910 – this was a striking success.

Squire's magazine found a transatlantic readership from the beginning, and its early readers included Wallace Stevens.[43]

In his 'Editorial Notes', Squire declares that the magazine's comprehensive coverage is unrivalled among other weekly papers and 'politico-literary monthlies'.[44] It had an Anglophone-centric but international scope, and it accumulated an impressive list of contributors. Poets and prose writers included Thomas Hardy, W. B. Yeats, Joseph Conrad, Robert Bridges, Robert Frost, Edward Thomas, Virginia Woolf, Katherine Mansfield, Laurence Binyon, Maurice Hewlett, D. H. Lawrence, E. M. Forster and Walter J. Turner. Essayists included Edmund Gosse, George Saintsbury, Max Beerbohm, G. K. Chesterton, Havelock Ellis, Hilaire Belloc and Vernon Lee. Each number contained the following sections, spanning about 130 pages in total: 'EDITORIAL NOTES', its section breaks adorned with three floating leaves; 'LITERARY INTELLIGENCE', consisting of brief news items; a section headed 'POETRY'; prose fiction and long essays, each piece headed by capitalised titles; 'CORRESPONDENCE'; 'BIBLIOGRAPHICAL NOTES & NEWS'; 'BOOK-PRODUCTION NOTES'; 'CHRONICLES', in which short reviews were organised by genre, such as the Drama, the Fine Arts, Music, Poetry, Fiction, Belles-Lettres, Literary History and Criticism, Biography and Memoirs, the Classics, and Science; and, less regularly, foreign correspondence (for example, 'A LETTER FROM FRANCE' by the Geneva School critic Albert Thibaudet). Its contents were presented in a neat, consistent format. The beginning of each section, even each poem, was typographically marked with an ample drop cap initial. All were printed in single-column pages. In a letter dated 26 March 1920, T. S. Eliot admitted to John Quinn that Squire's magazine was 'a despicable volume, but it is well arranged and its appearance is attractive'.[45]

The London Mercury championed literary pursuits, with a particular emphasis on criticism and book-production. In the inaugural number, one correspondent implores the magazine to lead by example and by instruction in literary taste and publishing standards.[46] This hope for the magazine was coupled with a shared sense of crisis. In its March 1925 number, for instance, J. B. Priestley expresses a grave view: 'we are in some danger of losing our hold, at least in public if not in private, upon a very sure and sensible method of judging critics and criticism'.[47] The magazine's conspicuous literariness and attention to quality are also reflected by the contents of its relatively few advertisements. Interspersed among the lists from book sellers and publishers are promotions of sectional bookcases, fountain pens, superior whisky, order-made hunting hats, courses for aspiring freelance journalists and short story writers ('Join the ranks of well-paid contributors'), and Hilaire Belloc's *Land & Water* magazine, which claims to make 'a serious attempt to supply WELL-WRITTEN FICTION and, particularly, to revive the lost art of short-story writing'.[48] The magazine's target audience included book collectors and writers of all levels: readers who valued quality products and the preservation of literature both as an art and as a physical object.

The magazine has been predominantly interpreted as a 'conservative, market-driven, middlebrow organ' of Squire's circles.[49] Raymond MacKenzie concludes that the magazine was an anachronism for its exclusive 'Georgianism'.[50] Patrick Collier modifies this by pointing out that the magazine represents a later phase of the divide between 'the emerging Eliot-Pound version of modernism' and the Georgian poets, who in the 1910s were 'perceived as pursuing a separate, equally experimental, poetic agenda from the Imagists'.[51] At the same time, Collier argues, the magazine attempted 'to ground and stabilise value in solid objects', particularly high-end textual objects.[52] J. Matthew Huculak revises the narrative that the magazine was increasingly reactionary, seeing it as an 'experiment' in itself, 'undertaken to solidify a common sense of cultural unity and to provide a universally understood touchstone of taste', when changing forms of cultural production and market demands threatened the integrity of the evaluation of literature.[53] It sought to address both a readership attentive to avant-garde coteries and the general public with middlebrow inclination.

These accounts tend to view *The London Mercury* as one body, operating under a unified aesthetic ideology. In its general editorial choices, the magazine did aspire to provide a universal touchstone of taste. But within Squire's broad criteria, contributors could express various aesthetic opinions that at times led to slight paradoxes. For instance, in July 1924, Priestley criticised L. P. Hartley's first volume of short stories, *Night Fears*, as having 'a kind of false *subtlety* in the telling, a nod and wink manner, a trick of referring to a background that is not really there'. He laments that 'what might be called the "high brow" short story is rapidly becoming as standardised, as much a mere bag of tricks as the despised "low brow" magazine tale'.[54] Just a month earlier, however, the magazine had published one story out of Hartley's book, 'The Island'.[55] Rather than acting as an organ for a single voice, the magazine was shaped by its community of readers and writers. Notably, starting from the June 1920 issue, the contents page included the names of each letter writer in the 'Correspondence' section, which suggests Squire's interest in fostering an active, participatory readership.[56] Readers could argue back against reviews (in 'An Accusation of Neglect', a reader demanded more attention be paid to Noël Coward's *The Vortex*), contribute commentary of their own (in 'A de la Mare episode', a reader discovered the source for a curious phrase quoted in de la Mare's *Memoirs of a Midget*) or even create a new section of the magazine: Squire followed a subscriber's suggestion and made 'Book-Production Notes' a regular feature from the second number onwards.[57] Although his taste did define the magazine overall, Squire allowed room for individual writers to experiment and, in the case of de la Mare's and Bowen's stories, attempt to realign the standards of good writing in the magazine, to influence the readers' expectations of what a short story could do.

The aesthetic debates in the magazine and its commitment to literary value invite us to find a deeper resonance between the metafictional dimensions of the parrot stories in light of their authors' poetics of the short story. Laden with literary allusions and defining the characters by their literary tastes, both stories highlight their own self-conscious literariness.[58] Moreover, the magazine's positioning of short stories endows them with an ulterior function of commenting, however implicitly, about the art of writing. Each number printed one or two stories without a section heading, preceding the longer essays, which followed the same format. The stories and essays thus appear in the same category, and in the indices to bound volumes, they are listed together under 'Occasional Contributions in Prose'. Squire himself wrote a story that contains some literary criticism for the June 1924 number, attacking the 'trick of incomprehensibility' practised by 'second-rate' poets of free verse.[59] In a much more implicit manner than the overt parody and commentary in Squire's story, de la Mare's and Bowen's stories participate in the magazine's conversations concerning the aesthetics of the short story form.

In 1898, Henry James classified short stories into two kinds: one is 'the detached incident, single and sharp, as clear as a pistol-shot'; the rarer performance is 'the impression [...] of a complexity or a continuity'.[60] James's distinction anticipates the categories used in debates about the short story in the early twentieth century: craft/art, middlebrow/highbrow, plot-dependent/plotless, mainstream/avant-garde, or popular magazine stories/modernist stories. Although *The London Mercury* was a popular magazine, often labelled as conservative and commercial, its contents blur the boundary between such dichotomies. For instance, it published Virginia Woolf's short story 'An Unwritten Novel' in July 1920 (another 'Minnie' in the magazine) among more traditional stories; her experimentalism and the work of the Hogarth Press were generally highly regarded in its reviews.

The parrot stories are markedly different in their inner workings from the majority of short fiction that surrounds them in the magazine, and to borrow James's phrasing, they leave an impression of an unresolved continuity. In many stories – such as C. K. Scott-Moncrief's 'The Mouse in the Dovecot', a story about a divorce which immediately follows de la Mare's 'Pretty Poll' – the narrative ends abruptly with a climactic incident, or leads up to something that provides an explanation. Death, or the revelation of it, is a typical ending in the magazine's fiction. Ethel Rolt-Wheeler's 'Wireless', in which broadcasting experiments make the dead audible to the living, ends with the wife's discovery of her husband struck by lightning.[61] M. R. James's 'A Warning to the Curious' neatly concludes with the haunted man's death and inquest.[62] Hartley's 'The Island' draws the curtains as soon as a flash of lightning illuminates the pitch-black library and the corpse of the wife.

In contrast, de la Mare's story begins distinctly *in medias res*. The first sentence focuses on a particular auditory impression: 'In her odd impulsive fashion [. . .] Judy had laughed out: and the sound of it had a faint far-away resemblance to bells – bells muffled, in the sea.'[63] The story proceeds by gradual, convoluted disclosures. Bowen begins her story swiftly and suddenly: 'When Mrs Willesden's parrot escaped, it rocketed in a pale-green streak across the sky.'[64] The most striking difference between their stories and others lies in the way they end. The two stories' denouements share a certain insubstantial or ineffectual quality. There are no substantive consequences of the stories' incidents; this subtly deflates the reader's expectations. After what can be taken as the climax – in 'Pretty Poll', Minnie's murder of the parrot; and in 'The Parrot', the bird's capture – the stories taper off without really explaining anything, leaving an odd aftertaste. At the end of de la Mare's story, the narrative's attention takes an unlikely turn towards Stella, as she watches the moon about to set, suggesting some hidden story of her life that is neither indicated in the story nor elucidated by the last sentence: 'the moon of her own secret waters had long ago set for ever'.[65] Tressider sees the end of the parrot and his own tale as irrational and meaningless: 'the tragic – the absurd – *finale*'.[66] His lethargy and Stella's disinterested remark make a bathetic conclusion: 'I am a little too grown-up for fairy tales. And as for morals; I can find my own.'[67] At the end of Bowen's story, the parrot has the last word, calling to the unknown Minnie.

The final sentences are bare statements that suggest some significance without elaborating on it: 'It ended on a note of regret and bewilderment. And Eleanor put down its cage quickly and walked over to the window. It was like the crowing of the cock.'[68] The 'And', which begins a new paragraph, makes the transition slightly disjointed, as if to express Eleanor's confusion. The parrot's 'crowing' is an ill omen – but of what, the story does not divulge. Both stories foreground mood and impression over plot, ending on an open note which cannot be fully assimilated.

Bowen describes her own inconclusive stories as 'questions posed – some end with a shrug, others with an impatient or a dismissing sigh'.[69] In the parrot stories, it is difficult even to put one's finger on the questions posed. By experimenting with such endings, the stories explore alternative forms to much of the fiction in *The London Mercury*, which has a definite sense of closure and tacitly realigns certain judgements made by the magazine's critics. In 'Truth and Fiction' in the October 1923 number, the poet Dyneley Hussey discusses de la Mare's novel *Memoirs of a Midget* (1921) and the 'obscurity in its crucial incident'. In his assessment, the story's 'emotional climax' remains 'so vague in meaning as to convey almost none'; 'we are left with a sense of bewilderment and of incompleteness, which is not the effect proper to a work of art'. He suggests that the attempted idea could only have been fully realised in 'its proper medium of pure lyric'.[70] Such an impression of 'bewilderment' and 'incompleteness', however, is exactly what de la Mare's short stories convey, and this 'obscurity' is essential to their themes and narrative effects. Read in this way, the obscurity that Hussey identifies as a defect turns into the implicit subject of the story. The parrot stories can thus be interpreted as an indirect rejoinder to Hussey and a readjustment of the general view that the short story should have a clear plot and closure. The incompleteness of both stories is an integral part of their subject, analogous to the parrot's cry that ends on a note of bewilderment: vague and mystifying, yet crucial to the sense of unresolvable complexity that the stories impart to the reader.

The attention to birdcalls is a key element of the stories' experimentation with the impressionistic, open-ended story. In 'Atmosphere in Fiction', an unpublished essay from the late 1910s, de la Mare treats atmosphere not as a mere ornament but as part of a novel's 'conceptive nucleus': 'a mood, a certain condition of mind, a certain tone [. . .] may itself be for its writer the actual theme of his story'.[71] This is precisely what motivates the parrot stories: the possibility of a 'tone', or a 'certain condition of mind', to be the subject of a story. This takes on a particular significance because of their place in *The London Mercury*, for they form a curious tangent to Squire's view of language. One of Squire's tenets was that language is a means of communication. In a short review of *The Waste Land* in October 1923, he demands: 'what is language but communication, or art but selection and arrangement? I give it up.'[72] The parrot stories explore the narrative possibilities of tone: tones that convey meaning, and even become the central stimulus of the stories, without giving voice to any intelligible words. The parrots' cries, which occasion de la Mare's story and which introduce enigmas into Bowen's story, pose the question: what can tones detached from actual words do in a short story?

The parrots are described as mindless, but their cries waver between a dramatic range of tones: contempt, regret, bewilderment and even ecstasy. De la Mare's fascination with tones is apparent from the very first time Bysshe and Tressider hear the parrot's two voices from behind a closed door. What haunts them most persistently is not the parrot's words, but a 'remembrance of the execrable *tone* of its speech'. More than once in the story, the 'tone' is emphasised over 'the words, the mere language'.[73] It is the parrot's mindlessness – in other words, its unawareness of the actual meaning of the words – that brings out the pure sound, or the pure tone of its utterances. The 'inmost sense [. . .] comes out the better because the speaker is not taking any notice of it', says Tressider.[74] The story asks what makes birdsong so ethereally entrancing, and whether it is possible to evoke its pure tone in language. The parrot's seraphic song is '[a] voice innocent of the meaning [. . .] of its longing'.[75] The story itself, by embodying Bysshe's obsession, seems to emulate the quality of this voice, letting the dynamic tones of his longing permeate its sentences. The emotional tone of his nauseating 'expectation', accompanied by a 'terror of having that expectation fulfilled', is the story's theme itself.[76] The words of Bowen's parrot also carry no meaning, only tones. By writing stories about parrots – birds that can speak in human language, but only mindlessly – de la Mare and Bowen draw the reader's attention to the dramatic effects of tones: tones that are meaningful and affective even apart from their words. They put into practice their own theorisations about taking a tone, or a mood, as the theme of a story, working around Squire's expectation that the language of a literary work needs to communicate lucidly in words, or Hussey's that a story in prose should not leave an impression of vagueness.

The tone and emotion of longing, shared by the two stories, bring us back to Bowen's interest in the possibility of the modern short story to do in prose what had formerly only been done in poetry. Bysshe longs to discover the original of the parrot's voice. Eleanor longs for the open air, the vigorous, liberating experience of the Lennicotts' rooftop. Considering the emergence of the poetic short story in the early twentieth century, and the magazine's emphasis on the juxtaposition of poetry and prose in its pages, it is significant that Bysshe's longing for 'the ghost of a voice', or the 'impossible She', is figured in distinctly literary, poetic terms.[77] The 'impossible She', calling to mind Richard Crashaw's 'Wishes to his (Supposed) Mistress', connects Bysshe's impulse to the pursuit of beauty in poetry, and the poet's listening for a voice. The story itself makes this explicit when Tressider remarks: 'There is a bit, you remember, in one of Conrad's novels about a voice – Lena's. There is another bit in Shakespeare, and in Coleridge; in almost every poet, of course.'[78] To take this metaphor further, Bysshe's story doubles as a story of a poet haunted by an imagined voice, longing to capture it and to substantiate what he listens for in his imagination. For Bowen, the emotional condition of longing was one of the key driving forces of the short story. The short story form, she writes, 'allows for what is crazy about humanity: obstinacies, inordinate heroisms, "immortal longings"'.[79] 'Immortal longings' may be an expression better suited to Bysshe's overpowering longing than to Eleanor's nebulous, objectless wistfulness, but hers is still 'immortal' in the sense that it is universal. De la Mare's story, then, presents a way of dramatising Bowen's later ideas about the poetic potentials of the short story: to express timeless longings, as well as to take tones, emotions or fleeting moments as its subject, in a manner that approaches lyric poetry. The stories' original proximity in *The London Mercury* enables this as one of innumerable interpretations.

For Bowen, who saw the evolving short story as a prose form of poetry, and for de la Mare, who saw poetry in prose as much as in verse, *The London Mercury* offered an opportune space in which to attempt to expand the possibilities of the short story form. The publication context of the parrot stories invites us to explore the connections between the writers and the affinity of the stories that would otherwise remain unnoticed. Moreover, reading the stories in their original context brings out their metafictional engagement with questions of the short story form, as they participate in the aesthetic debates in *The London Mercury*. They subtly readjust the aesthetic judgements made by some reviewers and story writers in the magazine, and thereby endeavour to shift the expectations and criteria that the magazine's readers may have had for short stories. They push towards an aesthetic of incompleteness, which allows for narratives that leave questions open, giving an impression of unknowableness that is bewildering yet meaningful. They develop the potentials of taking a 'tone', or a condition of mind, as their subject. This becomes especially explicit because of the figure of the parrot, which conveys meaning not in words but in tones. The magazine provided a platform of communication between the writers, readers, and writers as readers of each other's works. Its professed aim of passing on the torch of literary culture stimulated them to pursue questions of literary form. Just as reading de la Mare's story in *The London Mercury* would have affected the ways in which Bowen responded to it, encountering their parrot stories in this context shapes the reader's understanding of them, as stories that posed questions about their own evolving medium and explored the intersections of poetry and prose.

Notes

1. Bowen, 'Coming to London', p. 88.
2. Glendinning, *Elizabeth Bowen*, p. 53.
3. Bowen, 'Coming to London', p. 88.
4. The reputations of de la Mare (1873–1956) and Bowen (1899–1973) draw a comparable arc from respected prominence during their lifetimes to academic neglect. See Leighton, *Hearing Things*, pp. 117–20; Lee, *Elizabeth Bowen*, pp. 1–2.
5. Bowen, 'Letters', p. 193.
6. Bowen, 'The Short Story in England', in *People, Places, Things*, p. 312.
7. Ibid. p. 310.
8. Bowen, *Afterthought*, pp. 103–4.
9. Bowen, 'The Back Drawing-Room', p. 222).
10. Walter de la Mare, 'Pretty Poll', *The London Mercury*, 11.66 (April 1925), pp. 580–93; Elizabeth Bowen, 'The Parrot', *The London Mercury*, 12.69 (July 1925), pp. 242–52. Quotations are taken from later collected editions.
11. His earliest known publication is 'Kismet' (1895), in *The Sketch*.
12. Anonymous, 'The Riddle and Other Stories (Book Review)', *The New Statesman*, 21.528 (26 May 1923), p. 201; Anonymous, 'Encounters (Book Review)', *The New Statesman*, 21.528 (26 May 1923), p. 201.
13. De la Mare, 'Pretty Poll', in Giles de la Mare (ed.), *Short Stories*, p. 326.
14. Ibid. p. 329.

15. Ibid. p. 331.
16. Ibid. p. 328.
17. Bowen, *Afterthought*, p. 93.
18. Bowen, 'The Parrot', in *Collected Stories*, pp. 121, 126.
19. Ibid. p. 126.
20. Ibid. p. 115.
21. Ibid. p. 127.
22. De la Mare quotes from Newman's hymn in the poem 'Strangers' and the short stories 'The Rejection of the Rector' (1901) and 'The Lost Track' (1926).
23. Lee, *Elizabeth Bowen*, p. 51; Thomas, 'Walter de la Mare as a Prose Writer', p. 111.
24. De la Mare, 'Pretty Poll', in *Short Stories*, p. 327.
25. Ibid. 325–6.
26. Ibid. p. 336.
27. Bowen, 'The Parrot', in *Collected Stories*, pp. 118, 117, 123.
28. Ibid. p. 121.
29. Ibid. p. 117.
30. Ibid. p. 123.
31. Oliver Lodge, 'The Ethics of Suicide', *Fortnightly Review*, 110.658 (October 1921), pp. 594–600 (p. 594).
32. De la Mare, Early One Morning, pp. 289–90; Elizabeth Bowen, 'The Mulberry Tree', in Lee, *The Mulberry Tree*, pp. 13–21 (p. 15).
33. Bowen, 'The Parrot', in *Collected Stories*, p. 127.
34. J. C. Squire, 'Editorial Notes', *The London Mercury*, 1.1 (November 1919), pp. 1–6 (p. 1).
35. Ibid. p. 1.
36. Anonymous, 'Literary Notes', *The Athenaeum*, 4662 (5 September 1919), p. 847.
37. Anonymous, 'Notes of the Week', *Saturday Review of Politics, Literature, Science and Art*, 128.3338 (18 October 1919), pp. 353–6 (p. 356).
38. J. C. Squire, 'Editorial Notes', *The London Mercury*, 1.2 (December 1919), pp. 129–34 (p. 131).
39. Anonymous, 'A New Literary Magazine: The "London Mercury": Mr. Squire Outlines His Programme', *The Observer* (28 September 1919), p. 10.
40. Quoted in Diepeveen, *Mock Modernism*, p. 31.
41. See Edmund Blunden and Clare L. Taylor, 'Squire, Sir John Collings (1884–1958), poet and literary editor', *Oxford Dictionary of National Biography*, Oxford University Press, 21 May 2009, <https://www.oxforddnb.com/view/10.1093/ref:odnb/9780198614128.001.0001/odnb-9780198614128-e-36227> (last accessed 1 September 2020); Hyams, *The New Statesman*, p. 17; Smith, *The New Statesman*, pp. 23–4, 29.

42. See Huculak, 'The London Mercury (1919–39) and Other Moderns'; MacKenzie, 'The London Mercury'.
43. For details on the circulation and prices, see Brooker and Thacker, Oxford Critical and Cultural History of Modernist Magazines, pp. 24, 226–39. Wallace Stevens' copies of the first four issues of The London Mercury are in the Huntington Library, California.
44. Squire, 'Editorial Notes', 1.1 (November 1919), p. 2.
45. Eliot, 'To John Quinn'.
46. Original Subscriber, 'Correspondence', The London Mercury, 1.1 (November 1919), p. 77.
47. J. B. Priestley, 'Contemporary Criticism', The London Mercury, 11.65 (March 1925), pp. 496–504 (pp. 496, 502).
48. The quoted advertisements are from The London Mercury, 1.3 (January 1920), pp. v, xi, and the inside back cover. This issue contains eleven pages of advertisements, each item neatly arranged.
49. Huculak, 'The London Mercury (1919–39) and Other Moderns', p. 242.
50. MacKenzie, 'The London Mercury', p. 254.
51. Patrick Collier, 'Reactionary Materialism: Book Collecting, Connoisseurship and the Reading Life in J. C. Squire's London Mercury', in Collier, Modern Print Artefacts, pp. 141–79 (p. 142).
52. Ibid. p. 143.
53. Huculak, 'The London Mercury (1919–39) and Other Moderns', p. 246.
54. J. B. Priestley, 'Fiction', The London Mercury, 10.57 (July 1924), pp. 427–9 (p. 429).
55. L. P. Hartley, 'The Island', The London Mercury, 10.56 (June 1924), pp. 138–49.
56. Regarding The New Age, Robert Scholes and Clifford Wulfman note that it is unusual for the correspondents' names to appear in the contents page, and it is an indication of the magazine's special interest in constructing an active readership. Scholes and Wulfman, Modernism in the Magazines, pp. 152–3.
57. John Tudor, 'An Accusation of Neglect', The London Mercury, 12.69 (July 1925), p. 297; A. C. Crookshank, 'A de la Mare Episode', The London Mercury, 10.57 (July 1924), p. 299; Original Subscriber, 'Correspondence', The London Mercury, 1.1 (November 1919), p. 77.
58. For instance, Bysshe's nickname is chosen for its 'romantic associations', recalling Shelley and James Thomson (also known as Bysshe Vanolis), and his obsession is compared to 'some "morbid affection"' of Keats (de la Mare, 'Pretty Poll', in Short Stories, pp. 324, 334). When Eleanor first encounters Mrs Lennicott, she is reading a poetry book with large print and looks at Eleanor 'uncomprehendingly, but with an air of earnest effort, as though she were a verse of Georgian poetry that

one could not possibly understand' (Bowen, 'The Parrot', in *Collected Stories*, p. 119).
59. Squire, 'The Man who Wrote Free Verse', p. 197.
60. Henry James, 'The Story-Teller at Large: Mr. Henry Harland', *Fortnightly Review*, 63.374 (April 1898), pp. 650–4 (p. 652).
61. Ethel Rolt-Wheeler, 'Wireless', *The London Mercury*, 12.67 (May 1925), pp. 31–43.
62. M. R. James, 'A Warning to the Curious', *The London Mercury*, 12.70 (August 1925), pp. 354–65.
63. De la Mare, 'Pretty Poll', in *Short Stories*, p. 322.
64. Bowen, 'The Parrot', in *Collected Stories*, p. 114.
65. De la Mare, 'Pretty Poll', in *Short Stories*, p. 337.
66. Ibid. p. 324.
67. Ibid. p. 336.
68. Bowen, 'The Parrot', in *Collected Stories*, p. 127.
69. Bowen, *Afterthought*, p. 94.
70. Dyneley Hussey, 'Truth and Fiction', *The London Mercury*, 8.48 (October 1923), pp. 600–11 (p. 611).
71. De la Mare's formulation of 'atmosphere' is strikingly consonant with Bowen's later writing on tone in the short stories of the early twentieth century, such as in her preface to *The Faber Book of Modern Stories*. De la Mare, 'Atmosphere in Fiction', Walter de la Mare Papers, Special Collections, Bodleian Library, Oxford, A115 (b), pp. 18–19. I am grateful to Giles de la Mare of the Literary Trustees of Walter de la Mare, the Society of Authors as their representative, and the Bodleian Library for granting me permission to quote from de la Mare's published and unpublished works.
72. J. C. Squire, 'Poetry', *The London Mercury*, 8.48 (October 1923), pp. 655–7 (p. 656).
73. De la Mare, 'Pretty Poll', in *Short Stories*, p. 329.
74. Ibid. p. 329.
75. Ibid. p. 331.
76. Ibid. p. 333.
77. De la Mare, 'Pretty Poll', in *Short Stories*, pp. 334, 333.
78. Ibid. pp. 330–1.
79. Bowen, *Afterthought*, p. 80.

Chapter 9

Virginia Woolf and Aldous Huxley in *Good Housekeeping* Magazine

Saskia McCracken

In 1931, Virginia Woolf was commissioned to write a series of six articles for *Good Housekeeping* magazine, and critics have typically read these as five essays and a short story. Woolf's series takes her readers on a tour of the sites of commerce and power in London which she visited that year, from 'The Docks of London', published in December 1931, in which 'beauty begins to steal in' to the utilitarian docklands; to 'Oxford Street Tide', in which 'everything glitters and twinkles'; and on to the 'raucous bawling' of politicians in 'This is the House of Commons'.[1] The tour includes 'Great Men's Houses' – in which she depicts Thomas Carlyle's home as a domestic 'battlefield' – and the 'Abbeys and Cathedrals' of St Paul's and Westminster. The series ends in December 1932 with 'Portrait of a Londoner', where the 'innumerable fragments of the vast metropolis seemed to come together' at the tea table of the fictional hostess Mrs Crowe.[2]

This chapter has three aims. The first section suggests that Woolf's *Good Housekeeping* publications can be read not simply as five essays and a short story as scholars have tended to interpret them, but as a series of short stories or, as the magazine editors introduced them, 'word pictures' (December 1931 and January 1932) and 'scenes' (all but 'Portrait of a Londoner'). I will consider the series in its magazine context, bearing in mind its editorial history and focusing on what Christine Reynier calls Virginia Woolf's 'ethics of the short story' in order to justify my reading of the series as generically unstable scenes.[3] In the second section I will argue that Woolf's *Good Housekeeping* series responds to, and resists the totalitarian politics of, Aldous Huxley's series of four essays on England, published in 1931 in *Nash's Pall Mall Magazine*. Analysing her engagement with Huxley's work depends on an understanding of the ethical stakes of Woolf's series, both in terms of form (as Reynier argues) and ideology (that is, in relation to Huxley's politics), and is made possible by original archival research which reveals that she submitted her series for publication later than previously recognised. Several critics have engaged with Woolf's *Good Housekeeping* series as feminist texts which engage with issues of class, gender and empire.[4] These are important and useful readings, but these topics are not central to this chapter. Taking into account the magazine format, ideology, illustrations and advertisements juxtaposed with Woolf's texts is crucial to understanding the ethical stakes of the series, as I aim to do in this chapter. I will engage with criticism by Woolf scholars Alice Wood and Jeanette McVicker, both of whom discuss the series in its magazine context. Finally, in the third section, I will analyse a critically neglected short story by Ambrose O'Neill, 'The Astounding History of Albert Orange', published in February 1932 in *Good Housekeeping*, which features both Woolf and Huxley as characters and which critiques, satirises and destabilises the boundaries of highbrow literary culture. Thus, I turn the focus from highbrow writers' short stories to a story about highbrow writing, all published in the supposedly middlebrow *Good Housekeeping*, demonstrating the rich complexity of the magazine and its generically hybrid publications.

Good Housekeeping magazine

Good Housekeeping was established in 1922 as a women's magazine which featured fiction, opinion pieces, interviews and articles on a range of topics including housekeeping, furnishing, cookery and fashion. Advertisements (which took up approximately 60 per cent of each issue in the early 1930s), photographs and illustrations accompanied the magazine text.[5] When Woolf's series was published, the magazine was edited and directed by suffragist Alice Maud Head, who commissioned work by famous female politicians and suffragettes including Millicent Fawcett and Ellen Wilkinson.[6] *Good Housekeeping*, however, is generally regarded as a middlebrow magazine, aiming to 'teach middle class women how to run their homes'.[7] Woolf scholars have observed, as Wood points out, that the magazine's 'interests and concerns were far more diverse than are often assumed', and Jeanette McVicker affirms that it is 'crucial that this context be given greater elaboration'.[8] The magazine featured numerous articles on unemployment, capitalism and politics, although some were couched in homely terms, such as Mary Agnes Hamilton's 'Mother of Westminster', which offered a portrait of the 'Labour ex-Member for Blackburn – who has a housewife's eye for domestic improvements in St Stephen's!'[9] Woolf's publications were categorised in the *Good Housekeeping* contents page as special articles, an umbrella term which covered interviews, opinion pieces, myths and profiles (of Labour Prime Minister Ramsay MacDonald, for example), as well as essays such as 'Women in Music' by composer and suffragette (and friend of Woolf's) Ethel Smyth.[10] The magazine was evidently a platform for a diverse range of topics and writers.

Good Housekeeping is mentioned only in passing in the three-volume *Oxford Critical and Cultural History of Modernist Magazines*, as one of several women's magazines dedicated to 'mindless femininity and weak creativity'.[11] This is not the case. *Good Housekeeping* was not a modernist magazine, but it did publish a broad range of literary works. The magazine contained articles encouraging women to go into publishing, with an article for 'the girl who likes books and can appreciate them as commodities', and ran a feature on 'Literary Lodgings'.[12] Fiction content included short stories, and ranged from a middlebrow serial by O. Douglas about '[t]he everyday experiences of a very young family, told with all her endearing charm', to work by prominent writers including Woolf, Huxley, John Galsworthy, W. Somerset Maugham and H. E. Bates.[13] The magazine ran a 'Ladies of Literature' series from February 1932, featuring profiles by Mary Craik of Vita Sackville-West, Virginia Woolf, Rebecca West, Vera Brittain and other famous authors. These profiles were published on alternating months to Woolf's *Good Housekeeping* series, and Woolf herself was featured in the second Ladies of Literature publication. The magazine also juxtaposed highbrow articles with advertisements for consumer goods. The article on Sackville-West, for example, was published alongside adverts for cod liver oil, cots, HP sauce, ink, and the Elsan Chemical Closet.[14] *Good Housekeeping*, then, was hardly 'mindless', and covered a far more diverse range of highbrow and middlebrow topics than it is credited with.

Woolf's *Good Housekeeping* publications engaged with the production and distribution of the commodities being advertised in the magazine, including fashion furs, wine, creams, and woollen rugs and clothes (each issue opened with an advertisement for baby underwear 'of the Finest Empire Wool'). In 'The Docks of London' Woolf writes, 'We demand shoes, furs, bags, stoves, oils, rice puddings, candles; they are brought to us [. . .] we demand woollen overcoats in winter', and if 'we gave up drinking claret [. . .] the whole machinery of production would rock and reel and adapt itself afresh'.[15] She lists commodities for sale in 'Oxford Street Tide', such as tobacco, wool, scented cream, satin dresses and even tortoises. Her further publications in the series not only engaged with such commodities, but also were printed alongside numerous advertisements for products similar to those she described. 'This is the House of Commons', for example, was accompanied by advertisements for cookbooks, sanitary towels, bed sheets, the *Good Housekeeping* shopping service, a coat dyeing service, a polishing cloth and duster, and casserole dishes.[16] The magazine, then, was a space where cultural artefacts and criticism were brought together for consumption by the wider public. Wood observes that, although 'Woolf could never have guessed exactly what would appear alongside her contributions to *Good Housekeeping*, she appears to have known enough of this publication to anticipate the type of articles and advertising material that would surround her contributions'.[17] Woolf engaged with these anticipated materials, stating that it is 'we – our tastes, our fashions, our needs [...] that call the ships from the sea'.[18] She empowers her female readership as consumers, as numerous critics have observed, but she does more than this, and understanding the unstable genre of her series is key to understanding the ethical implications of her magazine writing.

Short stories, scenes, word pictures

The *Good Housekeeping* editorial headers used mixed terminology to introduce each of Woolf's publications. Her contemporaries evidently found her work difficult to categorise, as Mary Craik makes clear in her Ladies of Letters article on Woolf:

> But how is one to classify Virginia Woolf? She is not exactly a novelist although she writes novels, nor is she a poet in that she does not write verse although she has the poet's keen sense of the beauty which is inherent in everyday things. What is she then? I give it up.[19]

The word 'scene' appears in multiple editorial headers for Woolf's *Good Housekeeping* series. The second and third instalments (and the March 1932 proofs of the fourth) were introduced as 'The London Scene'; 'This is the House of Commons' is described as 'the Westminster scene'; and 'The Docks of London' was introduced as a 'finely etched *word picture* of London River, first in a gallery of *scenes* made vividly alive by the brilliant pen of Virginia Woolf' (emphases added); while 'Oxford Street Tide' was introduced as a 'brilliant word picture'.[20] The term 'word picture' was not applied to any other writer's work in the magazine, and may refer not only to the images Woolf describes, but to the etchings of the docklands which accompanied 'The Docks of London', the illustrations which accompanied 'Oxford Street Tide' and 'Portrait of a Londoner', and the photographs of buildings which accompanied the remaining publications. 'Portrait of a Londoner', usually referred to as a short story, is the only piece the editors categorise as an essay.[21] Woolf was aware of these headers, as her handwritten annotations on the galley proofs of her series show. These editorial headers, then, suggest that Woolf's *Good Housekeeping* series defies categorisation, except perhaps loosely in the most commonly used term by the editors, that is, as a series of scenes. We shall see that 'scene' is a term Woolf used herself to discuss short stories.

Woolf's first five *Good Housekeeping* publications have consistently been read by scholars as essays or articles, and the sixth as a short story. The first five of Woolf's *Good Housekeeping* publications were posthumously reproduced as *The London Scene* (1975) and are included in the six-volume *Essays of Virginia Woolf*, and numerous essay collections.[22] These five pieces do not appear in Susan Dick's *The Complete Shorter Fiction of Virginia Woolf* (1985; revised 1989) or other story collections, including the forthcoming Cambridge edition of her collected short fiction.[23] The sixth publication in the series, 'Portrait of a Londoner', is consistently published as fiction in collections of her work, including *The Complete Shorter Fiction of Virginia Woolf*, probably because the title character is fictional. The predominant trend since Dick's edition is to collect (as with the forthcoming Cambridge edition of her *Collected Short Fiction*) or produce criticism regarding Woolf's short or shorter fiction, rather than short stories.[24] There are of course exceptions, such as David Bradshaw's collection *Carlyle's House and Other Sketches* (2003), Stella McNichol's collection *Mrs. Dalloway's Party: A Short Story Sequence* (1979) and Reynier's monograph *Virginia Woolf's Ethics of the Short Story*, but it is clear that the editorial choices of scholars have shaped the way we read the series as essays and a story.[25] I argue that Woolf's *Good Housekeeping* publications are hybrid texts, and that reading these as short stories (rather than fiction) or scenes can provide insight into the formal ethics of the series. First, though, it is worth discussing the generic instability of Woolf's short prose.

Numerous critics have observed that Woolf's short stories are difficult to categorise, and often blur generic boundaries. Different editors and scholars, as Reynier points out, continually 'highlight the affinities that the short story may have with another literary genre', including the essay (Susan Dick, Elena Gualtieri, and Dominic Head), the novel (Stella McNichol), impressionist pochades and tales (Jean Guiguet) and the sketch or journal (David Bradshaw, Amy Bromley, Gualtieri, Guiguet and Craig Morehead).[26] Woolf's manuscripts, which include sketches, essays and novel drafts within the same notebooks, suggest an openness to generic hybridity in her works. By borrowing from a range of genres Woolf, as Kathryn N. Benzel and Ruth Hoberman put it, 'questions the possibility of any single, inclusive definition for the short story'.[27] Dick, however, offers a definition of her fiction as 'works in which the characters, scenes, and actions are more imaginary than they are factual, and in which the narrator's voice is not necessarily identical with the author's'.[28] Woolf's *Good Housekeeping* publications feature real people and places, but also follow a narrative journey across London, featuring imagined scenes and actions, such as the 'perpetual struggle' of Thomas Carlyle's maid and his wife, or John Keats as he 'turned the page without haste though his time was short'.[29] The series also includes fictional characters such as the first-person perspectives of a tortoise salesman, a thief in 'Oxford Street Tide', and the protagonist of 'Portrait of a Londoner'. The series both resists and is closer to Dick's definition of fiction than it first appears; indeed, the 'proper stuff of fiction', Woolf says in her essay 'Modern Fiction' (1925), 'does not exist; everything is the proper stuff of fiction'.[30] More significantly perhaps, the series corresponds to Woolf's own understanding of the short story form.

Woolf engaged with short stories as both an author and a critic, reviewing work by writers including Anton Chekhov and Katherine Mansfield. Woolf's reviews, letters, essays and diaries provide some insight into her understanding of the short story form, despite the commonly cited claim that 'she left few direct statements about her theory of the short story; there are no manifestos'.[31] Woolf complained about 'the bore of writing out a story to make money', and dismissed such publications as 'pot boiling stories for America'.[32] But she was proud that these stories were a source of income, writing: 'Ladies' clothes and aristocrats playing golf don't affect my style [. . .] what I want [is] money.'[33] 'Happily', she writes in her diary in 1937, she can get '£500 for a 9.000 word story', although she received only £50 per publication for *Good Housekeeping*, minus 10% for her agent.[34] Woolf also worried about the critical reception of her short stories just as she did with her novels. She revised them substantially, as Dick's editorial notes to *The Complete Shorter Fiction of Virginia*

Woolf demonstrate, and wrote in her diary: 'I don't know that I can write stories.'[35] Anticipating the reception of her short story collection *Monday or Tuesday* (1921), she wrote in her diary that 'in the *Westminster, Pall Mall* and other serious evening papers I shall be treated very shortly with sarcasm'.[36] Thus, 'Woolf's anxiety and meticulous revisions', as Reynier puts it, 'show that she took short story writing more seriously than she chose to say'.[37]

There is no denying that Woolf herself referred to her *Good Housekeeping* series as articles, although I suggest that the series corresponds closely to her understanding of short stories. She wrote to Ethel Smyth in March 1931: 'I'm being bored to death by my London articles.'[38] A few weeks later she wrote to Smyth: 'I've written and written – so many articles – 8 to be exact. Five on London.'[39] On what grounds, then, might we call this a series of short stories? Rather than attempt a closed definition, I will point to the ways in which the *Good Housekeeping* publications can be read as generically hybrid scenes, which may be understood as forms or variants of the Chekhovian short story. As early as 1917, Woolf wrote in a letter that 'its [sic] easier to do a short thing, all in one flight than a novel', adding 'I daresay one ought to invent a completely new form'.[40] This form was already emerging in 1927, when she wrote in her diary: '[h]ow many little stories came into my head! [. . .] One might write a book of short significant separate scenes.'[41] The short significant scene, then, is aligned with the short story. The scene is also connected to her understanding of autobiography. In *A Sketch of the Past*, Woolf's autobiographical writings, she says: 'I find scene making is my natural way of marking the past.'[42] Woolf's *Good Housekeeping* series, like her understanding of short stories, comprises scenes that thread together memories of her London tour with fictional characters and scenes.

The ethics of form

Woolf's writing on Chekhov's short stories demonstrates what Reynier calls her 'ethics of the short story'.[43] This ethics, Reynier says, includes a commitment to generic hybridity, to inconclusiveness and to 'obscure figures'.[44] In 'The Russian Point of View' (1925), Woolf says that 'Chekov is successful as a short story writer' not 'because he is interested in social satire – even if he is', as she says, 'aware of the evils and injustices of the social state'.[45] Rather than being didactic, his stories are inconclusive, and Woolf had written on

Chekov earlier in 'The Russian Background' (1919), saying that his 'inconclusive stories are legitimate [. . .] they provide a resting point for the mind', for 'reflection and speculation'.[46] She elaborates on the function of this inconclusiveness in 'The Russian Point of View', writing that 'as we read these little stories about nothing at all, the horizon widens'.[47] This inconclusiveness and uncertainty is ethical in that it empowers the reader to reflect, to speculate, to consider, as she puts it in 'Modern Fiction', 'question after question which must be left to sound on and on after the story is over'.[48]

Woolf's series sketches out several inconclusive scenes. In 'Great Men's Houses' Woolf describes the homes of eminent men, 'bought for the nation and preserved entire'.[49] Instead of focusing on these great men, she imagines scenes from the lives of Carlyle's wife 'coughing in the large four-poster' and fighting bug infestations, and his maid carrying boiled water 'up three flights of stairs from the basement'.[50] Woolf depicts Carlyle's home as a 'battlefield where daily [. . .] mistress and maid fought against dirt and cold for cleanliness and warmth'.[51] In 'Oxford Street Tide' Woolf imagines the perspectives of obscure men and women: the tortoise salesman says (she writes) 'my chance of selling a tortoise is small; but courage! there may come along a buyer; my bed tonight depends on it'; a 'middle class woman' on a shopping spree says 'I grab and pounce with disgusting greed. But [. . .] I have only fifteen pounds a year to dress on; so here I come'; and a thief says she will steal a bag though it 'may contain only spectacles and old bus tickets'.[52] These scenes are inconclusive: the battle in Carlyle's House is not resolved, and the reader does not learn whether the tortoise seller makes a sale, what the shopper buys or what the thief finds in the bag. Indeed, Woolf says 'it is vain to try to come to a conclusion in Oxford Street'.[53] Her *Good Housekeeping* series speaks to her understanding of the inconclusive scenes of the Chekhovian short story.

This ethics is apparent too, Reynier says, in the generic hybridity of Woolf's short stories, where 'the fictional, the metafictional, the historical or the autobiographical are woven together in total disregard of generic laws; allusion, quotation, and creation are intertwined'.[54] This openness and generic hybridity is evident in her *Good Housekeeping* series, where each publication might be read as an individual unit fragmented by advertisements, or a fragment of a series; where each piece might be read as a word picture, a scene, an essay, an recollection or fictional short story. As generically unstable, inconclusive scenes, Woolf's short stories are 'site[s] of resistance against all forms of political and literary monologism and totality'; her short stories can therefore 'be read as a deeply committed form'.[55] This ethics is crucial to understanding the relationship between Woolf's *Good Housekeeping* series and Aldous Huxley's essay series, published in *Nash's Pall Mall Magazine*, which I will turn to now.

Woolf and Huxley

We have seen that Woolf's *Good Housekeeping* series may be read as short stories or scenes, and that these are committed to an ethics of inconclusiveness and formal, generic hybridity. The ethics of the scene is crucial to my comparative reading of Woolf and Huxley's work. In this section, I aim to demonstrate that Woolf's series engaged with, and resisted, the totalitarian ideology of Aldous Huxley's series of four articles published in 1931 in the literary monthly *Nash's Pall Mall Magazine*. I will call them his England essays: 'Abroad in England' (May), 'Sight-Seeing in Alien Englands' (June), 'The Victory of Art over Humanity' (July) and 'Greater and Lesser London' (October). *Nash's Pall Mall Magazine* was frequently advertised in *Good Housekeeping* (the two magazines were owned by the Hearst Corporation and merged in 1937), and Huxley was also published in *Good Housekeeping*, in 1932.[56] Huxley lived in France in the 1930s, and frequently travelled to England to write about his experiences there.[57] His essay series describes his tour of English mines and factories, London's docklands and the House of Commons, and offers his views on the relationship between production, consumption and mass unemployment – in 1931, 3.25 million people were officially unemployed in the UK – and his proposed solutions to these issues.[58]

Huxley felt 'distaste for mass society and parliamentary democracy', preferring the masses to be ruled by an 'intellectual aristocracy', as David Bradshaw explains.[59] Huxley was a proponent of eugenics, and wrote in 'The Future of the Past' (1927) that, '[i]n the future we envisage, eugenics will be practised in order to improve the human breed', reiterating this view in 'What is Happening to Our Population?' (1934), where he called for the 'compulsory sterilisation' of the poor.[60] Bradshaw suggests that the England essays were a turning point in Huxley's view of the masses from contempt to compassion, where Huxley 'spoke out more and more vociferously on behalf of those whose lives he had derided or ignored in the previous decade [. . .] whom he now regarded as the powerless victims of a bankrupt political system lumbering towards war'.[61] In 1933 Huxley was horrified by reports of book burning and the Jewish boycott in Hitler's Germany, and in 1934 'witnessed the thuggery' of Oswald Mosley's blackshirts at a British Union of Fascists (BUF) rally in London, which led to a 'sea change in Huxley's attitude to authoritarianism'.[62] He came to reject Nazism and dictatorships, went on to organise an exhibition of 'Artists Against Fascism and War' and became the first president of the anti-fascist organisation 'For Intellectual Liberty'.[63] In his 1931 essays published in *Nash's Pall Mall Magazine*, however, Huxley was still of the view that eugenics, a Soviet-style 'Five-Year Plan' and 'such reforms in procedure as those suggested by Sir Oswald Mosley', were legitimate solutions to the economic slump in the UK.[64] I want to suggest that although Woolf recognises some of the same issues as Huxley, she rejects and subverts his proposed solutions.

Huxley and his wife Maria were friends with the Woolfs and dined with them on 16 February 1931 after the London part of their tour.[65] The next day, Woolf wrote in her diary:

> I feel us, compared with Aldous & Maria, unsuccessful. They're off today to do mines, factories . . . [sic] black country; did the docks when they were here; must see England. [. . .] And I am to write 6 articles straight off about what?[66]

It is likely that dining with the Huxleys inspired her visit, organised by the Port of London Authority, to the docklands on 20 March 1931, with her husband Leonard Woolf and Vita Sackville-West.[67] The six articles Woolf mentions above became the *Good Housekeeping* series, the first of which describes her visit to the docklands. Woolf reiterated her interest in Huxley's tour a few days later, in a letter to Clive Bell written on 21 February 1931:

> Aldous astounds me – his energy, his modernity. [. . .] he spends his week in London visiting docks [. . .] and now is off on a tour of the Black Country, to visit works, to go down mines: and then to Moscow, and then America. I am very envious in my heart.[68]

Evidently, Huxley's visit made an impression, and the two writers discussed his tour of London and upcoming travels.

Huxley's first England essay, 'Abroad in England', covers his 1930 visit to Durham Cathedral and a nearby mining village, and concerns the 'crowds of unemployed men' who 'fill the streets'.[69] His solution to the unemployment crisis is a Soviet-style 'Five-Year Plan', and he considers 'national plans' proposed by BUF founder Oswald Mosley, which he considers 'doubtful'.[70] In 'Sight-Seeing in Alien Englands', Huxley discusses the 'sufferings and legitimate claims' of the factory worker, and the 'problems of urban growth and new industrial development', which 'can only be dealt with adequately on a national scale' and says that '[a]s usual, a plan is needed, and, as usual, there is no plan'.[71] In 'The Victory of Art over Humanity' Huxley visits a motor factory and the London docks, observing that '[h]igher production by fewer producers' means '[m]ore unemployed with less money to buy goods'.[72] He calls for 'world-wide agreements' on production and consumption, and the 'prompt assassination' of numerous politicians.[73] He calls for an organisation as efficient as the Port of London Authority to 'deal with the larger chaos of world trade'.[74] Huxley's final England series essay, 'Greater and Lesser London', is concerned with a visit to the House of Commons, which he calls a 'torture chamber' of 'Septic Boredom'.[75] He proposes that 'such reforms in procedure as those suggested by Sir Oswald Mosley', whose national plans he no longer seemed to consider doubtful, 'are obviously essential'.[76] Thus, while having a plan for getting people into work is not necessarily Stalinist or Mosleyan, Huxley's idea of national planning explicitly draws on the work of both these men. Woolf's *Good Housekeeping* series engages with these England essays, resisting Huxley's polemic with non-didactic narratives that feature and subvert his themes, language, similes and imagery. Rather than proposing reforms of her own (and thus writing essays), she resists monologism through hybrid form, turns her focus to the power of the female consumer (her *Good Housekeeping* readership) and asks 'question after question which must be left to sound on and on after the story is over'.[77]

The docklands

There is some question as to how useful reading Woolf and Huxley's London scenes together might be, as scholars have inaccurately stated that Woolf submitted the final drafts of her series to *Good Housekeeping* before Huxley's essays were published. Wood, who offers a comparative reading of the two writers' docklands publications, states that Woolf was 'inspired' by his work, but that, as 'Huxley's articles were not published in *Nash's Pall Mall Magazine* until after Woolf submitted her series to *Good Housekeeping*, any further parallels between the texts are presumably coincidental'.[78] Likewise, Jeanette McVicker states that Woolf submitted her series 'between February and early April 1931'.⁷⁹ Woolf did submit initial drafts of her series (dated March 1931) to *Good Housekeeping* in April 1931. I have discovered, however, that the galley proofs of the series are mostly dated 1932, with a letter to *Good Housekeeping* enclosing proofs of Woolf's 'Abbeys and Cathedrals' dated March 1932.⁸⁰ This discovery enables us to revise our understanding of the 'coincidental' parallels between Woolf and Huxley's magazine publications. Woolf was known to make 'significant substantive revisions' to her work 'even at proof stage'.⁸¹ I have evidence that Woolf made substantive revisions to her London scenes at proof stage, after reading Huxley's essays. All of Huxley's England essays had been published between May and October 1931, and Woolf's first *Good Housekeeping* publication was in December of that year, allowing plenty of time for revision. The significant parallels – numerous phrases, similes and images are identical, in both authors' published essays – may well be deliberate. The two writers, of course, may have shared views, phrases, images and similes over dinner. It is also possible that the language the two writers share is that of the Port of London Authority, who organised and perhaps guided their tours. But given that Woolf's revised drafts were submitted to *Good Housekeeping* after Huxley's full series had been published, it is highly likely that her series responded directly not only to Huxley's views regarding his tour, but specifically to his England series of publications.

Let us analyse some of these parallels. In their docklands publications both Woolf and Huxley use the simile 'ant-like activity' to describe the city; they liken the wine vaults to a 'vast cathedral' or an 'enormous cathedral'; both use the word 'mellow' to describe wine in 'swollen' or 'bulging' barrels; and both describe fungus using the similes 'cotton-wool-like' or 'sooty lacework'.⁸² With the exception of the sartorial fungus, none of these parallel similes appear in the March 1931 manuscript version of Woolf's 'The Docks of London', and were likely added after she read Huxley's description of the docks in 'The Victory of Art over Humanity'.⁸³ These similarities shed light on the significance of the differences between the two publications. Woolf writes that the 'only thing, one comes to feel, that can change the routine of the docks is a change in ourselves', and that '[b]ecause one chooses to light a cigarette, all those barrels of Virginia tobacco are swung on shore'.⁸⁴ Woolf concludes that '[o]ne feels an important, a complex, a necessary animal'.⁸⁵ This is a far cry from Huxley's claim that 'man is a lazy animal' in need of a five-year plan.⁸⁶ In a magazine that explicitly promoted consumerism, Woolf empowers women and, as Wood points out, 'prompts her readers to realize their potential individual influence as shoppers'.[87] On the other hand, as McVicker points out, Woolf seems 'uneasy about the way women's consumer driven desires are shaped and served by commodity capitalism', and how shopping 'inevitably supports the horrendous conditions of the labouring men [. . .] who live in the sordid tenements lining the docks'.[88] The affinities between Woolf and Huxley's docklands texts are striking, and Woolf, whether responding to Huxley's specific publication or to his wider views, resists the closure of national planning, identifying a degree of trade power in her female *Good Housekeeping* readership, while highlighting women's complicity in labour exploitation.

The House of Commons and the obscure

Woolf's 'This is the House of Commons' and Huxley's 'Greater and Lesser London' both focus on the writers' separate visits to the House of Commons, which Huxley calls a 'torture chamber' of 'Septic Boredom'.[89] He proposes that 'such reforms in procedure as those suggested by Sir Oswald Mosley are obviously essential'.[90] Both write of the 'bawling' of politicians, whom they align with oxen, and note the banality of the topics discussed – the status of osteopaths for Huxley; the speed limit in Hyde Park for Woolf – concluding that the House of Commons is, as Woolf puts it, 'not in the least noble or majestic or even dignified'.[91] Yet where Huxley calls for the retirement of the 'Grand Old Men' running the country, Woolf sees only a young graduate, a shopkeeper, businessmen and a country gentleman fresh from 'poking pigs' in the House of Commons. She says it is 'unthinkable' that these men will 'turn into statues' like those of their eminent predecessors, for the 'conduct of affairs has passed from the hands of individuals to the hands of committees'.[92] She asks, 'if the days of the small separate statue are over, why should not the age of architecture dawn?', adding, '[l]et us see whether democracy which makes halls cannot surpass aristocracy which carved statues [. . .] or that [. . .] both will be combined, the vast hall and the small, the particular, the individual human being'.[93] The replacement of aristocracy with democracy seems like a pointed reference to what Bradshaw calls Huxley's 'distaste for mass society and parliamentary democracy', and preference for a ruling 'intellectual aristocracy'.[94] Woolf counters Huxley's Grand Old Men and didactic reforms with anonymous committees and individual human beings, in what *Good*

Housekeeping called her 'Westminster scene'. The parallels between Woolf and Huxley's series, rather than being coincidental, suggest Woolf's sustained engagement with, and subversion of, Huxley's views.

Woolf's series also resists Huxley's on a formal and feminist level. Her *Good Housekeeping* publications comprise inconclusive scenes, in line with her understanding of the Chekhovian short story. This inconclusiveness is intimately connected to her focus on the importance of 'obscure figures', those who, Reynier says, 'have been forgotten by history, the unknown ones, most of the time, women'.[95] We have seen that Woolf's series sketches out scenes from the lives of obscure figures, mostly women, including Carlyle's wife and his maid, the tortoise seller, the shopper and the thief. The 'million Mr Smiths and Miss Browns', Woolf writes in 'Abbeys and Cathedrals', 'seem too many, too minute, too like each other to have each a name, a character, a separate life of their own', and yet Woolf offers these minute figures small scenes in her series. Thus the 'small, the particular, the individual human being' is cast not as a Grand Old Man or a labourer, or an unemployed man, but a range of unknown characters, mostly women.[96] Woolf's attention to obscure figures is most evident in the final instalment of her *Good Housekeeping* series, 'Portrait of a Londoner'. In this publication, the fictional hostess Mrs Crowe presides over her tea-table, as she has done for sixty years, and gossips. Each of the publications in Woolf's series focuses on centres of power, and Crowe's home, implicitly, is also such a centre of power, though clearly of a different kind from the docklands or House of Commons. Woolf therefore invites the reader to consider what power Crowe may wield. When Crowe dies at the end of the narrative, she makes way for a new generation of women, the *Good Housekeeping* readership perhaps, to wield what power they have, and to shape the scenes of London. Woolf's *Good Housekeeping* series maintains an ethics of generic hybridity, Chekhovian inconclusiveness and attention to obscure figures which resists the didactic politics of Huxley's magazine essays.

'The Astounding History of Albert Orange'

In this chapter I have suggested that Woolf's *Good Housekeeping* series may be read as hybrid short stories or scenes, and that this series responded to and resisted the didactic, national-planning-focused politics of Huxley's *Nash's Pall Mall Magazine* essays. Both writers were also the subject of a boundary-blurring short story, which I will focus on briefly in the final section of this chapter. 'The Astounding History of Albert Orange' by Ambrose O'Neill, published in *Good Housekeeping* in February 1932 (between Woolf's second and third *Good Housekeeping* publications), was introduced as 'A New Kind of Story about the Literary World with many Distinguished Living Authors among the characters'.[97] O'Neill's protagonists are fictional, but his secondary characters include Woolf, Huxley, Rebecca West and Vita Sackville-West. The story is experimental, combining fiction with non-fiction, and uses the strategies of popular fiction (in this case humour, intrigue and plot twists) to critique, satirise and destabilise the boundaries of highbrow and popular literature, in a magazine that acted as a complex cultural platform for high and middlebrow writers and topics. I use the term highbrow to refer to Woolf and Huxley's writing on the basis that Woolf is widely understood to be a high modernist writer, which I take to be a form of highbrow literature, and Huxley declared himself a highbrow in his essay 'I am a Highbrow'.[98]

O'Neill's protagonist, author Mrs Olive Raymond Opplethwaite, is a popular fiction writer who feels she has 'wasted her talent' on 'entertaining, sentimental stuff' read primarily by 'foolish, undeveloped people'.[99] Opplethwaite aspires to 'the noble austerity of Mrs. Woolf and Miss Sackville-West, Aldous Huxley and Richard Aldington', particularly 'the loneliness of the left-out adjective, the unexclamatory style, the glory of short and close-fitting words'.[100] She has evidently not read Woolf (the first two-page 'Interlude' of her 1931 novel *The Waves* has over thirty adjectives and twenty-six tri-syllabic or longer words) or Huxley ('Greater and Lesser London' contains ten exclamation marks).[101] When Opplethwaite tries 'paring down [her] adjectives' and emulating these writers, her editors complain that 'there is no *plot* in this story [...] your readers expect plot' (emphasis in original), an allusion perhaps to Woolf's own novels which resist conventional plotting, such as *The Waves*, and possibly her call, in 'Modern Fiction', for writing with 'no plot, no comedy, no tragedy, no love interest or catastrophe in the accepted style'.[102] Opplethwaite begins publishing her would-be highbrow writing successfully under the new pen name Albert Orange. She tells her editors that Orange has recently returned from a Burmese tea plantation and, like Huxley, is bespectacled, smokes, and – drawing satirical attention to Orange's status as a 'future highbrow' – has 'a Brow'.[103] Opplethwaite is 'a highly observant woman, with the greatness of heart that led all kinds of people to confide all kinds of secrets to her', who now 'granted herself the leisure to do her best'; her editors compare Orange's style to Woolf's and Huxley's, and he is hailed a 'true artist'.[104] O'Neill here implies that any observant woman with time and money – the *Good Housekeeping* reader, for instance – might become a true artist. Indeed, Ambrose O'Neill may well be the pen name of a woman writer. This passage, then, both empowers women to write and satirises such aspirations.

The illustration of Huxley and Woolf that accompanied the story (Figure 9.1) serves several functions. Firstly, as Orange's success is augmented by praise from 'avowed highbrow' Huxley, who 'considered Albert Orange full of promise', the image emphasises the dependence of prestigious writers on what Rachel Potter calls the 'literary and publishing networks which produced and disseminated modernism' and highbrow literature (for example, the Bloomsbury Group and the Hogarth Press for Woolf; or Huxley's intellectual network, which included Lytton Strachey, Bertrand Russell and D. H. Lawrence).[105] Secondly, the recognisability of the two writers in the illustration draws the eye of the reader, who may be flicking casually through the magazine pages, giving the image a practical as well as a critical function. Finally, the image was juxtaposed with illustrations of fictional characters, drawing attention to the experimental form of the story itself. Published in a popular magazine which featured work by Woolf and Huxley, and featuring these writers as characters, the story both critiques and satirises highbrow and modernist networks and writers, whilst at the same time demonstrating that these are not mutually exclusive from popular writing styles or publishing platforms. O'Neill's is a 'New Kind of Story' which destabilises the boundaries of fact and fiction, high and middlebrow culture; and, as a hybrid text which empowers women readers as writers, the story demonstrates a formal ethics not too distant from that of Woolf's *Good Housekeeping* series.[106]

In this chapter, I hope to have offered new approaches to reading Woolf's *Good Housekeeping* series – as hybrid short stories, word pictures, scenes – readings which take the magazine context of the publications seriously and create potential for understanding of the ethics of form and its relation to ideology in her series. I have suggested that the editorial headers in *Good Housekeeping* offer an alternative reading to that of Woolf scholars who categorise these six pieces as five essays and a short story. This chapter also demonstrates that the series responded to, and resisted, the didactic totalitarian politics of Aldous Huxley's England essays. This resistance is formal in nature, in accordance with the ethics of generic hybridity, and

Figure 9.1 Illustration accompanying Ambrose O'Neill's story 'The Astounding History of Albert Orange'.
© British Library Board, *Good Housekeeping* Magazine, February 1932.

twists Huxley's themes, language and imagery away from Stalinist five-year plans and Mosleyism, towards open questions that 'sound on and on', perhaps in the mind of the empowered female *Good Housekeeping* readership. Finally, this chapter has brought to light a previously overlooked short story which treats Woolf and Huxley not just as writers, but as characters that represent the world of highbrow literature whilst publishing work in mass-produced popular magazines. Ambrose O'Neill's 'The Astounding History of Albert Orange' destabilises the categories of high and middlebrow, of popular, modern and modernist writing, in a magazine which provided a platform for experimentation with these forms.

Notes

1. Virginia Woolf, 'The Docks of London', *Good Housekeeping*, 10.4 (December 1931), pp. 16–17, 114–17 (p. 116); 'Oxford Street Tide', *Good Housekeeping*, 10.5 (January 1932), pp. 18–19, 120 (p. 18); 'This is the House of Commons', *Good Housekeeping*, 12.2 (October 1932), pp. 18–19, 110–12 (p. 18).
2. Virginia Woolf, 'Great Men's Houses', *Good Housekeeping*, 11.1 (March 1932), pp. 10–11, 162–3 (p. 11); 'Abbeys and Cathedrals', *Good Housekeeping*, 11.3 (May 1932), pp. 18–19, 102; 'Portrait of a Londoner', *Good Housekeeping*, 12.4 (December 1932), pp. 28–9, 132.
3. Reynier, *Virginia Woolf's Ethics of the Short Story*.
4. Scholarship on Woolf's *Good Housekeeping* publications which I do not have space to discuss here includes: Caughie, 'Purpose and Play in Woolf's London Scene Essays'; Sarker, 'Locating a Native Englishness in Virginia Woolf's the London Scene'; Snaith and Whitworth, *Locating Woolf*; Squier, '"The London Scene": Gender and Class in Virginia Woolf's London'; Squier, *Virginia Woolf and London*.
5. Wood, 'Made to Measure', p. 18.
6. Ibid. p. 16.
7. Braithwaite et al., *Ragtime to Wartime*, p. 7.
8. Wood, 'Made to Measure', p. 12; McVicker, 'Virginia Woolf and American Writers', p. 315.
9. Woolf, 'Great Men's Houses', p. 19.
10. Woolf, 'Great Men's Houses', p. 2; 'This is the House of Commons', p. 2.
11. Dowson, 'Interventions in the Public Sphere', p. 536.
12. Woolf, 'Oxford Street Tide', p. 60; Clemence Dane, 'Literary Lodgings', *Good Housekeeping*, 20.6 (February 1932), pp. 22–3 (p. 2).

13. O. Douglas, 'Priorsford: A New Serial', *Good Housekeeping*, 20.4 (December 1931), pp. 6–8 (pp. 6–7); Baldwin, *Art and Commerce in the British Short Story*, p. lxi.
14. 'Advertisements: Cod Liver Oil, Cots, HP Sauce, Ink, Elsan Chemical Closet', *Good Housekeeping*, 20.6 (Feb 1932), p. 112.
15. Woolf, 'The Docks of London', p. 117.
16. Woolf, 'This is the House of Commons', pp. 110–12.
17. Wood, 'Made to Measure', p. 18.
18. Woolf, 'The Docks of London', p. 117.
19. Mary Craik, 'Ladies of Letters: Virginia Woolf', *Good Housekeeping*, 21.2 (April 1932), pp. 20–1, 104 (p. 20).
20. *The Virginia Woolf Manuscripts*, The Henry W. and Albert A. Berg Collection, New York Public Library [microfilm], Reel 5-12, M13-M135 (University of Glasgow, 2018), Reel 12 M133; Woolf, 'This is the House of Commons', p. 18; Woolf, 'The Docks of London', p. 16; Woolf, 'Oxford Street Tide', p. 18.
21. Woolf, 'Portrait of a Londoner', p. 28.
22. Woolf, *The London Scene*.
23. Woolf, *The Collected Short Fiction of Virginia Woolf* (forthcoming).
24. See: Baldwin, *Virginia Woolf*; Benzel and Hoberman, *Trespassing Boundaries*; Levy, *The Servants of Desire*; Marcus, 'The Short Fiction'; Skrbic, *Wild Outbursts of Freedom*.
25. Woolf, *Carlyle's House and Other Sketches*; Woolf, *Mrs. Dalloway's Party: A Short Story Sequence*; and Reynier, *Virginia Woolf's Ethics of the Short Story*.
26. Reynier, *Virginia Woolf's Ethics of the Short Story*, p. 8; Dick, 'Introduction', p. 3; Gualtieri, *Virginia Woolf's Essays*, p. 18; Head, *The Modernist Short Story*, p. 81; McNichol, 'Introduction', p. x; Guiguet, *Virginia Woolf et son œuvre*, pp. 326–38; Bradshaw, 'Introduction', p. xvii; Bromley, *Virginia Woolf and the Work of the Literary Sketch*, p. 4; Morehead, '"Rambling the Streets of London"', p. 19.
27. Benzel and Hoberman, *Trespassing Boundaries*, pp. 6–7.
28. Dick, 'Introduction', p. 2.
29. Woolf, 'Great Men's Houses', pp. 162, 163.
30. Woolf, 'Modern Fiction', in Woolf, *Essays*, vol. 4, pp. 157–65 (p. 164).
31. Baldwin, *Virginia Woolf*, p. xii.
32. Woolf, *Diary*, vol. 5, p. 189; Woolf, *Letters*, vol. 6, p. 252.
33. Woolf, *Letters*, vol. 3, p. 154.
34. Woolf, *Diary*, vol. 5, p. 107; Woolf, *Essays*, vol. 5, p. 663.
35. Woolf, *Diary*, vol. 2, p. 44.
36. Ibid. p. 98.
37. Reynier, *Virginia Woolf's Ethics of the Short Story*, p. 4.
38. Woolf, *Letters*, vol. 4, p. 301.

39. Ibid. p. 304.
40. Woolf, *Letters*, vol. 2, p. 167.
41. Woolf, *Diary*, vol. 3, p. 157.
42. Woolf, 'Sketch of the Past', p. 145.
43. Reynier, *Virginia Woolf's Ethics of the Short Story*, p. iii.
44. Dick, 'Introduction', p. 17; Reynier, *Virginia Woolf's Ethics of the Short Story*, p. 129.
45. Woolf, *Essays*, vol. 4, p. 185.
46. Woolf, *Essays*, vol. 3, p. 84.
47. Woolf, *Essays*, vol. 4, p. 185.
48. Ibid. p. 163.
49. Woolf, 'Great Men's Houses', p. 10.
50. Ibid. pp. 11, 10.
51. Ibid. p. 11.
52. Woolf, 'Oxford Street Tide', pp. 19, 120.
53. Ibid. p. 120.
54. Reynier, *Virginia Woolf's Ethics of the Short Story*, p. 32.
55. Ibid. p. 117.
56. Stouck, *As for Sinclair Ross*, p. 304; Dean Inge, 'Four eminent men consider what it would mean to the modern world If Christ Should Come', *Good Housekeeping*, 21.2 (April 1932), pp. 6–9 (pp. 6–7).
57. Huxley, *The Hidden Huxley*, p. vii.
58. McVicker, '"Six Essays on London Life"', p. 150.
59. Huxley, *The Hidden Huxley*, p. x.
60. Ibid. pp. xiii, xiv.
61. Ibid. pp. xvi, xxii.
62. Ibid. p. xxi.
63. Ibid. p. xxi.
64. Ibid. pp. 62, 91.
65. Woolf, *Diary*, vol. 4, p. 11, note 7.
66. Woolf, *Diary*, vol. 4, pp. 11–12.
67. Woolf, *Letters*, vol. 4, p. 301, note 2.
68. Woolf, *Letters*, vol. 4, pp. 293–4.
69. Huxley, *The Hidden Huxley*, p. 60.
70. Ibid. pp. 62–3.
71. Ibid. pp. 66, 67.
72. Ibid. p. 80.
73. Ibid. p. 83.
74. Ibid. p. 86.
75. Ibid. p. 88.
76. Ibid. p. 91.
77. Woolf, *Essays*, vol. 4, p. 163.
78. Wood, *Woolf's Late Cultural Criticism*, pp. 40, 36.
79. McVicker, '"Six Essays on London Life"', p. 150.
80. The rubber-stamped dates on the galley proofs of 'The Docks of

London', 'Oxford Street Tide' and 'Portrait of a Londoner' are indecipherable. Those of 'Great Men's Houses' are stamped '03 JAN 1932'; those of 'This is the House of Commons' are stamped '[05?] AUG 1932'; the typescript for 'Portrait of a Londoner' is dated 5 October; and the proofs of 'Abbeys & Cathedrals' are stamped '[16?] MAR 1932' and are accompanied by a letter to *Good Housekeeping* (19 March 1932) titled 'PROOFS: URGENT' (*The Virginia Woolf Manuscripts*, Reel 12 M130–135).
81. Hussey, 'Introduction', p. xlviii.
82. Woolf, 'The Docks of London', p. 114; Huxley, *The Hidden Huxley*, p. 86; Woolf, 'The Docks of London', p. 117; Huxley, *The Hidden Huxley*, p. 84; Woolf, 'The Docks of London', p. 117; Huxley, *The Hidden Huxley*, p. 85; Woolf, 'The Docks of London', p. 117; Huxley, *The Hidden Huxley*, p. 85.
83. Woolf does write 'in the cool white colourless cathedral room' (*The Virginia Woolf Manuscripts*, Reel 5 M13, p. 49).
84. Woolf, 'The Docks of London', p. 117.
85. Ibid. p. 117.
86. Huxley, *The Hidden Huxley*, p. 57.
87. Wood, *Woolf's Late Cultural Criticism*, p. 38.
88. McVicker, '"Six Essays on London Life"', p. 145.
89. Huxley, *The Hidden Huxley*, p. 88.
90. Ibid. p. 91.
91. Woolf, 'This is the House of Commons', p. 18; Huxley, 'Greater and Lesser London', p. 88.
92. Huxley, *The Hidden Huxley*, p. 92; Woolf, 'This is the House of Commons', pp. 110, 111.
93. Woolf, 'This is the House of Commons', p. 112.
94. Huxley, *The Hidden Huxley*, p. x.
95. Dick, 'Introduction', p. 17; Reynier, *Virginia Woolf's Ethics of the Short Story*, p. 134.
96. Woolf, 'Abbeys and Cathedrals', p. 18; Woolf, 'This is the House of Commons', p. 112.
97. Ambrose O'Neill, 'The Astounding History of Albert Orange', *Good Housekeeping*, 20.6 (February 1932), pp. 6–9, 133–8 (p. 6).
98. Aldous Huxley, 'I am a Highbrow', *Aldous Huxley Annual*, 7 (2007), pp. 126–8 (p. 126).
99. O'Neill, 'The Astounding History', pp. 8, 6.
100. Ibid. p. 6.
101. Woolf, *The Waves*, pp. 3–4.
102. O'Neill, 'The Astounding History', p. 8; Woolf, *Essays*, vol. 4, p. 160.
103. O'Neill, 'The Astounding History', pp. 9, 8.
104. Ibid. pp. 134 and 9.
105. Ibid. pp. 9 and 133; Potter, *Modernist Literature*, p. 30.
106. O'Neill, 'The Astounding History', p. 6.

Chapter 10

Virginia Woolf and the Magazines

Dean Baldwin

That Virginia Woolf built her reputation on the novel in no way diminishes her significant contributions to the short story. Between 1917 and 1943, she published over forty stories, nearly all of them appearing first not in periodicals but in book form, namely *Monday or Tuesday* (1921) and *A Haunted House and Other Stories* (1943). Only ten of the forty stories were published first in magazines. This is an extraordinarily low number given the fact that Woolf's writing career coincided with the most propitious period in British literary history for publishing stories in periodicals. Scores of magazines opened their pages to short fiction, many of them paying handsome fees for first serial rights. Savvy fiction writers exploited this market on both sides of the Atlantic, usually publishing simultaneously in America and Britain and collecting fees in both dollars and sterling.

Why she took so little advantage of the profitable market for stories is an open question. It was certainly not that she didn't want or need money. Her letters and diaries are peppered with references to her need for money. Nor can she be accused of focusing exclusively on her novels, for she produced reams of essays, reviews and other literary journalism, the writing of which she frequently resented for its hard work, low pay and frequent rejection. It may in fact be the fear of rejection or criticism that explains her reliance on the Hogarth Press as the publisher of her story pamphlets and collections. An exchange of letters between Woolf and H. G. Leach, editor of *The Forum* (New York), suggests as much. The magazine had offered her $250 for a story, so she sent 'The New Dress'. He rejected it, then changed his mind and published it in 1927.[1] However, when he asked for another story, she replied: 'It is very good of you to ask me to submit another story for your consideration, but I feel that it would only be a waste of your time. The stories I have at present are in much the same style as The New Dress and are open to the same objections.'² Nevertheless, she subsequently sent 'Moments of Being: Slater's Pins Have no Points', and *Forum* published it in January 1928. Moreover, as Julia Briggs points out, establishing the press gave Woolf the freedom to experiment, as well as protection from editors' comments and rejections.³

Another possibility is that she did not employ a literary agent until 1937, when she worked with Jacques Chambrun, an agent working in New York City, and then she apparently used him for only the three stories she published in *Harper's Bazaar* (US and UK) in 1938 and 1939. A savvy agent would surely have encouraged her to send all her stories to magazines and would have handled the tedious business of placing them and negotiating suitable payment.

A related possibility is that she wanted to appear only in the best magazines. I infer this from the observation that the stories she did publish in magazines were largely in 'highbrow' rather than popular venues. *The Athenaeum*, which published 'Solid Objects' in 1920, was one of the foremost literary periodicals of the day, with a history of publishing such writers as Thomas Hardy and T. S. Eliot.⁴ The same holds true for *The Criterion*, which published Woolf's 'In the Orchard' alongside such forward-looking poets as Ezra Pound, William Empson, W. H. Auden and Stephen Spender in 1923.⁵ The American journals *The Dial* and *The Forum* were equally selective and significant. *The Dial*, which featured 'Mrs. Dalloway in Bond Street' in 1923, 'printed virtually all the distinguished authors of the period'.⁶ *The Forum*, in which 'The New Dress' and 'Moments of Being: Slater's Pins Have no Points' appeared in 1927 and 1928 respectively, was an important organ of political and literary thought, especially under the editorship of H. G. Leach.⁷ Even *The London Mercury*, a magazine Woolf dismissed as a 'slop pail of stale tea',⁸ but which printed her story 'An Unwritten Novel' in 1920, included W. B. Yeats and D. H. Lawrence among its contributors.⁹ 'The Lady in the Looking Glass', on the other hand, appeared in 1929 in the important American magazine *Harper's* before landing in *Harper's Bazaar* (UK) in 1930. Thus, *Harper's Bazaar* was Woolf's only venture into non-literary journals, a movement that coincides with the change in her fictional technique from experimental to more conventional forms in the later stories.¹⁰

If fear of rejection, the lack of a literary agent, and a desire to be seen only in high-quality periodicals help explain Woolf's publishing history until 1930, followed by an eight-year hiatus until the three *Harper's Bazaar* stories, what accounts for the change in policy in 1938? One point, already noted, is that she employed Chambrun, who as her agent would have negotiated simultaneous publication in the US and UK. Moreover, we can surmise that early in her career, Woolf was concerned about the prestige of the journals in which her stories appeared, but by 1938, with her reputation secure, this consideration no longer carried much weight.

Another possibility explaining the change in policy can be found in an invitation in 1937 to submit a story: 'I had a cable from America, asking for a story – to which I replied, as you [Vanessa Bell] bade me, only if money is paid beforehand.'[11] According to the editors of her letters, Woolf was offered £200 for the story – a very good sum, indeed. Another clue can be found in a diary entry: 'This morning I had a moment of the old rapture – think of it – over copying The Duchess and the Jeweller for Chambrun NY. I had to send a synopsis. I expect he'll regret the synopsis. But there was the old excitement, even in that little extravagant flash – more than in criticism I think.'[12] In other words, the combination of a commission, plus the rediscovered excitement of writing stories, may help to explain her return to the genre. Moreover, as I pointed out above, Woolf adopted a more traditional narrative method for the *Harper's Bazaar* stories than she had used up to 'The Lady in the Looking Glass'. A letter to John Lehmann suggests that this was a deliberate choice: 'I loathe having to keep to dates and so many thousand words. Indeed, save for writing an occasional article for the Lit. Sup. and two pot boiling stories for America I've not written for any editor for years.'[13] The two 'pot boiling' stories would certainly be 'The Duchess and the Jeweller' and 'Lappin and Lapinova', already published at the time of this letter, but it is difficult to know how seriously she meant the derogatory term 'pot boiling'. Was this merely a self-deprecating gesture, a confession to writing for money, or a bit of anti-Americanism? That she harboured anti-American feelings is suggested by a comment to Vita Sackville-West a decade earlier: 'Sixty pounds just received from America for my little Sapphist story ['Slater's Pins Have no Points'] of which the Editor has not seen the point, though he's been looking for it in the Adirondacks.'[14]

Because she published only these ten stories in magazines, her voluminous correspondence and detailed diaries contain relatively few references to her stories and their publication in magazines, though some of these are revealing. A letter to Jacques Raverat contradicts my assertion that she preferred quality magazines:

> I have been engaged in a great wrangle with an old American called [Logan] Pearsall Smith on the ethics of writing articles at high rates for

fashion papers like vogue [sic]. He says it demeans one. He says one must write only for the Lit. Supplement and the Nation and Robert Bridges and prestige and posterity and set a high example. I say Bunkum. Ladies' clothes and aristocrats playing golf don't affect my style; and they would do his a world of good. Oh these Americans! How they always muddle everything up! What he wants is prestige; what I want, money.[15]

In a similar vein, she wrote to Vita Sackville West: 'And what's the objection to whoring after [Dorothy] Todd [Editor of *Vogue*]? Better whore, I think, than honestly and timidly and coolly and respectably copulate with the Times Lit. Sup.'[16] In the event, however, she did not publish fiction in *Vogue*, perhaps because Condé Nast fired editor Dorothy Todd for trying to improve the cultural level of the magazine.[17]

Finally, the period 1936 to 1940 was exhausting for Woolf. These were not only the years of rising fear of war and then its outbreak that have been so frequently remarked upon as weighing on her nerves. Julia Briggs also observes that in 1936 Woolf 'was overcome with the weight of *The Years*',[18] yet she forged ahead with *Three Guineas* (1938) and then almost immediately turned to work on her biography of Roger Fry, about which she remarked: 'I think I've mounted a barren nightmare in this book (R.F.) but shall finish the dreary round and then dismount and see what's the use of it. Odd what a grind biography is.'[19] As relief she rushed 'headlong into *Pointz Hall*', published as *Between the Acts* in 1941.[20] These pressures and another factor suggest a corollary motive for turning to short stories. In 1938, Woolf sold her share of Hogarth Press to John Lehmann – the very year she turned to the commercial publishing of her stories.[21] Freed now from her duties at Hogarth and the pressure to build her reputation as a 'serious' author, she could relax and enjoy writing these stories.

Selecting well-paying magazines over 'quality' ones brings both compensations and liabilities. The compensations are high pay and exposure to a wide but perhaps not very discriminating audience; the liabilities are exposing oneself to the charge of writing for money and allowing one's fiction to be printed beside fashion spreads, adverts for make-up and articles about socialites. Commercial magazines also carry the risk of implying that a short story is a commodity, equivalent to the products advertised in their pages. Another potential liability is that stories of this period were accompanied by illustrations which, as we shall see, carry interpretive messages over which the author has no control.

Harper's Bazaar

Harper's Bazaar in the late 1930s was an expensive, glossy, lavishly produced magazine for white, upper-middle-class women and those who aspired to imitate them. Each issue of the periodical in the late 1930s focused on a fashion theme, and the newest styles in clothes made up much of its contents. A typical issue would include photo spreads and drawn illustrations in both colour and black and white of stylish clothing – most often dresses (very few trousers) – and also hats, coats, gowns, furs, sportswear, accessories and shoes. Advertising followed this pattern, though unlike the features, it focused a great deal on what used to be called 'foundation garments'. Every issue of the period included an article called 'The Cosmetic Urge'. In addition to the advertisements scattered throughout the magazine, there was a large classified section devoted to schools and summer camps for girls, clearly aimed at an 'exclusive' audience.

The contents were not restricted to those mentioned above, however. Under the heading 'Fiction And Features', most issues included at least one article on travel, sometimes with a shopping emphasis, plus pictorial spreads on well-known women of fashion, Hollywood stars, society women, leisure and sport (especially golf and tennis). Articles never, so far as I can determine, ventured into the genuinely serious topics of politics, economics or social problems, despite the fact that it was the heart of the Great Depression and close to the outbreak of the Second World War. Every issue I have examined included three or four short stories and sometimes poems. Among the fiction writers who appeared in its pages were names known even today – E. M. Delafield, A. E. Coppard, Evelyn Waugh, Frank O'Connor, H. E. Bates, Thomas Wolf, John Dos Passos and others of similar rank. In other words, *Harper's Bazaar* was willing to pay substantial sums to writers who could enhance the magazine's aspirations for intellectual seriousness. Indeed, *The Writer's Market* for 1937 lists the magazine under the heading 'Women's Magazines – First Class' and says of its fiction: 'Does not use a great deal of fiction, but this must be very smart, with a lightly sophisticated, humorous touch.'[22] Critics would not regard this as an accurate account of Woolf's stories, but the description suggests a high standard of excellence.

Before proceeding to a discussion of the three stories that appeared in *Harper's Bazaar* (US), a discussion of the term 'context' is in order. I use the term to refer generally to the magazines and their implied audiences, but context is more complex than a brief description of a publication's general contents and readership. These features are important, but the specifics of a particular issue – its cover, the articles or advertisements immediately surrounding the story, and the illustrations accompanying the fiction – are also worth noting. Beyond the magazine itself are other contextual factors, such as the social, economic and political conditions of the time, plus relevant details from the author's biography. Just how far any discussion of these larger considerations should extend is impossible to specify, the danger on one hand being that we miss something essential, but on the other hand we can extend the discussion so far that the story becomes drowned in contextual detail. For this chapter, the focus will be mainly on the magazine and its readership in general, the specific issue and the materials directly surrounding the story, and very importantly, I believe, the illustration accompanying it. Some consideration will also be given to the international political situation, not because it is discussed in the magazine's pages, but because it is ignored. These are the features readers of the time would be aware of, and thus ones we can analyse with some confidence of their relevance. The burden of my argument will be that in their commercial magazine context, Woolf's three stories stand in ironic contrast to the implied values of the magazine and its readership.

'The Shooting Party'

The cover of the issue containing 'The Shooting Party', like others of that year, might be described as 'Modernist lite'.[23] The editors clearly wanted to align the magazine with contemporary art trends without challenging readers with something avant-garde. Apart from giving the title of the magazine and listing its price as 50 cents US, 15 FR in Paris, and 2/6 in London, the only clue to its contents is the phrase 'AMERICAN FASHIONS' (Figure 10.1). Significantly, and unlike many other magazines of its day, *Harper's Bazaar* in the late 1930s did not advertise the names of its famous contributors on the cover; it did in 1930, when printing 'The Lady in the Looking Glass', but at some later point abandoned the practice. Moreover, the magazine did not include any information about its fiction writers or their stories; readers were evidently expected to know who these writers were and to read the stories without editorial assistance. This policy would change in January 1939, when it began a column called 'The Editor's Guest Book', which featured that issue's contributors along with descriptions of their achievements and often photos of them.

Figure 10.1 Cover of *Harper's Bazaar*, March 1938.

During the depths of the Great Depression, the price of 50 cents would put the magazine out of reach for most women, except those at whom it was aimed: women of the upper middle class and those who aspired to imitate them.

In addition to 'The Shooting Party', fiction in the March issue included 'Madame De Malitourn's Cold' by F. L. Lucas, 'Sleeping Beauty' by John Collier, and 'Ouled-Nail' by Colette. One poem each by Ruth Lechlitner and Clinch Calkins completed the literary selections. Colette is familiar to readers today; F. L. Lucas, John Collier and the poets have faded into obscurity.

Of the three stories Woolf published in *Harper's Bazaar*, 'The Shooting Party' is formally the most challenging. It opens with a description of a woman entering a train carrying a small suitcase and a brace of pheasants. She is called only 'M.M.' We learn later she is Milly Masters, the housekeeper at a crumbling stately home, but her introduction here seems curiously vague and tentative, despite the omniscient point of view. Particularly mysterious is the sound she makes, '"Chk". "Chk".' at the back of her throat, a sound she heard from Miss Antonia and that she repeats in the last paragraph of the story as she leaves the train. This framing narrative and its relation to the central story present a challenge to readers accustomed to conventional narrative structure.

The body of the story is dominated by actions and images of age, dissolution, decay and impending doom. The main characters, Miss Antonia and Miss Rashleigh, are frail, elderly women, sisters of the Squire, who is hunting pheasant on this cold, rainy fall day. Meanwhile, the two old women sew, reminisce and finally sit down to a lunch of pheasant, while the wind howls outside, scattering leaves and dislodging a slate from the roof. The women's conversation turns to remembrances of deaths in the family: one man killed in a hunting accident, another while riding a horse, a third leading a charge in battle. Then the subject turns to seductions, including a girl at a mill, another at a pub, yet another woman who worked at a tailor's shop and whose son cleans the local church. Tantalisingly, we hear: '"Milly Masters in the still room", began old Miss Rashleigh. "She's our brother's [. . .]."'[24] The reader will ask: her brother's what? Mistress? Unacknowledged wife? Occasional lover?

At the end of the meal, Miss Antonia throws the pheasant's carcass under the table to feed the spaniel waiting there. Moments later, the Squire enters with three large dogs, who instantly attack the spaniel; this results in a melee that the Squire breaks up by whipping the dogs. During the chaos, a vase is broken and Miss Rashleigh is cut across the cheek by the Squire's whip; consequently, she falls back against the mantelpiece and her stick hits the plaster decorations, dislodging and smashing the family's crest. A framed photograph of King Edward also falls, as does a tree outside.

All the details in the story point to a stately home on the verge of collapse. Despite the philandering by men of the family, no male heir will inherit the property, which is clearly falling apart. Descriptions of the hunt and its mass slaughter of birds parallel the deaths discussed by the elderly women, who themselves are compared to the pheasants. Woolf says of the pheasants: 'The birds were dead now, their claws gripped tight, though they gripped nothing. The leathery eyelids were creased greyly over their eyes [...]. The pheasants looked smaller now, as if their bodies had shrunk together.'[25] The women are similarly described:

> Light faded from the carpet. Light faded in their eyes too, as they sat by the white ashes listening. Their eyes became like pebbles, taken from water, grey stones dulled and dried. And their hands gripped their hands like the claws of dead birds gripping nothing. And they shrivelled as if the bodies inside the clothes had shrunk.[26]

The decaying house, the prevalence of death, the ageing, heirless family, the fallen crest and photo of King Edward point unmistakably to a story preoccupied with a dead and irrelevant aristocracy. But Woolf goes beyond the symbolism of the decaying house and household to link the story to a wider theme. Returning to the imagery of eyes in the last paragraph, Woolf similarly describes Milly's eyes:

> Only her eyes gleamed, changed, lived all by themselves it seemed; eyes without a body; blue-grey eyes seeing something invisible [...]. Yet after all since there is nothing that does not leave some residue, and memory is a light that dances in the mind when the reality is buried, why should not the eyes there, gleaming, moving, be the ghost of a family, of an age, of a civilization dancing over the grave?[27]

When we remember that the year is 1938, with the Great Depression devastating the world's economies and Hitler in power and threatening war, we cannot help but note this wider context of a story ironically placed in a magazine devoted to fashion and published in the United States, where isolationism theoretically insulated its readers from concern about the gathering slaughter in Europe. Hermione Lee detects another contextual consideration, speculating that the story reflects Woolf's mourning of Julian Bell (killed in the Spanish Civil War) and her brother Thoby's untimely death from typhoid.[28]

Despite all this emphasis on decay and collapse, the illustration emphasises calm and stability (Figure 10.2). The two elderly women sipping their wine, with the spaniel contentedly gnawing the bones

Figure 10.2 Illustration accompanying Virginia Woolf's story 'The Shooting Party', *Harper's Bazaar*, March 1938.

under the table, are completely at odds with the story's themes. Perhaps the illustration is intended to depict the calm before the storm, but whatever the intention, the drawing ironically clashes with the story or at the very least creates an anticipation that the story does not satisfy. In hindsight, it may be seen as reflecting America's indifference to the frightening events happening on the continent, reinforcing the isolationist feelings among its readers. Unwittingly or consciously, the illustrator is reassuring readers that all is well, when in fact chaos reigns in the story and is about to break out in Europe. However one interprets it, the illustration is remarkable for its distance from the story it purports to depict.

'The Duchess and the Jeweler'

As noted above, an unusual aspect of *Harper's Bazaar* of the time was its understated approach to calling the reader's attention to its contributors. Many other magazines of the time trumpeted the fame of their contributors by splashing their names on their covers; some also included a 'Notes on Contributors' page or editorial comments, highlighting the accomplishments and/or fame of the writers who graced their pages. But *Harper's Bazaar* at this time did neither of these things. It is significant, therefore, that in the April 1938 issue is a half-page advertisement: 'A Must for May! Virginia Woolf's "**The Duchess and the Jeweler**" [sic.] May **Harper's BAZAAR**' (emphasis in original).[29] These words are printed over part of the illustration that would serve as background to the first two pages of the story. If not unique, this is the only such blurb I have seen in the magazine. Evidently, the editors considered Woolf's story a significant selling point for the May issue.[30]

The cover of the May 1938 issue of *Harper's Bazaar* announces the theme of the issue to be sports clothes, and indeed there are two articles, 'Now that It's May' and 'Pickin' Cotton' featuring informal wear, plus a travel essay, 'We Went to a Dude Ranch', that immediately precedes Woolf's story.[31] Perhaps by coincidence, there is also a feature on inexpensive clothes, 'Pearls of Little Price', that may refer slyly to Woolf's story, which concerns a Duchess who wants to sell her fake pearls to a social-climbing jeweller, more of which later.[32]

Technically, the story is traditional in its style and structure, beginning with a sketch of Oliver Bacon, the self-made jeweller, now the wealthiest in London, leisurely at breakfast, then striding to his shop in Piccadilly elegantly dressed, and finally entering his luxurious shop and gloating over the jewels in his safes. Throughout the story, Oliver recalls moments from his impoverished, hustling childhood to remind him of how far he has come. In contrast to these details, which can be interpreted as criticising his crass materialism, Woolf refers frequently to the jeweller with animal imagery, most obviously in his surname, but also in an extended passage that elaborates on that name:

> [H]e was the richest jeweller in England; but his nose, which was long and flexible, like an elephant's trunk, seemed to say by its curious quiver at the nostrils (but it seemed as if the whole nose quivered, not only the nostrils) that he was not satisfied yet; still smelt something under the ground a little further off. Imagine a giant hog in a pasture rich with truffles; after unearthing this truffle and that, still it smells a bigger, a blacker truffle under the ground further off. So Oliver snuffed always in the rich earth of Mayfair another truffle, a blacker, a bigger further off.[33]

Another extended image compares him to a camel. In yet another image he 'snorts'.

As the passage above shows and the story emphasises, he wants more than his current success, and it's on this desire that the Duchess plays and preys. Showing Oliver her ten pearls – which she needs to sell to cover gambling debts – she hints more than once that he might be invited to a long weekend at her home, where the rich and politically powerful will gather, and where her three lovely daughters, especially Diana, will be available. Succumbing to these blandishments, he writes a cheque for the full amount she wants, £20,000, despite fearing and later confirming that they are not genuine: 'This then was the truffle he had routed out of the earth! Rotten at the centre – rotten at the core!'[34]

Behind this story is a clichéd social situation in fact and fiction, the rich middle-class aspirant to privilege and prestige angling to marry into an aristocratic family, and the aristocratic family's acquiescing to such an arrangement for an infusion of needed cash. In this sense the story echoes 'The Shooting Party', with its depiction of an ancient house in financial and moral decay. In this case, however, much of the story's satire points to the hog-like greed and social climbing of the self-made man. The implied narrator harshly criticises Oliver's money-grubbing and social climbing, but then the Duchess doesn't fare much better:

> And Oliver, rising, could hear the rustle of the dress of the Duchess as she came down the passage. Then she loomed up, filling the door, filling the room with the aroma, the prestige, the arrogance, the pomp, the pride of all the Dukes and Duchesses swollen in one wave. And as a wave breaks, she broke, as she sat down, spreading and splashing and falling over Oliver Bacon the great jeweller, covering him with sparkling bright colours, green, rose violet; and odours; and iridescences; and rays shooting from fingers, nodding from plumes, flashing from silk; for she was very large, very fat; tightly girt in pink taffeta; and past her prime. As a parasol with many flounces, as a peacock with many feathers, shuts its flounces, folds its feathers, so she subsided and shut herself as she sank down in the leather armchair.[35]

Her excess contrasts sharply with Oliver's threadbare childhood and even his current dapper appearance, but it also overwhelms him and his defences, and, along with his social-climbing ambitions, helps explain the capitulation of his common sense and business acumen. Indeed, referring again to the article, 'A Pearl of Little Price', and also noting that a biblically literate reader might well recall Jesus' parable of 'The Pearl of Great Price' (Matthew 13:45–6), by placing the article next to Woolf's story, the magazine's editors may have helped

Woolf emphasise Oliver's foolishness in purchasing the phony pearls. In any case, the story's apparent condemnation of Oliver Bacon and his acquisitiveness and social climbing stands in ironic contrast to the magazine's blatant valorising of both these qualities, though it's doubtful that readers made the connection between the story and themselves.

There is yet another aspect, a disturbing one at that, relating both to the historical moment of the story and Woolf's biography, impinging on the story and its contexts – its latent anti-Semitism. On the one hand, this would seem to be a charge that could not apply to Woolf, as she married Leonard Woolf, a Jew. Yet her letters reveal ambivalence towards, sometimes even a dislike of, Leonard's relatives, particularly his mother, because of their Jewishness. Turning again to a biographical context, Lee notes that Jacques Chambrun saved Woolf from publishing a version of 'The Duchess and the Jeweller' that was overtly anti-Semitic:

> In the summer of 1937 she wrote a story called 'The Duchess and the Jeweller', and sent it to a New York agent, Jacques Chambrun, who offered to place it for her. But the story of 'Isidore Oliver', a 'little Jew boy' with a hooked nose and a doting mother, who begins life in a 'filthy little alley', and makes his way through Whitechapel and Hatton Garden to become the richest jeweller in England, cheating and being cheated by duchesses, was not acceptable to the American market. 'COULD YOU CHANGE RACE OF JEWELLER SINCE THERE IS TERRIFIC RACIAL PREJUDICE IN AMERICA' Chambrun cabled her [...]. The story was published in *Harper's Bazaar* once she had changed some of the details: 'Isidore' became 'Oliver', little Jew boy became little boy, and so on, but his nose was still 'long and flexible, like an elephant's trunk': the 'jew' in 'jeweller' was still pronounced.[36]

Even with revisions, echoes of that prejudice remain in the name Oliver Bacon and in the extended pig metaphor quoted above. It seems safe to say that Chambrun and the magazine that rejected the story saved Woolf from acute embarrassment, not only at the time, but also for posterity, a rare instance of editorial squeamishness that turned out to be correct.

If the illustration for 'The Shooting Party' stands in ironic contrast to that story's content, the illustration for 'The Duchess and the Jeweller' is more complicated. On the surface, it appears simple enough, depicting the ten pearls on a blotting paper background, just as the story says, and including the jeweller's loupe (Figure 10.3). The difficulty with the drawing concerns its source of light. The

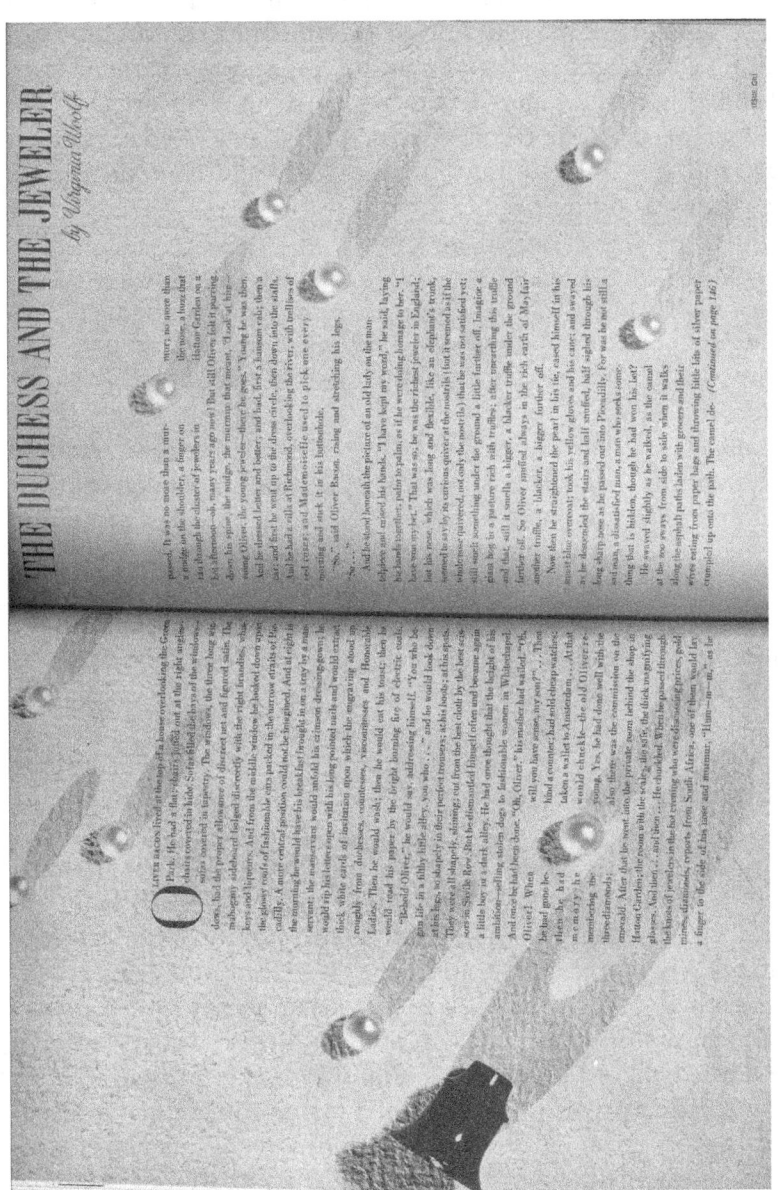

Figure 10.3 Leslie Gill's illustration accompanying Virginia Woolf's story 'The Duchess and the Jeweler', *Harper's Bazaar*, May 1938.

bright spot on each pearl and the loupe, and the dark shadow and different texture in the blotting paper to the left of each, suggest a source of light from the right side of the illustration, but then to the right of each pearl and the loupe is a long, light shadow, indicating a source of light from the left side of the illustration. An alternate explanation of this light shadow could be that the pearls themselves are emitting this light. Indeed, Oliver sees them as 'lustrous', but Woolf's description as the Duchess presents them to Oliver is almost grotesque, and it is unlikely that fake pearls would emit such light, even if real ones could:

> And with a sigh, but no words, she took from her bag a long wash-leather pouch – it looked like a lean yellow ferret. And from a slit in the ferret's belly, she dropped pearls – ten pearls. They rolled from the slit in the ferret's belly – one, two, three, four – like the eggs of some heavenly bird.[37]

Woolf's imagery, perhaps reflecting Oliver's own perception, emphasises Bacon's ambivalence: he strongly suspects they are fake, yet their attraction and value lie outside themselves in the repeated invitation to a long weekend at the Duchess's estate. Has the illustrator Leslie Gill's use of light captured the ambiguity in the pearls themselves and Oliver's dilemma as he examines them in the handling of light in the illustration? It is tempting to think so; and, if so, the illustrator has guided the reader to the heart of the story.

'Lappin and Lapinova'

'Lappin and Lapinova' joins two other stories by British writers, 'A Devil of a Cook' by A. E. Coppard and 'It's All Too Difficult' by E. M. Delafield.[38] A fourth story, 'Love is not Love', is by American writer Lionel Wiggam but is set in England. Indeed, it is worth mentioning that a high percentage of stories in the magazine over the years were by British writers. The inclusion of many British writers suggests that the editors believed that readers would associate Britain with the upper classes, the aristocracy and refined taste. Immediately preceding Woolf's story is an elaborate feature on ready-made fashions from Paris, and immediately following that is a pictorial on wedding gowns, perhaps not coincidentally alluding to the theme of marriage in Woolf's story; though, if so, the juxtaposition is once again ironic.

As noted above, beginning in January 1939, *Harper's Bazaar* included a monthly feature, 'The Editor's Guest Book', which highlighted some of the writers and illustrators included in the issue. It is worth noting what was said about Virginia Woolf in the April issue:

> Again *Harper's Bazaar* proudly publishes a story by **VIRGINIA WOOLF**. Last March we published her first short story in years – one she wrote especially for us. She is, of course, one of the greatest of women writers in our day, and her history is a fascinating one. In her father's home, she knew Meredith and Stevenson and Ruskin; with her husband, Leonard Woolf, she founded the Hogarth Press, and formed the center of the forever memorable Bloomsbury Group.[39] (emphasis in original)

Interestingly, this introduction emphasises that Woolf's previous story was her first in years and written especially for *Harper's Bazaar*, touting the magazine's exclusivity and prestige (actually, the editor should have said that 'The Shooting Party' was her first in years). In the same vein, the editor drops the names of famous British authors. Overall, it illustrates the bargain between well-known writers and middlebrow magazines: the author receives good pay and a large audience; the magazine gets the reflected glory of the author's fame and literary reputation.

Superficially, 'Lappin and Lapinova' is a typical story for a women's magazine, featuring love and marriage. However, since this is also the story of a marriage that eventually endures a significant rupture, it cuts across the grain of stereotypical 'women's stories'. 'Lappin and Lapinova' begins where most women's stories end – with a happy couple and a delightful wedding. For the first two years, the marriage is blissful, in part because the lovers invent a private fantasy world in which Ernest is Lappin and Rosalind is Lapinova:

> He was King Lappin; she was Queen Lapinova. They were the very opposite of each other; he was bold and determined; she wary and undependable. He ruled over the busy world of rabbits; her world was a desolate, mysterious place, which she ranged mostly by moonlight. All the same, their territories touched; they were King and Queen.[40]

Significantly, they are not king and queen of the same realm – 'their territories touched'. Theirs is a private world, a kind of game, that for Rosalind becomes a lifeline: 'Without that world, how, Rosalind wondered, that winter could she have lived at all?'[41] The necessity of that imaginary world to her is illustrated by a celebration of her in-laws' fiftieth wedding anniversary party, at which Rosalind feels alienated from Ernest's large, wealthy family, as she is an only child from a family of modest means. This in itself creates an ironic contrast between her and the implied readers of the story, for the readers would feel perfectly comfortable in Ernest's family's world of wealth and material comfort. Luckily, she is pulled back into the celebration when a brother-in-law mentions rabbits and she incorporates members of the family into her world of Lappin and Lapinova and sees the family as part of a decaying aristocratic tradition, recalling both 'The Shooting Party' and 'The Duchess and the Jeweller':

> 'Oh, King Lappin!' she cried as they went home together in the fog. 'If your nose hadn't twitched just at that moment, I should have been trapped!'
> 'But you're safe,' said King Lappin, pressing her paw.
> 'Quite safe,' she answered.
> And they drove back through the Park, King and Queen of the marsh, of the mist, and of the gorse-scented moor.[42]

Two years after the anniversary, Rosalind is still taking refuge in the fantasy world of Lappin and Lapinova, but it is beginning to slip away. When she confides this to Ernest, it takes him several minutes to recall his part in the game, during which time Rosalind 'felt a load on the back of her neck, as if somebody were about to wring it'.[43] That night in bed, she has trouble seeing Ernest as Lappin, wakes him to tell of her fears, and is firmly rebuked for talking 'such rubbish'.

The next day, she is restless and worried, so she takes a walk and ends up in the Natural History Museum, where the first thing she sees is a stuffed hare with pink glass eyes standing on artificial snow. That evening at home, trying to conjure up the world of Lappin and Lapinova, she cannot fully enter it. When Ernest returns from work, his key in the door sounds like a gunshot. She cries out that Lappinova is dead:

> Ernest frowned. He pressed his lips tight together. 'Oh, that's what's up, is it?' he said, smiling rather grimly at his wife. For ten seconds he stood there, silent; and she waited, feeling hands tightening at the back of her neck.
> 'Yes', he said at length. 'Poor Lapinova . . .' He straightened his tie at the looking glass over the mantelpiece.
> 'Caught in a trap,' he said, 'killed,' and sat down and read the newspaper.
> So that was the end of that marriage.[44]

Although the form and structure of the story are highly conventional, it presents real difficulties of interpretation, particularly because of its last line, 'So that was the end of that marriage.' In what sense is the marriage ended? It is ended probably not in the legal sense of divorce, given the laws of England at the time. Nevertheless, the story clearly traces the growing rift between Rosalind and Ernest as she clings desperately to the fantasy of the rabbit kingdom, even as it gradually slips from her. But part of the reason it slips away is Ernest's reluctance or inability to re-enter it with her and finally his cold rejection of it. Are we, therefore, watching a sensitive woman, out of place in Ernest's world of stolid reality, gradually losing her sanity? Or are we simply watching a marriage go through the normal diminishing of passion and intimacy as symbolised by the gradual demise of the Lappin and Lapinova world? Or was this simply an ill-advised marriage to begin with, especially as Rosalind believed at the outset that her husband did not look like an Ernest: 'The name suggested the Albert Memorial, mahogany sideboards, steel engravings of the Prince Consort with his family – her mother-in-law's dining room in Porchester Terrace in short.'[45] However, she gradually realises that he is Ernest indeed:

> Was it possible that he was really Ernest; and that she was married to Ernest? A vision of her mother-in-law's dining room came before her; and there they sat, she and Ernest, grown old, under the engravings, in front of the sideboard . . . It was their golden wedding day. She could not bear it.[46]

As suggested earlier, this story is anything but the conventional woman's story of 'They lived happily ever after', and its presence in a woman's magazine, surrounded by advertisements for clothing, cosmetics and other feminine products, themselves often framed in scenes of domestic comfort, including stylish living rooms, bathrooms or dining rooms, is pointedly ironic.

Once again, the illustrations for the story enter the interpretive dilemma. Across pages 90 and 91 is the title of the story in large block capitals, with the 'L' of 'Lappin' depicted as two vertical sticks and some grass-like vegetation, supporting a king's crown and topped with two hearts (Figure 10.4). On page 91, the final 'A' of 'Lapinova' is formed of the same sort of vegetation, supporting a queen's crown and topped by only a single heart – one heart has been removed. The 'L' with two hearts suggests the two lovers, bound together by the king's crown, but what are we to make of the terminal 'A' with its queen's crown and only one heart? The last line of the story might have suggested to the illustrator no crown and no

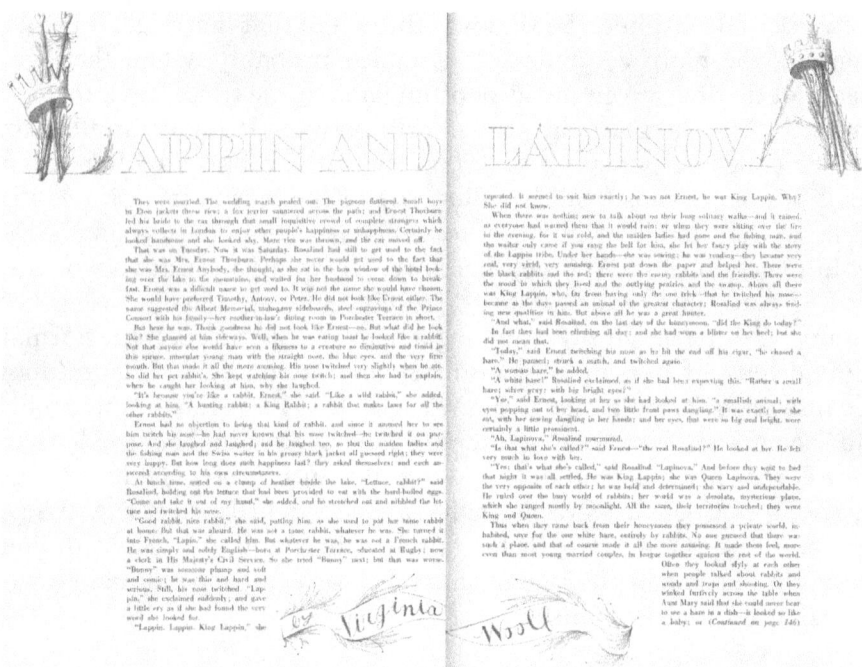

Figure 10.4 Illustrations accompanying Virginia Woolf's story 'Lappin and Lapinova', *Harper's Bazaar*, April 1939.

heart, but what does the queen's crown and one heart imply? Clearly, one half of the couple is missing from this picture, but which half? If it's Ernest that's missing, and the fantasy of Lappin and Lapinova has died, how can Rosalind be depicted still wearing the crown and her heart intact? If Rosalind is the one missing from the 'A', then does the illustration suggest that Ernest's heart is unbroken and the queen's crown remains as his misguided understanding of the marriage? Alternatively, the ambiguity of the illustration may reflect the illustrator's understanding of the story as ambiguous, or it may be that the illustrator misunderstood the story and depicted in that capital 'A' a Rosalind that the story does not support. In any event, the illustration has perhaps unwittingly introduced an interpretive debate that may have puzzled the story's contemporary readers.

Conclusions

Reading these stories in book form eighty years or more after their first publication must be significantly different from reading them when they appeared in *Harper's Bazaar*. But exactly how and in what ways that difference can be understood and appreciated by contemporary readers is difficult to assess. Obviously, we are not upper-middle-class women of the late 1930s. One point we can make with some certainty, however, is that in each of these three cases, magazine publication created an ironic tension between the story, its context, and its readers that does not exist when we read them in a collected edition. I would not go so far as to say that context creates a different text, but it does make us aware that magazine context can bring to light aspects of the story that book form can mute. In the case of 'The Shooting Party', reading the story in *Harper's Bazaar* emphasises the historical moment of its creation and publication – the coming threat of violence and chaos – a point we might miss or remember only with effort in a modern edition. The lingering aspect of anti-Semitism in 'The Duchess and the Jeweller' is likewise especially striking in the *Harper's Bazaar* context, and knowing Woolf's conflicted feelings about her Jewish family complicates the story just as the story complicates her biography. And once more, seeing 'Lappin and Lapinova' in a woman's magazine, regardless of its aspirations to sophistication, increases our understanding of how sharply that story contrasts with stereotypical 'women's fiction'. More subtle factors include materials immediately preceding and following a story, such as the article 'Pearls of Little Price' near 'The Duchess and the Jeweller'. It also seems likely that illustrations influenced how contemporary readers read and interpreted the stories. Finally, seeing these stories in a magazine like *Harper's Bazaar* emphasises how they deliberately insulated readers from the realities of the Great Depression and the sufferings it caused. Fiction is often seen as an escape from reality; here, a whole magazine is dedicated to suppressing it.

Notes

1. Woolf, *Letters*, vol. 3, p. 193, note 1.
2. Ibid. p. 217.
3. Briggs, *Virginia Woolf: An Inner Life*, pp. 58–62.
4. Drabble, *Oxford Companion to English Literature*, p. 48.
5. Ibid. pp. 240–1.
6. Hart, *Oxford Companion to American Literature*, p. 200.
7. Ibid. p. 258–9.
8. Woolf, *Diary*, vol. 2, p. 404.
9. Drabble, *Oxford Companion to English Literature*, p. 584.
10. Baldwin, *Virginia Woolf*, pp. 61–74.

11. Woolf, *Letters*, vol. 6, p. 257.
12. Woolf, *Diary*, vol. 5, p. 107.
13. Woolf, *Letters*, vol. 6, p. 252.
14. Woolf, *Letters*, vol. 3, p. 431.
15. Ibid. p. 154.
16. Ibid. p. 200.
17. Ibid. p. 295, note 2.
18. Briggs, *Virginia Woolf: An Inner Life*, p. 338.
19. Woolf, *Letters*, vol. 6, p. 262.
20. Ibid. p. 294.
21. Dubino, 'Introduction', p. 6.
22. *The Writer's Market*, p. 35.
23. Virginia Woolf, 'The Shooting Party', *Harper's Bazaar* (March 1938), pp. 76–7, 124, 176.
24. Virginia Woolf, 'The Shooting Party', in *The Complete Shorter Fiction of Virginia Woolf*, ed. by Susan Dick (London: Harcourt, 1989), p. 253. For convenience, all quotations from Woolf's stories will be from Dick's edition.
25. Ibid. pp. 250–1.
26. Ibid. p. 253.
27. Ibid. p. 254.
28. Lee, *Virginia Woolf*, p. 691.
29. *Harper's Bazaar* (April 1938), p. 173.
30. Virginia Woolf, 'The Duchess and the Jeweller', *Harper's Bazaar* (May 1938), pp. 74–5, 146–7.
31. *Harper's Bazaar* (May 1938), pp. 80–3; 96–9; 72–3.
32. 'Pearls of Little Price', *Harper's Bazaar* (May 1938), pp. 102–3.
33. Woolf, *Complete Shorter Fiction*, p. 243.
34. Ibid. p. 247.
35. Ibid. p. 245.
36. Lee, *Virginia Woolf*, pp. 668–9.
37. Woolf, *Complete Shorter Fiction*, pp. 245–6.
38. Virginia Woolf, 'Lappin and Lapinova', *Harper's Bazaar* (April 1939), pp. 90–1, 146, 148.
39. *Harper's Bazaar* (April 1939), p. 32.
40. Woolf, *Complete Shorter Fiction*, p. 257.
41. Ibid. pp. 257–8.
42. Ibid. pp. 259–60.
43. Ibid. p. 260.
44. Ibid. p. 262.
45. Ibid. p. 255.
46. Ibid. pp. 260–1.

Chapter 11

Horizon Magazine and the Wartime Short Story, 1940–1945

Ann-Marie Einhaus

In his editorial for the June 1940 number of *Horizon*, Cyril Connolly took an optimistic approach to wartime paper shortage as an opportunity rather than a challenge, arguing that it was 'a secret of good writing that it takes up very little room and expands in the remembering', and that the shortage would rid the country 'of the books not worth publishing and the news not worth printing'.[1] Besides poetry, Connolly commended 'economical' forms of writing such as 'the short story, the critical essay, and, where we can find it, the imaginative writing which was once known as the prose poem' as suitable literature for a wartime magazine.[2] Short fiction was thus embedded into the editorial programme of *Horizon* from its beginnings, as was its treatment as an 'economical' type of contribution. The selection of short fiction published in *Horizon* is a reflection of the uneasy and often inconsistent positioning of *Horizon* in between mainstream and modernist, literary and commercial, and also insular and international interests. The magazine's commissioning of short fiction was determined by two factors. The first of these was Connolly's personal connections. *Horizon* helped a handful of young short story writers to break into professional writing careers and published a small number of foreign authors, but the majority of its short fiction content was sourced from authors who were either already well established, part of Connolly's circle of friends and acquaintances, or both, and shared his public school and Oxbridge background.[3]

The editorial direction of the magazine was almost exclusively driven by Connolly. Although Stephen Spender was the magazine's co-editor until 1942, he was a silent partner and, as Sean Latham notes, Spender did not significantly influence the magazine's political or aesthetic direction despite Connolly's later claims to the contrary.[4] Sonia Brownell, the other silent editor of *Horizon* for its duration, remained almost entirely unacknowledged, though Connolly dedicated his later compilation *The Golden Horizon* (1953) to her. The second factor in the selection of short fiction was financial considerations. Latham argues that although Connolly 'saw himself in essentially heroic terms as the embattled guardian of a collapsing culture', he was also aware that diversity of contributors and contributions were necessary to secure the magazine's economic survival.[5] Only readability and diversity could ensure a steady readership for the new magazine, notwithstanding the war-related decimation of competition for *Horizon* in the literary magazine market.

This chapter explores the relationship between the 'uneven yet brilliantly eclectic editorial policy' of *Horizon* between 1940 and 1945 and the magazine's selection of short story content.[6] *Horizon* as an editorial venture sat, at times rather awkwardly, between a magazine that engaged with current affairs and one that ostentatiously disavowed them in favour of prioritising literary and artistic concerns; an ambivalence which Sam Cutting has described as *Horizon*'s 'complex and sometimes contradictory ethos'.[7] Connolly alternated opportunistically between these two approaches in his editorial practice and commentary depending on the current moment, and, as Gill Plain points out, his editorial pronouncements were 'consistent only in their contrariness'.[8] Likewise, *Horizon* alternated between highbrow or 'little magazine' ideas, and instances of anti-modernist rhetoric. Latham has argued that *Horizon* 'deliberately and sometimes melodramatically staged the end of the modernist "little magazine"'.[9] The short fiction selection in the first five years of *Horizon* mirrors this uneasy editorial relationship to (late) modernism. A survey of five years' worth of short fiction content in *Horizon* reveals a split between short stories as entertainment and those that are pitched as 'literary' short fiction, as well as between those that address the war and those that ignore it.

Short stories published in *Horizon* reflected the eclecticism and/or inconsistency of the magazine's political, ideological and aesthetic allegiances. Next to late modernist notables like Elizabeth Bowen, William Sansom and Anna Kavan, *Horizon* published writers of far more straightforwardly popular fiction like Fred Urquhart, a small number of international authors including Arturo Barea and Franz Kafka,[10] and hitherto unknown soldier writers like Julian Maclaren-Ross and Alun Lewis. This chapter scrutinises short fiction in the first five years of *Horizon*, and concludes that the criteria that qualified a short story for inclusion in the magazine shifted constantly as the magazine developed and were determined largely by opportunity and availability. It also considers the contribution of short fiction to covering topical concerns about the ongoing war and its effects at home and abroad.

A brief survey of short fiction in *Horizon*, 1940–1945

Between its first issue in December 1939/January 1940 and the seventy-second number in December 1945, *Horizon* published fifty-six short stories, as well as a small number of prose sketches or extracts from longer works that one could potentially include in the category of short fiction.[11] For the first nineteen months of the journal's life, each number carried at least one short story, and six numbers carried two, despite deteriorating paper quality and supplies from March 1941 onwards. However, from August 1941 onwards, short fiction ceased to be a staple monthly element. The August, November and December numbers for 1941 included no short stories, and though short fiction remained a semi-regular feature, only one more number after this point (in May 1943) ran more than one short story at a time. In 1942, four out of twelve numbers included no short fiction; in 1943, this rose to six out of twelve. 1944 saw a slight recovery, with only two numbers without short fiction, but in 1945, seven out of twelve numbers did not include any short stories.

In part, these trends can be explained by external factors. For the latter part of 1944, from the D-Day landings onward, and for most of 1945, rapid developments in the war and a preoccupation with newly liberated France meant that space that could have been devoted to short fiction was given over to either coverage of topical events, or content that showcased French literature and culture after several years of isolation from France. Paper rationing meant that *Horizon* was working with a fixed number of pages, and could not make extra room for these additional features, so something had to give. At the same time, external factors are clearly not the only explanation for the haphazard inclusion of short fiction. The July 1941 issue was published at the height of a paper supply crisis, reflected in the very poor quality paper on which this number was printed, and yet it carried not one but two short stories, William Sansom's 'The Wall' and Roger Roughton's 'The Human House'. It is more likely, then, that the reduced number of short stories in subsequent years was down to an editorial policy that did not see short fiction as a crucial type of contribution, but was happy to include short stories as and when convenient or opportune. In the case of Sansom's 'The Wall' and Roughton's 'The Human House', both stories engaged (directly and indirectly) with the war. 'The Wall' formed part of a dedicated 'War Symposium' section, pointing to the topicality value of these stories at a point when German air raids on London were still in full swing. Moreover, 'The Human House' was published posthumously, after Roughton's suicide earlier the same year, in homage to a fellow magazine editor and poet who moved in the same circles as the editors and regular contributors of *Horizon*.[12]

To put its inclusion of short fiction into context, the first five years of *Horizon* saw the publication of 189 poems, including some sets of poems by the same author (for example, an April 1944 selection of poems by Hölderlin in both the original German and English translation) and several 'anthology' sections (for example, the 'Christmas Anthology' of recent poetry compiled by Stephen Spender for the December 1944 number). Only eleven out of the seventy-two numbers surveyed did not include any poetry, and the remaining numbers vary between one and in the region of twenty poems, with an average number of three to four shorter poems per number. Though it was a more consistent feature than short fiction, poetry too could fall victim to pressing topical demands, and in moments of extreme pressure on space, Connolly and his editorial team tended to prioritise criticism and reportage. The dip in short fiction in 1944 and 1945 is also visible in the poetry published, especially in the spring and early summer of 1945. Yet where absence of short fiction in some numbers was rarely made up for in others, in most cases a dearth of poetry in one issue was balanced by a larger selection in the next, perhaps more easily achieved due to the smaller space poetry tended to take up.

Most authors contributed only one or two short stories during the time span surveyed, though several of these one-time short story contributors also supplied copy in other categories. Diana Witherby, for instance, contributed not only two short stories, but also book reviews and poetry. It is possible that she was asked to be a repeat contributor because she was related to Anthony Witherby, an acquaintance of Connolly's whose family firm printed the early numbers of *Horizon*.[13] Apart from Diana Witherby, only eight other authors contributed more than a single short story between 1940 and 1945: Anna Kavan, Alun Lewis, William Sansom, Fred Urquhart and Eudora Welty contributed two each, while Elizabeth Bowen, Julian Maclaren-Ross and Philip Toynbee contributed three stories each. Not all repeat contributors were particularly well known at the time (indeed, Maclaren-Ross made his name through his *Horizon* short stories as one of Connolly's 'finest discoveries' alongside Denton

Welch and Angus Wilson),[14] and not all of them were offering war-related material either, though topicality may have been a factor in the inclusion of some of these stories. In Welty's case, her appeal was the local colour quality of her writing, and *Horizon* explicitly took credit for being the first magazine in England to publish stories by this emerging American writer.[15] It is hard, however, even from this list of comparatively favoured authors, to draw any overarching conclusions as to the kind of short fiction preferred by Connolly. Though the majority of authors whose short stories were published were in some way connected with Connolly, he also took a gamble on a few unknowns; some wrote about the war, others did not; some were traditional storytellers, others were perceived as strikingly modern writers. The upshot is that short stories included in *Horizon* were a mixture and sometimes an amalgam of the well-made magazine story tradition and the modernist 'slice of life' conception of the short story.

Roland Lushington's story 'Happy All Alone', published in January 1941, is a case in point. Lushington's story relates a married couple's arrival in the fictional Swiss health resort of Monte Sano, where the husband is to be treated for tuberculosis. Their marriage of only two years is already troubled, and the plot somewhat conventional, but the story is rendered interesting by Lushington's deft use of shifts in narrative perspective. The focalisation of the third-person narrative shifts constantly between the husband and wife, reverting at intervals to a third, neutral viewpoint that withholds information from the reader and reduces them to an outside view. This is particularly noticeable when, having been privy to a private conversation between the wife, Marcia, and her husband's doctor concerning the husband's dangerous state of health, the story switches abruptly to a distant observation of the doctor escorting Marcia out of the building and the information that '[h]e was telling her something that was a relief to her, although she was ashamed of feeling relieved'.[16] The reader is left to infer from the rest of the story that the 'something' is the instruction to leave her husband behind and return to the ordinary world outside of Monte Sano. The central conflict of the story, which one is led to assume centres on whether or not Marcia will remain faithful to her husband, is likewise left unspoken. The ending is inconclusive, and the story thus combines rather clichéd features (the troubled marriage, the spectre of death and of an illicit affair, the husband's anxiety) with a modernist interest in psychology, with complex narrative perspectives and with an open ending.

Out of the fifty-six short stories published between January 1940 and December 1945, only five were written in languages other than English, or at least by writers whose first language was not English: Alfred Perlès's 'I Live On My Wits' and Arturo Barea's 'The Scissors' (the latter translated from Spanish but with no translator stated) in July and November 1940 respectively; Franz Kafka's 'In the Penal Colony' (1942, translated from the French version previously published in the *Cahiers du Sud* by Eugene Jolas), and Alberto Moravia's 'In the Country' (1945, translated by Vivian Praz), as well as one prose sketch published in the original French, Francis Ponge's 'La Pomme de Terre' (also 1945), which appeared in a special post-liberation issue dedicated to French literature and culture. Perlès and Barea also contributed other material to *Horizon*, and were both known to Connolly personally, whereas the publication of the stories by Kafka and Moravia signalled *Horizon*'s interest in widening its readers' access to foreign literature and culture. An editorial note in the April 1945 issue stressed that an 'article by [Benedetto] Croce, specially written for HORIZON, and the story by Alberto Moravia mark the beginning of our cultural relations with the new Italy', while the next issue was to be 'devoted to France' with the inclusion of 'unpublished work by Paul Valéry, Paul Eluard and many others'.[17] Five out of fifty-six short stories may not seem like a particularly determined attempt, in Connolly's words, to 'represent the best writing available; the deepest imagination, the clearest thought of the English, American, French, Spanish, German and Hungarian writers'.[18] Yet this figure has to be seen in relation to the much higher number of contributions in other categories that either dealt with foreign literature and culture, or were work in translation, or indeed in untranslated French.

Short fiction and editorial policy

Connolly used the editor's comments which prefaced most issues to subject the progress of *Horizon* to perpetual scrutiny. Every milestone issue prompted self-reflection, and Latham outlines succinctly the constant posturing and positioning of Connolly's editorials in relation to both elite and mainstream culture. The distinction between what he had termed 'Mandarin' and 'vernacular' styles of writing in *Enemies of Promise* (1938) appears to inform Connolly's selections for *Horizon*, too, as he tried to strike a balance between the two modes, intending to showcase the best contemporary examples of both. This balance was linked directly to Connolly's ambition to reach a wider audience than was usual for little magazines, a consideration visible, for instance, in his discussion of the kind of 'larger though still cultured' audience achieved by modern writers such as E. M. Forster.[19] In his regular editorial column, Connolly also occasionally commented explicitly on short fiction. His June 1940 comment not only took stock of *Horizon*'s career to date but reflected on the kinds of literature suitable for wartime publishing. Connolly acknowledged the preponderance of poetry among the material submitted, but identified short fiction, criticism and prose sketches as desirable prose forms for wartime consumption.[20]

Connolly also championed short forms of prose writing when, in October 1941, he proposed (half-seriously, half-jokingly) the institution of a 'word controller' to counteract the ambiguity and waste of wartime language: he argued that in wartime, 'a writer should not be able to put down more than two or three lines without making it obvious whether he has anything to say'.[21] This seems to suggest a preference for an economy of style that could find expression in the most limited of spaces. Yet some of the wartime stories published – first and foremost Franz Kafka's 'In the Penal Colony' in March 1942, Osbert Sitwell's 'The True Story of Dick Whittington' in March 1945 and Bowen's 'Ivy Gripped the Steps' in September 1945 – were in fact rather lengthy examples of short fiction at twenty-five, thirty-six and thirty pages respectively. Clearly, where Connolly and his editorial team felt a story had sufficient merit or where suitable copy was needed, the space could be found.

Horizon's pronouncements on short fiction and the selection of short stories it published were every bit as eclectic as the magazine's contents overall. Part of the reason for the sheer diversity of short fiction in *Horizon* was availability, given Connolly's repeated observations on the scantiness of good quality copy forcing him to pick writers and contributions that might not otherwise have made the cut. For instance, Connolly lamented in October 1942 that there was a dearth of military-age (and implicitly male) writers owing to their absorption into war service and that the magazine was increasingly dependent on women and old men for copy.[22] In December of the same year, Connolly joked that *Horizon*, at the age of thirty-six numbers, had become 'a magazine which to defeat the call-up has learnt to appear without writers',[23] a remark not necessarily flattering to those whose work was thus dismissed. In April 1941, Connolly stated that short stories selected for *Horizon* were 'not intended to be masterpieces', since the 'day of the great short story' was over in any case: in Connolly's professed view, there were 'too few authors who are capable of reducing life to the proportions and unities' of the short story's confined form.[24] There were, however, 'still many very readable short stories, often written by beginners who have had beginner's luck', which Connolly declared himself happy to publish 'for their vitality and as comic relief'.[25] What did the writers published in *Horizon* in 1941 make of this dismissal of their work as merely 'readable' and as 'comic relief'? Connolly's observations read like deliberate provocation, and the criteria for short fiction he outlined in his April 1941 editorial seem to be at odds with what Cutting has described as 'Connolly's commitment to the notion that art and culture should not [...] be sacrificed in times of war' because they were 'part of what is being defended'.[26] Yet such contradictions were not out of character for Connolly, and it is likely that he got away with his dismissive comments not only because the magazine market for short fiction had been decimated by the war,[27] but also because the majority of writers who contributed short fiction to *Horizon* were either his long-standing friends, acquaintances or sometime collaborators (including Bowen, Osbert Sitwell, Violet Trefusis and Connolly's former employer Logan Pearsall Smith), or aspiring writers like Maclaren-Ross, who could not afford to feel offended by an editor who was willing to give them a break in his magazine.

In 1941, *Horizon* published eleven short stories authored by ten different writers, four of them across two double short story issues in February and July 1941. Of the ten authors whose short fiction was published in 1941, only three will be readily recognised by most readers today: Alun Lewis, Elizabeth Bowen and William Sansom. Of these three, only Bowen was a well-established writer.[28] Lewis and Sansom were unknown young authors on whose short fiction Connolly took a successful gamble, much as he did with Maclaren-Ross. The other short story writers included in this year were mostly in some way connected to Connolly and/or *Horizon*: Roland Lushington was likely to be linked to Connolly via mutual school friends; Roger Roughton was a fellow editor and poet; and Diana Witherby was connected to the magazine's first printers, while journalist and writer Inez Holden (whose novel *Night Shift* was also published in 1941) was known to Connolly via George Orwell. The Irish writer Patrick Kirwan was connected to *Horizon* via his then wife, Celia, who temporarily worked for the magazine, and the two remaining short story contributors were Connolly's friend Antonia White, whose novel *Frost in May* had been published to critical acclaim in 1933, and White's husband, the journalist and *Picture Post* editor Tom Hopkinson.

The eclectic and erratic inclusion of short fiction was also a result of Connolly's ambivalent ideas as to the remit and mission of *Horizon*. In his opening comment for the first number of *Horizon*, Connolly had laid out his aim to publish a magazine for the 'archaistic, conservative and irresponsible' time in which he and his readers lived, a time in which war put increasing strain on cultural production and reception.[29] Other qualities that Connolly identified as crucial for inclusion in *Horizon* were adherence to the magazine's status as 'an adult periodical', which Connolly argued did 'not exist to give young writers their first chance', though it subsequently did just this in cases like Maclaren-Ross's.[30] Connolly's professed rejection of the highbrow versus lowbrow divide discourages an approach that splits the short fiction included in *Horizon* along these rather arbitrary lines,[31] though one might get a little further by applying Connolly's own distinction between fiction written in a wordy, literary 'Mandarin' style and the more journalistic 'vernacular' approach of realist fiction. It is possible to identify some broader characteristics shared by most *Horizon* short stories whilst acknowledging that not all stories the magazine published necessarily fitted smoothly into only one of these categories. *Horizon* showed a preference for comedy and particularly satire, war stories, psychological stories and especially those that dealt with mental illness, as well as local colour stories, with some autobiographical fiction thrown in the mix. Barely any stories are formally experimental, and where some level of experimentation occurred, as in Nicholas Moore's 'The Light Days' (1940) or Sansom's 'The Wall', it did not take radical forms but mostly amounted to a blurring of narrative perspectives or unsignalled time shifts that challenge boundaries between what is real and what is imagined. Although Bowen is generally considered a late modernist writer, her prose is subtle and psychologically complex rather than formally experimental in any notable way. This lack of radical formal innovation does seem to tally with Connolly's professed wariness of material that was 'revolutionary in opinions or original in technique' for a wartime magazine in a struggling market.[32]

Taking the short stories published in 1941 as a sample, all eleven are broadly speaking realist fiction, albeit with excursions into the symbolic or allegorical. However, the tone, narrative voice and structure of these stories are as diverse as their topics. Narrative perspective ranges from a long monologue reported via a third-person frame narrator in Roughton's 'The Human House' to first-person narrators in Holden's sketch of factory life, 'Fellow Travellers in Factory' (February) and Hopkinson's 'The Third Secretary's Story' (April).

Sansom's two stories (the hallucinatory 'The Wall' and the allegorical 'The Long Sheet') differ significantly from each other in terms of narrative voice, length and style as well as subject matter. Generally speaking, these stories cover a great range of topics, from studies of troubled marriages in Antonia White's 'The Moment of Truth' (June) and Lushington's 'Happy All Alone' to Alun Lewis's army comedy in 'The Last Inspection' (February) and Patrick Kirwan's satire of Soviet society in 'Comrades, Be Gay!' (May). Witherby's 'Abnormality' (March) adopts a restrained third-person narrative approach to condemn the conservative boarding school system that labels a healthy young girl as 'abnormal' for discussing bodily and reproductive functions, while Hopkinson's 'The Third Secretary's Story' is an old-fashioned tale that centres on a brief but life-changing love affair between a young English diplomat and a country doctor's wife in an unspecified Balkan capital. While realist in technique, many of these stories, with their focus on protagonists' minds and careful dissection of their relationships, nevertheless evidence the 'persistent vitality of modernist tropes' that Plain observes of 1940s literature.[33]

Cutting speaks of Connolly's desire to achieve a 'diversity of cultural voices in the magazine' and his 'need to simultaneously accommodate the popular and the serious, the literary and the accessible, maintaining the kind of challenge and style that characterized the best modernist texts'.[34] At the same time, Cutting notes that the everyday quality of stories such as Maclaren-Ross's and their 'vernacular' qualities appealed both to readers interested in 'plain English' and to highbrow critics in search of originality in writing.[35] Perhaps *Horizon*'s short story selection can best be described in light of cultural and practical compromise. Short fiction was not a key element of editorial policy, but rather complemented other types of content and was used as and when convenient. This could be to illustrate particular points, as with Paul Goodman's 'Iddings Clark' (1944), a story centred on the rapid mental breakdown of a high school teacher, published in an issue dedicated to exploring schizophrenia and neuroses. Short fiction could also be included to enhance the overall diversity of offerings, such as the few instances of short stories published in translation – although Latham rightly observes that '[d]espite its editor's own cosmopolitanism', the magazine 'proved to be [. . .] essentially British',[36] or at any rate focused on English-speaking nations. Ireland, Britain's neutral neighbour, was the subject of many contributions, including short fiction. Indeed, the January 1942 issue of *Horizon* was a special 'Irish number', and set out to explain the situation in Ireland for an English readership that, as Connolly recognised, was likely to be ignorant on Irish matters.[37] Edward Sheehy's short story 'Prothalamion' was part of the effort to educate the British reading public about Ireland and dispel limiting stereotypes.[38] It outlines the doubts assailing a middle-aged, agnostic, well-living country solicitor when his wife-to-be demands that he go to confession before the wedding. The story illustrates social tensions in a modern Ireland where conservative religious views clash with the secular outlook of a modern professional class. The special Irish number was of a piece with the efforts of *Horizon*'s sister magazine venture in Ireland, *The Bell*, edited by Seán O'Faoláin and Frank O'Connor, which set out to 'complicate idealized versions of Irish identity put forward in the Revival era'.[39] The two magazines shared several contributors, and both O'Faoláin and O'Connor contributed critical essays to *Horizon*'s Irish number, though *The Bell* also reviewed *Horizon* in March 1946 in not entirely complimentary terms. The review especially noted the upper-class bias of *Horizon*, which persisted despite Connolly's professed desire to reach an audience beyond the usual suspects for a literary magazine.[40] Given Connolly's heavy reliance on his public-school, Oxbridge circles for contributors, and considering his earlier acknowledgement that his writing was unlikely to 'appeal to the working class' but rather targeted his 'educated fellow bourgeois',[41] this was a reasonably astute judgement of *Horizon*'s readership.

War stories in *Horizon*

Last but not least, short fiction was occasionally published to contribute to interrogating the effects of war in the pages of *Horizon*. While Connolly's professed goal was, rather capaciously, to 'give writers a place to express themselves, and to readers the best writing we can obtain', he acknowledged from the beginning that the secondary objective of leaving its (fashionably left-leaning and liberal) 'politics [...] in abeyance' would come under pressure from contributors' desire to respond to the unfolding events of the war.[42] Indeed, by September 1943, Connolly found himself observing that 'HORIZON has not done enough lately to bring the war home to its readers',[43] and announced contributions on German war crimes in the next number, including a hard-hitting (and, as it turned out, controversial) piece by Arthur Koestler detailing the deportation and murder of Jews and other groups the Nazis considered undesirable. The reasons Connolly cited for not having published enough war material lately were, on the one hand, adherence to the magazine's 'mission [...] to maintain cultural values for those who are fighting the war', and on the other a dearth of 'good war material'.[44]

Short fiction was rather incidental to achieving good coverage of the war, as it was incidental to the magazine's editorial policy generally. In his 1953 compilation *The Golden Horizon*, Connolly included only two short stories in the sections covering the war, Maclaren-Ross's 'This Mortal Coil' and Rollo Woolley's 'The Pupil'; the latter story quite likely in homage to Woolley, a promising young writer who had died in action after publishing only two short stories in his lifetime.[45] In addition, Ponge's sketch 'La Pomme de Terre' was included in a section on 'Liberation'. However, several important war stories that have stood the test of time, as well as several pieces that were of the moment and not destined to have a lasting reputation, were among the 'good war material' that *Horizon* published. Those short stories that are still well known today, by notable writers such as Bowen, Sansom or Maclaren-Ross, were republished in author collections and/or included in general short story anthologies. Sansom's 'The Wall' and Maclaren-Ross's 'I Had to Go Sick' were both included in Dan Davin's *Short Stories from the Second World War* (1982), and Bowen was the only female writer represented in Davin's anthology, though with a story not published in *Horizon*, her perhaps most famous Blitz story, 'Mysterious Kôr'. 'Mysterious Kôr' also features in Anne Boston's *Wave Me Goodbye: Stories of the Second World War* (1988), an anthology of women's short fiction. It appeared in Boston's anthology alongside Kavan's *Horizon* story 'Face of My People' and Diana Gardner's satirical story 'The Land Girl' (included in *Horizon* in December 1940), while Inez Holden was represented with a different story to the one she published in *Horizon*, 'According to the Directive'. Those *Horizon* war stories that are now forgotten are ones that were not republished in either an author collection or anthology, whether a general short story anthology or one of the rare anthologies of Second World War short stories.[46]

Bowen's wartime short stories are among the best known short fiction in the English language to have come out of the Second World War, and they are also typical of *Horizon*'s interest in plain writing, psychological investigation and a mixture of the ordinary and the exceptional. Her three short story contributions to the first five years of *Horizon*, 'A Love Story' (1940), 'In the Square' (1941) and 'Ivy Gripped the Steps' (1945) are about the effects of war on different places and sets of people: a rural hotel in neutral Ireland, a house in London, a deserted English seaside resort, and the people linked to them, either voluntarily or by necessity. Bowen's stories successfully captured the mood of the moment, and, in their attention to the mundane, exemplify Plain's observation that 'for most writers and readers, the public and historical could only be comprehended through the lens of the personal'.[47] War is not a central concern in any of these stories; rather, it is the catalyst that prompts the unravelling of relationships, conventions and even personal identity.

Whereas Bowen's was already a well-known literary name, both Alun Lewis and William Sansom first broke into the *Horizon* circle with war stories. In Lewis's case, his story 'The Last Inspection' was published as part of a new 'War Symposium' section in February 1941 alongside Holden's 'Fellow Travellers in Factory'. While Lewis was a newcomer, Holden was a well-connected young novelist, journalist and short story writer. She wrote articles and fiction for the *Daily Express*, the *Evening Standard* and the *Manchester Guardian* and worked in an aircraft factory during the war. Like Lewis's 'The Last Inspection', Holden's 'Fellow Travellers in Factory' is an autobiographically informed sketch, with no plot in the strict sense beyond relating everyday occurrences. Holden details the impressions of a 'sometimes pampered bourgeois' who is adjusting with difficulty to the routine of factory life and becomes acutely aware of the reality of working-class life in the process,[48] while 'The Last Inspection' ostensibly centres on two enlisted men operating a steam train that takes their Brigadier on his final retirement journey. The emphasis in both pieces is on getting to know the ordinary protagonists and their wartime lives, whether through the financial disaster of a stolen coat in 'Fellow Travellers in Factory',[49] or the ominous telegram awaiting one of the two men in the regimental office at the end of 'The Last Inspection'.[50] Both stories take a wartime slice-of-life approach, as commonplace incidents are lent significance by the heightened drama of their wartime setting.

The interest of *Horizon* in publishing such snippets of ordinary wartime life is of a piece with the debates about class and the impact of war on social hierarchies sparked in the latter part of 1941 by an anonymous 'War Symposium' contribution on 'The Creation of a Class', an acerbic attack on the notion of a 'People's Army'.[51] This article sparked several retorts, and clearly hit a nerve with the magazine's readers and contributors. Earlier in the magazine's existence, Connolly had taken great pride in the fact that according to a survey of readers and subscribers in January 1941 roughly half of its audience appeared to be middle- and lower-middle-class, though his definition of middle- and lower-middle-class as in possession of an income of under £500 may be rather generous.[52] However, Connolly's emphasis on having a large proportion of lower-income readers demonstrates the magazine's desire to be in touch with ordinary people, 'the man-in-the-street income groups'.[53] This pride in a diverse readership that crossed class boundaries was expressive of a broader political shift, outlined by Marina MacKay, that saw Britain transformed 'from a class-bound empire into a medium-sized welfare state'.[54] The inclusion of short stories such as Holden's glimpse of factory life likely reflected this shift.

Sansom's *Horizon* debut, 'The Wall', also captures a piece of everyday reality, but in contrast to the relative uneventfulness of Holden's and Lewis's stories, 'The Wall' centres on an event that stands out from the mundane. The incident of a wall collapsing onto the narrator and his fellow firemen is related with the clinical precision and repetitiveness of traumatic recall, pulling the reader into the dramatic moment. It is easy to see why Connolly and his editorial team felt readers would receive Sansom's story with interest, given that it was published as the Blitz was still ongoing and volunteer firemen were celebrated as national heroes. Writing from the vantage point of 1941, Sansom had the credentials of being one of the thousands of ordinary men, the 'solicitors, journalists, salesmen and labourers', who tackled fires under the most dangerous conditions in the early stages of the Blitz before the wartime fire services were nationalised and professionalised.[55] The publication of Sansom's short story was thus timely and topical. By January 1944, Connolly announced that short fiction dealing with 'experiences connected with the blitz [sic]' and other everyday aspects of the war on the home front offered too ordinary a fare, and would only be published if the 'workmanship' were 'outstanding'.[56]

Where Sansom's first contribution to *Horizon* was likely picked for its topical appeal and because it contributed to the magazine's commitment to challenging class barriers, his second appealed for other reasons. Reviewing Sansom's collection *Fireman Flower* in the April 1944 number of *Horizon*, Anna Kavan compared Sansom to Kafka, noting that the majority of stories included in the collection 'take one into that dangerous territory of dream symbolism where all laws are incomprehensible, all authorities incalculable; where the hidden threat feeds in every rose and all simplicity hides the ominous complication'.[57] This is certainly true of 'The Long Sheet', Sansom's other story published in *Horizon* in October 1941. Where 'The Wall' directly engaged with the war and gave a fascinating insight into the experience of those fighting the war at home, 'The Long Sheet' clearly engages with topical concepts such as autonomy, freedom and totalitarian rule, but the meaning behind the 'rather obscure' allegory of the sheet, to borrow Kavan's terms, remains veiled to the reader.[58]

In his 1944 New Year's message 'to our contributors and would-be contributors', Connolly appealed for help in varying the magazine's contents. Concerning short story writers, he observed that they 'stand more chance if there is some unusual content in their stories – either an unusual background or treatment or point of view'.[59] This is reflected in the war stories published after this point. Many of the war stories in *Horizon*, particularly those published from 1944 onwards, contribute to what Plain has called a necessary 'rethinking [of] the parameters of "war writing"', by showcasing the diversity of responses to wartime crisis.[60] Though Dennis Boykins perhaps goes a little far when he argues that any short stories published in *Horizon*, whether or not they directly address the war, are 'war stories' because they were published and read 'in the context of war',[61] even those *Horizon* stories that did address the war did not necessarily do so in explicit and straightforward ways.

After January 1944, only four more short stories that either explicitly dealt with or were set recognisably during the war were included in *Horizon*: Kavan's 'Face of My People' (1944), Anthony Cotterell's 'Completely in the Air' (1944), Bowen's 'Ivy Gripped the Steps' (1945) and Georgina Dix's 'American Conversation Piece' (1945). In part this reflects the overall decline in short story contributions in the final two years of the war, but those stories included also begin to deviate from the slice-of-life quality of most earlier *Horizon* war stories. The four stories each offer something more than just an insight into everyday occurrence. As discussed above, Bowen's story uses its wartime setting to explore matters other than the war, in this case the links between early experiences and personal identity. Her protagonist, a middle-aged man who revisits a bleak seaside resort marked by the effects of several years of wartime isolation, is driven by the lifting of the ban for civilian visitors to revisit the scene of memorable and (to him) traumatic childhood experiences. The majority of the story is devoted to outlining the protagonist's recollections of fictional Southstone, though these are contrasted with its changed appearance in the wartime present. In the case of Cotterell's 'Completely in the Air', the experience at the heart of this piece of autobiographical fiction is indeed out of the ordinary for the average reader, as Cotterell's narrator is shown to accompany an American bomber squad on a mission to Germany. The piece is hard to categorise, as it is evidently based on Cotterell's own experience as a Public Relations Officer attached to the air force (in which capacity he was killed in the Netherlands in September 1944), but likely embellished and fictionalised. For the readers of *Horizon*, Cotterell's account of an American 'Flying Fortress' in action would certainly have held topical appeal as the war gathered momentum on the Allied side. Kavan's 'Face of My People' also takes readers beyond their lived reality, though in more troubling than exhilarating ways. The story combines her characteristic emphasis on those excluded from or marginalised in English society and her interest in mental illness, which also inform her earlier *Horizon* story, 'I Am Lazarus' (1943). 'Face of My People' centres on a continental European refugee hospitalised in England, isolated both by his foreignness and by his inability to deal with his traumatic past. Kavan's story offered readers ambivalent insights into modern psychiatric methods as well as hinting at Nazi atrocities in occupied Europe. Finally, Dix's 'American Conversation Piece' only touches on the war incidentally, as an Englishwoman visiting the USA becomes embroiled in a debate over the importance of history with her American host.

Conclusion

How important were short stories to *Horizon*, and what impact, if any, did *Horizon* have on the short fiction of its time? By its very opportunistic and erratic nature, short fiction in the first ten volumes of *Horizon* is emblematic of the wartime disruption of ordinary life, the unstable 'microclimate' of the first half of the 1940s, a 'period when the conditions of life and the creative imagination were radically disrupted' and when 'the continuity of literary development [was] fragmented'.[62] Connolly's inconsistent criteria for selecting short fiction contributions did not necessarily result in the emergence of a particular type of *Horizon* short story, but they do showcase the eclectic tastes of the period and display a strong preference for psychological exploration and introspection. The war stories included in *Horizon* certainly exemplify Plain's observation that '[w]ar's impact was refracted through personal relations and the incremental minutiae of daily life'.[63] While one might rightly feel wary about taking the short stories published in a literary magazine like *Horizon* to be a representative sample of wartime short fiction, it does give a reasonably good insight into the tastes of the time, not least thanks to Connolly's desire to appeal to diverse audiences beyond 'little magazine' readerships; though Donat O'Donnell perhaps rightly noted that *Horizon* eschewed 'the rather gritty slices of life offered by such a characteristic product' of the 1930s as John Lehmann's *New Writing*.[64] Mainstream magazines like *The Strand* or *Cornhill Magazine* were still publishing short fiction despite paper shortages, as did newspapers such as *The Daily Mail* and *The Observer*. The same contributors might appear in both kinds of magazine: Inez Holden, for instance, placed her 'Fellow Travellers in Factory' in *Horizon*, and another story, 'According to the Directive', in *Cornhill Magazine*. The same applied to most other *Horizon* short story contributors, and many, like Bowen and V. S. Pritchett (whose short story 'The Saint' appeared in the April 1940 number of *Horizon*), also wrote for the new mass medium of the wireless.[65] The kind of short fiction published in *Horizon* was thus not necessarily different from short fiction published in less artistically ambitious mainstream magazines, though a magazine like *The Strand* would publish not only a higher proportion of short stories than *Horizon*, but more that fell into the category of genre fiction, from romance to adventure and mystery tales.

Unlike other magazine editors, Connolly cannot be said to have shaped the short fiction included in *Horizon* through editorial interventions. He was prepared to accept short fiction of wildly varying length, from two pages to over thirty, depending on space and requirements of individual numbers. Rather, the value of *Horizon* to understanding short fiction of the 1940s is its showcasing of the variety of short stories in terms of both style and content. Short fiction included in the first ten volumes covers a broad and eclectic range of stories, from popular comedy in John Bryan's 'The Suitcase Hunt' (1940) or Fred Urquhart's 'Grandma Was A Land Girl' (1942) to old-fashioned yarns like Arthur Calder-Marshall's 'The Cap and the Bantam' (September 1940), to the charged symbolism of Kafka's 'In the Penal Colony' and Sansom's 'The Long Sheet', and the psychological acuity of Kavan's stories, especially 'I Am Lazarus'.

Yet despite the quality and variety of short fiction published in *Horizon*, it seems to have occupied a rather marginal role in Connolly's estimation. This is not only reflected in his fairly dismissive editorial comments, but also in the negligible number of short stories included in his *Horizon* swan song, the anthology *The Golden Horizon*. Out of over one hundred pieces, only eleven were short stories or sketches, and this was after Connolly had already decided against including political articles or art criticism.[66] Eight of these eleven stories appeared in a section titled 'Entertainments', selected based on 'the straightforward desire to please without which any magazine must founder', implying Connolly's view of short fiction as a crowd-pleasing concession rather than part of the core literary and cultural mission of *Horizon*. No short stories made it into Connolly's 'Personal Anthology' section, which was reserved exclusively for poetry.

Alongside *New Writing*, *The Penguin New Writing* and *New Writing and Daylight*, *Horizon* is one of the most cited publications of the period among literary and cultural scholars. It is seen as central to understanding literary culture of the 1940s partly because it pitched itself as such. Its collectible format, rhetoric of cultural authority and Connolly's connection with the influential critical circles of his day all guaranteed it a favourable critical reception and a lasting reputation – not least because many of the late modernist writers and critics he published had become 'figures of cultural authority' by the 1940s.[67] While short fiction published in *Horizon* was not a central part of Connolly's editorial strategy, the stories included in the magazine complemented other types of content and contributed to securing the diverse readership and economic viability desired by Connolly and his backers. At the same time, and despite Connolly's pronouncements about short fiction as primarily a medium for entertainment, *Horizon*'s short fiction showcases the diversity and strengths of wartime short fiction. The magazine's relationship to its short fiction is thus best described as a cultural and practical compromise.

Notes

1. Cyril Connolly, 'Comment', *Horizon*, 1.6 (June 1940), pp. 389–92 (p. 392).
2. Ibid. p. 392.
3. Donat O'Donnell noted in a March 1946 review of *Horizon* that he had tracked seven recently published contributors in *Who's Who* and identified them as fellow old Etonians, old Oxonians, or both: O'Donnell, 'Horizon', *The Bell*, 11.6 (March 1946), pp. 1030–8 (p. 1038).
4. See Latham, 'Cyril Connolly's *Horizon* (1940–50)', p. 860.
5. Ibid. p. 859.
6. Ibid. p. 859.
7. Cutting, 'The Short Story, Censorship, and Wartime Publishing', p. 26.
8. Plain, *Literature of the 1940s: War, Postwar and 'Peace'*, p. 40.
9. Latham, 'Cyril Connolly's *Horizon* (1940–50)', p. 856.
10. Kafka was an unusual writer to be included, not only in terms of being one of relatively few foreign-language writers to be published by the

magazine in translation, but also because the vast majority of writers published by *Horizon* were still alive.
11. These include pieces such as Violet Trefusis's 'Tryptich', Evelyn Waugh's 'My Father's House', and Seumas Boy Phelan's 'Naughty Mans', an experimental piece in which the author recorded his young son's conversations verbatim.
12. David Gascoyne and Roger Scott, 'Roughton, Roger Edmund Heude', *Oxford Dictionary of National Biography*, Oxford University Press, 28 May 2015, <https://www.oxforddnb.com/view/10.1093/ref:odnb/9780198614128.001.0001/odnb-9780198614128-e-60669> (last accessed 1 September 2020).
13. Lewis, *Cyril Connolly*, p. 337. H. F. & G. Witherby published at least two volumes of poems by Diana Witherby, suggesting a potential family connection.
14. Lewis, *Cyril Connolly*, p. 351. See also Cutting, 'The Short Story, Censorship, and Wartime Publishing', p. 26.
15. 'About this Number', *Horizon*, 6.31 (July 1942), p. 4 (p. 4).
16. Roland Lushington, 'Happy All Alone', *Horizon*, 3.13 (January 1941), pp. 33–8 (p. 36).
17. Cyril Connolly, 'Comment', *Horizon*, 11.64 (April 1945), pp. 223–4 (p. 224).
18. Cyril Connolly, 'Comment', *Horizon*, 4.24 (December 1941), pp. 375–7 (p. 376).
19. Connolly, *Enemies of Promise*, p. 27.
20. Connolly, 'Comment' (June 1940), p. 392.
21. Cyril Connolly, 'Comment', *Horizon*, 4.22 (October 1941), pp. 229–31 (p. 231).
22. Cyril Connolly, 'Comment', *Horizon*, 6.34 (October 1942), pp. 224–6 (p. 224).
23. Cyril Connolly, 'Comment', *Horizon*, 6.36 (December 1942), pp. 370–1 (p. 370).
24. Cyril Connolly, 'Comment', *Horizon*, 3.16 (April 1941), pp. 231–7 (p. 235).
25. Ibid. p. 235.
26. Cutting, 'The Short Story, Censorship, and Wartime Publishing', p. 29.
27. Latham, 'Cyril Connolly's *Horizon* (1940–50)', p. 361.
28. Lewis, *Cyril Connolly*, p. 176.
29. Cyril Connolly, 'Comment', *Horizon*, 1.1 (January 1940), pp. 5–6 (p. 5).
30. Cyril Connolly, 'Comment', *Horizon*, 4.24 (December 1941), pp. 375–7 (p. 376).
31. See Latham, 'Cyril Connolly's *Horizon* (1940–50)', p. 863.
32. Connolly, 'Comment' (January 1940), p. 5.
33. Plain, *Literature of the 1940s: War, Postwar and 'Peace'*, p. 42.
34. Cutting, 'The Short Story, Censorship, and Wartime Publishing', p. 31.

35. Ibid. p. 31.
36. Latham, 'Cyril Connolly's *Horizon* (1940–50)', p. 861.
37. Cyril Connolly, 'Comment', *Horizon*, 5.25 (January 1942), pp. 2–4 (p. 3).
38. Edward Sheehy, 'Prothalamion', *Horizon*, 5.25 (January 1942), pp. 63–72.
39. Matthews, '"Something Solid to Put Your Heels On"', p. 107.
40. O'Donnell, 'Horizon', p. 1038.
41. Connolly, *Enemies of Promise*, p. 5.
42. Connolly, 'Comment' (January 1940), p. 5.
43. Cyril Connolly, 'Comment', *Horizon*, 8.45 (September 1943), p. 149.
44. Ibid. p. 149.
45. In his April 1943 comment, Connolly had offered wistful reflections on the young generation who, like the recently killed Woolley, had never had the chance to develop their writing to its full potential because they were absorbed into the war immediately upon leaving school or university. Cyril Connolly, 'Comment', *Horizon*, 7.40 (April 1943), pp. 220–1.
46. There are hardly any dedicated anthologies of Second World War short fiction. The two most notable ones that actually collect short fiction (as opposed to extracts from longer prose works) – Dan Davin's *Short Stories from the Second World War* (1982) and Anne Boston's *Wave Me Goodbye: Stories of the Second World War* (1988) – are both out of print. In 2017, I edited a short anthology of Second World War stories for the British Library, which is now also out of print.
47. Plain, *Literature of the 1940s: War, Postwar and 'Peace'*, p. 44.
48. Inez Holden, 'Fellow Travellers in Factory', *Horizon*, 3.14 (February 1941), pp. 117–22 (p. 120).
49. Ibid. p. 121.
50. Alun Lewis, 'The Last Inspection', *Horizon*, 3.14 (February 1941), pp. 122–7 (p. 127).
51. 'The Creation of a Class', *Horizon*, 4.21 (September 1941), pp. 166–72.
52. '*Horizon*'s Questionnaire', *Horizon*, 3.16 (April 1941), pp. 292–6 (p. 293).
53. Ibid.
54. MacKay, *Modernism and World War II*, p. 3.
55. Robb, '"The Front Line"', p. 181.
56. Cyril Connolly, 'Comment', *Horizon*, 9.49 (January 1944), pp. 5–6 (p. 5).
57. Anna Kavan, 'Selected Notices', *Horizon*, 9.52 (April 1944), pp. 283–4 (p. 284).
58. Ibid. p. 284.
59. Cyril Connolly, 'Comment', *Horizon*, 9.49 (January 1944), pp. 5–6 (p. 5).

60. Plain, *Literature of the 1940s: War, Postwar and 'Peace'*, p. 7.
61. Boykins, 'Wartime Text and Context', p. 151, cited in Cutting, 'The Short Story, Censorship, and Wartime Publishing', p. 30.
62. Plain, *Literature of the 1940s: War, Postwar and 'Peace'*, p. 33.
63. Ibid. p. 44.
64. O'Donnell, 'Horizon', p. 1034.
65. For a fascinating account of Bowen's work for the BBC, see Hepburn, *Listening In: Broadcasts, Speeches, and Interviews by Elizabeth Bowen*.
66. Connolly, 'Introduction', *The Golden Horizon*, p. ix.
67. MacKay, *Modernism and World War II*, p. 13.

John Lehmann's War Effort: The Penguin New Writing (1940–1950)

Tessa Thorniley

Short story writing enjoyed a heyday in Britain during the Second World War, before a slump in the following years. After an initial 'grand slaughter of magazines' in the years 1939–40, which was one part of a cultural hiatus that also halted theatres and cinemas immediately after war was declared, publishers gradually found clever ways around paper rationing, and a mushrooming of new magazines ensured that writers had a healthy choice of outlets in which to print their work.[1] In his memoir of the 1940s, the writer Julian Maclaren-Ross recalled that excluding the literary journals *The Penguin New Writing* (1940–50) and *Horizon* (1940–50) there were 'no less than 16 markets for a short-story writer to choose from' by 1942.[2] Few literary editors were better placed than John Lehmann, the autocratic head of *The Penguin New Writing*, to take advantage of the shift in market conditions or to convene the new short story writers who began to emerge shortly after the outbreak of war. It was because of the literary success of Lehmann's 1930s *New Writing* journals, which promoted the work of left-wing writers such as Christopher Isherwood and W. H. Auden, that Allen Lane, the founder of Penguin Books, agreed to back his new venture in 1940.[3] Lehmann would go on to leave an equally indelible stamp on wartime literature, particularly on one of its 'hardiest blooms', the short story.[4]

Critical studies of the period provide a wealth of reasons for this wartime golden age of short stories. A marked slump in the production and sale of books, partly as a result of paper rationing, cut the incomes of novelists. Canny editors were able to circumvent wartime confusion over the precise definition of a magazine (new magazines were not permitted after May 1940) by publishing anthologies of short stories in a magazine format, providing new outlets for writers.[5] There was also a remarkable public appetite for short stories, with literary historian Ann-Marie Einhaus suggesting that the form offered a compromise for a 'time-strapped and anxious reading public' seeking distraction during blackouts and while huddled in bomb shelters, but unable to commit to the greater investment in time or attention required by a novel.[6] Writers were also drawn to short stories. Acclaimed novelists such as Elizabeth Bowen adopted it as their preferred format during the war. For Bowen, whose short story 'Mysterious Kôr' (first published in issue 20 of *The Penguin New Writing*) remains one of the most emblematic of the Blitz, short story writing was a psychological balm. She commented that her failure to grasp a clear perspective on events and an inability to process the trauma of war or to interpret what was happening imaginatively created a block only relieved by writing short stories. She did not publish a new novel until 1949. In an essay published in 1945 in *Britain Today*, she wrote:

> I suggest that we should not expect any *comprehensive* war novel until five, even ten years after hostilities cease. The short storyist is in a better position. First, he shares – or should share – to an extent the faculties of the poet: he can render the great significance of a small event. He can register the emotional colour of a moment. He gains rather than loses by being close up to what is immediately happening. He can take, for the theme of his story, a face glimpsed in the street, an unexplained incident, a snatch of talk overheard in a bus or train.[7]

Bowen declared the short story to be the 'ideal *prose* medium for war-time creative writing'.[8] Lehmann noticed a similar approach in the work of his sister, the novelist Rosamond Lehmann (a regular contributor to *The Penguin New Writing*), commenting in his memoir that on the outbreak of war she 'made up her mind, as Virginia [Woolf] had, to treat the whole situation as a challenge to her creative powers, and had settled to work at a series of short stories'.[9] Observing these shifts, Lehmann was in a powerful position to respond to writers' changes in direction, to guide them and provide them with a literary space in which to explore a new form and ultimately, to help them reach a broader readership than ever before.

The Penguin New Writing remains a source of short stories that are still considered today to be among some of the finest to have emerged from the Second World War, or in some cases the entirety of the twentieth century. These include works by Elizabeth Bowen, V. S. Pritchett, William Sansom, Rosamond Lehmann, Graham Greene, William Plomer, James Stern, Julian Maclaren-Ross, John Sommerfield, Dylan Thomas, Henry Green and, to a lesser extent, writers such as Alun Lewis and Denton Welch, who both died during the war. Their subject matter – the war, life in the forces, the civilian experience, the inner workings of ministries and life in hospital wards at home and abroad – sought to capture the essence of the wartime experience in Britain and around the world. H. E. Bates, who was described by Stephen Spender as the professional 'short story teller *par excellence*' (although this was not entirely meant as a compliment), singled out *New Writing* and publications of its kind as providing a bright spot in the market for the short form as early as 1941.[10] Bates's remark chimes with accounts that suggest the boom in short stories took some time to emerge after the outbreak of war and was much easier to delineate in hindsight.

It was more than serendipity that John Lehmann and Allen Lane were, respectively, the figurehead and patron of a publication that made such a significant and lasting contribution to the short story form. Both Lane and Lehmann had family ties with publications that had the development of the short story in Britain at the core of their existence. Lane launched his publishing career at The Bodley Head, in the employ of John Lane (a distant relative on his mother's side), and would have been only too aware of his 'uncle's' legacy as the publisher, along with Elkin Mathews, of the clothbound periodical which became an icon of 1890s aestheticism and decadence, *The Yellow Book*. Lehmann's *New Writing* venture (which began in 1936) was a deliberate reincarnation of the spirit of *The Yellow Book*, in so far as both publications sought to appear unapologetically modern and anti-establishment and vowed to publish short stories that did not conform, in either length or style, to contemporary literary conventions. It was with evident pride that, in the foreword to the first volume of *The Penguin New Writing*, Lehmann cited a review of the original *New Writing*, describing the magazine as 'The Yellow Book of the thirties'.[11] This helps to explain why Lane was inclined to back Lehmann's *New Writing* venture. Lehmann also had a more direct family connection to the short story genre via his father, who had been one of the founding members of *Granta* magazine as a student at Cambridge University before going on to write for the satirical magazine *Punch*.

'Friendly rivalry' in literary circles

The Penguin New Writing and Cyril Connolly's *Horizon* were the most influential literary magazines of the wartime period. Dan Davin, the New Zealand author of Irish Catholic descent, whose short story was published in 1942 in issue 13 of *The Penguin New Writing*, providing him with his first taste of literary success, described these two periodicals as 'the most sustained and notable wartime outlets for literature'.[12] The cultural historian Robert Hewison notes that even though the Cambridge *Bibliography* lists just over a hundred new magazine (or little magazine) titles between 1939 and 1945, '*The Penguin New Writing* and *Horizon* dominated.'[13] The parallel lifespans of the two publications mean they are often compared. Both were dedicated to keeping contemporary, imaginative writing alive during wartime and many writers published work in both journals. The role of Stephen Spender as contributor and advisor to both publications in the early years also brought them closer together than was comfortable for Lehmann, who himself noted the 'friendly rivalry with *Horizon*'.[14]

However, blending the two publications in this way brushes over their respective literary contributions and the very different goals and instincts of their respective editors. Where *The Penguin New Writing* most clearly had an edge over *Horizon* was in its circulation. Sales of Lehmann's journal, at its peak shortly after the war, reached 100,000 (compared with 80,000 in its first year), a figure that Lehmann not implausibly suggested may have reflected a readership closer to 250,000 given the extent to which the paperback journal, which could be tucked into a pocket or bag, was passed around between civilians and servicemen. When *The Penguin New Writing* closed, its sales had slipped to 40,000, a figure that was still high for a literary periodical. By comparison, *Horizon*'s sales never exceeded 10,000, which it reached in 1947, although the magazine maintained a strict monthly publication that *The Penguin New Writing*, despite Lehmann's best efforts and repeatedly tense negotiations with Lane, never quite achieved. *Horizon* was less hamstrung financially than *The Penguin New Writing*, as the wealthy arts benefactor, Peter Watson, backed the journal. But Penguin Books benefited from a generous paper allowance following wartime rationing (as paper rationing was based on pre-war usage), which meant that Lane could offer up to five tons of paper to Lehmann for each edition of *The Penguin New Writing* (roughly enough for 75,000 copies).

For short story writers seeking to build careers, refine their talents and find new readers, *The Penguin New Writing* had a great deal to offer. As Davin acknowledged, there was a 'certain status' to being published in *The Penguin New Writing*.[15] Jeremy Lewis also notes in his biography of Allen Lane that 'though less remembered and less liked than Connolly, Lehmann was, perhaps, the finer and bolder editor' and he always kept his door wide open to newcomers.[16] The forty forewords that Lehmann wrote during the lifespan of *The Penguin New Writing* provide evidence of the lengths to which he went to encourage writers from all walks of life, regardless of whether they had been published before. He issued repeated pleas for manuscripts, often with detailed complaints for writers to respond to; through these, readers could glimpse where Lehmann perceived the gaps or failings in the literature of the time. Lehmann's forewords also signposted writers' shifts in style, content and focus throughout the decade.

Even if Lehmann lamented the quality of the submissions he was receiving at times, as in the ninth issue of *The Penguin New Writing*, he never suggested that aspiring and existing writers should stop sending the 'flood levels' of manuscripts that crossed his desk.[17] Although Lehmann sought to maintain high standards and aspired to a certain spirit of writing for publication, he also assiduously cultivated a space where a certain amount of new, unorthodox experimentation could flourish. Lehmann set himself in opposition to Cyril Connolly's unashamedly 'ivory tower' attitude that had led him to conclude that the 'only thing writers could do while the war was going on was to concentrate on technique and shut their ears'.[18] Alan Ross, writing in the *Times Literary Supplement* in 1949, noted that *Horizon*, certainly in the early years, had a 'narrower' range in its writing.[19] In his editorial to issue 49 of *Horizon*, published in 1944, Connolly laid down some boundaries for would-be contributors:

> We take the line that experiences connected with the Blitz, the shopping queues, the home front, deserted wives, deceived husbands, broken homes, dull jobs, bad schools, group squabbles, are so much a picture of our ordinary lives that unless the workmanship is outstanding we are prejudiced against them.[20]

By contrast, Lehmann had a different view of ordinary lives and a particular sympathy for working-class writers. In his detailed analysis of the democratisation of writing in Britain, Christopher Hilliard notes that on at least one occasion Lehmann rejected a story that was highly 'successful technically' because 'to many readers of *New Writing* it would seem like a direct attack on the young unemployed'.[21] Hilliard also comments that Lehmann 'took pains to coax what he regarded as art out of their [the working-class writers'] manuscripts'.[22] As we shall see, Lehmann's ideas about literature were not confined to established working-class writers, but frequently extended to less well-known writers in whom he detected talent.

As the cultural and literary historian Paul Fussell comments in his analysis of the psychological and emotional culture of the British and American people during the Second World War:

> Compared with *Horizon*, which could seem precious, remote, and merely aesthetic, *Penguin New Writing* appeared 'committed' to the reality of the active life, to the necessity of politics in all its vulgarity, and to the redemption of postwar life by new imperatives of fairness and decency.[23]

Dan Davin suggests that it was Lehmann's 'wider sympathy and receptiveness that made *Penguin New Writing* the most truly representative of all wartime publications, the one most hospitable to talent from all over the world, whether already famous or still obscure'.[24] Lehmann's 'committed' and more political approach also extended to his readers, particularly any who could be converted into contributors, with whom he maintained a constant dialogue, inviting their correspondence, comments, feedback and manuscripts.[25]

When Lehmann first received backing for *New Writing* in 1936, he immediately fired off a letter to Isherwood and other authors who had provisionally agreed to contribute, stating: 'You can write anything between 3,000 and 12,000 words long.'[26] It was the first indication that he was not about to let writers be stymied by the literary conventions of the day, where average story length ran to no more than about 7,000 words. A 'Manifesto' which accompanied the first issue stressed that the publication aimed 'at providing an outlet for those prose writers, among others, whose work is too unorthodox in length or style to be suitable for the established monthly and quarterly magazines'.[27] Prose, Lehmann added, would 'form the bulk of the contributions' and writers from 'colonial and foreign countries' were to be included.[28] At once, the breadth and ambition of Lehmann's vision for the magazine is evident and it was one to which he remained remarkably loyal throughout the life of the venture.

A 'fragmentary vision' in wartime

In the fifth volume of *The Penguin New Writing*, published in April 1941, Stephen Spender waded into a spirited literary debate about the merits and demerits of certain kinds of short story. The debate had been sparked by some scathing comments about contemporary short stories made by George Orwell in a review for *The New Statesman and Nation* in January of the same year.[29] In his response, Spender set out his recipe for the ideal short story while also defining the kinds of stories that he felt lacked interest. Orwell's attack on the uniformity and banality of the modern short story, particularly as it appeared in anthologies of short stories or short story magazines, had, Spender argued, unfairly neglected to acknowledge the 'very considerable achievement' of a handful of short story writers, including Elizabeth Bowen and V. S. Pritchett (who were published in *The Penguin New Writing*) and Ernest Hemingway and H. E. Bates (who were not). In the essay, Spender argues that there are two prominent forms of the short story. Either it is an exercise, a miniature, in which the writer performs the 'delicate and minute task of creating his tiny world', which Spender has no time for; or, the short story is a 'fragment of the writer's whole experience'.[30] In his defence of writers in the latter camp, Spender comments: 'Their fragments may seem rough at the edges, the material may seem too large for the stone, the story may appear like a torso, or a limb even, but they have the great merit of being interesting.'[31] He goes on to suggest that:

> If a short story is not a miniature done by a miniaturist, or an exercise done by a novelist; if it is a fragmentary vision of a philosophy of life and of an experience, then, so far from being an exhausted form, we would expect it to be one of the most vital forms of prose writing to-day. Given the world to-day, we can hardly expect writers to 'see life steadily and see it whole'.[32]

Spender is not suggesting that short stories that could be defined as incomplete or part of a 'fragmentary vision' were necessarily born out of war, but he does imply strongly that stories written in this way were best suited to the exigencies of wartime.

Indeed, what Spender here identifies is an approach to the short story that helps to unite and identify a group of Blitz-generation writers (including one major adherent who had yet to emerge fully by 1941) whose work was, or would be, strongly in evidence in the pages of *The Penguin New Writing*. Such was the demand for short stories during the Second World War that *The Penguin New Writing* was rarely the exclusive domain of any one writer and most wrote for several publications simultaneously. But *The Penguin New Writing* did successfully capture a certain style from the early 1940s onwards in the works of writers such as Elizabeth Bowen, Henry Green and, when he emerged on the literary scene, William Sansom. Lehmann provided these writers with a platform on which they could try out and experiment with the short story form and the new impulses and instincts emerging in creative writing during the war. Although both Bowen and Green were already established novelists when the war began, Lehmann undeniably played a crucial role in teasing out short stories from them, and a great many other writers, during the war.[33] Lehmann's editorial archive in Austin, Texas, contains begging and cajoling letters to just about every short story writer, poet and several literary critics of note in Britain and a great many elsewhere.

William Sansom's 'hallucinations'

William Sansom is a good example of a writer whom Lehmann targeted, and letters between the two cited in Lehmann's memoirs and elsewhere show how much input he had into Sansom's writing. The short stories by Sansom which appeared from issue 14 of *The Penguin New Writing*, published in November 1942, are in many ways the closest in spirit to the writing that Spender had sought to define in the magazine eighteen months earlier. In several of the eleven short stories that Sansom published in *The Penguin New Writing*, the action takes place over a minute, or a moment, or fleetingly in the mind of an individual, which strongly suggests that he is not a writer concerned with presenting readers with a whole narrative sequence.[34] This technique also enables him to play with the tension and pace of his stories and to expand and contract time within the narrative. Sansom's wartime stories frequently suggest not merely the difficulty of processing and even recalling events which overwhelm the senses and are in constant flux, but also the inadequacy of previous narrative approaches in communicating the effect of war on (and in) the mind. Sansom is known for his highly descriptive prose style that is super-charged with a density of information, and the hallucinatory detail with which he describes scenes of terror. Describing events or moments in time as 'hallucinations' became a way for wartime writers to convey something of the unreality of the times they found themselves living through. The word itself appears repeatedly in short stories, including Bowen's and Sansom's, and in critical writing of the time.

At the outbreak of war, Sansom left his job in advertising and joined the Auxiliary Fire Service (AFS) as a full-time London firefighter. His experience in the AFS both inspired and informed his writing and enabled him to give voice to the non-combatant experience in wartime, which very much fell into Lehmann's sphere of interest. Sansom's first short story was published in *Horizon*, but it was in *The Penguin New Writing* that he published some of his best-regarded short works, such as 'Various Temptations', a grim tale about a psychopathic murderer who befriends a lonely, naïve young woman (published in issue 31), 'The Witnesses', one of Sansom's haunting stories about firefighters in which a fireman needlessly throws himself to his death (published in issue 17) and 'In the Morning', in which a firefighter muses on the jarring shift in his daily transformation from civilian to serviceman and the elemental terror of his wartime work (published in issue 20). Sansom's characters frequently inhabit a place on the boundary between life and death, whether a firefighter operating perilously close to a raging fire following a bombing raid or a man walking along the edge of a cliff. And while men in his stories often appear to be at the mercy of unconscious, destructive and violent desires, equally loaded with dark portent are inanimate structures such as a wall, the rocks of a cliff or a boiler in a school basement, which become sinister and strange by his pen. This may help to explain why Sansom has been described as the English equivalent to Kafka, whose writing was much in vogue in the early 1940s. In his memoirs, Lehmann commented on the publication of Sansom's first collection of short stories (published on Lehmann's insistence by the Hogarth Press in 1944) that:

> Of the stories in that volume, only one, *The Wall*, was a straight reportage of fire-fighting experience. In the rest, if he [Sansom] used the setting and paraphernalia of the London fires it was to illustrate some subtle problem of psychology or to establish some symbolic truth.[35]

Here Lehmann touches on one of Sansom's qualities as a writer that Elizabeth Bowen had also identified in her 1945 article on the short story in England. Bowen commented that she was struck by 'how much imagination has been able to add to experiences that might, one would have thought, exceed it' in wartime writing and she singled out Sansom's firemen stories as an example of this trait.[36]

In an appraisal of Sansom's art and of the short story in general that accompanied the publication of a collection of his stories in 1963, Bowen distinguished between short story practitioners whose stories are mere by-products of their longer works and the comparatively few, like Sansom, 'whose faculties not only suit the short story but are suited by it – suited and one may feel, enhanced'.[37] She also commented that:

Also, the short story, though it high-lights what appears to be reality, is not – cannot wish or afford to be – realistic: it relies on devices, foreshortenings, 'effects'. In the narration there must be an element of conjury and of that William Sansom is an evident master.[38]

In Sansom, then, Lehmann found a new voice and talent, capable of translating extraordinary times and events into powerful and haunting short stories. Sansom is that new writer 'capable of adding something to the terrific effort of the mind and imagination needed to grasp and dominate what is happening to us' for whom Lehmann had cried out in the conclusion of his foreword to issue 9 of *The Penguin New Writing*.[39] After the war, Sansom wrote novels and criticism, but it is for his short stories that he is best remembered. His 1963 collection of stories was, for example, republished in 2011 under the Faber Finds imprint. Sadly, his strong association with the form may also explain why Sansom is not better remembered overall.

'Articulating the real' by resisting reality: Sansom, Green and Bowen

As the war wore on, Lehmann was among the first to witness a change in writers' approaches to their art. In his foreword to issue 14 of *The Penguin New Writing*, published in 1942, he noted a shift 'from a rather extrovert, documentary type of realism to something more introvert, with a great deal more reflection and feeling in it'.[40] He singled out William Chappell's 'The Sky Makes Me Hate It', about the narrator's transformation from civilian to soldier, published in the previous issue of the magazine, and Henry Green's 'Mr Jonas', about a fire crew rescuing the story's eponymous unknown man, as examples of this shift. Lehmann had first printed the latter story in *Folios of New Writing*, and now published it again in issue 14 of *The Penguin New Writing*. It is worth noting that the documentary realism to which Lehmann refers had been a strong feature of his *New Writing* journals from the 1930s, particularly in the short stories of Isherwood, several of which were reprinted in *The Penguin New Writing*. As Rod Mengham points out, documentary realism in literature had already 'prompted a method of reading that would tolerate incompleteness, fragmentariness, on the understanding that a real and satisfying completeness would eventually supervene and as such it legitimated the abandonment of the novel as a means of articulating the real'.[41] In this sense, Mengham implies that Lehmann had, in no small measure, contributed to bringing about a moment in literary history when the novel was 'writing itself into the past, while the short story was writing itself into the future'.[42]

By the time the Blitz was underway and wartime conditions necessitated a fresh imaginative approach, what emerged in place of documentary realism was writing that suggested 'the need to complicate the terms of photographic realism and of radical present-ness'.[43] Mengham examines this shift in the work of Sansom, Bowen and Green, who were all published in *The Penguin New Writing*. In particular, Mengham notes that 'The Witnesses' examines the limits of conventional perception to the extent that 'even the relationship between the eye and brain is not taken for granted'.[44] The firefighting scene unfolds in jolts and starts and with an overload of detail: 'flashes of light', 'each line of the operator's uniform leaped into abrupt definition' and every feature of the pump operator's face 'could be distinguished'.[45] In this way, a fragment of time is 'saturated with incident'.[46] And, even as the eyes register events, they are unable to bring things properly into focus. Time too speeds up and is then made static. The narration, which shifts from first person plural to omniscient, describes the pause 'before every great catastrophe' in which moment 'time freezes solid' before 'the will to movement reasserts itself'.[47] And finally, readers are made aware that the senses cannot be trusted, 'we cannot be sure that the pressure [in the water pump which appeared to result in the fireman's death] really increased'.[48] The piece concludes that the fireman's own eyes may have deceived him, propelling him to a senseless death, 'the unreliable agent that informed us, the witnesses, his eyes'.[49] Meanwhile in the stories by Henry Green published in *The Penguin New Writing* ('A Rescue' in issue 4 and 'Mr Jonas' in issue 14) 'the whole question of completeness [supervening] is one they simply do not care about', with both stories simply fading away in the final few lines.[50] 'A Rescue' ends with 'He may have died', while all that remains to be said of Mr Jonas is that he is rescued from the hole in the ground that he fell into, 'whoever he might be'.

In Bowen's story of Blitz-time London ('Mysterious Kôr'), readers witness realism beginning to turn strange, so that 'what can be seen starting to infiltrate the writing is the logic of dream or nightmare'.[51] In the story, Arthur and Pepita, a young couple, wander the deserted moonlit streets of London during the blackout before returning to the apartment Pepita shares with her friend Callie. As they walk, London for Pepita becomes the abandoned city of Kôr, from

H. Rider Haggard's 1887 novel *She*, and the couple cite lines from a poem about Kôr that was commonly printed after the title page in the book. Bowen named her wartime stories 'resistance-fantasies'.[52] Indeed, at the conclusion of 'Mysterious Kôr' there is a strong sense that the reason and reasonableness proffered by Arthur and Callie has been no match for Pepita's imagination: imagination trumps all in the piece, even 'what's human'.[53] For Pepita, the end of the war could result in Kôr being 'the one city left: the abiding city'.[54] The theme of unreality comes through strongly in the short story and links it to a great many other wartime stories. Bowen's instinct to regard the world through distorted vision in her fiction is not dissimilar to Sansom's, but where in Sansom's firefighting stories hallucination suggests an inability to recall the real, which is simply too much for the mind to grasp, in Bowen's story the hallucinatory quality enables the author to segue from the real, or rather the fictional world which Arthur, Pepita and Callie inhabit, to a fantasy place (Kôr). It is the element of fantasy that provides Bowen with a release valve to explore the ideas that built up and pressed down on her so strongly in wartime. Collectively these works demonstrate what Mengham terms the 'spectacular failure of realism'.[55] In Bowen, realism has been supplanted by fantasy; in Sansom, documentary realism has been warped; and in Green, literary promises – that a sense of completeness will supervene in the story – have been shelved. With these stories a group of writers appeared to triumph over what Lehmann feared might otherwise have been the 'sterilizing aftermath of the "realism" of the thirties' on writers' imaginations.[56]

Even though similarities in the impulses and instincts of its writers emerged during the war, it must be emphasised that *The Penguin New Writing* was a magazine which never sought to identify with any one kind of writing. Overall, what defined it was a commitment to a wide variety of voices from around the world, capable of providing their own interpretation of the wartime condition, even in many of the stories that were not directly about the war. In the foreword to issue 14 of *The Penguin New Writing*, in which he notes the shift towards 'more introverted' writing, Lehmann also comments that other short story writers are sticking with a more 'hard-boiled realistic method' and others still with 'extreme lyricism'.[57] Here Lehmann effectively sums up the highly eclectic nature of *The Penguin New Writing*, and his own deliberate efforts to eliminate a hierarchy in the types of stories that he published. He sought instead to ensure that distorted realism, anti-elitism, introverted prose, hard-boiled realism and extreme lyricism could comfortably co-exist in the magazine. The short stories published in *The Penguin New Writing* were modern in so far as they were written in the 1940s, but they were never uniformly modernist in style or content. As Gill Plain comments in her analysis of the literature of the 1940s, the decade 'brought ways of reading into unexpected new conjunctions, and left a legacy of fiction that cannot be squeezed into the ill-fitting categories of modernism, the middlebrow and the popular'.[58] So too does *The Penguin New Writing* defy being squeezed too neatly into any one kind of journal ('modernist' or 'realist', for example), except that it sought to represent the breadth of wartime writing that met Lehmann's benchmarks for quality.

A 'deep exploration' of the past and the writing of Rosamond Lehmann

Among the variety of short stories identified by Stephen Spender in 1941, one is defined as 'an exercise by a novelist'.[59] Elizabeth Bowen similarly identified short stories that are 'by-products' from writers by nature given to 'greater space'.[60] What Spender and Bowen are alluding to are the kinds of short stories that might be more accurately defined as novels in the making, the beginnings of novels, or parts of a novel, rather than short stories that are wholly successful as standalone works of literary creation. In one sense, several of the nine short stories published by Rosamond Lehmann in *The Penguin New Writing* could be read in this way. Two of them in particular might be better described as novellas and had to be run across more than one issue of *The Penguin New Writing*.[61] It is also evident that the literary family, the Sandersons, in 'The Red-Haired Miss Daintreys' (published in issue 4 of *The Penguin New Writing*) provided much of the inspiration for the Landon family in Rosamond Lehmann's wartime novel *The Ballad and the Source* (1944).[62] Wendy Pollard cites correspondence between John and Rosamond which reveals that after reading the short story, he described it as being like the background for a novel and urged her to write more of it.[63] This strongly suggests that John Lehmann saw merit not only in the work of short story purists (such as Sansom) but also in stories that may have been novels in the making.

While Spender and Bowen might have considered certain of Rosamond Lehmann's stories lower down in the hierarchy of the ideal short story because they did not entirely escape the instincts of the novelist, this should not detract from the effect of Rosamond

Lehmann's work within the context of *The Penguin New Writing*. When John Lehmann approached his elder sister to urge her to contribute to *The Penguin New Writing* it was because he felt his literary periodical needed to publish 'stories that came out of the deep exploration of the past that so many people had found since the war broke out gave meaning and spiritual fortification to the dissolving present'.[64] Rosamond's pre-war novels had already marked her out as a writer preoccupied with the themes of childhood and the past and her brother was quick to see how her writing, if it could be harnessed in short story format, would counterbalance the prevalence in the magazine of actual and fictional reportage with its focus firmly on the present moment.

Two of Rosamond's stories, 'The Red-Haired Miss Daintreys' (published in issue 4) and 'The Gypsy's Baby' (serialised in issues 11 and 12), are told via a child narrator, or a narrator recalling childhood events. In another story, 'Letter to a Friend' (published in issue 5), Rosamond considers children's responses to the idea of death. Her longest contribution to the magazine, 'Wonderful Holidays' (serialised in issues 22 to 25), draws very heavily on her own childhood, which was privileged, but here is told through two fictional families, the Carmichaels and the Ritchies. In wartime, the need to re-examine the past is strongly in evidence in the high frequency of the related themes of autobiography and childhood in the novels and short stories published during and after the period. Hewison explains this trend:

> There is a reason for this outpouring of memory, and it is not simply that writers found it difficult to deal with the immediate present. The probing back into the past was in search of some explanation for the crisis of the times. Both fictional and autobiographical childhood took writers back to just before the First World War, and it was in the Edwardian period, seen part-nostalgically, part-critically, that causes were sought.[65]

The most explicit example of this is 'The Red-Haired Miss Daintreys', which is set in 1913. John Lehmann's memoirs note that many writers at the start of the war plunged 'back into the past of childhood and youth, times which now stood out in memory with a strange insulated intensity, an hallucinatory effulgence', and he cites his sister's work as an example.[66]

Wit, humour and satire in the stories of V. S. Pritchett, Graham Greene, Harold Acton and Zhang Tianyi

Although V. S. Pritchett was a published novelist as well as an established literary critic well before the war, it was not until the publication of 'Sense of Humour' in issue 2 of Lehmann's *New Writing* series that he began to make a name for himself as a talented short story writer. The tale, about a travelling salesman who starts a relationship with a young woman but finds that her ex-boyfriend is pursuing them on his motorbike, was reprinted in issue 1 of *The Penguin New Writing*, indicating strongly that Lehmann believed Pritchett's work would appeal to a wider readership. Lehmann went on to publish several of Pritchett's other best-known short stories in *The Penguin New Writing*, including 'Many are Disappointed' (in issue 5), 'The Sailor' (in issue 12) and 'The Chestnut Tree' (in issue 13). Pritchett has recalled in interviews the difficulty he had getting these stories published for the first time and his debt to Lehmann for doing so. In contrast to writers such as Bowen, Sansom and Green, whose depictions of the wartime experience in *The Penguin New Writing* conveyed the unreality, or warped reality, of the times, Pritchett's short stories almost exclusively focus on the actualities (and delusions) of lower-middle-class existence. It is worth noting that the stories by Pritchett mentioned here were written before or only shortly after the outbreak of war and hence cannot be read in quite the same way as the work of Sansom, Bowen and Green.

Of the nine short stories by Pritchett that Lehmann published in *The Penguin New Writing*, three were written exclusively for the magazine (rather than republished from previous issues of *New Writing*). The first is a fictionalised account of a neighbourhood Home Guard unit, included in the regular *The Penguin New Writing* feature 'The Way We Live Now' (in issue 7); the second is a piece of almost straight reportage, 'Workers Debate' (in issue 15); and the third, 'Night Worker' (in issue 23), is a darkly comic illustration of the inevitability of misunderstanding when a child interprets grown-up conversation. Pritchett's use of simple, direct narrative and his mastery of dialogue as a means of revealing character are strongly in evidence in these stories. Dean Baldwin has commented that Pritchett was among a handful of writers (Baldwin also counts Sansom among them) who rejected the elitism of modernism and preferred to focus on individuals at the margins of society. These writers, Baldwin notes, often took inspiration from among the people of small towns, away from the metropolitan centres, and they 'actively sought to cultivate, stimulate and challenge their middle class readers'.[67] Many of the stories by Pritchett published in *New Writing* and *The Penguin New Writing* were included in the story collection published in 1945 by Chatto & Windus, *It May Never Happen and Other Stories*, which Walter Allen critiqued in a 1948 essay for *The Penguin New Writing*, declaring them to be 'quite simply masterpieces'.[68] In particular, Allen noted Pritchett's ability to 'make the richest comedy' out of the lower-middle-class milieu 'without sneering at it', a skill that would undoubtedly have appealed to Lehmann.[69]

Pritchett performed another function for Lehmann within the pages of *The Penguin New Writing* and his other journals in that his short stories were rich in comedy, albeit most frequently a dark humour characterised by 'laconic understatement' or 'Cockney wit' rather than wry satire, which Lehmann felt English literature was sorely lacking in the early 1940s (excepting the novels of Evelyn Waugh).[70] Writing under the pseudonym 'Jack Marlowe' in issue 14 of *The Penguin New Writing*, Lehmann openly lamented the absence of comic figures in English literature drawn from the armed forces. More specifically, he bemoaned the lack of chroniclers of comic figures such as the Czech humourist Jaroslav Hašek, who had conjured *The Good Soldier Schwejk* (the abbreviated title of his unfinished work published in 1923) about a hapless soldier adrift in Austria-Hungary during the First World War.[71] Hašek's satirical and broadly anti-war novel, about a little man caught up in a vast bureaucratic machine, highlighted among other themes the futility of military discipline and featured characters who did not always understand what they were fighting for.

Pritchett took up Lehmann's thread two years later in issue 22 of *The Penguin New Writing* in a piece of criticism entitled 'The Undying Schweik' (the name has multiple spellings even within the pages of *The Penguin New Writing*) in which he noted that, in the present war, 'Schweik's patriotic significance has returned and also he has become the ridiculous hero of the muddle of war-time bureaucracy and military discipline.'[72] While Lehmann and Pritchett are signalling to writers or would-be writers of the comic novel, Lehmann also did what he could, via the medium of the short story and a good deal of reportage, to redress this literary imbalance in the pages of *The Penguin New Writing*. Lehmann persuaded Graham Greene to contribute 'one delicious glimpse' of his experiences working for the Ministry of Information in the story 'Men At Work' in issue 9 of *The Penguin New Writing*.[73] The story describes a futile day of memos and meetings and delightfully exposes the absurdities of the inner workings of the state publicity and propaganda machine.

In the same volume of *The Penguin New Writing* as Pritchett's critical work about Schweik, Harold Acton, whose satirical novel set in Peking, *Peonies and Ponies,* had been published in 1941, contributed a sketch about a colonialist in India who is 'rabidly allergic' to Indians and is awaiting discharge from a military hospital (although he has not apparently served in the armed forces).[74] In 'A Monopolist', published in issue 22 of *The Penguin New Writing*, the humour arises in Acton's depiction of a man who still clings to the illusion of the strength of the British Empire (and the inferiority of its subject people), seemingly oblivious that its foundations are crumbling around him. The story was inspired by Acton's own experience of being posted to India for the Royal Air Force during the war. The posting was a scandalous waste of his talents as a Chinese speaker with potentially useful contacts in Beijing (then Peking), where he had lived prior to the outbreak of the Second World War. Acton acted as a bridge between China and Britain for Lehmann by helping to translate a selection of short stories by Chinese writers that had been sent to Lehmann in the late 1930s. Acton and the Chinese writer Xiao Qian (Hsiao Ch'ien) had retranslated a satirical sketch entitled 'Mr Hua Wei' by the Chinese writer Chang T'ien-Yi (Zhang Tianyi, the pen name of Zhang Yuanding) which appeared in issue 15 of *The Penguin New Writing*. The short story parodies a certain type of official that Zhang had encountered in China's Nationalist Government, who is more concerned with fighting the Left than fighting the Japanese with whom the country is at war. Evidently Lehmann considered that Zhang's satire of the Chinese wartime experience could withstand comparison with Greene's or Acton's in the magazine and had significance for and relevance to his Anglophone readers.

Despite Lehmann's efforts to seek out more stories by Zhang, he was never able to get his hands on them.[75] However, Lehmann published ten short stories on or about China in the pages of *The Penguin New Writing* throughout its decade of existence – just one element of the international outlook of the magazine, which also published short stories from writers in France, Germany, Czechoslovakia, Greece, Poland, Italy and India, among other countries. Lehmann's memoirs testify to the various instincts that drove him to promote short stories by foreign writers in his magazines, including, initially, a desire to rejuvenate English literature and, later, his belief in the power of imaginative prose to capture 'the conception of an effective brotherhood born between victims of oppression'.[76] Lehmann also confessed to the grandiose idea that he might create 'a new international literature'.[77] What he did create was a platform for discovering writers from around the world, who merited publication alongside some of the finest names writing in English at that time.

Lehmann, the good shepherd

When considering the role of *The Penguin New Writing* in promoting the short story, an exploration of how its editor actively, but quietly, interacted with the writers he published is vital. Lehmann was committed to teasing and coaxing stories out of his writers, to the extent that it is reasonable to argue that without him a great number of the short stories that were eventually published in *The Penguin New Writing* might never have been written. Glancing down the contents page of any volume of *The Penguin New Writing*, the stories marked with an asterisk are ones which were written exclusively for that particular volume of the magazine. These were commissioned after 'careful discussion between author and editor', as Lehmann felt the need to explain to his readers in the foreword to issue 26. Several stories by William Sansom were commissioned in this way, as well as Graham Greene's story based on the Ministry of Information, Henry Green's 'A Rescue', works by Alun Lewis, Inez Holden, William Chappell, V. S. Pritchett, Laurie Lee and John Sommerfield, as well as most of the critical essays and sections that featured reportage. In the postscript to her collection of short stories (which includes 'Mysterious Kôr'), Elizabeth Bowen emphasised the vital role of the editor in the genesis of her wartime short stories:

> During these last years, I did not always write a story when I was asked for one; but I did not write any story that I was not asked for. [. . .] Does this suggest that these *Demon Lover* stories have been in any way forced or unwilling work? If so, that is quite untrue. Actually, the stimulus of being asked for a story and the compulsion created by having promised to write one were both good – I mean, they acted as releases. Each time I sat down to write a story I opened a door; and the pressure against the other side of that door must have been very great, for things – ideas, images, emotions – came through with force and rapidity, sometimes violence.[78]

She essentially describes that she needed to be compelled to write her short stories. Lehmann's own memoirs comment at some length about his support for the unknown (as he was then) writer William Sansom. Lehmann wrote:

> Bill continually sent me batches of the stories that now began to pour out of him; many of them I accepted straight away, but many others I sent back with critical letters trying to explain where I thought the weak spots were. Sometimes he re-wrote them, and I eventually printed these too; others he scrapped, others were printed elsewhere. It was extremely stimulating for me, whatever it may have been for him, because I had rarely before, if ever, had to do with an author so eager to learn from his experiments and to perfect them, and so little disposed to bite the hand that wanted to feed him – with the satisfaction of print.[79]

In Dylan Thomas too, Lehmann found a struggling writer whom he was willing to go to considerable lengths to support, both financially and with encouragement. Thomas, however, ungratefully rebuffed and mocked Lehmann and never delivered any stories to him. Archived correspondence between Lehmann and the Chinese writer Ye Junjian (whose short stories were published in issue 26 of *The Penguin New Writing* under the pen name Chun-Chan Yeh and in issue 38 under C. C. Yeh) similarly reveals the encouragement and sharp but well-intentioned criticism that Lehmann offered up to a writer who was seeking 'consecration' in the Anglophone literary centre of London, to borrow a phrase from Pascale Casanova.[80] In Ye's case, it was primarily Lehmann's endorsement of his short stories, which were written in English, that set him on the path to becoming 'an English writer', as one reviewer of Ye's career defined him in the 1980s.[81] Following Lehmann's initial support of his career, Ye's short stories and novels were published in Britain to critical acclaim and then translated into other European languages and disseminated abroad.

In his account of working-class writers in Britain, Hilliard provides ample detail about Lehmann's approach to the working-class writers whose short stories he published, including B. L. Coombes, Jim Phelan, George Garrett and Sid Chaplin (who all contributed to *The Penguin New Writing*) and the extent of his support, both financial and editorial, whether or not it was appreciated. Lehmann's indiscriminate and at times extravagant editorial support for writers in whom he detected talent is surely one feature of his approach that led Jeremy Lewis, in his biography of Allen Lane, to describe Lehmann as an 'incomparable' editor.[82]

Postscript: the legacy of *The Penguin New Writing*

If any doubt remains over the contribution that Lehmann and *The Penguin New Writing* made to the short story genre, consider the number of writers who were published in the journal who went on to publish short story collections of their own or to edit anthologies of the works of others, several of which are still in print today. The contribution of *The Penguin New Writing* can also be seen in the collapse of the short story form after the magazine ceased publication in 1950. In his foreword to the final number of the magazine, Lehmann himself predicted dark days ahead. Lamenting the demise of *Horizon* and *Life and Letters*, he wrote: 'Soon there will hardly be any address at all to which a young poet or writer of short stories can send his MSS in the hope of advice and publication – and that immediate and so necessary setting of roots that publication can give'.[83]

The ramifications of the closure of *The Penguin New Writing* and other magazines like it were still being felt and openly lamented in literary circles almost twenty years later. Even though Lehmann himself launched *The London Magazine* in 1954 and published short stories, he had fallen out of touch with the new writers and was much less effective at promoting their work. In a 1956 review of a new short story collection, Maclaren-Ross suggested that, in the absence of outlets to publish their work, short story writers could no longer make a living and he predicted the possible extinction of the form unless conditions changed.[84] However, things evidently failed to improve and in 1969, an editorial in the *TLS* again picked up the thread:

> A few weeks ago one of our fiction reviewers was lamenting the lack in this country of outlets for the writer of short stories: at best, a handful of small circulation magazines, a few benevolent and hopeful publishers, the B.B.C. Little wonder, he concluded, that the genre is beginning to look played out here. An English short story writer wishing to make a living from his work is now obliged to run his attention to the American market and even to concoct accordingly.[85]

Nor were there many editors left who could assist short story writers in their efforts to seek out that elusive formula. Without a flourishing market for literary magazines, short story writers lost both their source of income and a literary space in which to experiment, develop and pit their literary wits against each other.

Notes

1. Hewison, *Under Siege*, p. 11.
2. Maclaren-Ross, *Memoirs of the Forties*, p. 105.
3. Lehmann's *New Writing* venture spanned fourteen years from 1936 to 1950, involved five different publishers and included: *New Writing, New Writing (New Series), Folios of New Writing, Daylight, New Writing and Daylight* and *The Penguin New Writing*.
4. Davin, 'Introduction', p. ix.
5. As *The Penguin New Writing* was considered an extension of Penguin Book's book publishing business it was able to skirt restrictions on magazine publishing entirely.
6. Einhaus, 'War Stories', p.152.
7. Bowen, 'The Short Story in England', in Lassner, *Elizabeth Bowen*, p. 143.
8. Ibid. p. 143.
9. Lehmann, *I Am My Brother*, p. 36.
10. Stephen Spender, 'Books and the War IV – The Short Story Today', in John Lehmann (ed.), *The Penguin New Writing*, 5 (1941), pp. 131–42 (p. 134); Bates, *The Modern Short Story*, p. 221.
11. John Lehmann, 'Foreword', *The Penguin New Writing*, 1 (December 1940), pp. vii–viii (p. viii).
12. Davin, 'Introduction', p. x.
13. Hewison, *Under Siege*, p. 81.
14. Lehmann, *I Am My Brother*, p. 42.
15. Davin, *Selected Stories*, p.13.
16. Lewis, *Penguin Special*, p. 177.
17. John Lehmann, 'Foreword', *The Penguin New Writing*, 9 (October 1941), pp. 7–8 (p. 7).
18. Lehmann, *I Am My Brother*, pp. 42–43.
19. Alan Ross, 'Review of Reviews', *The Times Literary Supplement*, 2449 (8 January 1949), p. 32.
20. Cyril Connolly, 'Commentary', *Horizon*, 49 (January 1944), pp. 5–6 (p. 5).
21. Cited in Hilliard, *To Exercise Our Talents*, pp. 139–40.
22. Ibid. p. 141.
23. Paul Fussell, *Wartime*, p. 244.
24. Davin, 'Introduction', p. x.
25. For an account of Lehmann's dialogue with his readers during wartime see Bort, 'John Lehmann's *New Writing* in Wartime'.
26. Lehmann, *The Whispering Gallery*, p. 234.
27. Ibid. p. 236.
28. Ibid. p. 236.

29. Reprinted in Davison et al., *Complete Works of George Orwell*, Vol. 12, pp. 371–4.
30. Spender, 'Books and the War IV', p. 138.
31. Ibid. pp. 138–9.
32. Ibid. p. 139.
33. On Lehmann's insistence, Henry Green's third novel, *Party Going*, had been published in 1939 by the Hogarth Press (where Lehmann was general manager). The press also published Green's novels *Pack My Bag* (1940) and *Caught* (1943).
34. As well as short stories, Sansom published one critical essay in *The Penguin New Writing*, 33 (1948), on the art of Edgar Allen Poe's short stories.
35. Lehmann, *I Am My Brother*, p. 167. Sansom's short story 'The Wall' was first published in *Horizon*, so by singling the story out Lehmann is being somewhat catty here.
36. Bowen, 'The Short Story in England', in Lassner, *Elizabeth Bowen*, p. 142.
37. Bowen, 'Introduction', *The Stories of William Sansom*, pp. 7–12 (p. 8).
38. Ibid. p 8.
39. John Lehmann, 'Foreword', *The Penguin New Writing*, 9 (October, 1941), pp. 7–8 (p. 8).
40. John Lehmann, 'Foreword', *The Penguin New Writing*, 14 (November 1942), pp. 7–8 (p. 7).
41. Mengham, 'Broken Glass', p. 126.
42. Ibid. p. 126.
43. Ibid. p. 126.
44. Ibid. p. 127.
45. William Sansom, 'The Witnesses', *The Penguin New Writing*, 17 (November 1943), pp. 9–14 (p. 13).
46. Mengham, 'Broken Glass', p. 127.
47. Sansom, 'The Witnesses', pp. 13–14.
48. Ibid. p. 14.
49. Ibid. p. 14.
50. Mengham, 'Broken Glass', p. 128.
51. Ibid. p. 130.
52. Elizabeth Bowen refers to her stories as 'resistance-fantasies' in 'Postscript by the Author', *The Demon Lover and Other Stories*, p. 221.
53. Elizabeth Bowen, 'Mysterious Kôr', *The Penguin New Writing*, 20 (August 1944), pp. 53–67 (p. 65).
54. Ibid. p. 55.
55. Mengham, 'Broken Glass', p. 129.
56. Lehmann, 'Foreword', *The Penguin New Writing*, 9 (October 1941), p. 8.

57. Lehmann, 'Foreword', *The Penguin New Writing*, 14 (November, 1942), p. 7.
58. Plain, *Literature of the 1940s: War, Postwar and 'Peace'*, p. 26.
59. Spender, 'Books and the War IV', p. 139.
60. Bowen, 'Introduction', *The Stories of William Sansom*, p. 7.
61. *The Gypsy's Baby* ran across two volumes of *The Penguin New Writing*, and *Wonderful Holidays* ran across four volumes.
62. Pollard, *Rosamond Lehmann and Her Critics*, p. 102. Note the name of the 'Sanderson' family in *The Penguin New Writing*, 4 is changed to 'Ellison' when the story is republished in *The Gypsy's Baby and Other Stories* (1946). Pollard refers to the Ellisons.
63. Pollard, *Rosamond Lehmann and Her Critics*, p. 102.
64. Lehmann, *I Am My Brother*, p. 95.
65. Hewison, *Under Siege*, p. 90.
66. Lehmann, *I Am My Brother*, p 32.
67. Baldwin, 'The Understated Art, English Style', pp. 235–6.
68. Walter Allen, 'The Art of V. S. Pritchett', *The Penguin New Writing*, 34 (1948), pp. 80–92 (p. 90).
69. Ibid. p. 90.
70. Jack Marlowe [John Lehmann], 'A Reader's Notebook – II', *The Penguin New Writing*, 14 (November 1942), pp. 133–40 (p. 139).
71. Ibid. p. 134.
72. V. S. Pritchett, 'The Undying Schweik', *The Penguin New Writing*, 22 (December 1944), pp. 135–9 (p. 136).
73. Lehmann, *I Am My Brother*, p. 170.
74. Harold Acton, 'A Monopolist', *The Penguin New Writing*, 22 (December 1944), pp. 43–52 (p. 44).
75. Lehmann published two stories by Tchang T'ien-Yih/Chang T'ien-Yi (Zhang Tianyi) in issues 1 and 15 of *The Penguin New Writing*.
76. Lehmann, *The Whispering Gallery*, p. 238. Lehmann here cites at length from a review of the first issues of *New Writing* in *The Times Literary Supplement*.
77. Lehmann, *The Whispering Gallery*, p. 242.
78. Bowen, 'Postscript by the Author', p. 216.
79. Lehmann, *I Am My Brother*, p. 166.
80. Casanova, *The World Republic of Letters*, p. 118.
81. Michael Scammell, 'A Chinaman in Bloomsbury', *Times Literary Supplement* (10 July 1981), p. xx.
82. Lewis, *Penguin Special*, p. 181.
83. John Lehmann, 'Foreword', *The Penguin New Writing*, 40 (1950), pp. 7–8.
84. Julian Maclaren-Ross, 'A Beginning, a Middle and an End', *Times Literary Supplement*, 2850 (12 October 1956), p. 600.
85. 'Commentary', *Times Literary Supplement*, 3519 (7 August 1969), p. 880.

Chapter 13

Voicing 'the native tang of idiom': *Lagan* Magazine, 1943–1946

Tara McEvoy

> It must be realised by writers that now is the time to take new bearings, to try new paths, to explore new terrain; that the central problem is to interpret the complex spiritual life of this province. To do this, a writer must be conscious of the changing attitudes of the common people, that is, of the governed to their governors; he must be conscious of the inherent contradictions of our society, and of the intricate relationship between a maladjusted society and a maladjusted individual; he must be conscious of the social use of literature as drug or antiseptic: in short, he must be conscious that the struggle for a way of writing is part of the struggle for a way of life.[1]

With the above declaration, John Boyd set out his stall for *Lagan* magazine, the short-lived annual Northern Irish periodical that he founded and edited between 1943 and 1946. Against the backdrop of the Second World War, economic instability and lingering tensions over partition, Boyd sought to provide a space for 'exploration of new terrain' – importantly, of *home* terrain, stridently advocating for the fosterage of a 'vital tradition' of Ulster writing.[2] As the magazine's dates suggest, the space was a difficult one to maintain. The title shuttered after its fourth annual issue, in part as a result of the attendant difficulties of fulfilling this ambitious mission statement, but primarily due to a rapid decline in circulation.[3] In time, new publications would fill the void created by the magazine's departure: Roy McFadden, a former contributor to *Lagan*, co-founded *Rann*, 'An Ulster Quarterly of Poetry and Comment', alongside Barbara Hunter in 1948; in the 1950s Mary O'Malley established *Threshold*, the journal of Belfast's Lyric Theatre. Of course, the 1960s would see an explosion in literary journal production in Northern Ireland, from *Gorgon*, *Q*, and Stewart Parker's *Interest* (all three affiliated with Queen's University Belfast) to James Simmons's iconoclastic

Honest Ulsterman, famously subtitled a 'Monthly Handbook for Revolution'.[4]

In a context where discussion of Northern Irish periodical culture has largely been focused on these later efforts, *Lagan*'s importance has been obscured. Notwithstanding a few important contributions to the critical landscape surrounding the magazine,[5] there exists a paucity of scholarship on its production and intervention in the North's literary tradition. If it is discussed at all, it is largely as a relic or a curio; a less successful counterpart to Southern publications like *The Bell*. Undoubtedly, the quality of the material included is variable, yet while *Lagan* may never have scaled the heights of O'Faoláin's publication (recently the subject of two book-length studies),[6] there remains much to commend it. Not least amongst *Lagan*'s achievements is the space it carved out for short fiction from Northern Ireland. In addition to printing discursive essays, poetry and reviews, *Lagan* prioritised the short story, an emphasis often absent from other literary magazines in the North. Nicholas Allen comments that 'Belfast found her voice in *Lagan*' and some of the city's (and the province's) most enduringly important fiction writers did so too, among them Michael McLaverty, Sam Hanna Bell and Joseph Tomelty.[7] As such, the time is ripe for a reconsideration of the magazine's contribution to Northern Irish writing, and fiction in particular. Examining the trajectory of *Lagan* also enables a more nuanced understanding of the development of Northern Irish literature, both during and after the Second World War.

Towards an 'Ulster literary tradition': founding *Lagan*

Reflecting on the foundation of *Lagan*, Boyd recounts that his friend and collaborator Sam Hanna Bell was the real driving force behind the magazine; in contrast to Boyd's own reticence about the venture (he recalls that he had previously 'regarded Belfast as an incredibly provincial city which could only produce provincial writers of small consequence whose work could not possibly hold any interest for [him]'),[8] Bell was fuelled by 'the notion that if Dublin could produce a lively literary magazine like *The Bell*, we three in Belfast [Boyd, Bell and Robert Davidson] might be able to produce something just as good'.[9] In this endeavour, *Lagan* was informed by Northern precursors which were also defined in contradistinction to their Southern counterparts: in the introduction to the magazine's third issue, Boyd draws attention to *Ulad*, a publication of the Ulster Literary Theatre, as a 'forerunner' of *Lagan*.[10] Parallels between the two magazines are readily discernible; indeed, the introductory remarks to the first issue of *Ulad* are not dissimilar to the proclamations that Boyd would make some forty years later:

> *Ulad* means Ulster. It is still often necessary to state as much; we intend to insist. Draw an imaginary line across Ireland from that great bight, Donegal Bay, in the west, to Carlingford Lough, on the east, and draw it not too rigidly; north of that you have Ulster. This Ulster has its own way of things, which may be taken as the great contrast to the Munster way of things, still keeping on Irish lands [. . .] Exactly what [Ulster's] local temperament and artistic aptitude are *Ulad* wants to discuss. *Ulad* would also influence them, direct and inform them.[11]

Despite the bold claims made in *Lagan*'s opening salvo, it was not the only little magazine in Northern Ireland at the time; competitors included the university magazine *The New Northman* (1932) and *The Ulster Parade* (1942), a publication from Quota Press described by Tom Clyde as 'a wartime morale-boosting exercise'.[12] *Young Ulster*, the magazine of the Young Ulster Society, which had appeared in 1938, was another recent precursor and an instructive model for *Lagan*: although only one issue of the magazine appeared, *Young Ulster* contributors would go on to write for *Lagan*; its editorial expressed similar aims to those with which Boyd would introduce his publication; and the only issue of *Young Ulster* even included an essay entitled 'Rivers of Belfast', perhaps sowing the seed for *Lagan*'s title.[13]

Lagan's ambitions, however, were on a grander scale than those of its fellow journals and close precursors. Boyd set his sights on publishing the work of established writers (such as W. R. Rodgers, Roy McFadden and Michael McLaverty) alongside newcomers, and in *Lagan*'s first issue reprinted material from *Routledge*, *The Adelphi* and *The New Statesman*. From the outset, then, *Lagan*'s writers already had a readership that expanded beyond Northern Ireland – and indeed the island of Ireland. Malcolm Ballin notes that *Lagan* was distinguished not only by the quality of its writing, but also by its high production values: 'It immediately impresses the reader by an ambitious presentation [. . .] [It] comprises nearly a hundred pages with a good standard of print and paper.'[14] All of these elements combined to create the impression that a copy of *Lagan* was a thing of value.

The first issue of *Lagan* appeared in 1943, after Boyd gathered money for printing ('£10 each' from himself, Davidson and Bell).[15]

The geographical specificity of the magazine's title reveals something of its wider editorial approach. According to Boyd, Bell suggested the title; both men believed that the River Lagan (which flows from Slieve Croob Mountain, County Down, to Belfast Lough, bisecting Belfast) 'awaited its celebrant. Had not Joyce immortalised the Liffey in *Anna Livia Plurabelle*?'[16] *Lagan*, then, would emerge as a champion of the river, its towns and the entire province, seeking not only to act as a record of an Ulster literary tradition, but also to facilitate the development of that tradition.[17]

While Sean McMahon rightly notes that '*Lagan* was perhaps more of an anthology than a magazine of original material', as 'indicated by the acknowledgements made to other publishers' (and as is, perhaps, suggested by its original subtitle, 'A Collection of Ulster Writing'),[18] it fulfilled an important role in commissioning, as well as curating, material, and accepted submissions from readers. As such, even if not all of its material was original, *Lagan* can be categorised as a little magazine.

Employment of Ulster idiom, Boyd proposed, would be fundamental to *Lagan*: '[Our] idiom [. . .] must, I am convinced,' he writes in the introduction to the first issue, 'be revivified and used as the basis of a regional literature [. . .] An Ulster literary tradition that is capable of developing and enriching itself must spring out of the life and speech of the province.'[19] A significant factor that had prevented such a tradition's prior emergence, Boyd argued, was the 'tendency for writers to leave Ulster – they have been a kind of invisible export'.[20] These professed aims would find lengthier explanation in the now-famous essay by John Hewitt, 'The Bitter Gourd', published in the magazine's third issue; for Hewitt, the writer 'must be a *rooted* man, must carry the native tang of his idiom like the native dust on his sleeve: otherwise he is an airy internationalist, thistledown, a twig in a stream'.[21]

Hewitt's aspirations were being realised from the time of *Lagan*'s inception in the short fiction the magazine published. The first issue alone offered readers multiple fictional vignettes of Northern Irish life, with Belfast as their primary setting: Michael McLaverty's 'Evening in Winter' offers a child's perspective on the snow-covered city; Gerry Morrow's 'The Pub' takes as its setting a public house on the Ormeau Road; Robert Davidson's 'Speak Against Bonds' follows a young women's journey from Linenhall Street across town to the Bloomcroft Road; Joseph Tomelty's 'Destiny' centres on Fruithill Barracks; and John Boyd's 'Dying Day' is set on the Shankill Road. Sam Hanna Bell's story 'The Broken Tree' is the only fictional piece in the issue which is concerned with life in rural Northern Ireland, as is made evident in its opening sentence: 'Hans eased the clear cotter of the plough on to the rig and swung the horse to the downward furrow.'[22]

Hugh Shearman's 'Only Solution', meanwhile, moves further away again from *Lagan*'s geographical heartland, documenting military offensives taking place along the banks of the Dutch River Yssel. It is here important to note that if at first the story appears anomalous in the context of the issue, it is indicative of what will be published in later issues – and of the internationalist editorial bent Boyd sought to maintain alongside his advocacy for certain elements of regionalism. What emerges through studying the four issues of *Lagan* is not a tension between internationalism and regionalism, but the sense that Boyd conceived of the philosophies as interdependent; his implicit belief that a vibrant, outward-looking regionalism could act as a springboard for solidarity with international liberal and leftist causes, and artistic movements.[23]

Shearman's contribution notwithstanding, the fiction gathered in the first issue of *Lagan* abounds with Ulster 'idiom'. This, for example, is a representative passage from Bell's 'The Broken Tree':

> They were near the farm when William asked 'Did she cost ye much?' There was a pause. 'Twenty poun'' answered Hans. 'It's a risk' said William sagely. Suddenly he stopped at a gate, hooking his heel on the bottom bar. 'Hans,' he said urgently, 'Hans, before we go in.' Hans stopped and the horse sidled in the narrow lane, leaning his head over his mater's shoulder. 'What is it, William?' asked Hans, running his fingers up Darkie's jaw. 'How would ye like a job in town? I'm draining off slobland for an aerodrome, an' I could give ye a start as a ganger. What d'ye say?' 'I told ye before. I won't hear tell av it. I've a farm an' I'm workin' it. I know damn fine Maisie's been at Aggie. William, don't ask me again. Your work's building; my work's farmin'.'[24]

Despite the story's fictionalised location (it references an invented town called Newtowndullard), it utilises a recognisable rural Ulster English dialect, and is peppered with highly specific rural and agricultural language (Hans hears his visitor approaching on the 'loanen'; later William volunteers: 'Will ye give me an oul pair av breeks an I'll hag wood for ye?').[25] Bell provides other hints towards the story being set in Northern Ireland; one character is referred to as 'the Man from the Lough' (presumably Lough Neagh), and the aerodrome mentioned in the above passage might be surmised to be one of those built on the Lough's banks during the Second World War.[26]

This reference, therefore, while ostensibly inconsequential within the story (important only in so far as it represents the opportunity of employment in a more urban environment than the farm), situates the story temporally as well as geographically, and would have resonated with readers of the time. It is an example of another characteristic of many of *Lagan*'s stories – a close engagement with the war as subject matter: a characteristic to which I will devote further attention later in this chapter.

Of the issue's fiction, 'The Broken Tree' is most obviously attuned to what Boyd calls 'the unique swing of our speech',[27] but this is not to say that the other stories eschew the employment of an Ulster speech. Rather, they draw heavily on different types of idiom. We meet McLaverty's child protagonist sitting by the fire with his 'daddie and mammie'; after an adventure which takes him to the local church he is described colloquially as 'dying with sleep'.[28] The young policeman of Joseph Tomelty's story, transferred from a small village to a Belfast city barracks, encounters a new, urban vernacular upon his relocation – 'Jaze it's a Bobby,'[29] remarks a woman he meets at a dancehall – while John Boyd's protagonist recalls his mother and father arguing, idiomatically, about his grandmother:

> 'M'ma never done you no harm,' his mother repeated.
> 'She niver got the chance.'
> 'Then what's the matter wi' her?'[30]

Gerry Morrow's story, the only fictional piece in the issue written in the first person, draws less heavily on idiom than some of the others, but does not entirely dispense with it: 'For years now I have been knocking around the pubs up at our end of the town, and there's hardly one left where you could be sure that you wouldn't have to put up with somebody who talks as if they owned the place', says the protagonist, who regularly refers to his favoured haunt as a 'wee pub'.[31] Robert Davidson's 'Speak Against Bonds' offers a different perspective on the city with its view of an upper-middle-class household. The protagonist, Matty, a warehouse worker from a lower socioeconomic background than the family she visits, considers the disparity between the McCulloughs' home and her own:

> Her mind flicked back the pages of memory to the days when she had been determined to have a house just like this one. A house without basements. The basement at home was so gloomy and its atmosphere of damp seemed to permeate the whole house. She touched wistfully the soft cushions; her hands smoothed the fine worn leather of the upholstery.[32]

Here, the family's father figure is referred to not as 'daddie' but 'Dada', a signifier of class rather than geography, yet phrases and patterns of speech characteristic of an Ulster 'idiom' still surface; 'Is that yourself, Matty Cochrane?' asks Mrs McCullough, her son later describing Matty as 'full of crack'.[33] The import of these uses of idiom is twofold: on one hand, they ensured that the magazine was pitched, in the first instance, to resonate with an Ulster readership already familiar with such language and its nuances, with the dialectal shifts between regions, cities and towns, and with the markers of differing class backgrounds. On the other hand, one might surmise that Boyd hoped this very specificity would carve out a niche for *Lagan* in the wider little magazine marketplace of the UK and Ireland, offering a realist glimpse into life in the province, and the artwork arising from it.

Significantly, fiction appears to be the form best suited to accommodating the aspirations Boyd outlines in his introduction. The short stories, more so than any of the other writings included, might be said to 'spring out of the life and speech of the province' in the way Boyd envisages.[34] Ulster dialect is largely absent from the poetry and nonfiction included, and neither the issue's poems nor its articles, on the whole, are as rooted in Ulster as its short stories. The trend continues in subsequent issues of the magazine – from Arnold Hill's 'Jonesy' to Joseph Sherlock's 'Michin'', Edward Sheehy's 'Obit Episcopus' to Tomelty's 'Germs'. However, as will be discussed later in this chapter, it proves difficult for *Lagan* to maintain this linguistic focus; as he produces more issues, it becomes harder for Boyd to gather consistently a wealth of stories which employ Ulster idiom. We need only consider the introductory remarks to the publication's second issue for evidence of this fact. Here, Boyd appears to be backtracking after a bold opening gambit, conscious of managing readers' expectations. Ulster, he writes, has given rise to 'several promising works' of writing, but the statement is qualified: 'a handful of blades is no more a harvest than a handful of "slim volumes" is a renaissance'.[35]

Boyd's initial characterisation of the literary landscape of Northern Ireland in 1943, however, is telling in its prioritisation of prose: 'That Ulster prose is now richer and more realistic; poetry freer and more imaginative; criticism more radical and illuminating: these are all assertions which could be safely made.'[36] It seems that a key element of Ulster prose's 'realism' is its inclusion of a variety of idiomatic language largely absent from other genres. Prose writers, too, are the focus of the larger editorial, which cites Arnold Bennett, James Joyce, St John Ervine, Thomas Hardy, Lewis Grassic Gibbon, Jean

Giono, Forrest Reid and George Shiels: writers, in the main, best known for their contributions to fiction. Hardy, Gibbon and Giono, for example, are lauded as standard-bearers for the way in which their work is seen to draw on the 'common coinage' of their speech.[37]

In part, the emphasis *Lagan* places on the short story might owe something to the contemporaneous vogue for the form. As Heather Ingman records, the popularity of the short story had risen sharply in the preceding decades:

> Financial necessity [. . .] impelled writers like Wilde and Yeats to make forays into short fiction at the end of the nineteenth century when the demise of the three-volume novel in England and the rise of small literary magazines encouraged writers' work in the genre. In the twentieth century, the lucrative nature of the American magazine market stimulated development of short fiction generally and a large Irish American readership encouraged Irish writers towards the form.[38]

While Northern Irish fiction writers were not published as prolifically in American periodicals as their Southern peers, there can be little doubt that the forces that shaped the mid-century Southern short story boom had some influence north of the border.[39] But Boyd's dedication to the form transcends mere adherence to fashion; rather, it appears that he thinks of the short story as uniquely poised to achieve the style of realism he values, to foreground Ulster idiom as the basis for a new regional literature. To follow *Lagan*'s trajectory is to develop a sense of Boyd's belief in a dynamic that Edna Longley would explicitly theorise some years later: that 'prose-writers, particularising character and scene, can perhaps do more than poets to preserve local words'.[40] While Boyd nowhere gestures towards a generic hierarchy, in *Lagan*'s first issue, at least, fiction lies at the heart of the magazine (offering a platform for the genre seems to be its *raison d'être*), and a unifying aspect of much of this fiction is its incorporation of the cadences and colloquialisms of Ulster speech.

Lagan and the Second World War

As touched upon above, if the determination to convey a sense of its place is integral to *Lagan*, an engagement with the time of its production is no less important. I want to return to a consideration of *Lagan* in the context of its social, political and historical moment. What confluence of conditions facilitated *Lagan*'s arrival? How did the magazine speak back to these conditions? Why did the impetus – and the readership – exist, at that moment in time, for a magazine that announced itself as the harbinger of a new, regional literary tradition, and what were the political underpinnings of the regionalism it espoused? To begin answering these questions, it might be fruitful to reflect more deeply on the publication's form. In a valuable survey of what he terms the 'Irish cultural journal', Richard Kearney maps the development of 'the journal format as a literary genre' with specific reference to *The Nation*, *The United Irishman*, *The Irish Statesman*, *An Claidheamh Soluis* and *The Bell* – in terms which are nonetheless applicable to *Lagan*.[41] Kearney delineates the distinctions between the *journal intime* and the journalistic newspaper, positioning periodicals such as the aforementioned as hybrids – 'journal-magazines' – falling somewhere between the two poles:

> The journal-magazine was, as the root Arabic word, *makhazan*, reminds us, a storehouse. But here we are concerned with a storehouse which records both factual and fictional experience, and which combines the resources of subjectivity (as cultivated by the *journal intime*) and objectivity (as invoked by newspaper journalism).[42]

The attempt to combine the resources of subjectivity and objectivity is crucial to the project of *Lagan*, which seeks to offer a multitude of perspectives on Ulster – and the concerns of writers in or from the region – incorporating both factual and fictional approaches. The magazine's second issue is of particular interest in this regard, as it dispenses with section headings for each genre: rather than being grouped together, stories are interspersed with poems and pieces of non-fiction. A conversation across genres begins to occur, and is informed by another key element of the magazine form to which Kearney draws attention: its periodicity, and how this influences the material included:

> While newspapers appeared daily and dealt with topical matters and while novels were almost 'timeless' by virtue of the unconditioned freedoms enjoyed by the artist, magazines appeared on a 'periodical' basis, that is, at regular intervals of a week, a month, every three months, every year etc. [...] The purpose was not just to view but to re-view.[43]

The compulsion to 're-view' recent history perhaps most obviously animates *Lagan*'s non-fiction, of all the genres included, yet the frequency of the magazine's publication does appear to have some bearing on the subject matter of its fiction also. A dialogue emerges between the two categories, as both essayists and short story writers are compelled to address the existential threat, and practical consequences, of the war. Arriving in the recent aftermath of the Belfast Blitz, *Lagan* occasionally appears to be inspired by the same kind of morbid curiosity that the novelist Brian Moore would attribute to the young protagonist of *The Emperor of Ice-cream*, Gavin Burke, who initially derives a kind of perverse delight from witnessing the bombing campaign inflicted on the city: 'The world and the war had come to him at last [. . .] Tonight, history had conferred the drama of war on this dull, dead town in which he had been born.'[44]

Contributions are gathered from serving members of the armed forces; notably, a whole section, 'From the Forces', is dedicated to their poetry and fiction in *Lagan*'s third issue (including contributions from Patrick Maybin and Jack McQuoid, and a short story from Alan Prior), and the issue also includes a piece of reportage, 'Trainee: A day in the life of a munition worker', by Martin Morrison. The role of literature in a time of war unfolds as a question of central importance. In Robert Greacen's slightly overstated formulation, 'The poet guarding the fragrance of surrendered pasts/ Watches our faith slither to hell one fine morning'.[45] Other contributors, if they rely less on such dramatic rhetoric, are no less concerned with what they consider to be their responsibilities. Many of *Lagan*'s short stories pay close, careful attention to the effects of war on the lives of individuals.

In 'The Broken Tree', as discussed earlier, Sam Hanna Bell's characters are somewhat insulated from the threats posed by the war by virtue of living rurally; their attitude, it seems, mirrors that of the speaker of Patrick Kavanagh's 'Epic':

> I have lived in important places, times
> When great events were decided; who owned
> That half a rood of rock, a no-man's land
> Surrounded by our pitchfork-armed claims.
> [. . .]
> That was the year of the Munich bother. Which
> Was more important?[46]

A certain detachment is characteristic of the occasional story in the magazine, but in other fictive pieces, the Second World War is pulled into closer focus. The wail of the air-raid siren reverberates across the pages of *Lagan*, and even ghosts the last issue, published after the war has ended. The protagonist of Gerard Keenan's 'A Disappointing Day' returns to Belfast after an extended period of time living in the countryside as an evacuee, and is exhilarated to be back amidst 'ridges and ridges of rooftops, terminating in bare gantries, the vast meccano-set of the shipyard – a lovely sight after two years of looking at tattered, damp fields'.[47] Boyd's own 'Homecoming' stands out as exemplary of the kind of fiction he leans towards publishing. Even more than his editorials, it gives readers a sense of his tastes and intentions for *Lagan*'s broader fiction offering, as a story which combines a regional focus with an international context. 'Homecoming' follows a young soldier's visit to Belfast, his hometown, after a prolonged period of military service in the Middle East, and evokes his sense of alienation in a place he once knew intimately, amongst a people from whom he now feels a growing separation:

> He felt his heart warm as he listened to three soldiers who stopped beside him [. . .] They were all Ulstermen, and Matthew, hearing their voices, suddenly felt he was at last near home. He smiled. Their accent seemed slightly queer to him, harsh and yet attractive. He had done all his soldiering with an English regiment and had acquired a half-English intonation in his speech. He felt curiously happy listening to his native accent and he suddenly wanted to join in the conversation. But he allowed his impulse to pass.[48]

Less successful are contributions such as Shearman's 'Only Solution' and David Kennedy's 'Continental Sunday' (an account of a 'day's spree' an Irishman goes on in Kehl with German students), which bypass complexity for shock value.[49] Both set in mainland Europe, these stories fall back on lazy stereotypes, and seem to value topicality over depth of imaginative engagement with the war. As more issues appear, Boyd's initial focus seems to dissipate. Note how the focus shifts from fiction as early as the second issue; the editor's initial ambitions to prioritise fiction have dwindled, his interests have shifted towards poetry. While downplaying suggestions that *Lagan* is part of a 'renaissance' in Ulster writing, Boyd comments:

> Instead of vaunting small beginnings we prefer to understand the word as it is interpreted by the rest of the world. But we feel confident that some of the poetry which will come out of Ulster will be considered major work in centres of appreciation abroad, just as the work of our southern fellow-countrymen, forty years ago, resounded far beyond Ireland.[50]

By the third issue, the prognosis is even worse – not only for fiction, but for all genres: 'The editors know what they want', says Boyd, 'and they seldom get it.'[51] In issue 4, Boyd significantly reframes *Lagan*'s purpose:

> [A] regionalist publication like *Lagan* desires to have a deep interest not only in its own writers but in those of other regions [. . .] Such an extension of policy is to be viewed not as a contradiction but as a natural evolution of the policy outlined in the first issue.[52]

While this new expansiveness, the impulse to look outside Northern Ireland, is to be commended, the editorial reveals a shift in *Lagan*'s aims and a certain defensiveness on Boyd's part. A 'regional' agenda appears to be disappearing entirely. In microcosm, here, we can already see beginning to appear the cracks that Richard Kirkland astutely perceives in his survey of Belfast poetry of the 1940s:

> It is not that the Belfast poets of the 1940s failed to identify the problems of aesthetics, culture, and politics that poetry in the North had to face during this period. Indeed the need for creative renewal was often powerfully felt and articulated. Unfortunately, however, it is in their ultimate failure to refashion these antinomies that their interest now resides.[53]

The Second World War had been important to *Lagan* not only in terms of its provision of subject matter, but because in essence it had given the magazine a reason to exist. Tom Clyde perceptively comments that *Lagan*'s regionalist agenda was 'to a large extent inspired by wartime isolation [. . .] waving the name of the province like a flag of identity [had] never before been so prevalent, and cannot be coincidental'.[54] The war had inspired Boyd and his colleagues to interrogate their regional identities, and had awoken in them the desire to find a sense of belonging, figured along regional lines, in the midst of chaos. The magazine, informed by Boyd's own liberal, socialist outlook, was to be a non-sectarian endeavour, a space for enlightened discourse. As the war dragged on, however, *Lagan* struggled to consolidate its own identity; with the war's cessation, the magazine's death knell sounded.

Cessation and legacy: 'a golden age of Ulster writing'

In the same year that the publication of *Lagan* ceased, Frederick J. Hoffman, Charles Allen and Carolyn F. Ulrich published *The Little Magazine: A History and A Bibliography*, a survey of the period's literary magazines which focuses mainly on periodicals produced in America. While the authors' assertion that 'regionalism is synonymous with ruralism' does not necessarily map effectively onto a Northern Irish context, certain of the criticisms they make of regional literature might nonetheless be applied to some of *Lagan*'s stories; 'it is not the theory, but the literary practice – the value of the fiction produced – among other things, that leads to dispute', they write:

> Too often the regionalist fails to probe beyond the 'specific fact' to the universals. He is too preoccupied with the region's peculiarity, its eccentric detail, its uniqueness. Regionalism has, in effect, thrown too heavy a stress on the particular, and it would seem that this is a danger inherent in regional theory [. . .] Another serious defect [. . .] is a drabness of style.[55]

Further criticisms include the 'unhealthy heritage of sentimentalised pastoralism' and the 'nostalgic wish to preserve an outmoded cultural pattern' which the editors perceive as a plague upon regionalist fiction.[56] Such attacks would have come as little surprise to Boyd, who had been defending the quality of the writing in *Lagan* since his introduction to the magazine's second issue:

> After the first issue of *Lagan*, a number of people commented on the motif of depression which seemed to run through most of the work [. . .] That most of our young writers should be preoccupied with the seamy side of life may be unfortunate, but it would seem to be none the less a fact.[57]

Beneath their surface defensiveness, Boyd's comments imply an anxiety about 'a drabness of style'; perhaps it would have been untenable for *Lagan* to continue in this vein, regardless of the end of the war.

Other problems arose. Despite a strong start, *Lagan* failed to catch the attention of a significant number of readers outside Northern Ireland. McMahon, in Sam Hanna Bell's biography, reveals that:

> In retrospect Bell was not entirely happy about the final title. As he admitted to Deborah Keys, the word *Lagan* meant nothing outside Northern Ireland. There was no reason why *Lagan* should have any potential significance for readers in Cork or Galway, let alone in Britain.[58]

Ironically, Boyd's focus on showcasing Ulster idiom might well have contributed to its failure to travel – rendering it inaccessible to the 'general reader' outside Ulster, and perhaps advertising a perceived insularity which Boyd had been at pains to avoid. Furthermore, soliciting readers in Northern Ireland proved challenging, too; a fact which may have had something to do with the magazine's relatively high cover price, and, as the war ended, with a renewed anxiety amongst the general populace about their economic horizons.[59]

Perhaps these practical obstacles to the magazine's success could have been overcome, if not for the most grievous issue *Lagan* faced – the dissolution of its editorial focus, and the difficulty of soliciting 'relevant' material, as has been suggested earlier. Those compiling *Lagan* strove to include only material that they deemed to be of sufficient quality, but, as we have seen, this proved a struggle. The magazine dwindled in size, featuring work by eight contributors in its last iteration, as opposed to seventeen in its first. Of the pieces in the final issue, there were two short stories, where there had been seven in issue 1, and only one of these pieces, 'A Disappointing Day', is based in Ulster.

Implicit in *Lagan*'s final editorial is the suggestion that the magazine had not achieved as much as Boyd hoped it might. The piece is ambivalent, if quietly hopeful about the publishing prospects of writers from Northern Ireland, but importantly the focus seems to have shifted away from creating this tradition towards the less ambitious aim of simply providing a space for new work:

> [F]our years is a short period to allow for much growth in either a single writer or in a movement; and it is, I suppose, questionable whether the main contributors to *Lagan* feel sufficient kinship in methods and aims to regard themselves, in any sense, as a literary movement. Each is an individual with an independent view of a way of writing as well as a way of life; each differs with the others in questions of literary judgement; but each, I think, feels fundamentally the same about the conditions and problems of writers, scholars and artists in this province, and believes that the future of literature, scholarship, and art need not be as unsatisfactory as in the past.[60]

So how might we measure *Lagan*'s success? Its focus may have waned, the project may not have been long-lasting, but what did it achieve? Once again, it is instructive to bear in mind Kearney's discussion of the magazine form. As the form developed, he posits, it 'strove towards the creation of a sense of community, as [a] mediating link between the idioms of individualism and collectivism'.[61] The magazine's purpose is 'dialogue, and by extension, community', and for this reason 'it seems fair to say that the possibility of a journal always exceeds its actuality, it is of its nature to promise more than it can deliver'.[62] *Lagan*, however briefly, fulfilled such a purpose: trying to capture something of the pluralism of Ulster society; celebrating established writers and encouraging emerging ones; and building a community of writers and readers. As McMahon notes: 'The period of *Lagan* [...] and later *Rann*, seems in retrospect a kind of golden age of Ulster writing. So much of the work done then has lasted, and the names of the period still glitter.'[63]

When *Lagan* ran aground, this community lost a vital platform for their work – a loss for which the appearance of *Rann*, with its focus on poetry, could not completely compensate – but the lives and work of its members continued to overlap and intersect. Offering a brief overview of the careers of his colleagues post-*Lagan*, Boyd writes:

> Sam Hanna Bell [. . .] joined the BBC; Michael McLaverty became headmaster of a Catholic school; Roy McFadden continued to practise law; Robert Greacen went to Dublin and then settled in London; John Hewitt left Belfast in anger against discrimination and took a job in Coventry; newcomers like Brian Friel, a teacher in Derry, Seamus Heaney, a teacher (under the aegis of McLaverty) in Belfast, Michael Longley, James Simmons, Derek Mahon and others appeared. Altogether something was stirring in the North, but exactly what would be the outcome of the sectarianism, the discrimination and the scab of unemployment that festered throughout the area we could only guess.[64]

Lagan's abiding achievement may well be the influence it had on these 'newcomers'. In the 1964 essay 'Our Own Dour Way' (itself printed in a short-lived publication, *Trench*, a production of the students of St Joseph's Teacher Training College), a young Seamus Heaney calls readers' attention to *Lagan* as an important example of a magazine where emerging writers could 'flex their talent in the company of their established seniors', that 'gave the North a literary identity and encouraged a lively crop of local writing'.[65] Derek Mahon, invoking the periodical as part of a wider discussion of the literary culture of the Belfast in which he was raised, is rather less complimentary; considering the influence of John Hewitt (latterly one of *Lagan*'s associate editors) and his essay 'The Bitter Gourd', Mahon writes that 'there was something profoundly unsexy about his persona and attitudes that proved less than fascinating to us adolescent cynics'.[66] He recalls being dismissive of the regionalist agenda which the magazine promoted: 'To us citified provincial dandies, the real question was: what's happening in England?'[67]

Yet despite their differences in tone, both references to *Lagan* point towards the important position it occupied in 1940s Northern Ireland. Whether new writers were enlivened by, or reacting against, what they had read in *Lagan*, it was a cultural touchstone. In few places is *Lagan*'s influence more clear, for example, than in the introduction to its most obvious successor, *The Honest Ulsterman*:

The second half of the title of this magazine is Ulsterman [...] [T]he emphasis on Ulster seems easy to understand; the magazine originates in Ulster, it provides a special opportunity for Ulster writers and Ulster readers. It will be read here and there about the world; but if it has any profound effects they are most likely to be seen in Ulster [...] Just as it is necessary for each individual to claim his own freedom and make his own decisions, so it is important for the regions.[68]

Echoes of Boyd's mission statement resonate as evidently here as echoes of *Ulad*'s editorials had in *Lagan* (despite the different flavour of regionalism to which each publication aspires). The ripple effect of *Lagan*'s influence on subsequent generations is addressed by Tom Clyde, who notes that its 'example was extremely useful to the 1960s generation of writers in their own, more confident, rebellion (in particular, Heaney and Simmons)',[69] and by Edna Longley, in her assertions that 'some progress can be measured by the multiple links between what might be termed the first phase of a literary movement and subsequent developments',[70] and that '*Lagan* broke the repressive silences of the North in a way that had long-term repercussions'.[71]

It is crucial to note that discussions of *Lagan*'s influence take as their concern the space it would open up for poets working in Northern Ireland, suggesting that it had failed to offer any significant legacy for prose writers. Critical discourse on the literature of the so-called 'Ulster Renaissance', beginning in the 1960s, would focus primarily on the work of poets – most of whom were associated with the so-called 'Belfast Group' – while no comparable claims were made for any movement in Northern Irish fiction.[72] *Lagan*'s success was, therefore, limited: it stands as a magazine whose ambitions were only partially realised – refracted through poetry, but not borne out in an abundance of Northern short stories.

Notes

1. John Boyd, 'Introduction', *Lagan*, 1 (1943), pp. 5–7 (p. 6).
2. The Second World War had radically reconfigured Northern Ireland's identity; when *Lagan* appeared, the province was still reeling from the Belfast Blitz, which had taken place in 1941. Brian Barton writes that 'Northern Ireland had greatness thrust upon it: it became a base for convoys, escorts, maritime reconnaissance, costal command, and anti-submarine craft, as well as a launching pad for the American forces'; that 'its role in Allied victory became a vital one'. Barton, *The Blitz*, p. 286.

3. Boyd notes that the magazine's circulation dropped steeply with its last issue; while 2,000 copies of the first issue of *Lagan* had sold out, the last 'failed to sell even 500 copies'. Boyd, *The Middle of My Journey*, p. 27. According to Edna Longley, the magazine's initial circulation had been boosted by visiting members of the services – their departure, therefore, might partially explain the reduction. Longley, 'Progressive Bookmen', p. 53.
4. This subtitle was introduced with the magazine's second issue; the first had borne the subtitle 'A Magazine of Revolution'.
5. See, for example, Edna Longley's discussion of *Lagan* in the aforementioned essay 'Progressive Bookmen', and Allen, 'Out of Time', as well as analyses of the magazine in Ballin, *Irish Periodical Culture, 1937–1972*; Clyde, *Irish Literary Magazines*; and Shovlin, *The Irish Literary Periodical*. Richard Kirkland's chapter in the *Oxford Handbook of Modern Irish Poetry* also provides a useful discussion of the magazine and the era of its production (Kirkland, 'The Poetics of Partition').
6. See Matthews, *The Bell Magazine*, and Carson, *Rebel by Vocation*.
7. Allen, 'Out of Time', p. 94.
8. Boyd, *The Middle of My Journey*, p. 25.
9. *The Bell* first appeared in 1940.
10. John Boyd, 'Comment', *Lagan*, 3 (1945), p. 11.
11. 'Editorial Notes', *Ulad*, 1 (November 1904), pp. 1–3 (p. 1). *The Ulsterman*, which was founded in 1933 and ran for four issues, serves as an unacknowledged link between the two publications, its introduction reading as follows: 'The histories of pagan Greece and Rome receive scrupulous attention in the majority of our Ulster colleges, academies, and schools. On the other hand, with a fatuity that is as singular as it is amazing, the study of our own history and native culture is woefully neglected [. . .] The plain truth is that during the Victorian era we in Ulster were too busy making money to bother whether we had a history or a culture, or not [. . .] The result is that, culturally and historically speaking, we do not know where we stand. The subject is of first-rate importance to a journal calling itself *The Ulsterman*, and we shall return to it in future numbers.' 'Notes and Comments', *The Ulsterman*, 1.1 (April 1933), pp. 1–4 (p. 1).
12. Clyde, *Irish Literary Magazines*, p. 200. *The New Northman* was the revised title for the magazine formerly known as *The Northman*, which had been founded in December 1926.
13. The magazine's editorial makes the case that: 'The spirit of a people is expressed in their songs and sayings, their history and language, their bearing in a national crisis [. . .] The moment we remove our provincial dialect from our literature and drama, so soon will we develop into a second-rate English country.' *Young Ulster*, 1 (October 1938), pp. 1–2 (p. 1).
14. Ballin, *Irish Periodical Culture, 1937–1972*, p. 120. These production

values are particularly impressive given the constraints imposed upon publishers during the Second World War; for a comprehensive overview of the difficulties faced by presses during the period, see Holman, *Print for Victory*, p. 1: 'Fewer and fewer [books] could be produced when manpower, raw materials, fuel and transport were all in short supply. On a daily basis publishers had to fight for the status of their profession, the economic survival of the book trade and even the paper rations that were their due.'
15. Boyd, *The Middle of My Journey*, p. 27.
16. Ibid. p. 27.
17. Frank Shovlin draws attention to the political specificity of the way in which 'Ulster' is used by *Lagan*; by the time of the publication's inception, he writes, 'the term "Ulster" has become problematised. The historic notion of a nine-county province does not sit easily with the magazine,' and more often than not the designation 'Ulster' is used as a synonym for 'Northern Ireland'. Shovlin, *The Irish Literary Periodical*, p. 162.
18. By issue 3, the subtitle has changed to 'A Miscellany of Ulster Writing', perhaps suggesting a looser editorial grip, or a new diversity of intent and broadness of scope.
19. Boyd, 'Introduction', *Lagan*, 1, p. 6.
20. Ibid. p. 5.
21. John Hewitt, 'The Bitter Gourd', *Lagan*, 3 (1945), pp. 93–105 (p. 99).
22. Sam Hanna Bell, 'The Broken Tree', *Lagan*, 1 (1943), pp. 33–42 (p. 33).
23. Like John Hewitt, Boyd seems to conceive of the world as expanding outwards from the region; consider, for example, Hewitt's famous declaration to this effect: 'I'm an Ulsterman, of planter stock. I was born in the island of Ireland, so secondarily I'm an Irishman. I was born in the British archipelago, and English is my native tongue, so I'm British. The British archipelago consists of off-shore islands to the continent of Europe, so I'm European. This is my hierarchy of values and so far as I am concerned, anyone who omits one step in that sequence of values is falsifying the situation.' John Hewitt, 'The Clash of Identities – 1', *The Irish Times* (4 July 1974), p. 12.
24. Bell, 'The Broken Tree', p. 34.
25. Ibid. pp. 33–6. *The Concise Ulster Dictionary* defines a 'loanen' as 'a lane; a track; a by-road', and 'hag' as a verb meaning, 'hew, cut with an axe'. Macafee, *Concise Ulster Dictionary*, pp. 208, 160.
26. For an overview of the construction of aerodromes in Northern Ireland during the Second World War, see, for example, Blake, *Northern Ireland in the Second World War*.
27. Boyd, 'Introduction', *Lagan*, 1, p. 6.
28. Michael McLaverty, 'Evening in Winter', *Lagan*, 1 (1943), pp. 8–11.

29. Joseph Tomelty, 'Destiny', *Lagan*, 1 (1943), pp. 43–51 (p. 46).
30. John Boyd, 'Dying Day', *Lagan*, 1 (1943), pp. 52–62 (p. 55).
31. Gerry Morrow, 'The Pub', *Lagan*, 1 (1943), pp. 21–4 (p. 21).
32. Robert Davidson, 'Speak Against Bonds', *Lagan*, 1 (1943), pp. 25–32 (p. 28).
33. Ibid. p. 27.
34. Boyd, 'Introduction', *Lagan*, 1, p. 6.
35. John Boyd, 'Comment', *Lagan*, 2 (1944), pp. 11–12 (p. 12).
36. Ibid. p. 7.
37. Ibid. p. 6.
38. Ingman, *A History of the Irish Short Story*, pp. 4–5.
39. This being said, it is important to note that Belfast didn't entertain a flourishing wartime literary culture on the same scale as Dublin. See Wills, *That Neutral Island*, p. 425: 'The growth of a confident, independent Irish cultural sphere which went beyond the GAA and official Irish-language concerns [...] was one of the most striking outcomes of the Emergency [...] Small publishing houses, magazines, amateur theatre, Irish-language presses, art exhibitions, film-making, all testified to a new vitality in Irish culture.'
40. Edna Longley, 'Poetry and Politics in Northern Ireland', *The Crane Bag*, 9.1 (1985), pp. 26–40 (p. 31).
41. Richard Kearney, 'Between Politics and Literature: The Irish Cultural Journal', *The Crane Bag*, 7.2 (1983), pp. 160–71 (p. 160).
42. Ibid. p. 161.
43. Ibid.
44. Moore, *The Emperor of Ice-cream*, p. 199.
45. Robert Greacen, 'The Poet', *Lagan*, 1 (1943), pp. 74–5 (p. 74).
46. Kavanagh, *Collected Poems*, p. 184.
47. Gerard Keenan, 'A Disappointing Day', *Lagan*, 4 (1946), pp. 45–50 (p. 45).
48. John Boyd, 'Homecoming', *Lagan*, 3 (1945), pp. 44–9 (p. 44).
49. David Kennedy, 'Continental Sunday', *Lagan*, 2 (1944), pp. 21–3 (p. 22).
50. John Boyd, 'Comment', *Lagan*, 2 (1944), pp. 11–12 (p. 12).
51. John Boyd, 'Comment', *Lagan*, 3 (1945), p. 11.
52. John Boyd, 'Comment', *Lagan*, 4 (1946), pp. 9–12 (p. 11).
53. Kirkland, 'The Poetics of Partition', p. 224.
54. Clyde, *Irish Literary Magazines*, p. 44.
55. Hoffman et al., *The Little Magazine*, pp. 128, 134.
56. Ibid. p. 136.
57. Boyd, 'Comment', *Lagan*, 2, p. 11.
58. McMahon, *Sam Hanna Bell*, p. 29. For those who were aware of the etymology of the word 'lagan' as divorced from its connection to the river, the connotations would not have been positive; the *Oxford English Dictionary* definition for the word is 'Goods or wreckage lying

on the bed of the sea'. *Oxford English Dictionary*, < https://www.oed.com> (last accessed 1 September 2020).
59. Brian Barton documents the precarious position into which Northern Ireland was plunged with the end of the war: 'For all the suffering that had occurred, the conflict also brought a level of prosperity not known since World War I. The declaration of peace on 8 May 1945 should have brought an uncomplicated sense of relief. Instead it revived for many in Northern Ireland disturbing memories of the Depression.' Barton, *The Blitz*, p. 296. The magazine's cover price alternated between three shillings and sixpence (issues one and three) and two shillings and sixpence (issues two and four).
60. John Boyd, 'Comment', *Lagan*, 4 (1946), pp. 9–12 (p. 11–12).
61. Richard Kearney, 'Between Politics and Literature: The Irish Cultural Journal', *The Crane Bag*, 7.2 (1983), pp. 160–71 (p. 161).
62. Ibid. p. 161.
63. McMahon, *Sam Hanna Bell*, p. 31.
64. Boyd, *The Middle of My Journey*, p. 102.
65. Seamus Heaney, 'Our Own Dour Way', *Trench*, 1 (1964), pp. 3–4. *Lagan* is commended in contrast with O'Malley's *Threshold*; while Heaney recognises the latter as a more 'accomplished' effort, he argues that it 'might as well be published in Dublin. In fact, put a copy of "Threshold" inside a "Kilkenny Magazine" cover and very few people could tell the difference.' Heaney had published a short story in the Queen's University Belfast magazine *Gorgon* three years before this essay appeared, which reflects this concern with building a 'regional' literature; 'There's Rosemary' centres on a protagonist, Sean, who has recently graduated from the same institution.
66. Derek Mahon, 'Memoir: 1941–1980', Derek Mahon Papers 1948–2017, Irish Literary Collection, Stuart A. Rose Manuscript, Archives and Rare Book Library, Robert W. Woodruff Library, Emory University, Atlanta, GA, Collection Number 689, Box 25, Folder 31, Item Number 28.
67. Ibid.
68. James Simmons, 'Editorial: First Steps in Revolution', *The Honest Ulsterman*, 1 (May 1968), pp. 2–6 (pp. 5–6).
69. Clyde, *Irish Literary Magazines*, p. 45.
70. Longley, 'Progressive Bookmen', p. 56.
71. Longley, '"Between the Saxon Smile and Yankee Yawp"', p. 209.
72. For a comprehensive overview of the 'Ulster Renaissance', see Clark, *The Ulster Renaissance*.

Chapter 14

The Short Story in *Wales* (1937–1949): 'Though we write in English, we are rooted in Wales'

Daniel Hughes

Wales, initially a little modernist magazine, announced itself to the world by boldly placing the opening of Dylan Thomas's surreal short story 'Prologue to an Adventure' on its front cover, thus wearing its tonal, ideological and thematic identities on its sleeve.[1] It demonstrates that the first sustained manifestation of English-language writing in Wales (often referred to as 'the Golden Generation') was modernist at its point of inception. The brainchild of the journalist and poet Keidrych Rhys, Dylan Thomas, and the short story writer and poet Glyn Jones, the magazine's contradictory position – Anglophone yet Welsh-nationalist – is not only inferred by its use of the nation's anglicised name as its title but is also expressed in a subscription notice at the end of the first issue: 'We publish this journal in English so that it may spread far beyond the frontiers of Wales, and because we realise the beauty of the English language better than the English themselves [. . .] Though we write in English, we are rooted in Wales.'[2]

Indeed, it is significant that *Wales* inaugurates itself with an experimental, modernist short story by Wales's most famous writer, which sets the tone of the magazine. This tone is indicative of a modernist writing which – while corresponding with other, more familiar, modernist literatures – stems from a deliberately non-Anglocentric source. During *Wales*'s run of publication, numerous writers operate within these tonal, thematic and ideological paradigms, exploring and articulating both the cultural tensions and creative possibilities inherent in writing Welsh short stories in English. As John Harris has demonstrated, there were also tensions between the organisers of *Wales* when it came to the political and aesthetic ambitions of the magazine.[3] This chapter will demonstrate the ways in which the short stories featured in *Wales* reflected, and were inflected by, the magazine's ideological and thematic concerns: by its commitment to new

Welsh culture written in English, its position as Welsh-nationalist without the Welsh language (the primary drive of the Welsh nationalist movement at the time), and the ways in which its short fiction engages with European modernist paradigms originating in Ireland, France and Germany. To this end, the chapter will survey an array of the short fiction published both in *Wales*'s initial 1937–40 run, as a little modernist magazine, before tracing the shifts and continuities in its selection of short fiction as the magazine returned as a cultural miscellany in 1943. I will suggest that, while *Wales* certainly shifts focus as a magazine, it continues to engage in national and intranational modernist paradigms, as evidenced by some of the short stories published.

A home-grown modernist aesthetic

Wales has its origins in a correspondence initiated by Keidrych Rhys in July 1936, when he wrote to the Swansea-born poet Dylan Thomas, then and indeed now Wales's most famous literary scion. Thomas had already been discussing a potential Anglophone Welsh magazine with his friend and fellow writer Glyn Jones, and put Rhys in touch with Jones.[4] While Rhys wished that the magazine would be overtly Welsh nationalist, Thomas felt that the magazine's priority ought to be to provide a home to advanced, experimental literature from Wales. However, the magazine ultimately had 'a wider social mission: no less than to raise the national consciousness and political commitment of a new generation of writers'.[5] As Christopher Hopkins argues, *Wales* also articulated itself as a place 'where an energetic, distinctive yet submerged and youthful literary voice could make itself better heard'.[6] In his seminal critical and personal history of what was once commonly called 'Anglo-Welsh' writing, Glyn Jones addresses his book to Rhys, the one 'who started it all', and notes that, while Jones had previously considered his 'literary nationality', it was 'the founding that year [1937] of your sensational Anglo-Welsh magazine, *Wales*, [which] brought it up sharply for me then'.[7] *Wales* was therefore both aesthetically experimental and in some senses Welsh nationalist, though it was a nationalism which intended to promote Wales's emergent Anglophone literature on an international stage. These two directions inform the magazine's first two runs, with its latter, 1943 run shifting away from the little magazine format into a cultural miscellany, while its initial 1937 run prioritised the promotion of a home-grown modernist aesthetic.

As Jones goes on to note, 1937 was a memorable year in Welsh publishing, especially in the English language.[8] Not only was *Wales* founded, but other key texts were published as well, including Jones's surreal short story collection *The Blue Bed*, David Jones's epic modernist war poem *In Parenthesis*, Lewis Jones's industrial novel *Cwmardy* and the Faber-published anthology *Welsh Short Stories*. Given the subject of this volume, the Faber anthology is a notable development, pointing to the strength of Welsh short fiction. Indeed, Glyn Jones suggests that Anglophone Welsh writers were particularly attracted to the short story form throughout the twentieth century.[9] Jones identifies two major attractions of the short story during the 1930s and 1940s in particular. On the one hand, there was a 'large number of periodicals of some standing [. . .] prepared to publish short stories', and on the other, few Welsh writers were able to earn a living purely as writers:

> Perhaps amateurism in literature succeeds better when shorter works are attempted, since, for a man or a woman who has another job, writing a novel requires commitment and steadiness of vision and a quite unusual degree of stamina over a long period.[10]

While Jones points to publishing and economic realities as driving forces behind Welsh writers' attraction to the short story, Tony Brown has suggested that the particular cultural conditions of Anglophone Welsh writing also led to an affinity with the form:

> [T]he short story has been constructed by a number of critics as a form which frequently deals with what Clare Hanson sees as the 'ex-centric', the experience of those individuals and groups 'not part of official or "high" cultural hegemony' – in other words marginal groups or individuals who are outside the main centres of power.[11]

As Brown goes on to demonstrate, Anglophone Welsh writers often operated outside or on the edges of the 'main centres of power', such as the London-based publishing industry, and were further marginalised by their lack of Welsh-language skills in their bilingual nation. Writers such as Dylan Thomas and Glyn Jones were not taught Welsh by their Welsh-speaking parents, because 'English was the language of social advancement [as well as] the language to make money in'.[12] In some senses, the cultural climate denied writers like Jones and Thomas the chance to operate within the centuries-old literary tradition of Wales's native language. Alongside publishing realities and economic practicalities, Wales's particular cultural conditions meant that the short story was a form well suited to the needs of Welsh writers in the modern era.

While the late 1930s provided a number of literary outlets for Welsh writers – Jones identifies Gwyn Jones's *The Welsh Review*, as well as *Life and Letters To-day*, *The Adelphi* and *This Quarter*, as magazines which provided some exposure for him and his contemporaries – this was in fact a new development. As Jones remarked in his biography, referring to *Wales* and Gwyn Jones's *The Welsh Review*:

> One felt a great sense of relief, almost of self-indulgence, at having two literary magazines to which one could submit one's own work, when for years and years one had, perforce to send it to often indifferent, hostile or uncomprehending editors in London or America.[13]

Rather than having to appeal to 'hostile' or 'uncomprehending' editors in conventional literary publishing centres, *Wales* (and later *The Welsh Review*) provided Jones and his contemporaries with an 'ex-centric' outlet. Indeed, if Bloomsbury was in some ways the home of the 'official', 'high', hegemonic English literary culture (to borrow Clare Hanson's register), *Wales* initially positioned itself in contradistinction to it. For example, in a letter to *The Western Mail*, Keidrych Rhys argues that the new generation of Anglophone Welsh writers were not content to become a 'footnote in a monograph on the Auden age'.[14] The editorial notices in early issues of *Wales* confirm this combative stance. The final page of the first issue reveals that the choice of the name *Wales* aims to defy 'parasitical adoption' by the English, while the second issue's editorial announces that the magazine aims 'to print the work by our younger writers',[15] who are denied publishing opportunities in 'the English Literary Map of log-rolling, cocktail parties, book clubs, knighthoods, O.M.'s, and superannuated effeminacy in Bloomsbury editorial chairs'.[16] Indeed, in a letter to Rhys, Glyn Jones argued that *Wales* should seek to distance itself from the likes of T. S. Eliot, Ezra Pound and 'Windbag Lewis' (Wyndham Lewis) politically – the 'Fascists', as Jones called them – and should make it clear that 'we in Wales are on the side of socialism, the people'.[17]

Malcolm Ballin's history of Anglophone periodicals in Wales demonstrates that Rhys's magazine served not just to give Welsh writers an outlet denied to them in London, but also within the Welsh public sphere. The closure of the long-running *The Welsh Outlook* in 1933 left English-language writers in Wales without a meaningful publishing route into the Welsh public sphere for several years.[18] *Wales* aimed to fill that vacuum and Ballin suggests that it also marked 'a Welsh entry into the world of twentieth-century modernism'.[19] I have argued elsewhere that the writers centred around *Wales* constituted a modernist cultural formation, and that it is in fact Caradoc Evans's highly controversial 1915 short story collection *My People* which marks Wales's entry into modernism, as M. Wynn Thomas and Anthony Conran have also both suggested.[20] I will expand on the significance of this shortly, but it is worth noting that the same cultural conditions which attuned 'Anglo-Welsh' writers to the possibilities of the short story also lent themselves to a particularly Welsh expression of modernism. As Laura Wainwright's *New Territories in Modernism* persuasively demonstrates, a conventionally modernist 'crisis of language' is lent 'new resonance' when considering the particular cultural realities of the modern Welsh writer faced with a divide between 'a new social discourse derived from English-speaking Wales, and an established literary discourse rooted in native Welsh-language culture'.[21] *Wales* channels the creative possibilities of these cultural conditions; it is made 'ex-centric' by its position as an Anglophone magazine in the bilingual, paranational space of Wales, whilst also positioning itself as the heir to the explosive short fiction of Caradoc Evans.[22]

Indeed, both Thomas and Jones had visited Caradoc Evans early in the 1930s, suggesting that the pair saw Evans as their literary antecedent.[23] This feeling is strengthened by the second issue of *Wales*, which features Evans as the first writer in its series of bibliographies of 'Modern Welsh Authors'. Keidrych Rhys, editor of the fledgling magazine, also saw Evans's literary experiment and insurrectionism as a model paradigm: 'The older writer's stand against the Welsh establishment had long inspired Keidrych.'[24] Rhys wrote to Evans, sending him copies of the initial issues, offering to print some work of Evans's, and later printed Evans's praise for the magazine.[25] As I suggested, it is notable that Rhys places Dylan Thomas's modernist short story 'Prologue to an Adventure' on the cover of *Wales*'s debut number. It is a statement that voices both the aesthetic ambitions of *Wales* as well as the creative possibilities that the short story as a form and modernism as a mode offer to the young 'Anglo-Welsh' writers. Furthermore, it is in some ways an implicit acknowledgement of the debt owed to Caradoc Evans's short stories by this new generation of writers.

The use of 'Prologue' as the magazine's first cover publication is also an admission and appropriation of Thomas's commercial profile:

he was the best-established Welsh writer of his day, though younger and 'newer' than Rhys Davies. *Wales* pushes the reader immediately into the short story, with the 'Prologue' starting on the cover, breaking off after half a sentence: 'As I walked through the wilderness of this world, as I walked through the wilderness, as I walked through the city with loud electric faces and the crowded petrols.'[26] When the reader turns the page, the 'Prologue' begins again, this time with the complete sentence and the remaining five pages of Thomas's apocalyptic, biblically allusive text. The text follows two figures, an unnamed figure and Daniel, both of whom appear to be artists, journeying through this space that is, as the opening sentence tells us, both wilderness and city. There is also a very strong sense of artificiality; the city is 'lamped by its own red-waxed and iron stars, with a moon built above it' and there is a 'painted shadow'.[27] This space is also described in obviously literary terms: there is a 'literate light' shining around the city and there are 'the trees of a new scripture', suggesting that the story itself is a textual stand-in for the magazine which publishes it.[28]

Thomas's story also evokes familiar tropes of the short story and modernism. The two central figures are typical of the conditions of marginalisation and ambiguity which Frank O'Connor saw as essential to the form: 'Always in the short story there is the sense of outlawed figures wandering about the fringes of society.'[29] Relatedly, Thomas's wanderers can be seen as alienating variants of the flâneur, a trope first categorised by Charles Baudelaire and subsequently reimagined by James Joyce and Marcel Proust.[30] These twin tropes shape Thomas's bewildering, lurid text, which features a variety of satanic spaces such as 'the Seven sins' and 'the Deadly Virtue', which are seemingly pubs the story's wanderers enter. Thomas emphasises the alienating scale of the unnamed metropolis:

> For them in the friendless houses in the streets of pennies and pleasures a million ladies and gentlemen move up in bed, time moved with the time practised moon over a million roofs that night, and grim policemen stood at each corner in the black wind.[31]

From the very first sentence, there is also the sense of this metropolis as a site of both ending and beginning. This adventure takes place on 'that winter night before the West died' with 'the faces of a noiseless million in the busyhood of heaven staring on the afterbirth'.[32] This might be the night before the West died – and I would suggest 'the West' is symbolised by the lurid wilderness-city – but there is also some kind of 'afterbirth', suggesting something else has just been born. Indeed, as the story ends, the wilderness-city is destroyed:

Daniel and I stood alone in the city. The sea of destruction lapped around our feet. We saw the starfall that broke the night up. The glass lights on iron went out, and the waves grew down into the pavements.[33]

In contrast to the earlier 'built' moon, the city is now lit by more natural starfall, and the two artists alone survive the cataclysm. 'Prologue' seems to promise – in highly obscure, modernist prose – an adventure through a hostile world, but one that will end in cleansing and redemption. As prologue to *Wales*'s adventure, this story promises aesthetically radical prose, much like Evans's stories.

Despite this promise, the rest of *Wales*'s debut number is given to poetry, yet short stories from Thomas and others feature across later numbers.[34] While Thomas lends both a strong commercial profile and a radical aesthetic to *Wales*, his 'Prologue' also becomes problematic for the fledgling magazine. Thomas was deeply supportive of the magazine, but, as John Harris notes, correspondents of Rhys felt there was too much in the way of content that aped Thomas's surrealist stories. With reference to issue 4, Julian Symonds wrote that '[t]here's perhaps a bit too much Dylan in the number[;] by other people, I mean', and Glyn Jones wrote to Rhys about Idris Davies's 'Land of my Mothers' (printed in that fourth number), asking: 'Why do you print such stuff? Don't you see how fatally easy it is to write like that?'[35] Indeed, one can see Thomas's influence creeping in as early as the second issue, with Davies's 'Souvenirs from Erin' adopting the trope of a marginalised urban wanderer, this time with a traveller heading across the Irish Sea to Dublin.[36] The brief story features a similar, though less linguistically effusive, present-tense, stream-of-consciousness narrative to 'Prologue', beginning, as 'Prologue' does, *in medias res*: 'We are half-way across the Irish Sea. The dawn is breaking. The sea is choppy.'[37] Davies's story is also generically ambiguous, standing somewhere between travelogue and story, remarking on the specific details of Dublin's street signs ('The names of all the streets in Dublin are given in Irish and in English [. . .] But very little Irish is heard in Dublin'), yet also giving way to metaphysical speculation: 'Why is the rain keeping away? I thought there was much rain in Erin. Are the great Irish gods asleep?'[38] As Harris suggests, Davies's prose published in *Wales* and the letters he wrote to Rhys in this period indicate a writer searching for new literary templates; suggesting on one hand he does not find Thomas's prose a useful template, yet on the other seemingly aping Thomas's prose across a number of stories published in Rhys's magazine.[39]

The brief length and fragmented structure of Davies's story also demonstrates another feature of the short stories published in *Wales*'s initial run: their concern with the fragment and fragmentation. Davies's story is split into eight numbered fragments and in the same issue James Hanley's three-page 'Black Gold' appears, featuring a similarly bleak tone to 'Prologue' and again evoking themes of marginalisation; both through the detached, observational third-person narrator seemingly at a remove from the alienated community it observes and the 'tattered human ribbon' the narrator describes picking coal on a 'mountain of black dirt'.[40] This 'tattered human ribbon' is itself both fragment and fragmented; it is 'the human debris of the new social hell'.[41] In their search for coal on the tip, the community are also in pursuit of fragments. Unlike 'Prologue', which features an anonymous metropolis, Hanley's story is more geographically specific, taking place in the South Wales coalfields. In issue 4, Charles Fisher's 'Where Dragons Dance' also utilises fragmentation as a literary strategy, fragmenting its narrative with parenthetical asides.[42]

Wales's fourth issue also features a fragment which earned the opprobrium of Nigel Heseltine, a frequent contributor to and, at one point, editor of *Wales*: Dylan Thomas's 'In the Direction of the Beginning'.[43] Heseltine had contributed a negative review of Thomas's *Twenty-five Poems* to *Wales*'s second issue and he regarded this fragment as 'not up to standard':

> I have enjoyed his stories in the past. This fragment which he is confident enough to put in as if we hung on his every word no matter how scribbled, proves that he is not yet enough a great artist to throw off fragments even if Joyce does.[44]

'In the Direction' is described as a 'Fragment of a work in progress' at the bottom of its first page. Indeed, in a letter to Rhys, Thomas describes it as 'the opening of a long story I've been working on' and writes: 'Hope this is ok. It's all I've got at the moment. I'd obviously give you every single thing I do, but I've got to be paid sometime.'[45] Rhys's need for high-profile contributions from Thomas seems to have led to the publication of this fragment. Heseltine's objections seemingly elide that *Wales*, as a fledgling, unstable magazine, needed whatever commercially viable material it could find. The inclusion of this fragment demonstrates *Wales*'s continued commitment to Welsh modernism, and two notable fragments included in the double issue 6/7 point to Rhys's desire to connect his magazine more widely to

European modernism. *Wales* 6/7 features – and boasts of this on its cover – 'Two Unpublished Fragments' by Franz Kafka, 'The Top' and 'Poseidon'.[46] Kafka's ascetic prose contrasts the effusive prose favoured by Thomas, but his inclusion in *Wales* – even in the form of fragments – demonstrates the international modernist leanings of the little magazine.

This is not to suggest that *Wales* was persistently and entirely indebted to Thomas, or reliant simply upon publishing whichever fragments it could find from famous – living or dead – writers. In the same issue that featured Kafka's fragments, *Wales* published short fiction by the Scottish-Welsh poet Robert Herring as well as a review of Mary Butts's final, posthumous story collection, demonstrating *Wales*'s connections to the intra-national modernist milieu of the UK.[47] Later, in the eleventh issue, stories by the Scottish writer J. F. Hendry and the English writer Celia Buckmaster appeared.[48] Advertisements for magazines such as *Life and Letters To-day*, *Poetry*, the Welsh-language *Tir Newydd* ('New Ground'), Hugh MacDiarmid's *The Voice of Scotland* and James Laughlin's *New Directions* anthologies, as well as booksellers such as the modernist New Books (Parton Street, London), all suggest *Wales*'s membership of an intra- and international coterie of modernist publications.[49] Glyn Jones's story 'The Four-loaded Man', published in the third issue of *Wales* (which featured 'Short Stories' as its sub-heading on the title page, despite the issue containing both prose and poetry) demonstrates that experimental, modernist work in *Wales* could depart from the paradigms offered by Thomas.[50] By presenting the world to his readers through the eyes of a child narrator, Jones offers a story that highlights tension between modernism and realism. The third-person narrative is inflected with the observations of the girl's mind and images are articulated in her register; a robin she sees is the size of 'an eggcupful', and it is 'brick-breasted'.[51] Typical of the modern short story, the girl is an isolated figure: she has no parents and lives alone in the mountains with her grandmother, who does not physically appear during the course of the story. The old man who visits the girl is a slightly grotesque figure, cartoonish in appearance, with 'a small grey tangle' of a beard, a yellow, wrinkled, 'shrunken' face. His nose is described as 'a thin pink claw' and his hands are 'high-veined down the backs like the underside of a rhubarb leaf'.[52] As Anthony Conran has argued, the grotesque is an essential component of Welsh modernism: 'modernism in Wales is most at home with the grotesque. It is there that modernism characteristically shows itself, in Saunders Lewis as much as in Caradoc Evans or

Dylan Thomas.'[53] In this brief story, Jones combines the vague, third-person narrative with the girl's observations to add a defamiliarising dimension to what is a relatively simple narrative.

The titular loads carried by the man are revealed to be his poverty, his loneliness, his illness and his old age. To each of these the little girl attempts to offer a solution, offering bread to alleviate the man's poverty, and a key to the house to relieve his loneliness. For the latter two burdens, the girl's solution relies on the wisdom of her grandmother – at least, the grandmother's wisdom as the girl understands it – and to cure the man's illness, she says she will help him jump off the wicker chair, as her grandmother does, 'to jerk a bean through her swallow'.[54] Finally, the girl offers to cure the old man's age by burning the clock face, because her grandmother has taught her that 'the clock brings birthdays in his hands'.[55] The girl's compassion – evident from the moment she allows this old man into her home – is tempered and informed by the teachings of her grandmother, and so the girl offers simple, literal solutions to timeless, endemic problems, based on a literal understanding of the metaphoric lessons her grandmother has taught her. Jones's prose style, the non-specific third-person narrative informed by the girl's mindset and language, offers a more subtle surrealism than that found in Dylan Thomas's stories. It is not the jump to 'jerk a bean' which cures the granny when she is ill, but rather the tablet or pill represented by the 'bean' she swallows. Similarly, burning the clock face will do nothing to stop the passage of time, but the girl misunderstands her granny, thinking that the clock controls, rather than marks, time. Jones combines this defamiliarising style with a final ambiguity, namely, whether or not the old man is simply a poor, cold beggar or 'Rhys y Mynydd'. Rhys y Mynydd is another metaphor of the grandmother's invention; in this case, the personification of the wind on the mountains. Jones's use of the child's perspective, which conflates the old man with Rhys y Mynydd, creates a subtle surrealism that unsettles realist readings of the story.

From modernist magazine to cultural miscellany: shifts and continuities

After the publication of eleven issues, from 1937 through to 1939, *Wales* briefly ended as the Second World War erupted. After momentarily returning as a single wartime broadsheet in 1940, featuring only poetry, *Wales* resumed with a new run in 1943 which would last for six years, with Rhys once again at the helm. As Ballin notes of the returning magazine, Rhys signals that 'the reader is to expect a more considered, more conventional version of the magazine'.[56] Gone is the emphasis on aesthetically experimental literature and the magazine now features a wider variety of essays, as well as a greater number of stylistically realist stories. Ballin also points to differences in the advertisements *Wales* features as well as its greater length and its eventual adoption, in June 1946, of the subtitle 'The National Magazine' as reasons to view this return as a clear break from the little modernist magazine discussed thus far.[57] While I will argue that there are clear signs of continuity between *Wales*'s initial run and its second run, and that this is evident in the short fiction published, it is worth briefly considering some of the issues and themes indicative of the shift in direction identified by Ballin as evidenced by a number of short stories.[58]

Ballin suggests that this shift away from modernist writing is clear in the first issue of *Wales*'s new run: 'A sense of endorsing the Old rather than the New appears in W. J. Gruffydd's short story, "Bethesda'r Fro" (45–50), where a patriarchal nineteenth-century figure foresees the forthcoming industrialisation of his valley.'[59] This is a simplification of the shifts *Wales* undergoes. Indeed, while some of the fiction is realist, a selection of vignettes depicting wartime life in rural Carmarthenshire by the Argentine-Welsh modernist Lynette Roberts appear in the March 1944 issue, echoing the earlier *Wales*'s experimental fragments.[60] Furthermore, even in the same issue as W. J. Gruffydd's story, a story by Nigel Heseltine appears, 'Cam-Vaughan's Shoot'.[61] This, and several other Heseltine stories, feature a modernist mode which revels in grotesque violence and farce, which may owe something to the Irish modernist Flann O'Brien, whose *At Swim-Two-Birds* Heseltine had praised in an early issue of *Wales*.[62]

Heseltine and Roberts are not the only echoes of the old *Wales*: the magazine continues to demonstrate its connections to the 'intra-national' dimensions of modernism across the UK, as evidenced by the publication of essays on the Scottish Renaissance by R. S. Thomas, as well as the publication of a short story by the noted modernist Wyndham Lewis.[63] Lewis's 'The Rot' further demonstrates *Wales*'s ongoing excursions into modernist territory. Relatedly, Glyn Jones's 'The Wanderer' clearly evokes 'Prologue' and flâneur tropes, but does so in a mode of modernist writing which intimately stems from Wales's particular cultural conditions; it is an example of what M. Wynn Thomas calls 'Christian Surrealism'.[64] 'The Wanderer' depicts one of Jones's darkest, most abject worlds and is shaped by the parable of the prodigal son, which suggests the lingering influence of both Kafka and Caradoc Evans.[65] The titular wanderer is immediately framed for us in grotesque terms typical of Welsh modernism; he ('it' in the narrative) is a 'hideous figure' who 'lay in profound sleep at the bottom of its darkness with the bone of its arm across its face', with 'a split carpet-slipper covering the corruption of its swollen feet'.[66] In a twist on the conventional flâneur story, this wanderer returns from a city, haunted by its memory, and moves through his home-village, which features disgusting, alienated individuals, including '[a] sick hag [who] had tarred the stump of her arm to destroy the white worms eating the meat of it', an 'imbecile barefooted dwarf with the gigantic brass head', and even a 'mangy-skinned horse'.[67] Yet, even moving through this community of alienated and alienating individuals, the wanderer is insulted by children 'jeering at his poverty'.[68] Like the younger brother from the parable, the wanderer is destitute. The wanderer stands in 'weariness and despair' listening to 'floor-rats' and the clamour of blasphemy from the 'idolatrous rooms' beneath him.[69] In an extended metaphor he remembers 'the rumour of a paradisal city', which, instead of being likened to a rotting corpse, is likened to a grotesque prostitute.[70] The rumoured paradisal city was the promise of the man's youth, the grotesque whore-city the realisation and perversion of that promise, illustrated in a surreal fashion. The man's alienation, it seems, stems from his time in a metropolis, and this decidedly modernist dilemma is given a distinctly Welsh twist: 'he saw the forgotten homely tongue that warned how the world had cheesed her traps among the nightly orders of her illuminations' seems to me a lament for the lost Welsh language, succinctly and fittingly voiced by a member of that pioneering generation who grew up and wrote within earshot of, but often without the discourse of, that 'homely tongue'.[71]

This despair-riddled cityscape may owe something to Jones's time as a teacher in 1920s Cardiff, at Wood Street School, in a slum known as Temperance Town. As Brown notes, '[p]rostitution was rife in the area' and '[i]n such an environment, inevitably, many of the children, as Jones knew, were subject to violence and to sexual abuse, including prostitution'.[72] Yet, European modernism also engages with the figure of the prostitute in numerous ways. For example, Pablo Picasso's *Les Demoiselles d'Avignon* depicts five prostitutes in a disconcerting and confrontational manner and in Joyce's *A Portrait of the Artist as a Young Man*, Stephen Dedalus wanders into 'a maze of narrow and dirty streets' in search of a prostitute and fulfilment through sex.[73] The symbolic imagery of Jones's story is therefore one more aspect of European modernism's artistic engagement with prostitution.

Tellingly, the cityscape in 'The Wanderer' is registered in terms of a surreal, negative, female sexuality: 'He saw the constellated glitter of her milk-white thorough-fares, her debauchery, her bare-bubbled harlots with sweet-tasting hair, her mockery.'[74] Jones's story actively rejects this threatening female sexuality and, consequently, demonstrates a desire to return to romantic, male love and, by extension, religion: the wanderer is 'homesick for the remembering fields of his innocent country and the assurance of his father's morning call, sweet as the dawn dream of the condemned'.[75] Seemingly, the wanderer hangs himself and this action is described in phallic terms that also foreshadow his redemption: 'groping with his fingers for the rope and arranging it carefully around his neck, he hung down rigid as the gong of a giant bell'.[76] Welsh chapel culture makes an overt appearance, as a former miner ('he had taken the curved layers of coal out of the hill') preaches at a chapel emblazoned with the words 'DUW CARIAD YW': God is love.[77] This is an overtly masculine and overtly Welsh Nonconformist love, though the use of a working-class preacher is notable, as it suggests a particular idealisation of the Welsh miner. Once again, however, the preacher is a grotesque figure, with 'bright blue veins [that] ran in all directions through the flesh of his large smashed face'.[78] Recalling the earlier bell imagery, the preacher notes in his sermon that '[t]he love of God is like the tolling of a bell', and hearing this, the 'old ferryman' (the wanderer's father) springs into action, leaving the service and ringing the bell.[79] This masculine exertion and act of religious male love has sexual tones: 'The blows of the iron tongue seemed to be falling upon his naked brain, stunning him with its clamour, but he pulled and pulled [. . .] as his bell sent out its penetrating notes.'[80] The sacred and sexual clamour awakens the wanderer, now described as a 'beggar' after his unsuccessful suicide attempt (he sobs at 'the memory of the hanging and the broken rope').[81] Like the prodigal son in the parable, this is described as a return from the dead: the sound of the bell is as 'solemn to him as the sound of the opening of graves'.[82] By the close of the story, the wanderer returns to the father, whose heart 'was filled with joy and a great tenderness for even in the darkness he knew the cause of his bell was answered'.[83] 'The Wanderer' utilises the grotesque to explore conventionally taboo topics – sexuality and homoerotically-charged male love – within an overtly religious paradigm.

'The Wanderer' could be said to encapsulate modernist short fiction published in *Wales*. While Ballin suggests an abrupt departure from one *Wales* to another, Jones's story is a manifestation of the creative and ideological ambitions most strongly articulated in those first eleven issues, yet still present in its 1940s incarnation. Like *Wales*, 'The Wanderer' overtly stems from the particular cultural conditions of Welsh modernity: the shadow of the Welsh language is present (the 'homely tongue') in this Anglophone tale and, more overtly, Welsh Nonconformity and industrial heritage form the basis of the story's homoerotically-charged rejection of female sexuality. In its adaptation of the flâneur and in its symbolic use of the prostitute, 'The Wanderer' not only echoes the Dylan Thomas story that launched *Wales*, but corresponds with a European modernist tradition reaching from Joyce and Proust to Baudelaire in mid-nineteenth-century France. By structuring his story after a parable, Jones engages with both Welsh and European modernist paradigms pioneered by two short story writers, Caradoc Evans and Franz Kafka. It seems that, while *Wales*'s writers had to engage with England's publishing industry, the most innovative Welsh short stories published by this magazine often looked beyond and around England to Europe: to France and Ireland; to Kafka, Proust, Baudelaire and Joyce. *Wales*'s stories looked back, too, within Welsh literature, to Caradoc Evans. While these stories were written in English, they were rooted in Wales.

Notes

1. *Wales* initially ran as a little modernist magazine from summer 1937 to late 1939, for eleven issues. It returned briefly in 1940 as a single wartime broadsheet and then resumed in 1943 as a cultural miscellany. *Wales*'s second run ended in 1949, but it returned one last time as an attempt at a popular magazine (this time edited from London) from 1959–60.
2. 'WALES: An independent pamphlet of creative work by the younger progressive Welsh writers', *Wales*, 1 (Summer 1937), unpaginated. Page numbers for the first eleven issues refer to the 1969 collected edition published by Frank Cass and Company.
3. John Harris, 'Not a Trysorfa fach', *New Welsh Review*, 3.3 (1990–1), pp. 28–33.
4. Ibid. p. 28.
5. Ibid. pp. 28–9.
6. Hopkins, '*Wales* (1937–39), *The Welsh Review* (1939–40)', p. 714.

7. Jones, *The Dragon Has Two Tongues*, p. 1. On page 32, Jones provides an autobiographical recollection of the meetings that led to the founding of *Wales*.
8. Ibid. p. 34.
9. Ibid. p. 49.
10. Ibid. p. 49.
11. Brown, 'The Ex-centric Voice', p. 26.
12. Ibid. p. 32. The assumption of English as the language of social advancement was largely due to the aftershock of the *Brad y Llyfrau Gleision*, or 'Treachery of the Blue Books', an 1847 report into the state of education in Wales which directly connected Welsh-language use and culture to poverty in Wales, often repeating the prejudices of landowners and Anglican clergy. See Roberts, *Embodying Identity*, for further study of the report's significance in Welsh literature.
13. Jones, *Setting Out*, p. 12.
14. Quoted by Harris, 'Letters from the Cultural Battlefront', p. 22.
15. 'WALES: An independent pamphlet', unpaginated.
16. 'EDITORIAL: As You Know', *Wales*, 2 (August 1937), pp. 35–7 (pp. 36–7).
17. Glyn Jones to Keidrych Rhys, undated letter, NLW MSS 22745D, National Library of Wales, Aberystwyth. Reproduced with the permission of Literature Wales.
18. Ballin, *Welsh Periodicals in English*, pp. 60–70.
19. Ibid. p. 71.
20. Conran describes Evans's stories as 'certainly the beginning of Anglo-Welsh modernism' in Conran, *Frontiers in Anglo-Welsh Poetry*, p. 112. M. Wynn Thomas earlier described Evans's 1915 collection *My People* as 'the first modernist work to have been produced by a Welshman' in 'My People and the Revenge of the Novel', p. 20. See also my own chapter, 'Welsh Literary Modernism, Lynette Roberts and David Jones: "unearthing a huge and very important culture"', in McAvoy, *Locating Lynette Roberts*, pp. 101–20, for a concise summary of the Welsh modernist formation.
21. Wainwright, *New Territories in Modernism*, p. 9.
22. Evans was so notorious during his day that in 1917 a reviewer of Joyce's *A Portrait of the Artist as a Young Man* pejoratively described Joyce as 'an Irish edition of Mr Caradoc Evans'. See Hopkins, 'James Joyce is an Irish edition of Mr Caradoc Evans', pp. 23–6.
23. Ferris, *Dylan Thomas*, p. 115. Thomas and Jones visited Evans in 1934, having begun corresponding with one another early in the same year. Jones reflects on the importance of Evans to the modern Welsh short story in *The Dragon Has Two Tongues*, pp. 50–1.
24. Harris, 'Not a Trysorfa fach', pp. 30–1.
25. Ibid. pp. 30–1.

26. Dylan Thomas, 'Prologue to an Adventure', *Wales*, 1 (Summer 1937), pp. 1–6 (p. 1).
27. Ibid. p. 5.
28. Ibid. pp. 1–2.
29. O'Connor, *The Lonely Voice*, p. 19. Brown insightfully applies O'Connor's notion of 'submerged population groups' to Welsh short stories in the previously cited essay.
30. See Baudelaire's 1863 essay 'The Painter of Modern Life', as well as Shaya, 'The Flâneur, the Badaud, and the Making of a Mass Public in France'.
31. Thomas, 'Prologue to an Adventure', p. 2.
32. Ibid. p. 1.
33. Ibid. p. 6.
34. Further Thomas stories published in the first eleven issues include 'The Map of Love', *Wales*, 3 (Autumn 1937), pp. 116–23; 'In the Direction of the Beginning', *Wales*, 4 (March 1938), pp. 147–8; and 'Just like Little Dogs', *Wales*, 10 (October 1939), pp. 255–60.
35. Harris, 'Not a Trysorfa fach', pp. 29–30. Idris Davies was a poet from Rhymney. His published works include the poetic sequence *Gwalia Deserta* (London: Dent, 1938); *The Angry Summer: A Poem of 1926* (London: Faber & Faber, 1943); *Tonypandy and Other Poems* (London: Faber & Faber, 1945); and *Selected Poems* (London: Faber & Faber, 1953).
36. Idris Davies, 'Souvenirs from Erin', *Wales*, 2 (August 1937), pp. 56–60.
37. Ibid. p. 56.
38. Ibid. p. 58.
39. Harris, 'Not a Trysorfa fach', p. 30. Two other Idris Davies stories featured in the first run of *Wales*: 'Shadows and Cakes', *Wales*, 3 (Autumn 1937), pp. 115–16; and 'Land of My Mothers', *Wales*, 4 (March 1938), pp. 141–4.
40. James Hanley, 'Black Gold', *Wales*, 2 (August 1937), pp. 38–40 (pp. 38–9). Hanley was a Liverpool-born writer of Irish descent who lived in Wales from 1931 until 1963. See Fordham, *James Hanley: Modernism and the Working Class* for a detailed study of this neglected writer.
41. Hanley, 'Black Gold', pp. 38–9.
42. Charles Fisher, 'Where Dragons Dance', *Wales*, 4 (March 1938), pp. 144–6. Charles Fisher was a Welsh writer and member of the 'Kermodah Group', writers and artists who frequented the Kermodah Café in 1930s Swansea. Dylan Thomas and the poet Vernon Watkins (a frequent contributor to *Wales*) were also members of this group.
43. Dylan Thomas, 'In the Direction of the Beginning', *Wales*, 4 (March 1938), pp. 147–8. Nigel Heseltine was the son of the composer Peter Warlock (Phillip Heseltine). Heseltine edited issues 8/9, 10 and 11 of

Wales and published poems, translations, short prose, a novel, and several volumes of travel writing.
44. Quoted in Rhian Davies, 'Scarred Background: Nigel Heseltine (1916–1995), A Biographical Introduction and Bibliography', *Welsh Writing in English: A Yearbook of Critical Essays*, 11 (2006–7), pp. 69–99 (p. 80).
45. Thomas, 'Keidrych Rhys – Monday 20th December 1937', p. 307.
46. Franz Kafka, 'The Top' and 'Poseidon', trans. by G. Humphrey Roberts, *Wales*, 6/7 (March 1939), pp. 194–5.
47. Robert Herring, 'Where I Come From', *Wales*, 6/7 (March 1939), pp. 199–200; Rhys Davies, 'A Note on Mary Butts', *Wales*, 6/7 (March 1939), p. 207.
48. James Findlay Hendry, 'From a Life of General Chunkledom', *Wales*, 11 (Winter 1939–40), pp. 294–5; Celia Buckmaster, 'Voyage Without End', *Wales*, 11 (Winter 1939–40), pp. 298–9.
49. For further information on Herring and *Life and Letters To-day*'s connection to Welsh literature, see Stephens, 'The Third Man'.
50. Glyn Jones, 'The Four-loaded Man', *Wales*, 3 (Autumn 1937), pp. 110–14.
51. Ibid. p. 111.
52. Ibid. p. 112.
53. Conran, *Frontiers in Anglo-Welsh Poetry*, pp. 112–13.
54. Jones, 'The Four-loaded Man', p. 113.
55. Ibid. p. 114.
56. Ballin, *Welsh Periodicals in English*, p. 75.
57. Ibid. pp. 74–5.
58. Unsurprisingly, a number of stories are war stories, though often they are stories of the Home Front. A partial list includes examples such as: John Pennant, 'Welsh "Oat-cakes" from the skies!', *Wales*, 3.4 (Summer 1944), pp. 63–5; Vyrian Miles, 'Exile – Short Story', *Wales*, 4.5 (Autumn 1944), pp. 51–5; Frank Thomas, 'Nobody's baby now', *Wales*, 4.5 (Autumn 1944), pp. 86–8; Elspeth Lloyd, 'Past', *Wales*, 4.6 (Winter 1945), pp. 29–34; A. Edward Richards, 'The Admiralty Regrets . . .', *Wales*, 4.6 (Winter 1945), pp. 40–6; Roland Mathias, 'One Bell Tolling', *Wales*, 5.8/9 (December 1945), pp. 53–60.
59. Ballin, *Welsh Periodicals in English*, p. 77.
60. Lynette Roberts, 'Village Dialect,' *Wales*, 3.3 (March 1944), pp. 51–71. Roberts was born in Buenos Aires, Argentina, to Australian parents of Welsh descent. Her *Poems* and the modernist epic *Gods with Stainless Ears* were edited by T. S. Eliot and published by Faber in 1944 and 1951 respectively. See also: Roberts, *Collected Poems*; Roberts, *Diaries, Letters and Recollections*; McAvoy, *Locating Lynette Roberts*.
61. Nigel Heseltine, 'Cam-Vaughan's Shoot', *Wales*, 3.1 (July 1943), pp. 33–7.
62. See *Wales*, 11 (Winter 1939–40), pp. 308–9. See also M. Wynn

Thomas, '"A Grand Harlequinade": The Border Writing of Nigel Heseltine', *Welsh Writing in English: A Yearbook of Critical Essays*, 11 (2006–2007), pp. 51–68 (p. 55).
63. R. S. Thomas, 'Some Contemporary Scottish Writing', *Wales*, 23 (Autumn 1946), pp. 98–103; R. S. Thomas, 'A Welsh View of the Scottish Renaissance', *Wales*, 30 (November 1948), pp. 600–4; Wyndham Lewis, 'The Rot', *Wales*, 30 (November 1948), pp. 574–89. 'The Rot' is one of the stories later featured in Lewis's 1951 collection *Rotting Hill*, which took its name from a joke by Ezra Pound.
64. Thomas, *In the Shadow of the Pulpit*, p. 278.
65. Glyn Jones, 'The Wanderer', *Wales*, 3.2 (October–December 1943), pp. 26–34.
66. Ibid. p. 26.
67. Ibid. pp. 28–9.
68. Ibid. p. 28.
69. Ibid.
70. Ibid. p. 29.
71. Ibid.
72. Brown, 'Introduction: The Making of a Writer', p. xxiv. See also Jones's own recollections in *The Dragon Has Two Tongues*, pp. 27–8.
73. Joyce, *A Portrait of the Artist as a Young Man*, pp. 106–9. A similar episode occurs in *Ulysses*, with Stephen and Leopold Bloom's journey into nighttown (Dublin's red-light district): Joyce, *Ulysses*, pp. 408–565. See also Austin Briggs, 'Whorehouse/Playhouse: The Brothel as Theater in the "Circe" chapter of *Ulysses*', *Journal of Modern Literature*, 26.1 (2002), pp. 42–57.
74. Jones, 'The Wanderer', p. 29.
75. Ibid. p. 29.
76. Ibid. p. 29.
77. Ibid. p. 30.
78. Ibid. p. 30.
79. Ibid. p. 31.
80. Ibid. p. 32.
81. Ibid. pp. 32–3.
82. Ibid. p. 33.
83. Ibid. p. 34.

Bibliography

Primary sources

Full references for magazine contributions and material held in archives or libraries are provided in chapter endnotes.

Arnold, Matthew, 'The Function of Criticism at the Present Time', in *Essays in Criticism* (London; Cambridge: Macmillan and Co., 1865), pp. 1–41.
Baily, Francis Evans, *Twenty-Nine Years' Hard Labour* (London: Hutchinson, 1934).
Bates, H. E., *The Modern Short Story from 1809 to 1953* ([1941] London: Robert Hale, 1988).
Baudelaire, Charles, *The Painter of Modern Life* ([1863] London: Penguin, 2010).
Beresford, J. D., 'The Other Thing', in *Nineteen Impressions* (London: Sidgwick and Jackson, 1918), pp. ix–xv, <https://archive.org/details/nineteenimpressi00bereiala/page/xiv/mode/2up> (last accessed 1 September 2020).
Bergson, Henri, *Time and Free Will* ([1913] New York: Dover, 2001).
Black, Helen C., *Pen, Pencil, Baton and Mask: Biographical Sketches* (London: Spotiswood, 1896).
Blake, John W., *Northern Ireland in the Second World War*, 2nd ed. (Belfast: The Blackstaff Press, 2000).
Bowen, Elizabeth, 'Postscript by the Author', *The Demon Lover and Other Stories* ([1945] London: Jonathan Cape, 1952), pp. 216–24.
Bowen, Elizabeth, *Afterthought: Pieces about Writing* (London: Longmans, 1962).
Bowen, Elizabeth, 'Introduction', in William Sansom, *The Stories of William Sansom* (London: Hogarth Press, 1963), pp. 7–12.
Bowen, Elizabeth, 'Coming to London', in Hermione Lee (ed.), *The Mulberry Tree: Writings of Elizabeth Bowen* (London: Virago Press, 1986), pp. 85–9.

Bowen, Elizabeth, 'Letters', in Hermione Lee (ed.), *The Mulberry Tree: Writings of Elizabeth Bowen* (London: Virago Press, 1986), pp. 189–229.

Bowen, Elizabeth, 'The Short Story in England', in Phyllis Lassner, *Elizabeth Bowen: A Study of the Short Fiction* (New York: Twayne, 1991), pp. 128–43.

Bowen, Elizabeth, 'The Back Drawing-Room', in *The Collected Stories of Elizabeth Bowen* (London: Vintage, 1999), pp. 214–27.

Bowen, Elizabeth, 'The Parrot', in *The Collected Stories of Elizabeth Bowen* (London: Vintage, 1999), pp. 114–27.

Bowen, Elizabeth, 'The Short Story in England', in *People, Places, Things: Essays by Elizabeth Bowen*, ed. by Allan Hepburn (Edinburgh: Edinburgh University Press, 2008), pp. 310–15.

Boyd, John, *The Middle of My Journey* (Belfast: The Blackstaff Press, 1990).

Conan Doyle, Arthur, *Memories and Adventures* (Boston: Little and Brown, 1924).

Connolly, Cyril, *Enemies of Promise*, rev. ed. (London: Routledge & Kegan Paul, 1949).

Connolly, Cyril, 'Introduction', in *The Golden Horizon* (London: Weidenfeld & Nicholson, 1953), p. ix.

Cournos, John, 'Introduction', in John Cournos and Edward J. O'Brien (eds), *The Best British Short Stories of 1923* (Boston: Small, Maynard & Company, 1923), pp. xiii–xvii.

Davin, Dan, *Selected Stories* (London: Robert Hale, 1981).

Davison, Peter, Ian Angus and Sheila Davison (eds), *The Complete Works of George Orwell, Volume 12: A Patriot After All 1940–1941* (London: Secker & Warburg, 1998).

De la Mare, Walter, *Early One Morning* (London: Faber & Faber, 1935).

De la Mare, Walter, 'Pretty Poll', in Giles de la Mare (ed.), *Short Stories, 1895–1926: Vol. 1* (London: Giles de la Mare Publishers, 1996), pp. 322–37.

Eliot, T. S., 'To John Quinn', in Valerie Eliot and Hugh Haughton (eds), *The Letters of T. S. Eliot: Volume 1: 1898–1922* (San Diego: Harcourt Brace Jovanovich, 1988), p. 378.

E.T. [Jessie Chambers], *D. H. Lawrence: A Personal Record* (London: Jonathan Cape, 1935).

Fisher, Barbara (ed.), *Joyce Cary Remembered: In Letters and Interviews by His Family and Others* (Gerrards Cross: Smyth, 1988).

Huxley, Aldous, *The Hidden Huxley: Contempt and Compassion for the Masses, 1920–36*, ed. by David Bradshaw (London: Faber and Faber, 1994).

James, Henry, *The Art of the Novel: Critical Prefaces by Henry James* (Chicago: University of Chicago Press, 2011).

James, William, *The Principles of Psychology: The Briefer Course* (New York: Dover, 1892).

Joyce, James, *A Portrait of the Artist as a Young Man* ([1916] London: Penguin, 1992).
Joyce, James, *Ulysses* ([1922] Oxford: Oxford University Press, 1993).
Kavanagh, Patrick, *Collected Poems*, ed. by Antoinette Quinn (London: Penguin Books, 2005).
Lawrence, D. H., *The Letters of D. H. Lawrence, Volume I: 1901–13*, ed. by James T. Boulton (Cambridge: Cambridge University Press, 1979).
Lawrence, D. H., *The Prussian Officer and Other Stories*, ed. by John Worthen (Cambridge: Cambridge University Press, 1983).
Lawrence, D. H., *Study of Thomas Hardy and Other Essays*, ed. by Bruce Steele (Cambridge: Cambridge University Press, 1985).
Lawrence, D. H., *Love Among the Haystacks and Other Stories*, ed. by John Worthen (Cambridge: Cambridge University Press, 1987).
Lehmann, John, *The Whispering Gallery* ([1955] London: Longmans, 1957).
Lehmann, John, *I Am My Brother* (London: Longmans, 1960).
Lyall, David, *The Consolation Bureau* (London: Hodder and Stoughton, 1915).
Macafee, C. I. (ed.), *The Concise Ulster Dictionary* (Oxford: Oxford University Press, 1996).
Maclaren-Ross, Julian, *Memoirs of the Forties* (London: Alan Ross, 1965).
Maugham, W. Somerset, *Points of View* (London: Heinemann 1958).
Moore, Brian, *The Emperor of Ice-cream* (London: André Deutsch, 1966).
Murry, John Middleton, *Between Two Worlds* (London: Jonathan Cape, 1935).
Nin, Anaïs, *Linotte: The Early Diary of Anaïs Nin, 1914–1920* (New York: Harcourt Brace Jovanovich, 1978).
Poe, E. A., 'Review of Twice-Told Tales' (1842), reprinted in Charles E. May (ed.), *The New Short Story Theories* (Athens: Ohio University Press, 1994), pp. 59–64.
Priestley, J. B., 'High, Low, Broad', in *Open House: A Book of Essays* (London: William Heinemann, 1929), pp. 162–7.
Roberts, Lynette, *Collected Poems*, ed. by Patrick McGuinness (Manchester: Carcanet, 2005).
Roberts, Lynette, *Diaries, Letters and Recollections*, ed. by Patrick McGuinness (Manchester: Carcanet, 2008).
Ruskin, John, 'Of Queen's Gardens', in John Ruskin, *Sesame and Lilies* (Toronto: W. J. Gage, 1890), pp. 83–133.
Saunders, Max, *Ford Madox Ford: A Dual Life, Volume I: The World Before the War* (Oxford: Oxford University Press, 1996).
Squire, J. C., 'The Man who Wrote Free Verse', in J. C. Squire, *The Grub Street Nights Entertainments* (London: Hodder and Stoughton, 1924), pp. 195–217.
Stouck, David, *As for Sinclair Ross* (Toronto: Toronto University Press, 2005).

Swan, Annie S., *Hester Lane* (London: Leng, 1928).
Swan, Annie S., *My Life: An Autobiography* (London: Nicholson & Watson, 1934).
The First Book of Eve (New York: Brentano's, 1916), <https://archive.org/details/firstbookofeve00fish/page/n0> (last accessed 1 September 2020).
The Writer's Market (Cincinnati: Writer's Digest, 1937).
Thomas, Dylan, 'Walter de la Mare as a Prose Writer', in Dylan Thomas, *Quite Early One Morning: Broadcasts* (London: Dent, 1954), pp. 106–11.
Thomas, Dylan, 'Keidrych Rhys – Monday 20th December 1937', in Paul Ferris (ed.), *Dylan Thomas: The Collected Letters Volume 1: 1931–39* (London: Weidenfeld and Nicolson, 2017), p. 307.
Wilkins, H. W., *The Alien Invasion* (London: Methuen, 1892).
Woolf, Virginia, *The London Scene* (London: Hogarth Press, 1975).
Woolf, Virginia, *The Letters of Virginia Woolf*, ed. by Nigel Nicholson, 6 vols (London: Hogarth Press, 1975–80).
Woolf, Virginia, *The Diary of Virginia Woolf*, ed. by Anne Olivier Bell, 5 vols (New York: Harcourt, 1977–84).
Woolf, Virginia, *The Complete Shorter Fiction of Virginia Woolf*, ed. by Susan Dick (New York: Harcourt Brace Jovanovich, 1985).
Woolf, Virginia, *The Essays of Virginia Woolf*, ed. by Andrew McNeillie and Stuart N. Clarke, 6 vols (London: Hogarth Press, 1986–2011).
Woolf, Virginia, 'Sketch of the Past', in Virginia Woolf, *Moments of Being: Autobiographical Writings*, ed. by Jeanne Schulkind (London: Pimlico, 2002), pp. 78–160.
Woolf, Virginia, *The Waves*, ed. by Michael Herbert and Susan Sellers (Cambridge: Cambridge University Press, 2011).
Woolf, Virginia, *The Collected Short Fiction of Virginia Woolf*, ed. by Laura Marcus and Bryony Randall (Cambridge: Cambridge University Press, forthcoming).

Secondary criticism

Abu-Manneh, Bashir, *Fiction of the New Statesman, 1913–1939* (Newark: University of Delaware Press, 2011).
Adams, Jad, 'The Drowning of Hubert Crackanthorpe and the Persecution of Leila Macdonald', *English Literature in Transition, 1880–1920*, 52.1 (2009), pp. 6–34.
Allen, Nicholas, 'Out of Time: Belfast and the Second World War', in Nicholas Allen and Aaron Kelly (eds), *The Cities of Belfast* (Dublin: Four Courts Press, 2003), pp. 88–100.
Alpers, Antony, *The Life of Katherine Mansfield* (Oxford: Oxford University Press, 1982).
Ardis, Ann, 'Staging the Public Sphere: Magazine Dialogism and the Prosthetics of Authorship at the Turn of the Twentieth Century', in

Ann Ardis and Patrick Collier (eds), *Transatlantic Print Culture, 1880–1940: Emerging Media, Emerging Modernisms* (Basingstoke: Palgrave Macmillan, 2008), pp. 30–47.

Ardis, Ann and Patrick Collier (eds), *Transatlantic Print Culture, 1880–1940: Emerging Media, Emerging Modernisms* (Basingstoke: Palgrave Macmillan, 2008).

Ashley, Mike, *The Age of the Storytellers: British Popular Fiction Magazines, 1880–1950* (London: British Library and Oak Knoll Press, 2006).

Ashley, Mike, *Adventures in the Strand: Arthur Conan Doyle and the* Strand *Magazine* (London: The British Library, 2016).

Attridge, John, 'Liberalism and Modernism in the Edwardian Era: New Liberals at Ford's *English Review*', in Jason Harding (ed.), *Ford Madox Ford: Modernist Magazines and Editing* (Amsterdam: Editions Rodopi, 2010), pp. 169–83.

Attridge, John, 'The Saddest Tory', *Modernism/modernity*, 19.4 (2013), pp. 799–803.

Awadalla, Maggie and Paul March-Russell (eds), *The Postcolonial Short Story* (Basingstoke: Palgrave Macmillan, 2013).

Bal, Mieke, *Narratology: Introduction to the Theory of Narrative* (Toronto: University of Toronto Press, 2009).

Baldwin, Dean, *Virginia Woolf: A Study of the Short Fiction* (Boston: Twayne Publishers, 1989).

Baldwin, Dean, *Art and Commerce in the British Short Story: 1880–1950* (London: Pickering & Chatto, 2013).

Baldwin, Dean, 'The Understated Art, English Style', in Dominic Head (ed.), *The Cambridge History of the English Short Story* (Cambridge: Cambridge University Press, 2016), pp. 235–51.

Ballin, Malcolm, *Irish Periodical Culture, 1937–1972: Genre in Ireland, Wales, and Scotland* (Basingstoke: Palgrave MacMillan, 2008).

Ballin, Malcolm, *Welsh Periodicals in English 1882–2012* (Cardiff: University of Wales Press, 2012).

Barton, Brian, *The Blitz: Belfast in the War Years* (Belfast: The Blackstaff Press, 1989).

Beckson, Karl and Mark Samuels Lasner, '*The Yellow Book* and Beyond: Selected Letters of Henry Harland to John Lane', *English Literature in Transition, 1880–1920*, 42.4 (1999), pp. 401–32.

Beetham, Margaret, 'Open and Closed: The Periodical as a Publishing Genre', *Victorian Periodicals Review*, 22.3 (1989), pp. 96–100.

Beetham, Margaret, *A Magazine of Her Own? Domesticity and Desire in the Woman's Magazine, 1800–1914* (London: Routledge, 1996).

Beetham, Margaret, 'Periodicals and the New Media: Women and Imagined Communities', *Women's Studies International Forum*, 29.3 (2006), pp. 231–40.

Beetham, Margaret, 'Time: Periodicals and the Time of the Now', *Victorian Periodicals Review*, 48.3 (2015), pp. 323–42.

Benzel, Kathryn N. and Ruth Hoberman (eds), *Trespassing Boundaries: Virginia Woolf's Short Fiction* (New York: Palgrave Macmillan, 2004).

Bernstein, George L., 'Liberalism and the Progressive Alliance in the Constituencies, 1900–1914: Three Case Studies', *The Historical Journal*, 26.3 (September 1983), pp. 617–40.

Binckes, Faith, *Modernism, Magazines, and the British Avant-Garde: Reading* Rhythm, *1910–1914* (Oxford: Oxford University Press, 2010).

Bornstein, George, 'What Is the Text of a Poem by Yeats?', in George Bornstein and Ralph G. Williams (eds), *Palimpsest: Editorial Theory in the Humanities* (Ann Arbor: University of Michigan Press, 1993), pp. 167–94.

Bort, Françoise, 'John Lehmann's *New Writing* in Wartime: A Forward to Postmodernism?', in Helene Aji, Celine Mansanti and Benoit Tadie (eds), *Revues Modernistes, Revues Engagées 1900–1939* (Rennes: Presses universitaires de Rennes, 2011), pp. 383–91.

Bourgault du Coudray, Chantal, 'Introduction', in *The Curse of the Werewolf: Fantasy, Horror, and the Beast Within* (New York: I. B. Tauris, 2006), pp. 1–10.

Boykins, Dennis, 'Wartime Text and Context: Cyril Connolly's *Horizon*' (unpublished doctoral thesis, University of Sydney, 2007).

Bradshaw, David, 'Introduction', in Virginia Woolf, *Carlyle's House and Other Sketches*, ed. by David Bradshaw (London: Hesperus Press, 2003), xiii–xxv.

Braithwaite, Brian, Noëlle Walsh and Glynn Davies (eds), *Ragtime to Wartime: The Best of* Good Housekeeping *1929–1939* (London: Ebury Press, 1986).

Brake, Laurel and Marysa Demoor (eds), *Dictionary of Nineteenth-Century Journalism in Great Britain and Ireland* (Gent and London: Academia Press and The British Library, 2009).

Briggs, Austin, 'Whorehouse/Playhouse: The Brothel as Theater in the "Circe" chapter of *Ulysses*', *Journal of Modern Literature*, 26.1 (2002), pp. 42–57.

Briggs, Julia, *Virginia Woolf: An Inner Life* (New York: Harcourt, 2005).

Bromley, Amy, *Virginia Woolf and the Work of the Literary Sketch: Scenes and Characters, Politics and Printing in* Monday or Tuesday *(1921)* (unpublished doctoral thesis, University of Glasgow, 2017).

Brooker, Peter and Andrew Thacker, 'Introduction', in Peter Brooker and Andrew Thacker (eds), *The Oxford Critical and Cultural History of Modernist Magazines: Volume I: Britain and Ireland 1880–1955* (Oxford: Oxford University Press, 2009), pp. 1–26.

Brown, Erica and Mary Grover (eds), *Middlebrow Literary Cultures: The Battle of the Brows, 1920–1960* (London: Palgrave Macmillan, 2012).

Brown, Tony, 'Introduction: The Making of a Writer', in Tony Brown (ed.), *The Collected Stories of Glyn Jones* (Cardiff: University of Wales Press, 1999), pp. xiii–lxvi.

Brown, Tony, 'The Ex-centric Voice: The English-Language Short Story in Wales', *North American Journal of Welsh Studies*, 1.1 (Winter 2001), pp. 25–41.

Carson, Niall, *Rebel by Vocation: Seán O'Faoláin and the Generation of* The Bell (Manchester: Manchester University Press, 2016).

Casanova, Pascale, *The World Republic of Letters* (Cambridge, MA: Harvard University Press, 2004).

Caughie, Pamela, 'Purpose and Play in Woolf's London Scene Essays', *Women's Studies: An Interdisciplinary Journal*, 16.3–4 (1989), pp. 389–408.

Chan, Winnie, *The Economy of the Short Story in British Periodicals of the 1890s* (London: Routledge, 2007).

Chan, Winnie, 'The Linked Excitements of L. T. Meade and . . . in the *Strand* Magazine', in Ellen Burton Harrington (ed.), *Scribbling Women and the Short Story Form: Approaches by American & British Women Writers* (New York: Peter Lang, 2008), pp. 60–73.

Clark, Heather, *The Ulster Renaissance: Poetry in Belfast 1962–1972* (Oxford: Oxford University Press, 2006).

Clay, Catherine, '"The Magazine Short Story and the Real Short Story": Consuming Fiction in the Feminist Weekly *Time and Tide*', in Catherine Clay, Maria DiCenzo, Barbara Green and Fiona Hackney (eds), *Women's Periodicals and Print Culture in Britain, 1918–1939, The Interwar Period* (Edinburgh: Edinburgh University Press, 2017), pp. 72–86.

Clyde, Tom, *Irish Literary Magazines: An Outline History and Descriptive Bibliography* (Dublin: Irish Academic Press, 2002).

Cohen, Margaret, 'Narratology in the Archive of Literature', *Representations*, 108.1 (2009), pp. 51–75.

Collier, Patrick, 'What Is Modern Periodical Studies?', *Journal of Modern Periodical Studies*, 6.2 (2015), pp. 92–111.

Collier, Patrick, *Modern Print Artefacts: Textual Materiality and Literary Value in British Print Culture, 1890–1930s* (Edinburgh: Edinburgh University Press, 2016).

Conran, Anthony, *Frontiers in Anglo-Welsh Poetry* (Cardiff: University of Wales Press, 1997).

Cook, Malcolm, *Early British Animation: From Page and Stage to Cinema Screens* (Basingstoke: Palgrave Macmillan, 2018).

Crackanthorpe, David, *Hubert Crackanthorpe and English Realism in the 1890s* (Columbia, MO; London: University of Missouri Press, 1977).

Cranfield, Jonathan, *Twentieth-Century Victorian: Arthur Conan Doyle and the* Strand *Magazine, 1891–1930* (Edinburgh: Edinburgh University Press, 2016).

Cutting, Sam, 'The Short Story, Censorship, and Wartime Publishing: Julian Maclaren-Ross and *Horizon* Magazine, 1940–42', *Journal of Modern Periodical Studies*, 7.1–2 (2016), pp. 26–47.

Davin, Dan, 'Introduction', in Dan Davin (ed.), *Short Stories from the Second World War* (Oxford: Oxford University Press, 1982), pp. i–xiv.

Dawson, Janis, '"Not for girls alone, but for anyone who can relish really good literature": L. T. Meade, *Atalanta*, and the Family Literary Magazine', *Victorian Periodicals Review*, 46.4 (Winter 2013), pp. 475–98.

Delaney, Paul and Adrian Hunter (eds), *The Edinburgh Companion to the Short Story in English* (Edinburgh: Edinburgh University Press, 2019).

Delap, Lucy, '*The Freewoman*, Periodical Communities, and the Feminist Reading Public', *Princeton University Library Chronicle*, 61 (2000), pp. 233–76.

Delap, Lucy and Maria DiCenzo, 'Transatlantic Print Culture: The Anglo-American Feminist Press and Emerging "Modernities"', in Ann Ardis and Patrick Collier (eds), *Transatlantic Print Culture, 1880–1940: Emerging Media, Emerging Modernisms* (Basingstoke: Palgrave Macmillan, 2008), pp. 48–65.

D'hoker, Elke, 'Artist Stories of the 1890s: Life, Art, and Sacrifice', in Bénédicte Coste, Catherine Delyfer and Christine Reynier (eds), *Reconnecting Aestheticism and Modernism: Continuities, Revisions, Speculations* (London: Routledge, 2016), pp. 92–106.

D'hoker, Elke and Stephanie Eggermont, 'Fin-de-Siècle Women Writers and the Modern Short Story', *English Literature in Transition, 1880–1920*, 3 (2015), pp. 291–312.

D'hoker, Elke and Stephanie Eggermont, 'The Short Fiction of New Woman Writers in Avant-Garde, Mainstream and Popular Periodicals of the Fin de Siècle', in Christoph Ehland and Cornelia Wächter (eds), *Middlebrow and Gender: 1880–1930* (Leiden and Boston: Brill, 2016), pp. 21–38.

Dick, Susan, 'Introduction', in Virginia Woolf, *The Complete Shorter Fiction of Virginia Woolf*, ed. by Susan Dick (London: Harcourt, 1989), pp. 1–6.

Diepeveen, Leonard (ed.), *Mock Modernism: An Anthology of Parodies, Travesties, Frauds, 1910–1935* (Toronto: University of Toronto Press, 2014).

Dillane, Fionnuala, 'Forms of Affect, Relationality, and Periodical Encounters, or "Pine-Apple for the Million"', *Journal of European Periodical Studies*, 1.1 (2016), pp. 5–24.

Dowson, Jane, 'Interventions in the Public Sphere: *Time and Tide* (1920–30) and *The Bermondsey Book* (1923–30)', in Peter Brooker and Andrew Thacker (eds), *The Oxford Critical and Cultural History of Modernist Magazines: Volume I: Britain and Ireland 1880–1955* (Oxford: Oxford University Press, 2013), pp. 530–51.

Drabble, Margaret (ed.), *The Oxford Companion to English Literature*, 5th ed. (New York: Oxford, 1985).

Dubino, Jeanne, 'Introduction' in Jeanne Dubino (ed.), *Virginia Woolf and the Literary Marketplace* (London: Palgrave Macmillan, 2010), pp. 1–23.

Dubino, Jeanne (ed.), *Virginia Woolf and the Literary Marketplace* (New York: Palgrave Macmillan, 2010).

Dugan, Sally, *Baroness Orczy's* The Scarlet Pimpernel: *A Publishing History* (Abingdon: Routledge, 2016).
Eco, Umberto, 'Interpreting Serials', *The Limits of Interpretation* (Bloomington: Indiana University Press, 1990), pp. 83–100.
Einhaus, Ann-Marie, *The Short Story and the First World War* (Cambridge: Cambridge University Press, 2013).
Einhaus, Ann-Marie, 'War Stories: The Short Story in the First and Second World Wars', in Dominic Head (ed.), *The Cambridge History of the English Short Story* (Cambridge: Cambridge University Press, 2016), pp. 152–67.
Ferris, Paul, *Dylan Thomas: The Biography* (London: Dent, 1999).
Fisher, Benjamin Franklin, IV, 'Hubert Crackanthorpe', in William B. Thesing (ed.), *British Short-Fiction Writers, 1880–1914: The Realist Tradition, Dictionary of Literary Biography*, vol. 135 (Detroit;Washington, DC; London: Bruccoli Clark Layman/Gale Research, 1994), pp. 60–74.
Fordham, John, *James Hanley: Modernism and the Working Class* (Cardiff: University of Wales Press, 2002).
Funke, Jana, 'Introduction', in Jana Funke (ed.), *'The World' and Other Unpublished Works of Radclyffe Hall* (Manchester: Manchester University Press, 2016), pp. 1–44.
Fussell, Paul, *Wartime: Understanding and Behavior in the Second World War* (Oxford: Oxford University Press, 1989).
Giles, Judy, *The Parlour and the Suburb: Domestic Identities, Class, Femininity and Modernity* (Oxford: Berg, 2004).
Glendinning, Victoria, *Elizabeth Bowen* (New York: Anchor Books, 2006).
Greenslade, William, 'Naturalism and Decadence: The Case of Hubert Crackanthorpe', in Jason David Hall and Alex Murray (eds), *Decadent Poetics: Literature and Form at the British Fin de Siècle* (Basingstoke: Palgrave Macmillan, 2013), pp. 163–80.
Griffin, Dustin H., *Satire: A Critical Reintroduction* (Lexington, KY: University Press of Kentucky, 1994).
Gualtieri, Elena, *Virginia Woolf's Essays: Sketching the Past* (Basingstoke: Macmillan, 2000).
Guerlac, Suzanne, *Thinking in Time: An Introduction to Henri Bergson* (London: Cornell University Press, 2006).
Guiguet, Jean, *Virginia Woolf et son œuvre. L'Art et la quête du réel* (Paris: Didier, 1962).
Hammill, Faye, Paul Hjartarson and Hannah McGregor, 'Introduction: Magazines and/as Media: Periodical Studies and the Question of Disciplinarity', *The Journal of Modern Periodical Studies*, 6.2 (2015), pp. iii–xiii.
Hammond, J. R. (ed.), *H. G. Wells and the Short Story* (Basingstoke: Macmillan, 1992).
Hanson, Clare, *Short Stories and Short Fictions, 1880–1980* (Basingstoke: Macmillan, 1985).

Harmon, Maurice, *Seán O'Faoláin: A Life* (London: Constable, 1994).
Harris, John, 'Letters from the Cultural Battlefront', *Planet*, 65 (Oct/Nov 1987), pp. 21–6.
Harris, John, 'Not a Trysorfa fach', *New Welsh Review*, 3.3 (1990–1), pp. 28–33.
Harrison, Andrew, *The Life of D. H. Lawrence: A Critical Biography* (Oxford: Wiley-Blackwell, 2016).
Hart, James D. (ed.), *The Oxford Companion to American Literature*, 5th ed. (New York: Oxford University Press, 1983).
Haugtvedt, Erica, 'The Victorian Serial Novel and Transfictional Character', *Victorian Studies*, 59.3 (2017), pp. 409–18.
Head, Dominic, *The Modernist Short Story: A Study in Theory and Practice* (Cambridge: Cambridge University Press, 1992).
Head, Dominic (ed.), *The Cambridge History of the English Short Story* (Cambridge: Cambridge University Press, 2016).
Hensley, Nathan, 'Network: Andrew Lang and the Distributed Agencies of Literary Production', *Victorian Periodicals Review*, 48.3 (2015), pp. 359–82.
Hepburn, Allan (ed.), *Listening In: Broadcasts, Speeches, and Interviews by Elizabeth Bowen* (Edinburgh: Edinburgh University Press, 2010).
Hewison, Robert, *Under Siege: Literary Life in London 1939–1945* (London: Weidenfeld and Nicholson, 1977).
Hilliard, Christopher, *To Exercise Our Talents: The Democratization of Writing in Britain* (Cambridge, MA: Harvard University Press, 2006).
Hoffman, Frederick J., Charles Allen and Carolyn F. Ulrich (eds), *The Little Magazine: A History and a Bibliography* (Princeton: Princeton University Press, 1946).
Holman, Valerie, *Print for Victory: Book Publishing in England 1939–1945* (London: The British Library, 2008).
Hopkins, Chris, 'James Joyce Is an Irish Edition of Mr Caradoc Evans: Two Celtic Naturalists', *Irish Studies Review*, 3.12 (Autumn 1995), pp. 23–6.
Hopkins, Christopher, '*Wales* (1937–39), *The Welsh Review* (1939–40)', in Peter Brooker and Andrew Thacker (eds), *The Oxford Critical and Cultural History of Modernist Magazines: Volume I: Britain and Ireland 1880–1955* (Oxford: Oxford University Press, 2013), pp. 714–34.
Huculak, J. Matthew, '*The London Mercury* (1919–39) and Other Moderns', in Peter Brooker and Andrew Thacker (eds), *The Oxford Critical and Cultural History of Modernist Magazines: Volume I: Britain and Ireland 1880–1955* (Oxford: Oxford University Press, 2009), pp. 240–59.
Hughes, Daniel, 'Welsh Literary Modernism, Lynette Roberts and David Jones: "unearthing a huge and very important culture"', in Siriol McAvoy (ed.), *Locating Lynette Roberts: Always Observant and Slightly Obscure* (Cardiff: University of Wales Press, 2019), pp. 101–20.
Hughes, Linda, 'A Club of Their Own: The "Literary Ladies," New Women

Writers, and "Fin-De-Siècle" Authorship', *Victorian Literature and Culture*, 35.1 (2007), pp. 233–60.

Hunter, Adrian, *The Cambridge Introduction to the Short Story in English* (Cambridge: Cambridge University Press, 2007).

Hussey, Mark, 'Introduction', Virginia Woolf, *Between the Acts* (Cambridge: Cambridge University Press, 2011), xxxix–lxxiii.

Hyams, Edward, The New Statesman: *The History of the First Fifty Years, 1913-1953* (London: Longmans, 1963).

Ingman, Heather, *A History of the Irish Short Story* (Cambridge: Cambridge University Press, 2009).

Jackson, Kate, *George Newnes and the New Journalism in Britain, 1880–1910: Culture and Profit* (Aldershot: Ashgate, 2001).

Jaillant, Lise, 'Sapper, Hodder Stoughton, and the Popular Literature of the Great War', *Book History*, 14.1 (2011), pp. 137–66.

Johnson, Lionel, *Poetry and Fiction: Reflections on Three Nineteenth Century Authors* (Edinburgh: The Tragera Press, 1982).

Jones, Glyn, *Setting Out: A Memoir of Literary Life in Wales* (Cardiff: Cardiff University College Press, 1982).

Jones, Glyn, *The Dragon Has Two Tongues: Essays on Anglo Welsh Writers and Writing*, ed. by Tony Brown (Cardiff: University of Wales Press, 2001).

Kane, Louise, 'Pre-War Writing', in Andrzej Gasiorek and Nathan Waddell (eds), *Wyndham Lewis: A Critical Guide* (Edinburgh: Edinburgh University Press, 2015), pp. 5–19.

Kearney, Richard, 'Between Politics and Literature: The Irish Cultural Journal', *The Crane Bag*, 7.2 (1983), pp. 160–71.

Kelleter, Frank, 'Five Ways of Looking at Popular Seriality', in Frank Kelleter (ed.), *Media of Serial Narrative* (Columbus: Ohio State University Press, 2017), pp. 7–34.

Kirkland, Richard, 'The Poetics of Partition: Poetry and Northern Ireland in the 1940s', in Fran Brearton and Alan Gillis (eds), *The Oxford Handbook of Modern Irish Poetry* (Oxford: Oxford University Press, 2012), pp. 210–24.

Krueger, Kate, '*The Woman at Home* in the World: Annie Swan's Lady Doctor and the Problem of the Fin de Siècle Working Woman', *Victorian Periodicals Review*, 50.3 (2017), pp. 517–33.

Latham, Sean, 'Cyril Connolly's *Horizon* (1940–50) and the End of Modernism', in Peter Brooker and Andrew Thacker (eds), *The Oxford Critical and Cultural History of Modernist Magazines: Volume I: Britain and Ireland 1880–1955* (Oxford: Oxford University Press, 2013), pp. 856–73.

Lee, Hermione, *Virginia Woolf* (New York: A. A. Knopf, 1998).

Lee, Hermione, *Elizabeth Bowen* (London: Vintage, 1999).

Leighton, Angela, *Hearing Things: The Work of Sound in Literature* (Cambridge: The Belknap Press of Harvard University Press, 2018).

Levy, Heather, *The Servants of Desire in Virginia Woolf's Shorter Fiction* (New York: Peter Lang, 2010).
Lewis, Jeremy, *Cyril Connolly: A Life* (London: Pimlico, 1998).
Lewis, Jeremy, *Penguin Special: The Life and Times of Allen Lane* (London: Penguin Books, 2006).
Lewis, Pericles, 'Modernism and Religion', in Michael Levenson (ed.), *The Cambridge Companion to Modernism* (Cambridge: Cambridge University Press, 2006), pp. 278–307.
Liddle, Dallas, 'Genre: "Distant Reading" and the Goals of Periodicals Research', *Victorian Periodicals Review*, 48.3 (2015), pp. 383–402.
Liggins, Emma, Andrew Maunder, Ruth Robbins, *The British Short Story* (Basingstoke: Palgrave Macmillan, 2011).
Light, Alison, *Forever England: Femininity, Literature, and Conservatism between the Wars* (London: Routledge, 1991).
Lohafer, Susan, *Coming to Terms with the Short Story* (Baton Rouge: Louisiana State University Press, 1983).
Lohafer, Susan and Jo Ellyn Clarey (eds), *Short Story Theory at a Crossroads* (Baton Rouge: Louisiana State University Press, 1989).
Longley, Edna, 'Poetry and Politics in Northern Ireland', *The Crane Bag*, 9.1 (1985), pp. 26–40.
Longley, Edna, 'Progressive Bookmen: Politics and Northern Protestant Writers since the 1930s', *The Irish Review*, 1 (1986), pp. 50–7.
Longley, Edna, '"Between the Saxon Smile and Yankee Yawp": Problems and Contexts of Literary Reviewing in Ireland', in Jeremy Treglown and Bridget Bennett (eds), *Grub Street and the Ivory Tower: Literary Journalism and Literary Scholarship from Fielding to the Internet* (Oxford: Clarendon Press, 1998), pp. 200–9.
MacKay, Marina, *Modernism and World War II* (New York; Cambridge: Cambridge University Press, 2007).
MacKenzie, Raymond, '*The London Mercury*', in Alvin Sullivan (ed.), *British Literary Magazines: The Modern Age, 1914–1984* (New York: Greenwood Press, 1986), pp. 250–5.
Malcolm, David, *The British and Irish Short Story Handbook* (Oxford; Malden, MA: Wiley-Blackwell, 2012).
Malcolm, David (ed.), *Hubert Crackanthorpe: Wreckage – Seven Studies* (Edinburgh: Edinburgh University Press, 2020).
Mao, Douglas and Rebecca L. Walkowitz, 'The New Modernist Studies', *PMLA*, 123.3 (2008), pp. 737–48.
Marcus, Laura, 'The Short Fiction', in Jessica Berman (ed.), *A Companion to Virginia Woolf* (Chichester: Wiley Blackwell, 2016), pp. 27–40.
Matthews, Brander, *The Philosophy of the Short-Story* (New York and London: Longmans, 1901).
Matthews, Kelly, '"Something Solid to Put Your Heels On": Representation and Transformation in *The Bell*', *Éire–Ireland*, 46.1–2 (2011), pp. 106–27.

Matthews, Kelly, The Bell *Magazine and the Representation of Irish Identity* (Dublin: Four Courts Press, 2012).
May, Charles E. (ed.), *Short Story Theories* (Athens: Ohio University Press, 1976).
May, Charles E. (ed.), *The New Short Story Theories* (Athens: Ohio University Press, 1994).
McAvoy, Siriol (ed.), *Locating Lynette Roberts: Always Observant and Slightly Obscure* (Cardiff: University of Wales Press, 2019).
McGann, Jerome, *The Textual Condition* (Princeton: Princeton University Press, 1991).
McGee, David (ed.), 'Feature', *The Bluegrass Special* (2010), <http://thebluegrassspecial.com/archive/2010/november10/leo-tolstoy-one-hundred.php> (last accessed 1 September 2020).
McMahon, Sean, *Sam Hanna Bell: A Biography* (Belfast: The Blackstaff Press, 1999).
McNichol, Stella, 'Introduction', in Virginia Woolf, *Mrs Dalloway's Party: A Short Story Sequence*, ed. by Stella McNichol (London: Harcourt, 1979), pp. ix–xvii.
McVicker, Jeanette, 'Virginia Woolf and American Writers', in Mark Hussey and Vara Neverow (eds), *Virginia Woolf: Emerging Perspectives: Selected Papers from the Third Annual Conference on Virginia Woolf, Lincoln University, Jefferson City, MO, June 10–13, 1993* (New York: Pace University Press, 1994), pp. 313–18.
McVicker, Jeanette, '"Six Essays on London Life": A History of Dispersal Part I', *Woolf Studies*, 9 (2003), pp. 143–65.
Mengham, Rod, 'Broken Glass', in Rod Mengham and N. H. Reeve (eds), *The Fiction of the 1940s: Stories of Survival* (Basingstoke: Palgrave, 2001), pp. 124–33.
Mitchell, Sally, *The New Girl: Girls' Culture In England 1880–1915* (New York: Columbia University Press, 1995).
Mittell, Jason, 'Operational Seriality and the Operation of Seriality', in Zara Dinnen and Robyn Warhol (eds), *Contemporary Narrative Theories* (Edinburgh: Edinburgh University Press, 2018), pp. 227–38.
Monfort, Bruno, 'La nouvelle et son mode de publication. Le cas américain', *Poétique*, 90 (1992), pp. 153–71.
Morehead, Craig, '"Rambling the Streets of London": Virginia Woolf and the London Sketch', *Virginia Woolf Miscellany*, 83 (2013), pp. 18–19.
Morrisson, Mark S., 'The Myth of the Whole: Ford's *English Review*, the "Mercure de France", and Early British Modernism', *ELH*, 63.2 (Summer 1996), pp. 513–33.
Morrisson, Mark S., *The Public Face of Modernism: Little Magazines, Audiences, and Reception, 1905–1920* (Wisconsin: University of Wisconsin Press, 2001).
Mourant, Chris, *Katherine Mansfield and Periodical Culture* (Edinburgh: Edinburgh University Press, 2019).

Mussell, James, 'Repetition: Or "In Our Last"', *Victorian Periodicals Review*, 48.3 (2015), pp. 343–58.

Neacey, Markus, 'Introduction', in *Selected Stories of Morley Roberts*, ed. by Markus Neacey (Brighton: Victorian Secrets, 2015), pp. 5–16.

O'Connor, Frank, *The Lonely Voice: A Study of the Short Story* (London: Macmillan, 1965).

Oxford Dictionary of National Biography, <https://www.oxforddnb.com/> (last accessed 1 September 2020).

Parkins, Ilya, '"Eve Goes Synthetic": Modernising Feminine Beauty, Renegotiating Masculinity in *Britannia and Eve*', in Catherine Clay, Maria DiCenzo, Barbara Green and Fiona Hackney (eds), *Women's Periodicals and Print Culture in Britain, 1918–1939: The Interwar Period* (Edinburgh: Edinburgh University Press, 2018), pp. 139–52.

Pasco, Allan H., 'On Defining Short Stories', *New Literary History*, 22.2 (Spring 1991), pp. 407–22.

Peppis, Paul, *Literature, Politics and the English Avant-garde: Nation and Empire, 1901–1918* (Cambridge: Cambridge University Press, 2000).

Philpotts, Matthew, 'The Role of the Periodical Editor: Literary Journals and Editorial Habitus', *Modern Language Review*, 107.1 (2012), pp. 39–64.

Philpotts, Matthew, 'A Return to Theory', *Victorian Periodicals Review*, 48.3 (2015), pp. 307–11.

Pittard, Christopher, '"Cheap, Healthful Literature": *The Strand Magazine*, Fictions of Crime, and Purified Reading Communities', *Victorian Periodicals Review*, 40.1 (Spring 2007), pp. 1–23.

Plain, Gill, *Literature of the 1940s: War, Postwar and 'Peace'* (Edinburgh: Edinburgh University Press, 2015).

Plock, Vike Martina, '"A Journal of the Period": Modernism and Conservative Modernity in *Eve: The Lady's Pictorial* (1919–29)', in Catherine Clay, Maria DiCenzo, Barbara Green and Fiona Hackney (eds), *Women's Periodicals and Print Culture in Britain, 1918–1939: The Interwar Period* (Edinburgh: Edinburgh University Press, 2018), pp. 28–41.

Pollard, Wendy, *Rosamond Lehmann and Her Critics: The Vagaries of Literary Reception* (Aldershot: Ashgate, 2004).

Pollentier, Caroline, 'Virginia Woolf and the Middlebrow Market of the Familiar Essay', in Jeanne Dubino (ed.), *Virginia Woolf and the Literary Marketplace* (New York: Palgrave Macmillan, 2010), pp. 137–50.

Pong, Beryl, 'The Short Story and the "Little Magazine"', in Paul Delaney and Adrian Hunter (eds), *The Edinburgh Companion to the Short Story in English* (Edinburgh: Edinburgh University Press, 2019), pp. 75–92.

Potter, Rachel, *Modernist Literature* (Edinburgh: Edinburgh University Press, 2012).

Pratt, Mary Louise, 'The Long and the Short of It', in Charles E. May (ed.),

The New Short Story Theories (Athens: Ohio University Press, 1994), pp. 91–113.
Punter, David, 'The Uncanny', in Catherine Spooner and Emma McEvoy (eds), *The Routledge Companion to the Gothic* (London: Routledge, 2007), pp. 129–36.
Purdue, Melissa, 'Clemence Housman's *The Were-Wolf*: A Cautionary Tale for the Progressive New Woman', *Revenant: Critical and Creative Studies of the Supernatural*, 3 (December 2016), pp. 42–55.
Reynier, Christine, *Virginia Woolf's Ethics of the Short Story* (New York: Palgrave Macmillan, 2009).
Rigel Daugherty, Beth, '"Young writers might do worse": Anne Thackeray Ritchie, Virginia Stephen and Virginia Woolf', in Gina Potts and Lisa Shahriari (eds), *Virginia Woolf's Bloomsbury, Volume 1* (London: Palgrave Macmillan, 2010), pp. 20–36.
Robb, Linsey, '"The Front Line": Firefighting in British Culture, 1939–1945', *Contemporary British History*, 29.2 (2015), pp. 179–98.
Roberts, Harri Garrod, *Embody Identity: Representations of the Body in Welsh Literature* (Cardiff: University of Wales Press, 2009).
Sarker, Sonita, 'Locating a Native Englishness in Virginia Woolf's "The London Scene"', *NWSA Journal: A Publication of the National Women's Studies Association*, 13.2 (2001), pp. 1–30.
Scholes, Robert and Clifford Wulfman, *Modernism in the Magazines: An Introduction* (New Haven: Yale University Press, 2010).
Shaya, Gregory, 'The Flâneur, the Badaud, and the Making of a Mass Public in France, circa 1860–1910', *American Historical Review*, 109.1 (February 2004), pp. 41–77.
Sheehan, Elizabeth M., 'Now and Forever? Fashion Magazines and the Temporality of the Interwar Period', in Catherine Clay, Maria DiCenzo, Barbara Green and Fiona Hackney (eds), *Women's Periodicals and Print Culture in Britain, 1918–1939: The Interwar Period* (Edinburgh: Edinburgh University Press, 2018), pp. 124–38.
Shovlin, Frank, *The Irish Literary Periodical, 1923–1958* (Oxford: Clarendon Press, 2003).
Showalter, Elaine, *A Literature of Their Own* (London: Virago, 1978).
Skrbic, Nena, *Wild Outbursts of Freedom: Reading Virginia Woolf's Short Fiction* (London: Praeger, 2004).
Smith, Adrian, *The New Statesman: Portrait of a Political Weekly, 1913–1931* (London: Routledge, 2013).
Smith, Angela, *Katherine Mansfield: A Literary Life* (Basingstoke: Palgrave, 2000).
Snaith, Anna and Michael H. Whitworth (eds), *Locating Woolf: The Politics of Space and Place* (New York: Palgrave Macmillan, 2007).
Snyder, Carey, 'Introduction to *Rhythm* and *The Blue Review*', *The Modernist Journals Project* (2012), <https://modjourn.org/introduction-to-rhythm-and-the-blue-review/> (last accessed 1 September 2020).

Sparks, Tabitha, *The Doctor in the Victorian Novel: Family Practices* (Aldershot: Ashgate, 2009).

Squier, Susan, '"The London Scene": Gender and Class in Virginia Woolf's London', *Twentieth Century Literature*, 29.4 (1983), pp. 488–500.

Squier, Susan, *Virginia Woolf and London: The Sexual Politics of the City* (London: North Carolina University Press, 1985).

Stephens, Meic, 'The Third Man: Robert Herring and *Life and Letters To-day*', *Welsh Writing in English: A Yearbook of Critical Essays*, 3 (1997), pp. 157–69.

Stephensen-Payne, Phil, *Galactic Central*, <http://www.philsp.com> (last accessed 1 September 2020).

Thomas, M. Wynn, 'My People and the Revenge of the Novel', *New Welsh Review*, 1 (Summer 1988), pp. 17–22.

Thomas, M. Wynn, *In the Shadow of the Pulpit: Literature and Nonconformist Wales* (Cardiff: University of Wales Press, 2010).

Tomalin, Claire, *Katherine Mansfield: A Secret Life* (London: Penguin Group, 1988).

Towheed, Shafquat, 'Reading the Life and Art of Hubert Crackanthorpe', *English Literature in Transition, 1880–1920*, 43.1 (2000), pp. 51–65.

Turner, Mark W., 'Periodical Time in the Nineteenth Century', *Media History*, 8.2 (2002), pp. 183–96.

Wainwright, Laura, *New Territories in Modernism: Anglophone Welsh Writing, 1930–1949* (Cardiff: University of Wales Press, 2018).

Warhol, Robyn, 'Making "Gay" and "Lesbian" into Household Words: How Serial Form Works in Armistead Maupin's "Tales of the City"', *Contemporary Literature*, 40.3 (1999), pp. 378–402.

Wees, William C., *Vorticism and the English Avant-Garde* (Toronto: University of Toronto Press, 1972).

West, Emma, 'Cover Stars and Covert Addresses: Strategies for Reading Magazines Across the "Great Divide"', in Bram Lambrecht and Matthias Somers (eds), *Writing Literary History* (Leuven: Peeters, 2018), pp. 85–102.

White, Cynthia L., *Women's Magazines 1693–1968* (London: Michael Joseph, 1970).

Wildon Carr, Herbert, *Henri Bergson: The Philosophy of Change* (New York: Dodge Publishing, 2004).

Williams, Raymond, *Television: Technology and Cultural Form* (London: Routledge, [1974] 2003).

Wills, Clair, *That Neutral Island: A Cultural History of Ireland During the Second World War* (London: Faber & Faber, 2007).

Wiltse, Ed, '"So Constant an Expectation": Sherlock Holmes and Seriality', *Narrative*, 6.2 (1998), pp. 105–22.

Wood, Alice, 'Made to Measure: Virginia Woolf in *Good Housekeeping* Magazine', *Prose Studies*, 32.1 (2010), pp. 12–24.

Wood, Alice, *Virginia Woolf's Late Cultural Criticism* (London: Bloomsbury, 2013).

Wood, Alice, *Modernism and Modernity in British Women's Magazines* (Abingdon: Routledge, 2020).

Wulfman, Cliff, 'Ford Madox Ford and *The English Review* (1908–37)', in Peter Brooker and Andrew Thacker (eds), *The Oxford Critical and Cultural History of Modernist Magazines: Volume I: Britain and Ireland 1880–1955* (Oxford: Oxford University Press, 2009), pp. 226–39.

Young, Emma, *Contemporary Feminism and Women's Short Stories* (Edinburgh: Edinburgh University Press, 2018).

Notes on Contributors

Dean Baldwin is Professor Emeritus of English at Penn State Behrend in Erie, Pennsylvania. His BA in English and History is from Capital University; his MA and PhD in Medieval Studies are from Ohio State University. In forty-four years of university-level teaching, he has taught a wide variety of courses, including composition, Chaucer, Shakespeare, British literature surveys, the novel and the short story. He has written books on the short stories of H. E. Bates, V. S. Pritchett and Virginia Woolf. His latest book is *Art and Commerce in the British Short Story, 1880–1950* (Pickering and Chatto, 2013). Among his other publications are two textbook anthologies: *The Riverside Anthology of Short Fiction* (Houghton Mifflin, 1997) and *An Anthology of Colonial and Postcolonial Short Fiction* (Houghton Mifflin, 2006).

Elke D'hoker is Professor of English Literature at the University of Leuven, where she co-directs the Leuven Centre for Irish Studies and the modern literature research group, MDRN. She is the author of *Visions of Alterity: Representation in the Works of John Banville* (Rodopi, 2004) and *Irish Women Writers and the Modern Short Story* (Palgrave, 2016). She has edited several essay collections, including *Unreliable Narration* (De Gruyter, 2008), *Mary Lavin* (Irish Academic Press, 2013) and *The Irish Short Story* (Lang, 2015).

Louise Edensor is Senior Lecturer in Creative Writing, Children's Literature and Global Journalism at Middlesex University Dubai. For the past four years she has also held the position of Programme Leader in Dubai for the International Foundation Programme. Louise's lifelong interest in Katherine Mansfield culminated in her PhD thesis, which was entitled 'Katherine Mansfield: Conceptualisations of the Self'. Louise has written on Katherine Mansfield and her associates, and current research interests centre around Mansfield's earliest writings published in little magazine contexts. Louise is also working on research relating to vignettes published in the little magazines of Australia in the early twentieth century.

Ann-Marie Einhaus is Associate Professor of Modern and Contemporary Literature at Northumbria University Newcastle. She is the author of *The Short Story and the First World War* (Cambridge University Press, 2013) and editor of *The Cambridge Companion to the English Short Story* (Cambridge University Press, 2016) among others. Her research interests and publications cover the early twentieth-century short story (modernist and mainstream), writing about the First World War from 1914 to the present day, the reception of foreign literature in Britain during the interwar period, and British wartime and interwar magazines. Her most recent work looks at the feminist periodical *Time and Tide* in the 1920s and 1930s, and at Cyril Connolly's wartime venture *Horizon*.

Annalise Grice is Lecturer in English at Nottingham Trent University. Her first monograph (forthcoming with Edinburgh University Press) focuses on the Edwardian literary marketplace and the ways in which D. H. Lawrence became a professional writer. The book examines Lawrence's engagement with newspapers, magazines and journals and considers publishing cultures, marketing and self-fashioning, literary networks and forms of patronage as well as collaborative writing, editing and production. Annalise has published several other book chapters and articles, including essays for the *D. H. Lawrence Review* and *D. H. Lawrence in Context* (Cambridge University Press).

Daniel Hughes completed his PhD in English Literature at Bangor University, where he taught modern and contemporary literature for four years. His research concentrates on modern Welsh literature in English and has been published in journals such as the *International Journal of Welsh Writing in English* and the *Yearbook of English Studies*. He is the editor of *A Day's Pleasure and Other Tales: Selected Stories by Nigel Heseltine* (Parthian, 2021) and is co-authoring the first book-length study of the poet, translator and essayist Tony Conran (1931–2013) for the University of Wales Press series Writers of Wales. Daniel is the recipient of a Fulbright All-Disciplines Scholar's Award, and is currently a postdoctoral teaching and research fellow at the University of Texas at Austin.

Yui Kajita is an independent research scholar of nineteenth- and twentieth-century literature. She completed her PhD at the University of Cambridge in 2019, for which she conducted extensive archival research on Thomas Hardy and Walter de la Mare. Her work has appeared in journals such as *English Literature in Transition: 1880–1920*, *Cambridge Quarterly* and *The Hardy Review*. She was awarded the Thomas Hardy Association's Student Essay Prize in 2018. She is currently co-editing the first ever collection of essays on de la Mare with Angela Leighton and Anna Nickerson. Based in California, she divides her time between researching, working as a translator in Japanese and English, and creating illustrations.

David Malcolm is a Professor at SWPS University of Social Sciences and Humanities in Warsaw. He is author of books on Ian McEwan, Graham Swift and John McGahern (all published by the University of South Carolina Press) and of *The British and Irish Short Story Handbook* (Wiley-Blackwell, 2012). He co-edited *The Wiley-Blackwell Companion to the British and Irish Short Story* (2008) and *On John Berger: Telling Stories* (Brill Rodopi, 2016). His edition of Hubert Crackanthorpe's *Wreckage* (1893) was published by Edinburgh University Press in 2020. He is co-editor of *A Companion to Contemporary Poetry, 1960–2015* (Wiley-Blackwell, 2020).

Saskia McCracken is a doctoral researcher at the University of Glasgow. Her thesis considers the politics of Virginia Woolf's Darwinian animal tropes. Her publications on Woolf, Darwin and animal studies appear in *Virginia Woolf, Europe, and Peace: Aesthetics and Theory* (2020), *Crossing Borders: Transnational Modernism Beyond the Human* (2021) and *Modernism/Modernity: Reading Modernism in the Sixth Extinction* (2021). She has also transcribed the earliest MS draft of *Flush: A Biography* for the Cambridge scholarly edition of Woolf's work (2022).

Tara McEvoy is a doctoral researcher at Queen's University Belfast. Her research interests include the politics of poetic form and publication culture. In 2017, she was awarded a short-term research fellowship at the Stuart A. Rose Library, Emory University, Atlanta, and a Helen Ramsey Turtle Scholarship from Queen's. In 2018, she won the Irish Studies Association of Australia and New Zealand Postgraduate Essay Prize, and her winning essay was published in the *Australasian Journal of Irish Studies*. She edits *The Tangerine*, a Belfast-based magazine of new writing, and was formerly a placement student and temporary education officer at Seamus Heaney HomePlace, Bellaghy.

Chris Mourant is Lecturer in Early Twentieth-Century English Literature at the University of Birmingham, where he co-directs the Centre for Modernist Cultures. Chris researches nineteenth- and twentieth-century literatures, with particular emphasis on modernism, print culture, media history and postcolonial criticism. He is the author of *Katherine Mansfield and Periodical Culture* (Edinburgh University Press, 2019) as well as numerous articles and book chapters on Mansfield and modern short fiction. Chris has served on the executive committee of the British Association for Modernist Studies (BAMS) and has co-organised several major international conferences, including 'Modernism Now!' (2014) and 'Modernist Life' (2017). He is an editor of the journal *Modernist Cultures*.

Whitney Standlee is Senior Lecturer in English Literature of the Long Nineteenth Century at the University of Worcester. Her research focuses on Irish women's writing, migrant narratives, the literature of the nineteenth century *fin de siècle*, and the intersection of literature, politics and popular culture. She is the author of *Power to Observe: Irish Women Novelists in Britain 1890–1916* (Peter Lang, 2015) and co-editor (with Anna Pilz) of *Irish Women's Writing 1878–1922: Advancing the Cause of Liberty* (Manchester University Press, 2016). A member of the board of the Irish Women's Writing 1880–1920 Network, she and Pilz are also co-originators and editors of the popular Research Pioneers series of online interviews for the network.

Tessa Thorniley is an early career researcher. Her doctoral studies considered a group of Chinese writers whose short stories were published in the literary journal *The Penguin New Writing* during and shortly after the Second World War. Her research interests include Second World War short stories, modernist magazines and modern Chinese literature (particularly its reception in the Anglophone world). Prior to embarking on a PhD at Westminster University, where she also taught in the Chinese Studies department, she spent seven years working as a freelance journalist in China.

Emma West is a British Academy Postdoctoral Fellow at the University of Birmingham. Her postdoctoral project, Revolutionary

Red Tape, examines how committees helped to commission, disseminate and popularise British modernist art, design, literature and performance. She has published essays on modernism, periodicals, fashion and theory and is the organiser of several conferences, including Alternative Modernisms (2013), A Century On (2015), Twentieth-Century British Periodicals: Word and Art on the Printed Page (2017) and Modernist Art Writing/Writing Modernist Art (2019). She was the Founder and inaugural Chair of Modernist Network Cymru (MONC), and is the organiser of Ways of Reading, a series of interactive workshops for postgraduate and early-career researchers on modern magazines.

Alice Wood is Senior Lecturer in English Literature at De Montfort University. She is the author of *Modernism and Modernity in British Women's Magazines* (Routledge, 2020) and *Virginia Woolf's Late Cultural Criticism* (Bloomsbury, 2013). She contributed a chapter on *Good Housekeeping* and *Modern Home* to *Women's Periodicals and Interwar Print Culture in Britain, 1918–1939: The Interwar War*, edited by Catherine Clay, Maria DiCenzo, Barbara Green and Fiona Hackney (Edinburgh University Press, 2018), and has written articles on short fiction and literary journalism in interwar *Harper's Bazaar* and *Good Housekeeping* for *Modernist Cultures* and *Women: A Cultural Review*.

Index

Acton, Harold, 20, 264, 266
Adelphi see *The Adelphi*
Albemarle see *The Albemarle*
Anderson, Jean, 155–6
anthology, 21–2, 170, 240, 245, 248n, 250, 256, 269, 295, 301
Ardis, Ann, 11, 18–19, 134,
Arnold, Matthew, 88–9
Ashley, Mike, 2, 5–6, 46, 130
Atalanta, 14, 259, 33–9
Athenaeum see *The Athenaeum*
Attridge, John, 86, 104
Auden, W. H., 209, 250, 296
avant-garde, 3, 4, 5–10, 42n, 71, 88, 113, 130, 132, 154, 177, 213

Baily, Francis, 132, 137–40, 142, 145–6
Baldwin, Dean, 2, 7, 9, 19, 130, 145, 264
Balfour Symington, Arthur, 37
Ballin, Malcolm, 275, 296–7, 303, 306–7
Barron, Oswald, 38
Baudelaire, Charles, 21, 298, 306
Beardsley, Aubrey, 74
Beetham, Margaret, 4, 10–11, 47, 50–1
Bell see *The Bell*
Bell, Sam Hanna, 274–7, 282, 285, 287
Bennett, Arnold, 86, 98, 110, 132, 279
Beresford, J. D., 109, 114, 123–5
Bergson, Henri, 16, 108–11, 114–17, 119–20, 122–4, 126
Besant, Walter, 6
Black and White, 2, 132

BLAST, 88, 130
Bornstein, George, 12
Bowen, Elizabeth, 17–18, 20, 151, 160–1, 169–74, 178–83, 230, 232, 235–7, 240–1, 243, 245, 251, 256–62, 264, 267
Boyd, John, 20, 273–80, 283–8
Brazil, Angela, 25, 39, 41
Briggs, Julia, 209, 211
Britain Today, 251
British Weekly see *The British Weekly*
Brooker, Peter, 12, 14

Caird, Mona, 26
Cannan, Gilbert, 109, 114, 119–21
Cary, Joyce, 17, 135–8, 141
Cassell's Magazine, 130, 131
Castle, Christine, 131, 139, 143, 145
Chambers, Jessie, 97–8, 101
Chan, Winnie, 2, 6–8, 130
class, 16, 35, 45, 49, 51–2, 68–9, 71, 73, 76–8, 80–3, 86–7, 93, 95–104, 139, 140, 150–3, 155, 158, 161, 164, 188, 194, 212, 214, 219, 227, 239, 241–2, 254–5, 264–5, 268, 278–9
Clay, Catherine, 4, 10
Cohen, Margaret, 13
Collier, Patrick, 4, 19, 134, 177
Conan Doyle, Arthur, 6, 15, 38, 44–7, 130, 135
Connolly, Cyril, 19–20, 229–30, 232–46, 252, 254
Conrad, Joseph, 86, 122, 176, 182
Contemporary Review, 88

Coolidge, Susan, 31–2
Coppard, A. E., 212, 222
Cornhill Magazine, 245
Cotterell, Anthony, 243–4
Cournos, John, 21–2
Crackanthorpe, David, 66–8
Crackanthorpe, Hubert, 15, 65–9, 71–2, 75–6, 78, 80–3
Criterion see *The Criterion*
Crossthwaite, Arthur, 109–13
Curle, Richard, 109, 122

D'Arcy, Ella, 72
D'hoker, Elke, 14, 28–9
Daily Mail see *The Daily Mail*
Daudet, Alphonse, 7
Davidson, Robert, 274–6, 178
Davin, Dan, 240, 252–3, 255
Dawson, Janis, 38
de Balzac, Honoré, 16, 91–2
Delafield, E. M., 152, 212, 222
de la Mare, Walter, 18, 114, 169–74, 178–83
Delaney, Paul, 3
Delap, Lucy, 4
de Maupassant, Guy, 7, 16, 66, 91–2, 100
Desart, Earl of (William Ulick O'Connor Cuffe), 68, 70–2, 79, 83
Dial see *The Dial*
DiCenzo, Maria, 4
Dickens, Charles, 28, 80, 122
Dillane, Fionnula, 12
Douglas, George, 70–1, 76, 81, 83
Dowson, Ernest, 7, 75

Eco, Umberto, 46
editorship, 10, 12–13, 50–1, 60n, 132, 136–7, 139, 140, 142, 145–6, 150–1, 153, 162, 165n, 169, 171, 175–7, 187, 190–1, 201–2, 209–11, 213, 218–20, 222–3, 269, 287–8, 296–7, 300
Egerton, George, 7, 71
Eggermont, Stephanie, 28–9
Einhaus, Ann-Marie, 2, 19–20, 250
English Review see *The English Review*

Evans, Caradoc, 21, 297, 299, 301, 304, 306
Eve, 17–18, 22, 150–68

Falconer, Lanoe, 25, 27–9, 38
feminism, 21, 29–38, 40, 48, 50–9, 74, 89, 130, 135, 141–3, 150–64, 188–9, 200, 303
 New Woman, 7, 35, 42n, 59, 135, 141–2, 151
Flaubert, Gustave, 91
Fleming, Alice, 68, 72, 74, 82–3
Ford, Ford Madox, 15–16, 21, 86–105, 175
Forster, E. M., 176, 235
Fortnightly Review, 8, 88, 174
Forum see *The Forum*

Galsworthy, John, 86, 95–6, 98, 131–2, 189
Garnett, Richard, 32–3
Gaskell, Elizabeth, 28
genre
 artist story, 130–46
 comedy, 70–2, 132–3, 137–8, 140–1, 160, 236–7, 238, 245, 264–6
 detective story, 7, 30, 38, 44, 152
 fairy tale, 31–2, 37, 163
 generic hybridity, 19, 28, 60, 188, 191–5, 197, 200–2
 irony, 55, 123, 155, 164, 213, 220–7
 romance story, 5, 31–2, 38, 49–50, 57–8, 100, 114–15, 133, 135, 137–8, 141–3, 152, 154–9, 245
 satire, 79, 96, 134, 137–8, 145, 150, 152, 155, 158–9, 188, 193, 201–2, 219, 237–8, 240, 264–6
 sketch, 87, 89, 93, 96, 103–4, 153, 192, 194, 231, 234–5, 237, 240–1, 245, 266
 war story, 239–44, 250–2, 260–1, 265, 267–78, 280–4, 309n
Glyn, Elinor, 140–1
Gogol, Nikolai, 7
Golden Hind see *The Golden Hind*
Good Housekeeping, 18–19, 130, 158, 187–204
Goodyear, Frederick, 109–12, 114, 120, 126

Granta, 252
Green, Barbara, 4
Green, Henry, 20, 251, 256–7, 259–61, 264, 267
Greene, Graham, 20, 251, 264–7
Greenhough-Smith, Herbert, 140, 146

Hall, Radclyffe, 17, 161–4
Hamlyn, Arnold, 30
Hammond, A., 38
Hankin, John, 96,
Hardy, Thomas, 7, 76, 87, 176, 209, 279–80
Harland, Henry, 8, 92
Harper's Bazaar, 19, 130, 20910, 212–15, 217–18, 220–3, 226–7
Harris, Frank, 109, 115–17
Harris, John, 293, 299
Harte, Bret, 7, 31
Hartley, L. P., 177, 179
Haugtvedt, Erica, 47
Head, Dominic, 3, 192
Heaney, Seamus, 21, 287–8, 331
Heseltine, Nigel, 300, 303
Hewitt, John, 276, 287
highbrow, 1, 4, 5–10, 21, 90, 132, 135–6, 188–9, 201–2, 204, 209, 230, 237, 238
Hodgson Burnett, Frances, 25
Holden, Inez, 236–7, 240–2, 245, 267
Holtby, Winifred, 17, 151
Horizon, 19–20, 229–46, 250, 252–5, 258, 269
Housman, Clemence, 25, 33–5, 37
Hughes, Linda, 26
Humphrey, Frances A., 30–2
Hunter, Adrian, 3, 28, 66–7, 72
Huxley, Aldous, 18–19, 169–70, 187–9, 195–205

Illustrated London News see *The Illustrated London News*
Ingelow, Jean, 25
Isherwood, Christopher, 250, 255, 259

Jackson, Kate, 130, 140
James, Henry, 7–9, 16, 66, 72, 76, 78, 86, 90, 92–3, 104, 169–70, 178–9
James, M. R., 179

Jameson, Storm, 17, 132, 151
Johnson, Lionel, 66, 69–72, 80, 82–3
Jones, Glyn, 21, 293–7, 299, 301–6
Joyce, James, 21, 170, 276, 279, 298, 300, 304, 306

Kafka, Franz, 21, 230, 234–5, 242, 245, 258, 301, 304, 306
Kavan, Anna, 230, 232, 240, 242–5
Kipling, Rudyard, 7, 72, 74, 92, 170
Krueger, Kate, 52

Lady's Realm, 132
Lagan Magazine, 20–1, 273–88
Lane, Allen, 250, 252–3, 268
Lane, John, 35
Latham, Sean, 134, 229–30, 234, 238
Lawrence, D. H., 16, 86–7, 89, 97–105, 114, 152, 169–70, 176, 202, 209
Le Gallienne, Richard, 66, 75
Lee, Vernon, 7, 86, 176
Lehmann, John, 20, 210–11, 245, 250–69
Lehmann, Rosamond, 20, 251, 262–4
Levy, Amy, 26
Lewis, Alun, 230, 232, 236, 238, 241–2, 252, 267
Lewis, Wyndham, 86, 93, 296, 303
Liddle, Dallas, 5
Life and Letters (also *Life and Letters To-day*), 296, 301
Lindsay, Caroline Blanche Elizabeth (Lady), 29–30
London Mercury see *The London Mercury*
Lushington, Roland, 233, 236, 238
Lyall, David see Swan, Annie S.

Macaulay, Rose, 17, 151, 169
MacDiarmid, Hugh, 21, 301
McFadden, Roy, 273, 275, 287
McGann, Jerome, 12
Maclaren-Ross, Julian, 230, 232, 236–8, 240, 250–1, 269
McLaverty, Michael, 274–6, 278, 287
McMahon, Sean, 276, 285–7
McNeile, H. C., 131, 139, 143–6
McVicker, Jeanette, 188, 197, 199
Magill, Robert, 17, 135, 138, 142–3

Mahon, Derek, 21, 287
Mansfield, Katherine, 9, 16, 108–9, 112, 114–15, 125, 170, 176, 192
Mansford, Charles J., 44
Matthews, Brander, 7
Meade, L. T., 6, 14, 25–9, 31, 33, 35–41, 44–5
Mengham, Rod, 259–61
Meynell, Alice, 26
middlebrow, 1, 2, 4, 5–10, 45, 59, 88, 90, 130, 136, 139, 144, 151, 164, 177–8, 188–9, 201–2, 204, 229, 234, 245, 262
Mittell, Jason, 50
modernism
  late modernism, 152, 164, 230, 246
  little magazine, 8, 10, 16, 88, 130, 137, 230, 253, 275–9, 284, 293–7, 302–3
  modernist short story, 2–3, 5, 8–10, 22n, 25, 28, 86, 90, 94, 101, 115–18, 122–5, 151–3, 178, 189, 213, 230, 233, 238, 262, 293–306
  proto-modernism, 2, 8, 25, 28
Monfort, Bruno, 2
Morgan, Gerda, 109, 117–19
Morrison, Arthur, 44, 71
Morrisson, Mark S., 88
Morrow, Gerry, 276, 278
Mourant, Chris, 134
Murry, John Middleton, 15–16, 21, 108–20, 124, 126, 137
Mussell, James, 11

Nash's Magazine, 9, 22
Nash's Pall Mall Magazine, 18–19, 187, 195–7, 200
Nation and the Athenaeum see *The Nation and the Athenaeum*
Nesbit, Edith, 6, 25, 35–6, 38
New Age see *The New Age*
New Statesman see *The New Statesman*
Newnes, George, 14, 140
Nicoll, William Robertson, 50

O'Brien, Edward J., 21–2
O'Connor, Frank, 170, 212, 239, 298
O'Faoláin, Sean, 10, 239, 274
O'Neill, Ambrose, 188, 201–4

Oliphant, Margaret, 38
Orwell, George, 236, 256

Pearson's Magazine, 9, 130, 131, 138
Penguin New Writing see *The Penguin New Writing*
Peppis, Paul, 88
periodicals
  periodical codes, 12, 48, 65, 72, 77, 80–3
  polyvocality, 2, 9, 11, 18, 77–8, 83, 87, 108–11, 123, 134, 147n
  theories of the periodical, 3–5, 10–13, 15, 47–8, 65, 131, 281
  see also little magazine; Victorian periodical
Philpotts, Matthew, 12–13
Plock, Vike M., 152, 161
Poe, Edgar Allan, 7, 93
popular, 1, 3, 4, 5–10, 21–2, 25–7, 38, 57–9, 90, 130–146, 178, 201–4, 209, 230, 237–8, 262, 306n
Pound, Ezra, 86, 177, 209, 296
Pound, Reginald, 140
Pratt, Mary Louise, 65
Priestley, J. B., 136, 176–7
Pritchett, V. S., 20, 245, 251, 256, 264–7
Proust, Marcel, 21, 91, 298, 306
Punch, 252

region, 94, 98, 99–100, 104, 276–7, 280–1, 283–5, 287–8, 290n
Reynier, Christine, 19, 187, 191–4
Rhys, Keidrych, 293–4, 296–300, 302–3
Rhythm, 15–17, 88, 108–26, 130, 137
Rider Haggard, H., 31, 261
Rigel Daugherty, Beth, 40
Roberts, Lynette, 21, 303
Roberts, Morley, 131–3, 137
Robinson, Frances Mabel, 36, 38, 68, 74, 77–8, 82–3
Roughton, Roger, 231–2, 236–7
Royal see *The Royal*

Sackville-West, Vita, 189, 196, 201, 210–11
Saki, 72

Sansom, William, 20, 230–2, 236–8, 240–2, 245, 251, 256–62, 264, 267–8
Saunders, Max, 94
Savoy see *The Savoy*
Scholes, Robert, 134
Schreiner, Olive, 7
Sharp, Evelyn J., 25, 35–41
Shaw, George Bernard, 76, 81–2, 132
short story
   short story cycle, 2, 3, 65
   short story series, 6, 38, 42n, 43n, 44–64, 98, 187, 191–3
   theories of the short story, 1–3, 7–9, 10, 46–7, 92, 169–70, 191–3, 285
   see also genre
Simmons, James, 21, 273, 287–8
Sinclair, May, 86
Sitwell, Edith, 17, 151, 169
Sitwell, Osbert, 235–6
Somerset Maugham, W., 14, 170, 189
Sparks, Tabitha, 50, 52
Spender, Stephen, 209, 229, 232, 252–3, 255–7, 262
Squire, J. C., 18, 169, 171, 175–8, 181, 215
Stevenson, Robert Louis, 7, 223
Stoddart, Jane T., 50
Strand see *The Strand*
Struther, Jan, 158–9
Stuart Phelps, Elizabeth, 32
Sullivan, Alvin, 67
Swan, Annie S., 15, 44–5, 47–60
Swinnerton, Frank, 114
Symons, Arthur, 7

T. P.'s and Cassell's Weekly, 22
Tatler see *The Tatler*
Thacker, Andrew, 12, 14
Thackeray, William Makepeace, 28
The Adelphi, 21, 275, 296
The Albemarle, 8, 15, 65–83
The Athenaeum, 21, 175, 209
The Bell, 239, 274, 281
The British Weekly, 50
The Criterion, 209
The Daily Mail, 245

The Dial, 209
The English Review, 2, 8, 13, 15–16, 21, 86–105, 175
The Forum, 208–9
The Golden Hind, 21
The Illustrated London News, 22
The London Mercury, 18, 21, 169–83
The Nation and the Athenaeum, 21
The New Age, 8, 21, 109, 123–4, 175
The New Statesman, 2, 171, 175, 256, 275
The Penguin New Writing, 20, 246, 250–69
The Royal, 17, 130–46
The Savoy, 2, 8, 76
The Strand, 2, 6–9, 14–15, 17, 25–7, 30, 37–8, 44–6, 48, 76, 130–46, 245
The Tatler, 22, 150, 155
The Voice of Scotland, 21, 301
The Welsh Review, 296
The Windsor, 9, 130–2
The Winter Owl, 21
The Woman at Home, 15, 44–5, 47–8, 50–2, 55–7, 59
The Yellow Book, 2–3, 8, 15–16, 39–40, 66
Thomas, Dylan, 21, 173, 251, 268, 293–5, 297–303, 306
Tianyi, Zhang, 20, 264, 266
Time and Tide, 4, 10, 21, 130
Tit-Bits, 76
Tomelty, Joseph, 274, 276, 278–9
Toynbee, Philip, 232
Transatlantic Review, 21
Troly-Curtin, Marthe, 156–8
Turgenev, Ivan, 7
Tynan, Katharine, 26

Urquhart, Fred, 230, 232, 245

Victorian
   fin-de-siècle short story, 2, 6–9, 28–9
   Victorian periodical, 3–4, 10
Victorian Magazine, 37
Vogue, 130, 152–3, 162, 211
Voice of Scotland see *The Voice of Scotland*

Wales, 21, 293–306
Warhol, Robyn, 57
Waugh, Evelyn, 212, 265
Welch, Denton, 232–3, 252
Wells, H. G., 9, 87, 96–7
Welsh Review see *The Welsh Review*
Welty, Eudora, 232–3
West, Rebecca, 189, 201
Wharton, Edith, 152
White, Antonia, 236, 238
White, Cynthia L., 152
Wilkins, W. H., 65, 67, 73, 80, 82
Williams, Raymond, 46
Wilson, Angus, 233
Wiltse, Ed, 46, 49
Windsor see *The Windsor*
Winter Owl see *The Winter Owl*
Witherby, Diana, 232, 236, 238
Wodehouse, P. G., 135, 136
Woman at Home see *The Woman at Home*
Wood, Alice, 188, 190, 197, 199
Woolf, Virginia, 9, 15, 18–19, 25, 40–1, 125, 151, 169, 176, 178, 187–204, 208–27, 251
World War One, 45, 132, 140, 144, 150, 152–3, 175, 263, 265
World War Two, 196, 220, 229, 231, 239–44, 250–2, 256–8, 260–1, 273, 277–8, 280–4, 288n, 302

Ye Junjian, 268
Yellow Book see *The Yellow Book*

Zola, Émile, 66, 76, 91

EU representative:
Easy Access System Europe
Mustamäe tee 50, 10621 Tallinn, Estonia
Gpsr.requests@easproject.com

www.ingramcontent.com/pod-product-compliance
Lightning Source LLC
Chambersburg PA
CBHW051557230426

43668CB00013B/1885